Martin Roberts

BRITAIN
AND
EUROPE
1848–1980

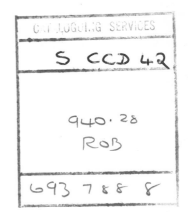
Longman

LONGMAN GROUP UK LIMITED
Longman House, Burnt Mill, Harlow, Essex
CM20 2JE, UK
and Associated Companies throughout the World.

Published in the United States of America
by Longman Inc., New York

© Longman Group UK Limited 1986

First published 1986
Second impression 1987
ISBN 0 582 22434 9

Set in 9/12pt Century Schoolbook Linotron 202
Produced by Longman Group (FE) Ltd
Printed in Hong Kong

British Library Cataloguing in Publication Data

Roberts, Martin, *1941–*
   Britain and Europe 1848–1980. –
   1. Europe – History – 19th century
   2. Europe – History – 20th century
   I. Title
   940.2′8   D359

   ISBN 0-582-22434-9

Library of Congress Cataloging-in-Publication Data

Roberts, Martin.
   Britain and Europe, 1848–1980.

   Includes index.
   Summary: Discusses the history and relationship of
Great Britain and Europe from the mid-nineteenth to the
late twentieth century.
   1. Europe – Foreign relations – Great Britain.
2. Great Britain – Foreign relations – Europe. 3. Europe –
History – 1789–1900. 4. Europe – History – 20th century.
[1. Europe – Foreign relations – Great Britain.
2. Great Britain – Foreign relations – Europe. 3. Europe –
History – 1789–1900. 4. Europe – History – 20th century]
I. Title. II. Series.

D34.G7R63 1986   327.4104   86-14724
   ISBN 0-582-22434-9

Acknowledgements

We are grateful to the following for permission to reproduce copy-right material:
Penguin Books Ltd for an extract from pp 38–39 *Nehru: A Political Biography* by Michael Edwardes (Allen Lane, The Penguin Press, 1971), copyright © Michael Edwardes, 1971; Weidenfeld & Nicolson Ltd for extracts from *The Labour Government 1964–70: A Personal Record* by Harold Wilson.

We are grateful to the following for permission to reproduce photographs:
Archiv Gerstenberg, Wietze, 5/F3 and 6/E5; L'Armée Française, Section Cinematographique, 7/G3; Associated Newspapers, 15/G2 and 17/G; BBC Hulton Picture Library, 2/A, 3/A1, 6/G2, 7/C5, 8/H1, 9/A1–3, 10/D2, 10/D3, 10/E1, 10/F2, 12/A2–4, 12/E, 12/G3 and 14/J1; Bildarchiv Preussicher Kulturbesitz, 5/A; Bolze and Ravin, Bulawayo, 16/G1; British Library, 3/D2–3; British Museum 3/C1; Bundesarchiv, Koblenz, 13/G2–3; Camera Press/Imperial War Museum, 14/E2, 14/F3 and 14/K2; Central Press, 17/D2; Documentation Française, 1/F1, 4/D (Musées Nationaux), 5/G2 (Holzapfel), 10/H4 (Holzapfel/©DACS 1986); Documentation Internationale, Paris, 8/I3; ECP/Armées, 7/C3; Fawcett Library/Mary Evans Picture Library, 2/G1; John Hillesson Agency/Capa/Magnum, 14/J4–5; Hoover, 10/E2; Illustrated London News Picture Library, 1/A2–3, 1/G2, 3/E4, 7/H1, 8/A1, 14/D7, 14/D8, 15/G1 and 17/I2 (UPI); International Defence and Aid Fund, 16/H5; Imperial War Museum, 6/A1, 7/C1–2, 7/C4, 7/D4, 7/E2, 7/F1, 7/G2, 7/I6, 13/A1 and 13/E4; David King Collection, 8/E4, 8/F2, 11/D6 and 11/H; Labour Party, 10/C1; Library of Congress, Washington, 15/C1; London Express News and Feature Services, 12/H5, 15/A2, 15/E2, 16/F2, 17/A1 and 17/E7; London School of Economics, 2/E1–2; Mansell Collection, 4/J1, 5/G1 and 6/B1; Novosti Press Agency, 3/A2–3, 3/E6, 8/A2, 8/B, 8/E3, 12/I1, 15/F5–6; Photosource/Keystone, 11/I3, 14/F2, 16/C1–2, 16/D6, 16/E and 17/D1; Popperfoto, 8/H3, 15/E3, 17/D3 and 17/H2; Punch Picture Library, 2/B4, 2/D4, 2/G5, 4/E, 5/H, 10/D6 and 14/F1; Roger-Viollet, Paris, 4/I4–5, 4/J4 and 4/K1–4; Simplicissimus/Scherz Verlag, Bern, 6/D1 and 17/E3; Society for Cultural Relations with the USSR, 8/H2, 11/D2 and 11/E1; Syndication International, 16/F3; Topham, 8/I2, 10/C2, 10/H3, 11/A1, 11/D4, 11/E2, 12/H3, 15/A1, 15/C2 and 16/F1; Ullstein Bilderdienst, 13/F2 and 13/G1; Ulster Museum, 2/E2 and 2/F1; Weimar Archiv, 13/A4 and 13/B1.

We are grateful to the following for permission to redraw maps and reproduce tables:
Hamlyn Publishing Group, R. Natkiel, *Atlas of Twentieth Century History*, 1982, 14/H1; Heinemann Educational Books, L. P. Morris, *Eastern Europe Since 1945*, 15/F1–3; Macdonald, *Purnell's History of the 20th Century*, 16/C3 and 16/D4; Rainbird Books/Robert Harding, Field Marshall Viscount Montgomery of Alamein, *A History of Warfare*, 1968, 14/E1 and 14/H2, and A. J. P. Taylor, *The First World War – An Illustrated History*, 1963, 7 pages 106, 107 and 7/H2; George Weidenfeld and Nicholson, M. Gilbert, *Recent History Atlas*, 10/I1.

Contents

Extracts taken from:

CHAPTER 1: D1: Harold U. Faulkner, *Politics, Reform and Expansion*, Harper and Row, 1959; H1: H. I. Priestley, *France Overseas*, D. Appleton-Century 1938; H2: E. Isichei, *History of Nigeria*, Longman 1983; H3: L. H. Gann and P. Duignan, *The Rulers of German Africa*, Stanford; H4: James Morris, *Pax Britannica*, Penguin 1979. CHAPTER 2: B1: *The Gladstone Diaries Vol. VI*, ed. H. C. G. Mathew, Clarendon Press 1978; B2 and C2: W. F. Moneypenny and G. F. Buckle, *The Life of Benjamin Disraeli*, John Murray 1929; D3: J. L. Garvin, *Life of Joseph Chamberlain Vol. II*, Macmillan 1933; F3: A. P. Ryan, *Mutiny at the Curragh*, Macmillan 1956; G2 and G3: R. Churchill, *Winston Churchill Vol. II*, Heinemann 1967; G4: J. Grigg, *Lloyd George from Peace to War 1912–16*, Methuen 1985. CHAPTER 3: A4, B1, B2, C2, E1, E2, E3, F1 and F2: *Source Book of Russian History Vol. III*, ed G. Vernadsky, Yale University Press 1972; E5: S. Harcave, *Years of the Golden Cockerel: The Last Romanov Tsars 1814–1917*, New York 1968. CHAPTER 4: B and F: D. Mack Smith (ed.), *Garibaldi*, Prentice Hall 1969; C: A. J. Whyte, *The Political Life and Letters of Cavour 1848–61*, Oxford University Press 1930; G: J. A. B. Corley, *Democratic Despot*, Barrie and Rockliff 1961; H: L. M. Case, *French Opinion on War and Diplomacy during the Second Empire*, University of Pennsylvania Press 1954; J2: *Encyclopaedia Britannica*, William Benton 1973; J3, J5 and J6: G. P. Gooch, *The Second Empire*, Longman 1964; I2 and I3: A. Horne, *The Fall of Paris*, St Martin's Press 1965. CHAPTER 5: E: O. Pflanze, *Bismarck and the Development of Germany Vol. I*, Princeton University Press 1971; F4 and F5: O. von Bismarck, *Reminiscences and Recollections Vol. II* trans. A. J. Butler, Smith Elder. CHAPTER 6: B2: F. von Holstein, *Memoirs*, ed. N. Rich and M. H. Fisher, Cambridge University Press 1955; C: F. Dorpalen, *H von Treitschke*, Yale University Press 1957; E1 and E2: G. A. Craig, *Europe 1815–1914*, The Dryden Press 1972; E4: A. J. Marder, *British Naval Policy 1880–1905*, Putnam 1941; F2: J. H. Baernreither, *Fragments of a Political Diary*, ed J. Redlich, Macmillan 1930; G1: *British Documents on the Origins of World War I Vol. XI*, ed. Gooch and Temperley, HMSO 1926. CHAPTER 7: A: *Source Book of Russian History Vol. III*, ed G. Vernadsky, Yale University Press 1972; B: *Purnell History of the Twentieth Century II*, BPC Publishing 1968; D1 and D2: M. Ferro, *The Great War*, Routledge and Kegan Paul 1973; D3: N. Stone, *The Eastern Front*, Hodder and Stoughton 1957; G1: A. Marwick, *Women at War*, Fontana 1977; G4: A. Marwick, *The Deluge*, Bodley Head 1965; I1, I2, I3, I4 and I5: D. Winter, *Death's Men*, Allen Lane 1978. CHAPTER 8: A3: N. Stone, *Europe Transformed*, Fontana 1983; C1, C2 and H4: D. Shub, *Lenin*, Doubleday 1948; D1, D2, E1, E2, F1, G1 and G2: *Source Book of Russian History Vol. III*, ed G. Vernadsky, Yale University Press 1972. CHAPTER 9: B2 and D2: R. Harrod, *Life of J. M. Keynes*, Penguin 1972; B3: *Encyclopaedia Britannica*, William Benton 1973; C2 and E1: G. Tabonis, *Life of Jules Cambon*, trans. C. F. Atkinson, Jonathan Cape 1938; C3: O. Bauer, *The Austrian Revolution*, trans. H. J. Stenning, L. Parsons 1925; C4: J. W. Bruegel, *Czechoslovakia before Munich*, Cambridge University Press 1973; E2 and E3: F. J. Berber, *Locarno. A Collection of Documents*, Hodge 1936; G2, G3 and G4: J. M. Maki, *Conflict and Tension in the Far East*, University of Washington 1961; G5 and G6: S. Roskill, *Hankey Vol. III*, Collins 1974. CHAPTER 10: B4 and D4: K. Middlemas and J. Barnes, *Baldwin*, Weidenfeld and Nicolson 1969; B1, B2 and B3: M. Kinnear, *The Fall of Lloyd George*, Macmillan 1973; B5: P. Snowden, *Autobiography Vol. II* Nicholson and Watson 1934; D1 and D5: M. Morris, *The General Strike*, Journeyman Press 1976; F1: R. Skidelsky, *Oswald Moseley*, Macmillan 1975; H1 and H4: J. Lacouture, *Leon Blum*, trans. G. Holoch, Holmes and Meier 1982; I2 and I3: B. Crick, *George Orwell:*

A Life, Secker and Warburg 1980. CHAPTER 11: A2: E. Yaroslavsky, *Landmarks in the Life of Stalin*, Lawrence and Wishart 1942; B1, B2, B3, C1, C2, D2 and G1: I. Deutscher, *Stalin*, Penguin 1966; D5 and J3: *An Illustrated History of the USSR*, Novosti 1977; F2 and F3: R. Conquest, *The Great Terror*, Macmillan 1973; G2: G. Vernadsky, *A History of Russia*, Yale University Press 1961; I1 and J1: N. Riasonovsky, *A History of Russia*, Oxford University Press 1969; J2: A. A. Zhdanov, *On Literature, Philosophy and Music*, Edition de la Nouvelle Critique 1950 (author's translation). CHAPTER 12: C2: A. Rossi, *The Rise of Italian Fascism*, London 1938; D: I. Kirkpatrick, *Mussolini*, Odhams 1964; G1: F. von Papen, *Memoirs*, Deutsch 1952; G2: Don Sturzo, *Italy and Fascism*, London 1926; G4 and G5: D. Mack Smith, *Mussolini*, Weidenfeld and Nicolson 1981; H2: E. Tannenbaum, *The Fascist Experience*, Basic Books 1972; H4: D. Mack Smith, *Mussolini's Roman Europe*, Longman 1976; I2: *Purnell History of the Twentieth Century IV*, BPC Publishing 1969. CHAPTER 13: A2: J. P, Nettl, *Rosa Luxemburg*, Oxford University Press 1966; B2: J. W. Hiden, *The Weimar Republic*, Longman 1974; C1 and C2: W. Shirer, *The Rise and Fall of the Third Reich*, Pan 1960; D1, D2 and D3: A. Hitler, *Mein Kampf*, trans. R. Manheim, Sentry Paperbacks 1943; E1 and H1: A. Speer, *Inside the Third Reich*, Weidenfeld and Nicolson 1970; E2 and E3: S. Taylor, *Germany 1918–1933*, Duckworth 1983; E6: *Purnell History of the Twentieth Century III*, BPC Publishing 1968; F1: D. G. Williamson, *The Third Reich*, Longman 1982; I1 and I2: H. W. Kern, *Hitler Youth*, Macdonald and Janes 1975. CHAPTER 14: A1 and A2: M. Gilbert, *Britain and Germany Between the Wars*, Longman 1964; B, H3, H4, H5, H6, I2 and L2: W. Shirer, *The Rise and Fall of the Third Reich*, Pan 1960; C: J. C. G. Röhl, *From Bismarck to Hitler*, Longman 1973; D2, D3, D4 and D5: K. Feiling, *Life of Neville Chamberlain*, Macmillan 1946; D6: P. Calvocoressi and G. Wint, *Total War*, Allen Lane 1972; E3: B. H. Liddell Hart, *History of the Second World War*, Pan 1973; I1: E. Wendel, *Hausfrau at War*, Odhams; I3 and L1: A. Speer, *Inside the Third Reich*, Weidenfeld and Nicolson 1970; J2: B. Crozier, *De Gaulle*, Eyre Methuen 1973; J3: D. Cook, *De Gaulle*, Secker and Warburg 1973; K1: P. Knightley, *The First Casualty*, Quartet 1975. CHAPTER 15: B2: N. Davies, *God's Playground*, Oxford University Press 1982; C3, C4, C5 and C6: F. L. Schuman, *Russia since 1917*, New York 1957; D: R. Medvedev, *Krushchev*, Blackwell 1982; F1: N. Riasonovsky, *A History of Russia*, Oxford University Press 1969, H: A. Crawley, *The Rise of West Germany*, Collins 1973. CHAPTER 16: A2 and H4: M. Benson, *The Struggle for a Birthright*, Penguin 1963; A3: B. Davidson, *Africa in Modern History*, Penguin 1978; A4: F. P. King, *The New Internationalism*, David and Charles 1973; A5, B2 and B3: C. Cross, *The Fall of the British Empire*, Hodder and Stoughton 1968; B1: M. Edwardes, *Nelson*, Penguin 1973; D1, D2 and D3: J. Lacouture, *Ho Chi Minh*, trans. P. Wiles, Allen Lane 1968; D7: A. Horne, in *Purnell History of the Twentieth Century V*, BPC Publishing 1972; G2: H. Wilson, *The Labour Government 1964–70: A Personal Record*, Weidenfeld and Nicolson 1971; H1, H2 and H3: A. Hepple, *Verwoerd*, Penguin 1967. CHAPTER 17: A2: A. Marwick, *Britain in Our Century*, Thames and Hudson 1984; B1, B2, B3 and B4: K. Harris, *Attlee*, Weidenfeld and Nicolson 1982; C2: M. Foot, *Aneurin Bevan*, Davis-Poynter 1973; E1, E5 and E6: N. Fisher, *Macmillan*, Weidenfeld and Nicolson 1982; E2: P. Williams, *Hugh Gaitskell*, Oxford University Press 1982; E4: D. Cook, *De Gaulle*, Secker and Warburg 1973; F1 and F2: H. Wilson, *The Labour Government 1964–70: A Personal Record*, Weidenfeld and Nicolson 1971; F3 and I1: R. Crossman, *Diaries of a Cabinet Minister Vol. II*, Hamish Hamilton/Jonathan Cape 1977; F4: A. Sked and C. Cook, *Post-War Britain*, Penguin 1977; H1: S. Cronin, *Irish Nationalism*, Continuum 1982.

1 Empire building 1870–1914

In barely forty years Europeans conquered Africa, brought much of Asia under their control, settled the habitable parts of the Americas and Australasia and reached the North and South Poles (see maps B1 and B2). Japan alone of the world's major nations stayed genuinely independent of Europe, yet this independence was kept only by the thorough imitation of European industry and technology. Never in history had a single continent so dominated the rest of the world.

Source A: The technology of imperial expansion

A1 *North Africa, 1880–1914.*

1 *The Sudan was a huge, wild and barren area. Use Source A1 and information on page 12 to explain why the British government should be worried about events there in the 1880s and 1890s.*

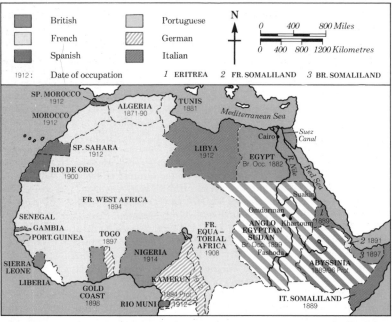

A2 *HMS* Euryalus (*centre*) *at Suakin. This picture appeared in the* Illustrated London News, *2 February 1884.*

The Illustrated London News *was first published in 1842 and was the most successful of a number of illustrated weekly news magazines which flourished in the nineteenth century. It was aimed at the educated and prosperous middle classes and gave considerable coverage of imperial affairs.*

Causes of imperialism

Technological advantages

This extraordinary expansion of European power is usually termed 'imperialism'.

It was possible because of the wide technological gap which the industrialisation of Europe had opened up between Europe and the rest of the world. A few hundred Europeans armed with machine guns and fast-firing rifles were far too strong for the Matabele tribesmen of Rhodesia, who were armed only with stabbing spears and leather shields, even though they fought fiercely in their thousands. In the Far East, the Chinese government stopped resisting European demands for ports and trading rights after their wooden sailing junks were smashed to pieces by steam-driven ironclads.

A3 *Modern naval technology on board the* Euryalus (Illustrated London News, *1 March 1884). The caption below read: '1. Visit of Friendly Sheikhs to the Euryalus: Firing the Nordenfeldt Gun. 2. Exploding a Gun-Cotton Torpedo. 3. Firing Main-Deck Guns by Electricity. 4. Escape of General Baker Pasha and Colonel Hay from the Fight at Tokar. (From particulars supplied to our Artist by Baker Pasha.)'*

Use sources A2 and A3.

2 *Why do you think that the* Euryalus *should have been at Suakin in 1884?*

3 a) *What weapons are the officers of the* Euryalus *showing off?*
   b) *To whom are they being shown?*
   c) *Why do you think that this display was held, especially when some of the visitors might have been friends of the Mahdi?*
   d) *What were the main weapons of the Sudanese?*

A4 *Winston Churchill, then aged twenty-three, fought at the Battle of Omdurman in 1898 and charged against the Mahdi's forces (the Dervishes) with his regiment, the 21st Lancers. He later described the battle in his book* The River War: An Account of the Reconquest of the Sudan, *published in 1899.*

Use source A4.

4 a) *What was a British army doing near Omdurman in 1898?*
   b) *What are 'infantry'? What was tedious for them about the battle?*
   c) *The Maxim gun had been patented in 1884. What sort of gun was it and why was it such an advance on previous guns?*
   d) *Using sources A2, A3 and A4, list the advantages in military technology which the British possessed and comment on the European view of the time that their over-*

A4

"The infantry fired steadily and stonily, without hurry or excitement, for the enemy was far away and the officers careful. Presently the physical act became tedious."

(*Elsewhere however the battle was going badly for the British Camel Corps so a gunboat on the river went into action.*)

"It began suddenly to blaze and flame from the Maxim guns, quick-firing guns and rifles. The river slopes of the Kerreri hills, crowded with advancing thousands, sprang up with clouds of dust and splinters of rock. The charging Dervishes sank down in tangled heaps. The masses in the rear paused irresolute. It was too hot even for them."

whelming victories were as much caused by bravery and discipline as by better weapons.
e) *There are a number of reasons why Churchill might be thought a good source for the events in Sudan in 1898. What are these reasons?*

Population increase

There were other reasons too. Between 1800 and 1914 Europe's population increased rapidly, from 200 million to about 600 million. This increase was faster than that of the rest of the world. In 1914 one in three people were European. In 1800 the ratio had been one to five. There were acute shortages of land in some rural areas of Europe and over-crowding in the new industrial cities. Consequently emigration to other continents was a major feature of nineteenth-century European life. The 1850s' average of 370,000 emigrants per year rose to nearly one million per year in the 1890s. Between 1890 and 1914, 40 million or more Europeans moved to new lives in different continents, perhaps the greatest ever mass movement of people. While most of them went to North America or from European to Asiatic Russia, millions went else-where, to Africa, to Australasia and to the Far East.

Economic reasons

There were also strong economic reasons for imperialism. Raw materials like rubber from the Congo, diamonds from South Africa or Persian oil were valuable to European businessmen. So too were the

Source B: Europe and the world

B1 *Europe and the world in 1878.*

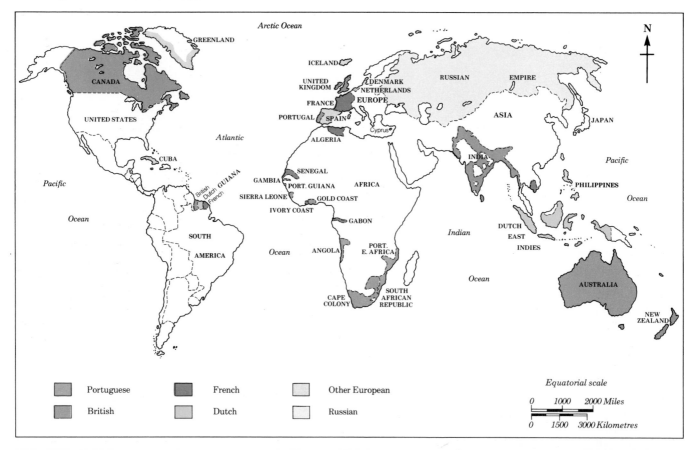

Lenin's ideas

markets ready to be developed for European manufactured goods. India, Britain's proudest possession, purchased 40 per cent of Lancashire's cotton goods and all the major European powers hoped to win the even larger Chinese market for their manufacturers. Some writers, notably the British economist J. A. Hobson (see source C) and the Russian communist, Lenin, believed that imperialism was entirely caused by the economic needs of European capitalist society by which they meant a society whose wealth or capital, whether it was in factories or trading companies, was concentrated in the hands of the middle classes. Without the new cheap raw materials and the new markets for the manufactures of capitalist-owned factories, capitalism, Lenin said, would have failed in Europe and the workers' revolutions (which Marx, the founder of Communism, had predicted) would have taken place (see page 122). Lenin described imperialism as capitalism's highest and final phase. In his opinion, colonies were conquered and their wealth used by Europeans so that the overthrow of bourgeois (middle class) capitalism by proletarian (working class) revolution could be postponed.

Compare the two maps.

1 *In which continent was there the most European expansion between 1870 and 1914?*

2 *What was the difference in 1914 between the position of Britain in Nigeria and her position in Persia (see page 15)?*

B2 *Europe and the world in 1914.*

3 *Name one European country which had no colonies in 1878 but at least one in 1914.*

4 *Why had there been no increase in European power in South America? (See page 18 for clue.)*

5 *Are maps primary or secondary sources?*

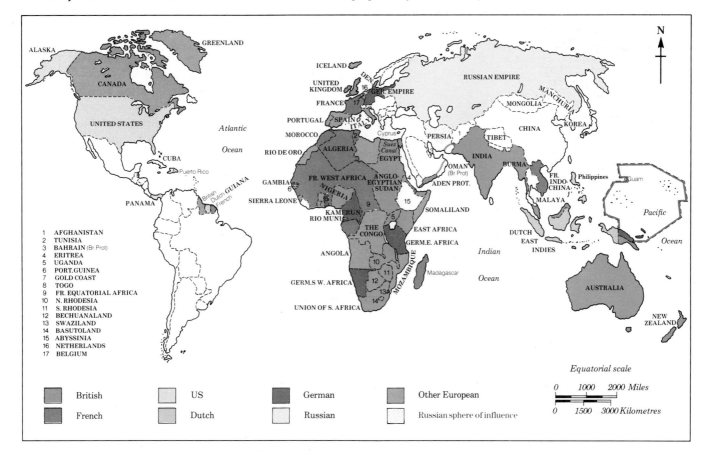

1 AFGHANISTAN
2 TUNISIA
3 BAHRAIN (Br Prot)
4 ERITREA
5 UGANDA
6 PORT. GUINEA
7 GOLD COAST
8 TOGO
9 FR. EQUATORIAL AFRICA
10 N. RHODESIA
11 S. RHODESIA
12 BECHUANALAND
13 SWAZILAND
14 BASUTOLAND
15 ABYSSINIA
16 NETHERLANDS
17 BELGIUM

British
French
US
Dutch
German
Russian
Other European
Russian sphere of influence

Equatorial scale

0   1000   2000 Miles

0   1500   3000 Kilometres

Similar ideas were voiced by politicians very different from Lenin. Some Conservatives liked imperial expansion, partly because it made possible the emigration of discontented workers and partly because successful colonial victories in excitingly distant lands were very popular and a distraction from social problems nearer home.

National rivalries

However, imperial expansion often took place for which there was no economic reason; e.g. Italy into Eritrea, Germany into the Cameroons and Britain into the Sudan. In the case of Italy and Germany, these conquests were made for reasons of national pride, while Britain's main concern in the Sudan was to keep other Europeans out. Imperialism therefore was partly the fierce national rivalries of the late nineteenth century in another form. Britain had a particular military reason for her Indian Empire. While she had a far larger navy than her European rivals, her army was much smaller. Consequently the Indian army, with British officers, had an important part to play in the defence of Britain's world-wide interests.

An influential book of the time was *The Influence of Seapower upon History,* written by A. T. Mahan, an American, and published in 1890. Mahan concluded that seapower and overseas possession were essential to any nation which wished to be a major power in the world.

Christian missionaries

The churches of Europe and the USA were also influential in the growth of empires (see source D). The early nineteenth century saw a great burst of missionary initiatives aimed not only at converting the pagan to Christianity, but at ending such evils as the slave trade and witchcraft. The missionaries had much support in Europe and, when they ran into difficulties in their work, their governments often took action on their behalf. In 1897, for example, after two German missionaries had been murdered, the German government not only protested to the Chinese government, but seized and kept the port of Kiaochow.

Soldiers and adventurers on the spot often set the pace with their governments following up behind – sometimes reluctantly. Louis Lyautey, commander of the French forces on the Algerian/Moroccan border between 1904 and 1910, decided where the frontier ran, while for Britain a private army of the millionaire, Cecil Rhodes, conquered the huge area of what is modern Zimbabwe between 1890 and 1896 (and called it Rhodesia!).

Rapid expansion, 1870–1914

Two separate events started the late-nineteenth-century scramble for colonies. In 1869 the Suez Canal was dug and in 1876 King Leopold II of Belgium set up the International Association of the Congo.

The Suez Canal, 1869

The Suez Canal was designed by the French engineer de Lesseps and paid for by British and French money. As a key section of the main sea route to India it was of vital importance to Britain and of great interest to France who had many commercial interests in the Near East. Its building soon caused these nations to become fierce rivals for influence in the areas near the canal.

Leopold II of Belgium

Leopold II was determined to expand the Belgian economy. He was sure that in the basin of the River Congo would be found valuable minerals. The International Association was the organisation which provided the explorer Stanley with the means to take possession of the Congo for the king. Portugal, with settlements in Angola to the south,

Source C: The economics of imperialism

C *This extract is from* Imperialism: A Study *by J. A. Hobson, 1905. Hobson (1858–1940) was a lively economist with an independent mind.*

1 *Is Hobson here stating facts or his opinion?*

2 *If imperialism has gained an increase in markets why then does he state that it is 'unsound business'?*

3 *Whom in Britain does he expect to do well out of imperialism and whom badly?*

4 *Why should a communist like Lenin find Hobson's ideas appealing?*

5 *Joseph Chamberlain (see pages 31–34) was Colonial Secretary when Hobson was writing his book. He believed that imperialism was 'sound business' and encouraged expansion. How might he have argued against the points which Hobson makes?*

C

"Seeing that the Imperialism of the last three decades is clearly condemned as a business policy, in that at enormous expense it has procured [gained] a small, bad, unsafe increase in markets, and has jeopardised [put at risk] the entire wealth of the nation in arousing the strong resentment [anger] of other nations, we may ask 'How did the British embark upon such unsound business?' The only possible answer is that the business interests of the nation as a whole are subordinated to those of a certain sectional interests . . ."

"[Imperialism means] the great expenditure of public money upon ships, guns, military and naval equipment . . . more posts for soldiers and sailors and in the diplomatic and consular offices . . . employment for engineers, missionaries, miners, ranchers and other emigrants . . ."

"With them stand the great manufacturers of export trade who gain a living by supplying the real and artificial wants of the new countries we annex or open up . . ."

Source D: The churches and imperial expansion: the USA and the Philippines

D *The USA has just defeated the Spanish whose colony the Philippine Islands had formerly been. The Filipinos now asked the American President, William McKinley, for their independence. What should he do?*

The italic words are from an article of 1903 by McKinley in the Christian Advocate *newspaper. It is quoted here by Harold U. Faulkner in his book* Politics, Reform and Expansion, *New York 1959.*

1 *Would you describe* a) *Faulkner's book and* b) *the* Christian Advocate *quotation used by Faulkner, as a primary or secondary source for McKinley and the problem of the independence of the Philippine islands? Explain your answer.*

2 *What evidence is there that the Church influenced McKinley's thinking?*

3 *What decision did he take and what were his main reasons for so deciding?*

D

"[McKinley] listened to imperialists, to the churches, to those businessmen who now saw in the Philippines the gateway to the China market and to the audience who greeted his expansionist speeches in the Middle West with shouts of enthusiasm. He later stressed the need *'to educate the Filipinos and uplift and civilize and Christianize them'*. Having prayed for guidance, he said, he discovered with the help of the Almighty that the United States could not hand the islands back to Spain nor turn them over to France or Germany nor let them go for they were *'unfit for self-government'*."

and Britain, with her South African colonies, became alarmed. At the Berlin Conference of 1884, the boundaries of Leopold's Congo Free State were decided, and agreement reached that any area of Africa not yet occupied by Europeans was there for the taking, simply by marching in and raising one's national flag.

The British Empire

The British were the most successful imperialists. They started with the largest empire and expanded it enormously. Much of this expansion was defensive. Britain's main interests were trade, India and sea routes. Large areas were occupied, often with genuine reluctance, to defend these interests.

British Africa – Egypt and the Sudan

In Africa, Britain took control of the Nile Valley (Egypt and the Sudan) in order to defend the Suez Canal which was a vital section of the sea route to India. The British government had, in fact, opposed the building of the canal, but once it existed, bent its efforts to control it. Though still in name part of the Turkish Empire, real power in Egypt in 1870 lay in the hands of the local ruler, Ismail, whose title was Khedive. He was keen to modernise his country and to increase his control of the Sudan and the shores of the Red Sea, but his ambitions got him heavily into debt. In 1875 Britain took advantage of his financial difficulties to buy his shares in the Suez Canal Company for £4 million and, with France, to take over the financial administration of Egypt ('dual control'). During the next twenty-five years Britain both elbowed out the French and increased her grasp first on Egypt and then on the Sudan. A nationalist rising led by Colonel Arabi against foreign influence was defeated by General Wolseley at the battle of Tel-el-Kebir in 1882, after Alexandria had been bombarded by the British fleet. Thereafter Egypt was under military occupation and its affairs were, to a large extent, directed by the British agent and consul-general, Sir Evelyn Baring (later Lord Cromer).

Egypt claimed the Sudan but the Mahdist rising of 1881 there had forced Anglo-Egyptian troops to withdraw and led to the death of General Gordon at Khartoum in January 1885. Britain only moved into the Upper Nile valley (see map A1) again when the area seemed to be under threat from Belgian, German, Italian and French expeditions. Of these, the French one led by Colonel Marchand was the most dangerous. Marchand occupied the village of Fashoda on the Nile and at the same time the French government declared that Egypt no longer had any claim to the Sudan since its troops had been absent since 1884. For Britain, General Kitchener defeated the Mahdist army at Omdurman in 1898 (see source A4) and then sailed further up the Nile to meet Marchand at Fashoda. After an acute international crisis, Marchand withdrew. The Fashoda incident was the closest Britain and France came to war in this period. In 1904 they patched things up in order to meet the common threat of Germany. In return for France leaving Egypt and the Sudan to Britain, Britain left Morocco to France.

West and Central Africa

In West and Central Africa, British colonies were created when the British government came to the aid of trading companies like the Royal Niger Company or the British East Africa Company, which were threatened by European rivals or by the native inhabitants. In West Africa the main threats came from the French and the Ashanti tribe; in East Africa from the German explorer Carl Peters, who had Bismarck's active support.

Southern Africa

In Southern Africa (see map E1) the British record was more obviously aggressive. There were two main competitors, the black tribes and the white Boers. The latter were descendants of Dutch settlers who had arrived in the seventeenth century. They were farmers who considered the area their home. Britain had won Cape Town from the Dutch at the end of the Napoleonic Wars and also held Durban, the other good port on the southern coast. Cape Colony, whose capital was Cape Town, was expanded at the expense of the Xhosa tribe. Natal, whose capital was Durban, bordered on Zululand. In 1879 the British provoked Cetewayo, the Zulu king, into war and, though a section of their army was ambushed and destroyed at Isandhlwana (1879), eventually won a decisive victory at Ulundi (1881) and annexed Zululand.

Many Boers had moved out of Cape Colony into the interior, in order to escape from British rule. There they had set up the independent republics of the Orange Free State and the South African Republic (Transvaal). Britain annexed the Transvaal in 1877 but, when one of her armies was defeated by the Boers at Majuba in 1881, withdrew. At home, a Liberal government led by William Gladstone was in power, which did not approve of the 1877 annexation.

Cecil Rhodes

The major personality in the expansion of British power in Southern Africa in the 1880s and 1890s was Cecil Rhodes. The son of a Hertfordshire vicar, he had been sent out to Africa in the hope that the climate would improve his poor health. He moved to Kimberley when diamonds were discovered there and by skilful business deals won a near-monopoly control of the diamond mines (about 90 per cent of the world's supply) and became a millionaire. He was also elected an MP in the parliament of Cape Colony and, at the age of thirty-seven, became Prime Minister.

Source E: Southern Africa

E1 *South Africa in 1899, on the eve of the Anglo-Boer War.*

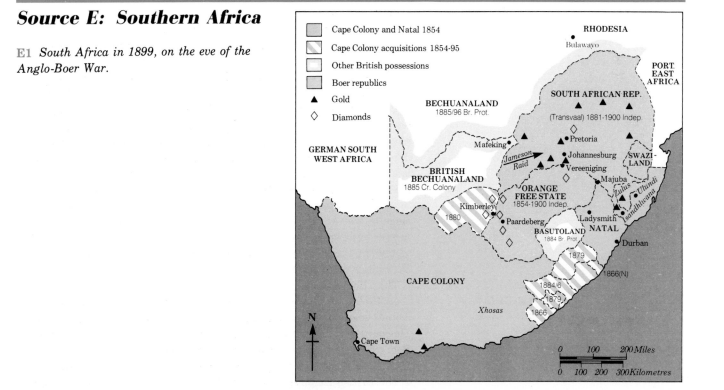

Rhodes was convinced that the Anglo-Saxon races (English, Germans, Americans) were superior to the rest of the world and the growth of the British Empire meant the spread of civilisation. He dreamt of a railway from the Cape to Cairo in Egypt running along its whole length through British colonies (see source E2). Rhodes's vision, energy, scheming and money not only brought Northern and Southern Rhodesia into the Empire, but also helped to secure Bechuanaland and to cause the Boer War. He was an extraordinary figure. Near the end of his short eventful life he went unarmed into the Matopo Hills and successfully negotiated peace terms with the Matabele chiefs who had risen in revolt in 1896. When he died in 1902 his body was buried high up in the Matopos with immense views over 'his' colony.

The Boer War, 1899–1902

The Boer republics were a major obstacle to Rhodes's ambitions. For their part, they felt increasingly hemmed in by his schemes (see source E2). The situation was made more tense by the discovery in the 1880s of the world's richest gold deposits in the Transvaal. The city of Johannesburg sprang out of nothing to develop the goldfields. Large financial investments were necessary and most of the new businessmen were foreigners (uitlanders), mainly Britons working for Rhodes or other British companies.

In 1895 Rhodes was plotting to overthrow the Transvaal government of Paul Kruger. He wanted the uitlanders in Johannesburg to rebel and had Dr Jameson, a close friend, ready to ride with a private army to assist them. The British Colonial Secretary, Joseph Chamberlain (see page 31), secretly supported the scheme. The Jameson raid did take place, but it was a fiasco. The Johannesburg rebels got cold feet and the Boers had no difficulty rounding up the invaders.

The Jameson raid convinced the Boers that war with Britain would come sooner or later. The two republics formed a military alliance and armed themselves as strongly as they could. In the Transvaal, Kruger refused to give political rights to the uitlanders who protested noisily to the British government. In 1899 Sir Alfred Milner, who also believed that war was unavoidable, used the protests as a way of provoking a war which he was sure would end in the British conquest of the republics and the goldfields.

In the first months the Boers nearly won. They had more troops ready for war. They knew the country intimately, rode fast, shot accurately and had some brilliant generals. In contrast, the British needed time to ship more troops from other parts of the Empire and were defeated time and again because of their unfamiliarity with the terrain and indecisive generals. However, the Boers lost the advantage of their first victories by delaying their advance on Cape Town and Durban in order to lay siege to Mafeking, Kimberley and Ladysmith (see map E1). The British armies built up an overwhelming advantage in numbers, won a decisive victory at Paardeberg, and by the end of 1900 had captured the major Boer cities of Johannesburg and Pretoria.

The Boers took to guerrilla warfare. Kitchener, the British commander, countered by herding Boer women and children into special camps where disease caused by poor sanitation killed 20,000 of them. He had their farms burnt so the guerrillas had no shelter. Eventually Boer resistance was worn down. By the Treaty of Vereeniging (1902), which ended the war, the Transvaal and Orange Free State became part of the British Empire.

Many Britons, including leading Liberals, felt guilty about the Boer

E2 *A cartoon of Cecil Rhodes, published in the* Review of Reviews, *February 1898.*

Cartoons are drawings exaggerated or presented in some unusual way to make a comment on a political or social event or trend. They became popular with the growth of a mass readership for newspapers and magazines during the nineteenth century.

Compare the cartoon E2 with the map E1 on page 13.

1 *In which colony is Rhodes's left foot, in which is his right? Why did the cartoonist place his feet so?*
2 *What are 'Zambezi', 'Nile', 'Orange', and 'Bulawayo'? Why did the cartoonist include them in his drawing?*
3 *What does 'Fort Folly' represent? Who is inside it? Explain its name and the way in which the artist has drawn it.*
4 *Where is the railway train going? Why is Rhodes pulling it?*
5 *What do you think is the point of view of the cartoonist?*

War. A Liberal government was elected in 1906 (see page 39) and created the Union of South Africa, which included Cape Colony, British Bechuanaland, Natal and the former Boer republics. Since there were more Boers than Britons in this new union they had the voting power to control the new state. What was a good deal for the Boers was a bad one for the non-whites. The Boers were fiercely opposed to racial equality and the British government took no steps to protect native interests in the new union.

The British in Asia

In Asia the defence of India and the Indian sea route was Britain's main concern. As the French moved into Indo-China, the British took Burma and Malaya. Rivalry with Russia along the northern frontier of India led to invasions of Tibet and Afghanistan and to the partition of Persia into three zones; a northern one (Russian influence), a southern one (British influence) and a neutral central zone. Britain also made sure that she got her fair share of China ports and Pacific islands. By 1914, the British Empire covered 20 per cent of the land surface of the globe, 27.2 million sq. km with 400 million inhabitants.

India

The East India Company

Britain's first links with India were trading ones. The British East India Company had set up trading bases in the seventeenth and eighteenth centuries and Britain had driven France out of the sub-continent and conquered part of it before the end of the eighteenth century in order to strengthen her trading position. By the mid nineteenth century all India was ruled either directly by Britain or by princes who were allied to her.

The 'Mutiny' of 1857–8

The so-called Indian Mutiny of 1857–8, which was not only a revolt of Indian troops against their British officers but a widespread explosion of anger against foreign rule, caused Britain to reform its methods of governing and also to increase the number of British troops within the Indian army. It also strengthened the belief of most Britons (see source H4) that Indians could not be trusted with political power.

The Indian National Congress

Not surprisingly, educated Indians found such an attitude unacceptable and began to organise themselves. The Indian National Congress was founded in 1885, dedicated to greater Indian unity and to self-government. The British tended to dismiss the nationalists as a tiny unimportant minority. Before 1909 the only political activity they would allow to Indians was to take part, as a minority, in provincial assemblies. The Morley-Minto reforms of 1909 introduced the election of Indians both to provincial councils and to the central Imperial Council. However, these councils could not make decisions, they could only advise.

The French Empire

During the Second Empire (see chapter 4) the French were also active in the colonising business. They had enlarged their Algerian colony and occupied part of Indo-China and of West Africa. After the humiliation in the Franco-Prussian War (1871) colonial successes were welcome.

West Africa

France's largest conquests were made in West Africa. From a base created in Senegal by Louis Faidherbe, who was Governor there from 1854 to 1865 (see source F), an immense area was occupied reaching across to the Sudan. The Fashoda incident (see page 12) was a setback but, with Britain's support, France took over Morocco in 1912, having already won Tunisia in 1881.

Indo-China

In Asia, Indo-China was her most important possession. French missionaries had been active there since the eighteenth century and the occupation of southern Indo-China in 1858–61 followed from the persecution of the Christian converts by the Indo-Chinese Emperor. The commercial possibilities of the area, its closeness to the China market and rivalry with Britain led to the conquest of the north (Tongking) and west (Laos and Cambodia) between 1884 and 1907.

She also won a share of the China trade (see source G) and a number of Pacific islands, including Tahiti. In 1914 the French Empire was the second largest in the world, 11.7 million sq. km in area with 52 million inhabitants.

Louis Lyautey

A leading figure in France's empire-building was Louis Lyautey. Trained as a cavalry officer, his first overseas experience was in Algeria. In his forties he saw active service in a senior post in Indo-China. He impressed his superiors not only by his military ability but by his firm belief in France's civilising mission through colonial conquest. In 1900 he was summoned to Madagascar and in two years conquered the south of the island. His most important work, however, was done in North

Africa. From 1904 to 1910 he was in Algeria, bringing frontier tribes under French rule and pushing the Algerian frontier westwards at the expense of Morocco. Then, in 1912, he was made President-General in Morocco, replaced one Sultan by another and brought an unsettled country firmly under French control. Lyautey both respected and was himself respected by the Moroccan Arabs. While doing much to develop Morocco economically, he made use of many traditional methods and local leaders in his government of the country.

Source F: The French Empire

F1 *Senegal became one of the more important of the French colonies in West Africa. This picture shows a trading-post near the mouth of the River Senegal in the 1850s. Published in the Parisian magazine L'Illustration in 1853, it was based on a sketch by the then Governor, Faidherbe. The main item of trade was 'arabic gum' which was used in the manufacture of paste, glue and artists' materials. At this early stage of empire-building the trade of the area was controlled by the Trarza Arabs.*

1 *Identify the three different races in this picture. What are they doing? How were you able to identify them?*

2 *To whom do the ships belong? How do you know?*

3 *Faidherbe brought Senegal more firmly under French control and attacked the neighbouring Arabs. From what you know about European empire-building and from the clues in this picture and on map A1, how and why do you think that he did so?*

4 *Comment on the reliability of Source F.*

Germany

Germany and Italy, recently unified, envied the success of Britain and France. Germany did quite well in the scramble for Africa, gaining Tanganyika, German South West Africa, Togo and the Cameroons. Many Pacific islands and some China ports also came her way. However, her empire of 2.6 million sq. km with 14 million inhabitants seemed disappointingly small compared with the British and French. Admiral von Tirpitz built his new navy to rival Britain's, with the express purpose of forcing Britain to allow Germany a larger empire. Its effect, however, was to encourage Britain and France, previously bitter colonial rivals, to sink their differences and combine against Germany. This they did most effectively in Morocco, first in 1905–6 and again in 1911. The new German fleet and colonial rivalries helped to bring about the First World War (see chapter 6).

Italy

Italy, whose southern provinces were badly overpopulated, hoped to have Tunisia, just a short voyage away across the Mediterranean. However, France got there first. Instead Italy had to be satisfied with Eritrea and Somaliland in East Africa. She then tried to conquer nearby Abyssinia, but met with a humiliating and decisive defeat at the hands of the Emperor Menelek at Adowa in 1896. The seizure of Tripolitania in 1911 from the Turkish Empire, weakened by internal revolution, was some compensation.

Russia

For Russia, imperialism meant pushing her Asiatic frontier eastwards and southwards and controlling and developing the vast areas thus opened up. Years of rivalry with Britain over Afghanistan nearly ended in war in 1885 when Russian troops occupied the town of Penjdeh and only withdrew after an ultimatum from Gladstone, the British Prime Minister. In the 1890s the government actively encouraged migration eastwards which, by 1907, was running at 500,000 per year. The building of the Trans-Siberian railway which linked European Russia with the Pacific port of Vladivostok was completed in 1902. The new emigrants produced wheat and textiles on a large scale and Russian businessmen and generals cast their greedy eyes further away into Korea and Manchuria which were rich in minerals and timber. Here, however, they met tough opponents in the Japanese. Commercial and military rivalries in the Far East eventually led to the Russo-Japanese war of 1904–5.

The USA

The USA had once herself been a British colony. The American tradition was anti-colonial and against the spread of European power, especially in the American continent. However, between 1898 and 1914 the USA appeared to be behaving as a colonial power. During the 1890s she greatly enlarged her fleet. A revolt in Cuba against Spanish rule and the mysterious destruction of one of her battleships, the Maine, in Havana harbour provided her with an excuse to go to war against Spain in 1898. Victory was quickly won and Cuba, the Philippines (see source D), Puerto Rico and Guam passed into American hands. While the Cubans were soon granted their independence, the Filipinos were not, and a rebellion against American rule was sternly put down. The USA also annexed many Pacific islands, including Hawaii, and helped the European powers to crush the Boxer rebellion in China. Simultaneously, American businesses expanded considerably in Central and South America and across the Pacific.

China

The First Opium War, 1839–42

Though the ancient civilisation of China avoided being partitioned like Africa by the nations of Europe, she suffered at their hands. From 1839 to 1842 she fought and lost the so-called First Opium War with Britain. British ironclads blew Chinese junks out of the water to prevent the profitable trade in the opium drug being banned by the Chinese government. By the Treaty of Nanking (1842) Britain gained the island of Hong Kong (see map) and five other ports 'treaty ports', were opened up for Europeans to trade on favourable terms.

British and French aggression

In European eyes China seemed likely to prove a large and profitable market so traders from all the major European nations flocked to the Chinese coast. Disputes with the Chinese government led to open war with Britain and France between 1856 and 1860. They not only seized Canton in the south but captured Tientsin in the north. Then they marched into the capital Peking and burnt the Emperor's summer palace. By the Treaty of Tientsin (1858) the privileges of the foreigners trading in China were extended.

British and French 'treaty ports' in China, 1890.

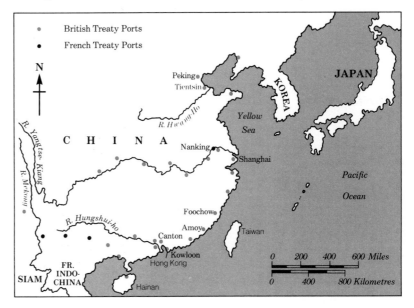

War with Japan, 1894–5

The power of the imperial government was never strong in the nineteenth century and it was gravely damaged by defeat in the war of 1894–5 with Japan. Between 1895 and 1914 there was a mini-scramble by Japan and the European powers for control of the best commercial areas in China. They also bullied the Chinese government into granting them special rights to undertake profitable schemes like railway building and mining.

The 'Boxer Rising', 1900

The methods, religion and success of the foreigners were hated by many Chinese. In 1898 a secret society which the British newspapers nicknamed the 'Boxers' organised a widespread rising directed mainly against Europeans and Chinese Christians. Thousands were slaughtered and in 1900 the European embassies in Peking besieged. An international expedition was organised, the embassies saved and the rising put down. The Chinese government was forced to pay the costs of the expedition.

Source G: China

G1 *The French attack on Foochow, China, in 1884 was described by the* Illustrated London News, *30 August 1884.*

G2 *A Chinese engraving of Foochow, showing an attack on a French gun boat* (Illustrated London News, *1 November 1884*)

G1

"Telegrams from Shanghai announced that the arsenal at Foochow was destroyed by Admiral Courbet on Saturday. The bombardment began at 2 o'clock in the afternoon and ended at night. Only one battery replied to the French fire. Seven gunboats were sunk .... Many hundreds of Chinese were killed by the French fire or drowned in the river. It is stated that the French fleet received little damage."

G3

G3 *This comment also came from the 1 November edition of the* Illustrated London News.

1 *Where and what was Foochow? Why should the French be interested in it and its arsenal? What might have caused the fighting?*

2 *What, according to the* Illustrated London News, *was the result of the fighting at Foochow? From whom did the magazine get its information?*

Study source G2 carefully.

3 a) *How can you tell the Chinese from the French?*
b) *What precisely is happening to the French, (i) on land and (ii) at sea?*
c) *Compare the arms of each side.*

"It had generally been supposed ... that the gunboats of the French naval squadron ... drove out the garrison with little difficulty ... and sank all the Chinese junks. But a Chinese artist in the sheet from which we have copied this engraving represents a different view .... History, at least that of Eastern Asia, seems liable to a considerable degree of variation, according to the point of view of the reporters and we should not be surprised to learn from some Chinese book that the allied French and British armies were once utterly defeated and destroyed in marching towards the city of Peking."

4 *In what ways does G2 contradict G1? How does the* Illustrated London News *explain the difference? Which source do you consider to be the more reliable?*

5 *How would a historian set about trying to discover what exactly happened in the fighting at Foochow in 1884?*

The balance-sheet of imperialism

The losses

Imperialism caused much suffering to the native peoples of the conquered lands. The conquests killed thousands, the suppression of later revolts thousands more. Guerrilla wars dragged on for years against the French in Indo-China and the Americans in the Philippines. The Boers suffered terribly in British concentration camps. As a punishment for rebelling in a desperate attempt to save their tribal lands, between 60,000 and 80,000 Hereros were slaughtered by the Germans in South West Africa (see source H3). Despite the great profits made from such raw materials as South African diamonds, Indo-Chinese bauxite and Congolese rubber, the wages of the local labour force were kept low, its hours long and its working conditions poor. So cruelly did King Leopold's officials treat the Congolese that an international outcry forced him to hand over the government of the Congo Free State to the Belgian parliament.

The best land was usually reserved for whites. The natives were seldom allowed political rights or to join a trade union. There was hardly any social mixing. Except for some Asian nobles, the whites regarded the natives as fit only to act as servants or labourers. That such attitudes might be open to criticism did not occur to many Europeans before 1914. They took it for granted that they were racially superior (see source H4). The biological ideas of Darwin were used (misused) to prove that races were bound to struggle for survival and that the fittest (the whites) would win. Whites like the Frenchman J. A. Gobineau and the English-born but German resident J. S. Chamberlain emphasised the importance of racial purity. Both believed that the Aryan or Germanic race, as long as it kept itself pure by not marrying other races, would rule the world.

The benefits

None the less European rule in the empires was not all take; there was some give too. Many missionaries and government officials were determined to improve the conditions of the native inhabitants and did so.

European rule often meant the end to tribal wars, to banditry, to witch-craft and to barbaric social customs. It started better medical, legal and educational services. It built railways, roads, irrigation schemes and power stations. The industries which it developed provided employment. Eventually some non-whites, mainly in Asia, became industrialists themselves and made their own use of European ideas and methods.

Through education the European ideals of liberty, equality and fraternity, of parliamentary democracy and of national independence became known to non-Europeans. These ideals made the imperial situation in which a tiny foreign minority ruled a huge unrepresented native majority quite unacceptable. Though the various nationalist risings against European rule were easily put down, they indicated that these huge empires so quickly and easily constructed might not last as long as their builders expected.

Source H: The colonised – some experiences of race-relations

H1 *An Annamite (Indo-Chinese) official friendly to the French talks to De Lannesan, a former colonial governor, in 1905.*

H1

"Discontent reigns in every class of the Annamite population. The king no longer has any authority; the mandarins are dissatisfied at not having [administrative] powers while the people are impoverished by taxes which mount ceaselessly and very rapidly. . . . This dull discontent has been excited by the recent victory of the Japanese."

H2 *The king and chiefs of the Brass people speak to Major Macdonald of the Royal Niger Company on 4 February 1895. The Company had established a trading monopoly along the Niger River which had hit the Brass people of the Niger Delta very hard.*

H2

"The ill-treatment of the Niger Company is very bad. They say that the Brassmen should eat dust . . . . Our boys fired, killed, plundered and even the innocent provision sellers were captured and killed likewise . . . instead of we Brass people die through hunger we had rather go to them and die in the sords [sic]."

H3 *A Herero leader to a German settler in South West Africa, 1904. The Herero were a grazing people and came into conflict with the German settlers over land. They rose in revolt in 1904 and were crushed mercilessly by a German army 17,000 strong. Their cattle were left to die and the whole colony made much poorer.*

H3

"Go back to your home country and tell your minister that you have erred and strayed from your path and lost your reason. The missionary says that we are the children of God. 'Like our White brothers', said another, 'but just look at us. Dogs, slaves, worse than baboons on the rocks . . . that is how you treat us'."

1 *List the various complaints made here about the Europeans.*

2 *What victory of the Japanese is being referred to? Why should it have excited the rest of Asia.*

3 *Sir John Kirk was sent by the British government to investigate the difficulties of the Brassmen. What sort of arguments*

would an official of the company have used to justify to Sir John its trading monopoly?

4 *All these primary non-European sources have reached us by way of Europeans: De Lannesan in Indo-China, Major Macdonald in Nigeria and a German settler in South West Africa. What problems do modern historians face in discovering the effects of imperial conquest on the conquered? How fair a picture do these extracts give?*

H4 *This extract comes from James Morris's* Pax Britannica, *London, 1968.*

1 *Explain the words and phrases 'concubinage', 'Empire-builder', 'confined within the cocoon of cantonment and family life', 'memsahib'.*

2 *In what ways had the home situation of the Englishman in India changed between 1750 and 1890?*

3 *What was the attitude of the average Englishwoman in India towards Indians?*

4 *The author seems to be suggesting that the wives were more racially prejudiced than the husbands. Is this not a trifle far-fetched? How would you measure racial prejudice and how would you set about finding out how widespread it was in India in the 1890s? How would you attempt to measure the extent of racial prejudice in modern Britain?*

H4

"In the early days of the East India Company social intercourse between white men and brown had been easy and respectful . . . .

In those days when Englishmen went out to the tropics alone, *concubinage* was one of life's great solaces. Most Englishmen in India took mistresses, and thus got close to the life and feelings of Indian people in a way that their successors seldom could . . . .

In the 1890s the attitude hardened. For one thing there were far more Englishwomen in the Empire. The steamship had seen to that, and the *Empire-builder* found himself far more closely *confined within the cocoon of cantonment and family life* . . . . In the multiracial Empire the white woman now occupied the same semi-divine status she had enjoyed in the slave states of the American South . . . . Fresh and fragile, pink and white . . . among the dark skins of the subject peoples she must have seemed exquisitely distinct. To those subjects she remained for the most part benevolent but aloof; as one *memsahib* wrote, 'It is best to treat them all as children who know no better, but . . . they are proud of their lies and the innate goodness of the Empire is not understood by them'."

2 Britain 1868–1914

In 1867 a Reform Act had been passed which doubled the number of men with the right to vote in British elections. Though a Conservative government had passed the Act, the inspiration of it was Gladstone, the Liberal leader. He gained his reward in the elections of 1868. The Liberals had a large majority and he became Prime Minister.

Britain's place in the world

His was among the most envied positions in the world. In 1868 Britain was more powerful in relation to the rest of the world than at any time before or since. She was economically the most advanced country, having pioneered modern manufacturing industry. She was also the leading trading nation with the largest fleet of merchant ships. To advance her trading interests she controlled a huge overseas empire which was still growing and was defended by a navy which was as big as the combined navies of her main competitors.

Nor was it just her economic and naval strength which foreigners envied. They were also impressed by the confident freedom of her people and the calm of her politics. Alone of the countries of Europe, Britain had achieved major social change in recent times without revolution (see source A).

There were problems. Rapid industrial growth combined with a fast-rising population had made Britain the most urbanised country in the world. Her cities, especially London, Birmingham, Glasgow, Manchester, Liverpool and Leeds, were large, crowded and blighted by appalling slums. Emigration was a popular escape from this overcrowding. The era of unquestioned economic dominance was ending. First the USA and then Germany successfully challenged and overtook her. In the late nineteenth century steel production was a good measure of industrial strength. Britain's output fell behind America's in 1886, and behind Germany's in 1893.

A particularly acute problem smouldered in the west. Ireland, John Bull's Other Island, posed questions which the British Parliament, as we shall see (pages 40–2), never satisfactorily answered.

Gladstone and Disraeli

From 1868 to 1880 British politics were dominated by the leaders of the two main parties, Gladstone for the Liberals and Disraeli for the Conservatives. They were both very able. They also detested one another.

Gladstone

The son of a wealthy Liverpool merchant, Gladstone had been educated at Eton and Oxford. He became an MP when he was only twenty-four. Exceptionally intelligent, energetic and industrious, a fervent Christian and expert economist, he was a skilful debater in Parliament and a fine public speaker. Though Queen Victoria heartily disliked him, he was popular both with his party and more generally in the country. Disraeli could hardly have been more different. Son of a Jewish stockbroker who had his children baptised Christians, he had no university education. In

Disraeli

his twenties he began writing novels but spent more of his energies making himself notorious for his extravagant dress, debts and party-going. He entered Parliament in 1837 and though his maiden speech was howled down, emerged within ten years among the Conservative leadership. He had a remarkable feel for the public mood and changed the party from a backward and aristocratic-looking party into one which had a genuine appeal to the new working-class voters. In his political novels he wrote understandingly about the 'Two Nations' in Britain. While One Nation enjoyed the benefits of the most powerful and rich country in the world, a Second Nation, millions of the poor and downtrodden, were sadly deprived. He made sure that the Conservatives were seen to be taking action to improve the situation of the poor and could genuinely claim to be working to make the Two Nations one. A cunning and skilful political operator, he had the party reorganised so that it was more effective at fighting elections. Witty and charming, particularly to women, he was adored by the Queen.

Liberalism and Conservatism, 1868–80

Gladstonian Liberalism meant free trade, freedom of opinion, particularly religious opinion, and the end of privilege. It favoured the extension of the franchise and expected moral principles to have some effect on foreign policy. It tended to disapprove of foreign and imperial adventures. The Conservatives were less ready to lay down firm principles and, under Disraeli's leadership, skilfully adapted their policies to changing needs. Conservatism generally favoured free trade and greater individual freedom but disapproved of excessive change. It saw itself as the Church of England party while Nonconformist churchgoers like the Methodists and Presbyterians were usually Liberal supporters. Conservatives considered the defence of national interests as the chief concern of foreign policy and took an earlier and more lively interest in imperial expansion. However, it would be wrong to exaggerate the differences between the parties or the fixed nature of their political principles. British society was changing fast. If they were to survive, politicians had to change too.

Gladstone's first ministry, 1868–74

Gladstone's first ministry lasted from 1868 to 1874. These were its main achievements. Merit, measured by competitive examination, replaced patronage for entry into the civil service. Forster's 1870 Education Act set up board schools to fill the great gaps in elementary education unfilled by the existing 'voluntary' mainly church schools. It brought education within reach of every child and was a major landmark in the development of state education. The army was rearmed and reorganised by Cardwell and the tradition that promotion could be purchased was abolished. Entry to Oxford and Cambridge universities was widened by the University Tests Act of 1871 which ended the religious tests which had allowed only Anglicans into the two universities. The law courts and administration of justice was thoroughly overhauled by the Judicature Act of 1873. In addition, there was the Ballot Act (see page 34) and measures affecting the trade unions (page 36) and Ireland (page 30).

Disraeli's ministry, 1874–80

The Conservatives won the 1874 election. Though Disraeli was ageing and, as the Earl of Beaconsfield, moved into the House of Lords for a quieter life, his government was also one of great achievement. He backed his Home Secretary, Cross, who was ready to meet the objections of trade unionists to some of Gladstone's legislation. Cross also made possible major housing improvements by his Artisans Dwellings Act of 1875. Other social reforms included the Public Health Act, the Food and Drugs Act, the Merchant Shipping Act, a Factory Act and an Education Act of 1876 which continued the developments begun by Forster.

Source A: British society in 1867

A The British Beehive. *The artist George Cruikshank published this picture in 1867.*

1 *Explain the phrases 'Freedom to all Religious Denominations'; 'Mercantile Marine'.*

2 *What features of British society does Cruikshank emphasise?*

3 *How content is he with the state of British society in 1867?*

4 *If you were to design a similar 'beehive' showing modern British society, what items shown by Cruikshank would you still include? What would be your main changes?*

5 *How useful a piece of evidence is this for the nature of British society in 1867?*

Disraeli's main interests, however, lay in imperial and foreign affairs, and here he had great sucess. In 1875 he bought a controlling interest in the Suez Canal off the Khedive of Egypt for £4 million (see page 12). The canal was an essential link in the sea route to India so Disraeli's purchase strengthened Britain's position in this vital strategic area. It also led to a greater involvement in Egyptian affairs and in Northern and Central Africa. Moreover he persuaded Parliament to allow Queen Victoria the title of Empress of India. This trivial gesture delighted both the Queen and public opinion. However, imperial adventures, though sure to capture the public imagination, sometimes ended in disaster. In South Africa, at Isandhlwana in 1879, there was defeat by the Zulus (see chapter 1). In Afghanistan, a mountainous and dangerous country positioned between the Russian Empire to the north and the British Empire in India to the south, an over-ambitious policy led to the violent death of the British representative and the defeat of a small British army, also in 1879.

The Eastern Question, 1875–8

The 'Eastern Question' is the shorthand form of the question 'what was to happen if and when the Turkish (Ottoman) Empire collapsed'. Since this empire was weak and getting weaker, and since it covered a large area including south-east Europe and the eastern Mediterranean (see map on page 28), its future greatly interested its neighbours. Of the European powers the most concerned were Russia, Austria-Hungary and Britain. Russia took every opportunity to increase her influence in south-

Source B: Gladstone and Disraeli

B1 *Gladstone's diary entry for 31 December 1868.*

1 a) *In source B1, what is meant by (i) '1852 Chancr. of Exr.', (ii) '1868 First Lord', and (iii) 'great year of opening, not alarming, change'.*
b) *What is Gladstone getting at in the section in italic? What career might he have preferred to politics? Explain your reasoning.*
c) *How useful are diaries as evidence of an individual's personality? What other evidence would you seek to get a rounded view?*

B1

"This month of December has been notable in my life as follows:

Dec. 1809 Born
     1827 Left Eton
     1831 Classes at Oxford
     1832 Elected to Parliament
     1838 Work on Ch. and State Published
     1834 Took Office, Lord of the Treasury [a junior minister]
     1846 Sec. of State [Minister for the Colonies]
     1852 Chancr. of Exr.
     1868 First Lord

Rather a frivolous enumeration [list] . . .

Swimming for his life a man does not see much of the country through which the river winds and I probably know little of the years through which I busily work and live, beyond this how sin and frailty deface them and how mercy crowns them.

But other years as I hope are to come a few at least on which yet ampler mercy will permit more of my own soul and *to live that kind of work which perhaps (I have never lost the belief) more specially belongs to me.*

It has been a special joy of this December that our son Stephen is given to the Church; 'whose shoe's latchet I am not worthy to unloose'.

Farewell great year of opening, not alarming, change; and welcome new year with promises and care'."

east Europe. She acted as champion of the Christian Slav peoples of the Balkans against their Muslim Turkish rulers. In the long run she hoped to gain Constantinople. Austria-Hungary wished to increase her own influence in the Balkans and viewed with anxiety Russia's activities. Also hostile to Russia was Britain. If Russia gained from a Turkish collapse, the eastern Mediterranean and the sea route to India would be threatened. British had gone to war with Russia in 1854–6 (the Crimean War, see page 45), to prevent such a collapse.

B2 *Disraeli writes to his wife from Osborne Palace in the Isle of Wight, 28 February 1868. He describes his first meeting with the Queen after Derby's resignation.*

B2

"I arrived [at Osborne] at 7 o'clock and had an audience about half an hour afterwards. The Queen came into her closet with a very radiant face holding out her hand, and saying 'You must kiss hands' which I did immediately and very heartily, falling on my knee. Then she sat down, which she never used to do, and only does to her First Minister and talked over affairs for half an hour (I standing) so that I scarcely had time to dress for dinner."

B3

"Yes, I have climbed to the top of the greasy pole."

B3 *Disraeli's comment to his friends congratulating him on becoming Prime Minister in 1868 (he was in office only a few months since the Liberals won the general election in the autumn).*

B4 Punch *cartoon, 3 January 1874. Mr Punch is in the chair of the manager of a theatre. Disraeli and Gladstone appear before him as writers of plays for him to choose. Punch, a weekly magazine of humorous political and social comment, was first published in 1841. It had a large middle-class readership and employed some of the outstanding cartoonists of the time.*

2 a) *In source B2 why was Disraeli at Osborne?*
b) *In source B3 what does he mean by the metaphor 'greasy pole'?*
c) *What sort of person does Gladstone appear to be from source B1 and Disraeli from sources B2 and B3?*

3 *Study the cartoon in source B4. 1874 was election year.*
a) *When Mr Punch asks the two leaders about 'the hits of the season', what actually is he requesting?*
b) *What characteristics of the two leaders does the cartoonist emphasise? Does he seem in any way biased?*
c) *How do the leaders in the cartoon compare with personalities of sources B1–3?*

THE MANAGER'S ROOM.

Mr. P. "WELL, MY DEAR DRAMATISTS, WHAT ARE TO BE OUR 'HITS' FOR THE SEASON?"
Mr. G. "I SHALL PROBABLY HAVE SOMETHING OF A VERY SERIOUS AND SENSATIONAL CHARACTER!"
Mr. D. "AND I'VE A CAPITAL NOTION FOR A BURLESQUE, ONLY THE PLOT ISN'T QUITE SETTLED!"

The Balkans, 1877–8.

▨	Austro-Hungarian Empire ⎫
▨	Ottoman Empire ⎬ after Congress of Berlin, 1878
▨	Russian Empire ⎭
—	Proposed boundaries (Treaty of San Stefano) 1878
1878	Date of autonomy ⎫ after Congress
1878	Date of Independence ⎬ of Berlin, 1878

The Bulgarian atrocities

In 1876 there was a revolt in Bulgaria which the Turks put down with great cruelty. This sparked off a major crisis in Europe and much controversy in Britain. The Russians marched to the aid of the Balkan Christians. While Gladstone toured the country speaking out passionately against the 'Bulgarian atrocities' and demanding that the Turks be expelled from Europe 'bag and baggage', Disraeli worked to limit the gains which Russia made in the eastern Mediterranean at the Turks' expense. In his opinion Britain's interests were better served if a weak Turkey rather than a strong Russia ruled in Constantinople. At a dangerous moment in the crisis Disraeli ordered the British fleet to set sail for Constantinople.

The Treaty of San Stefano, 1878

The Russians had already forced the defeated Turks to agree to the Treaty of San Stefano which much enlarged Bulgaria, Russia's ally, at Turkey's expense. However, so hostile were Britain and Austria-Hungary to this treaty that Russia agreed to a meeting of the major

Source C: The Bulgarian Atrocities and the Eastern Question crisis, 1876–8

C1 *In June 1876 British newspapers reported the razing to the ground of the Bulgarian hill town of Batak by Turks with the deaths of 5,000 including women and children. This news inspired Gladstone to write a pamphlet called* The Bulgarian Atrocities *and to lead a passionate campaign against Disraeli's pro-Turkish foreign policy. This is an extract from Gladstone's pamphlet.*

C1

"An old servant of crown and state, I entreat my fellow countrymen . . . to require and insist that our government which has been working in one direction shall work in the other . . . and shall apply all its vigour . . . in obtaining the extinction of the Turkish executive power in Bulgaria. Let the Turk now carry away their abuses in the only manner possible, namely by carrying off themselves. Their Zaptiehs and their Mudirs, their Bimbashis and their Yuzbashis, their Kaimahans and their Pashas, one and all bag and baggage shall I hope clear out of the province which they have desolated and profaned."

C2 *Gladstone's pamphlet caused an enormous stir. Disraeli, speaking at a Buckinghamshire by-election in 1876, made this comment:*

C2

"Under ordinary circumstances a British Minister [involved in a foreign crisis] would have the consolation of knowing that he was backed by the country . . . I do not think that there is any language which can denounce too strongly conduct [like Gladstone's]. He outrages the principle of patriotism . . . in the general havoc and ruin which [his conduct] may bring about, it may, I think be fairly described as worse than any of those Bulgarian atrocities which now occupy attention."

C3 *Gladstone speaks here to the House of Commons on 7 May 1877, at the end of a two and a half hour speech (reported in* Hansard*).*

C3

"Sir, there were other days when England was the hope of freedom . . . You talk to me of the established tradition and policy in regard to the Turks. I appeal to an established tradition, older, wider, nobler far – a tradition not which disregards British interests but which teaches you to seek the promotion of those interests in obeying the dictates of honour and justice."

C4 *Disraeli (Lord Beaconsfield) to the House of Lords, 1877.*

1 *What did Gladstone believe should be Britain's policy towards Bulgaria and south-east Europe? For what reasons? (See sources C1 and C3.)*

2 *Disraeli's policy was different. What was it? Why was he so angry with Gladstone in 1876? (See sources C2 and C4.)*

3 *Quite apart from the particular crisis of 1876–8, what do these extracts tell you about the main differences of principle between Liberal and Conservative foreign policy?*

4 *Who was most pleased with the outcome of the 1876–8 crisis – Disraeli or Gladstone? Explain your answer.*

5 *Having considered events in the Balkans between 1878 and 1914 (see pages 96–100), whose policy seems to you the most sensible – Disraeli's or Gladstone's? Explain your answer.*

C4

"I say absolutely the policy of Europe and not merely the policy of England . . . has been this – that by the maintenance of the territorial integrity and independence of the Ottoman Empire, great calamities may be averted in Europe, wars may be averted, and wars of no ordinary duration . . . . It has been said that the people of this country are deeply interested in the humanitarian and philanthropic considerations (i.e., the conditions of the Bulgarians) involved in the Eastern Question. All must appreciate such feelings. But I am mistaken if there be not yet a deeper sentiment on the part of the people of this country . . . and this is the determination to maintain the Empire of England."

(*From 1774 to 1828 the responsibility for printing a record of parliamentary debates was held by Luke Hansard who won a reputation for accuracy and speed of publication. His work was continued by his descendants until 1909, when the work was taken over by the government which published every word of business by the end of the following day. Hansard is still used as the name of the reports.*)

The Congress of Berlin, 1878

European powers to discuss the situation. A Congress was held in Berlin in 1878 with Bismarck in the chair.

Disraeli, supported by Bismarck, persuaded the Russians to agree to a less favourable treaty which left the Turks with a considerable foothold in Europe and transferred Cyprus to British control. Disraeli returned home in triumph claiming, with some justification, that he had gained 'peace with honour'.

Ireland to 1886

Catholics and Protestants

The Irish were part of the United Kingdom in 1868 but an unhappy part, profoundly divided from the other inhabitants of the British Isles. While two-thirds of the population were Irish and Catholic, one-third were of English or Scots descent and Protestant. The English and Scots had come as conquerors. Supported by the London governments they had stayed to control the best land and positions of power. Though reforms in the first half of the nineteenth century had at last made political careers possible for Irish Catholics, the hatred between the different groups was deepened by the catastrophe of the Great Hunger of 1847. The potato crop failed and hundreds of thousands of Irish peasants starved to death. Death and emigration, mainly to the USA, halved the population from 8 million to 4 million. So limited and ineffective were the efforts of the British government to head off the tragedy that many survivors came to believe that it had welcomed the suffering.

The Potato Famine, 1847

The Fenians

As in other parts of Europe, nationalism was a powerful force in nineteenth-century Ireland. More and more Irishmen decided that their best future lay either in complete independence from Britain or in greater self-government with their own parliament in Dublin. A secret society, the Fenians, helped by money and supplies from the USA, spread terror through Ireland and England to draw attention to their demand for independence.

Gladstone's first ministry

Gladstone, in his first ministry, aimed, he said, to 'pacify' Ireland. If the question of land ownership and religious difficulties could be settled, he believed that Ireland could be kept within the United Kingdom. In 1869 he 'disestablished' the Anglican (Protestant) Church in Ireland which meant ending its privileged position. His Land Act of 1870 gave to tenants (mainly Irish Catholics) better compensation if evicted by their landlords (mainly English Protestants). Roman Catholic opposition caused his plan to found a university in Dublin open to both Protestants and Catholics to fail.

Parnell

However, the Irish MPs at Westminster were not in the least pacified. They wanted Home Rule and from 1878 had a tough leader in Parnell. 'We shall never gain anything from England', he said 'unless we tread on her toes'. While he mounted a campaign to disrupt the workings of Parliament at Westminster, the Land League founded in Ireland by Davitt used violence to prevent tenants from being evicted. The Land League aimed to make all tenants the owners of their land.

Gladstone's second ministry

Gladstone returned to power in 1880. He passed another more far-reaching Land Act in 1881 which granted fair rents, fixity of tenure and free sale (the so-called three Fs). But violence continued. Parnell was temporarily imprisoned for his involvement in it and a new Irish Secretary, Lord Frederick Cavendish (who was also Gladstone's son-in-law) was knifed to death in Dublin's Phoenix Park. Parnell's Irish

The Home Rule crisis, 1885–6

Nationalists were absolutely committed to Home Rule and in the 1885 election were successful in the whole of Ireland except the Ulster city of Belfast. With 86 MPs they were in a strong bargaining position since the majority of the Liberals over the Conservatives was exactly that number. By this time Gladstone had realised that some form of Home Rule should be given to Ireland but the news of this change of mind slipped out in such a way as to suggest that he was simply buying the Irish Nationalist vote. The Liberal Party was badly shaken and 93 Liberal MPs followed Joseph Chamberlain when he opposed the Home Rule bill of 1886. The bill was defeated and Chamberlain's Liberal Unionists split off from Gladstone's party to vote usually with the Conservatives.

The split in the Liberal Party

Conservative domination, 1886–1905

The 1886 Liberal split led to a period of Conservative political domination which lasted for the best part of twenty years. Lord Salisbury succeeded Disraeli in 1880. He was Prime Minister from 1886 to 1892 when he lost the general election to Gladstone. The latter, having failed to get his Home Rule bill through the House of Lords, resigned in 1894 and Lord Rosebery, his successor as leader of the Liberal party, lost the general election of 1895 to Salisbury. The Conservatives remained in power until 1905 led first by Salisbury up to his resignation in 1902 and then by his nephew, A. J. Balfour, from 1902 to 1905.

Lord Salisbury

Salisbury was the last member of the House of Lords to be Prime Minister. Unusually he acted as his own Foreign Secretary for most of his years of office. In home affairs his instinct was to keep things running smoothly, to react to events, rather than put into effect new ideas. He was not at all enthusiastic about the increase in the franchise. Foreign affairs was his chief interest and he was a skilful negotiator in times of crisis. It was he who was mainly responsible for Britain's success at the Congress of Berlin in 1878, though Disraeli, his chief, took much of the credit.

Salisbury's foreign policy

He once wrote that 'English [foreign] policy is to float lazily downstream, occasionally putting out a diplomatic boat hook to avoid collisions' and the phrase 'splendid isolation' has often been used to describe Britain's relations with Europe while he was Foreign Secretary. In reality, however, Salisbury worked hard to keep Britain on good terms with the rest of the world, a far from easy task since the rivalry for colonies was at its most keen (see chapter 1). Particular successes were the sale of Heligoland to Germany in 1890 in return for Germany's agreement to Britain's expansion in East Africa, the settlement of a boundary dispute with Venezuela and British Guiana, despite the aggressive support of the USA for Venezuela (1895–9) and persuading France to back down over Fashoda in 1898 (see page 12). His last major decision was to sign an alliance with Japan in 1902 to protect Britain's interests in the Far East against Russia.

Joseph Chamberlain

Another important political figure of this era was Joseph Chamberlain, who had led the Liberal Unionists out of Gladstone's party in 1886 and who joined Salisbury's 1895 government as Colonial Secretary.

A Liberal in Birmingham

Though born in London, Chamberlain regarded himself as a citizen of Birmingham and insisted that he was buried there rather than in Westminster Abbey. It was in Birmingham that he made his fortune as a manufacturer of screws and where he began his political career. He first

Source D: The balance of power of the parties, 1880–6

D1

Election results

1880 General election Lib. 347, C. 240, Irish N. 65. Gladstone becomes Prime Minister.

1885 Lib. defeat in Commons, Lord Salisbury (C) forms government without an election. Parnell (Irish N. Leader) bargains with both parties to get Home Rule if he possibly can.

1885 (November) General election Lib. 335, C. 249, Irish N. 86 (Conservatives continue in power with Irish support).

1885 (December) Gladstone publicly in favour of Home Rule.

1886 (January) Cons. defeated by combination of Liberals and Irish Nationalists. Gladstone, Prime Minister again in February, tries to get Home Rule bill through Commons, defeated on 7 June.

1886 July general election, C. 316, Liberal Unionists (Chamberlain) 78, Liberals (Gladstone) 191, Irish N. 85.

D2 *Gladstone to the House of Commons, 1886, during the debate on Home Rule.*

D2

"Ireland stands at your bar, expectant, hopeful, almost suppliant. Her words are the words of truth and soberness . . . . You have been asked tonight to abide by the traditions of which we are heirs. What traditions? By Irish traditions? Go into the length and breadth of the world, ransack the literature of all countries, find if you can a single voice, a single book, in which the conduct of England in Ireland is anywhere treated with other than profound and bitter condemnation. Are these the traditions by which we are exhorted to stand? No, they are the sad exception to the glory of our country. They are a broad and black blot upon the pages of its history . . ."

D3 *Chamberlain to a meeting of the Birmingham Liberal Party explaining his objections to Home Rule.*

D3

"Was Home Rule to be allowed at last because of violence and menace? That is a cowardly argument and not to be addressed by Englishmen to Englishmen.

What of the situation under Home Rule in case of war? If that happens again, where shall we be? England may be struggling for her very existence; it may be in the throes of death; but Ireland will be unconcerned.

I should like to see the case of Ulster met in some form or other . . . having regard to the great distinctions which I have pointed out of race, religion and politics, I would be glad if there could be conceded to Ulster a separate assembly."

Study source D1.

1 a) *In 1885 who led (i) the Conservatives, (ii) the Liberals, (iii) the Irish Nationalists?*
b) *Who won the general elections of 1880, 1885 and 1886?*
c) *If the Irish Nationalists were so small a party why were both major parties keen to have their support?*
d) *Who were the Liberal Unionists? What part did they play in the 1886 crisis?*

Study sources D2 and D3.

2 a) *What were Gladstone's main Irish reforms between 1868 and 1874?*
b) *What is meant by Home Rule? Why did Gladstone believe Ireland should have it in 1886?*
c) *Summarise Gladstone's argument in source D2. What had he in mind when he* talked of 'a broad and black blot upon the pages of [England's] history'?
d) *What were Chamberlain's two main arguments against Home Rule?*
e) *Why was it important that he convinced the Birmingham Liberals that he was right?*
f) *How important was his part in the Home Rule crisis?*

made his mark as a local Liberal politician. He helped to turn the Birmingham Liberals into the best-organised local party in England and to found the National Liberal Association. Under the rule of his party Birmingham experienced great improvements. Water and gas supplies were taken over by the municipality from inefficient private suppliers. They were enlarged and run at a higher standard. Slums were demolished, parks created and a library, art gallery and eventually a university built.

Conflict with Gladstone

Chamberlain was elected to Parliament in 1876. His main interests were social reform and the expansion of the British Empire. He aimed to make the Liberal Party more committed to these interests. Gladstone neither sympathised with these interests nor liked Chamberlain personally. None the less he included him in his cabinet in 1882, but would not appoint him Irish Secretary, a position which, for all its difficulty and danger, Chamberlain was keen to have. Ireland soon caused a total break between the two men. Chamberlain could not bring himself to support Gladstone's Home Rule Bill of 1886. From Home Rule to complete Irish independence seemed to him a very short step and a real threat to the future of the British Empire. Consequently, as we have seen (page 31), he fiercely opposed Gladstone in 1886 and split the Liberal Party.

D4 *A* Punch *cartoon of 17 July 1886. Its caption was* 'The Finish'.

Study source D4.

3 a) *Who are the runners? When precisely did this race take place?*
   b) *Why does the winner wear the Union Jack and the loser 'Home Rule'?*

THE FINISH.

Colonial Secretary

Chamberlain's chief concern by now was the Empire and it was at his request that Lord Salisbury made him Colonial Secretary in 1895. Chamberlain favoured imperial expansion wherever possible and greater unity within the Empire. In South Africa he encouraged an aggressive policy against the Boer Republics of the Transvaal and Orange Free State. He secretly supported Rhodes and Jameson in the ill-fated raid on the Transvaal in 1895 (see page 14) and the Boer War of 1899 was caused in part by his desire to win the goldfields of the Transvaal for Britain. Though the war was won and the Boer Republics forced into the Empire, the costs were heavy and the long-term benefits either to Britain or to South Africa were far from clear.

Tariff reform

As he worked to strengthen the unity of the Empire, he became convinced that the traditional policy of free trade was no longer in Britain's or the Empire's interest. British agriculture had suffered badly as a result of cheap food being imported from overseas while British manufacturing industry was struggling against the competition of other recently industrialised nations. Many other countries were protecting their farmers and industries by tariffs (customs duties). Britain should do the same, Chamberlain argued, by a scheme of 'tariff reform', which would co-ordinate and protect imperial trade and production against foreign competition. Having failed to persuade the Conservatives to agree to such a major policy change, he resigned from the Cabinet and campaigned all over the country to swing public opinion in favour of 'tariff reform' (see source E1 and E2). He failed. In the 1906 election the Liberals, who presented themselves as the party of free trade, won a handsome majority. A few months after the election he had a serious stroke. Though he lived until 1914, he could no longer play an active part in politics.

Chamberlain was a powerful personality who liked to get things done his own way. With a clear mind and a crusading temperament, he found compromise difficult. Consequently his political career was frequently controversial. To disrupt two major parties in less than twenty years is quite an unusual feat! In Birmingham and the Colonial Office he was able to get things done. In his enthusiasm for social reform and imperialism he reflected important trends in public opinion.

Parliamentary reform and its effects

The 1867 Reform Act had increased the number of voters by reducing the value of the property which a man had to own or lease if he were to have the franchise. The number of men who could vote in 1867 was about one in three. Seats were redistributed so that the growing industrial areas were more fairly represented. A Ballot Act followed in 1872 which made voting secret and so greatly reduced the ability of the rich and powerful to influence elections. In addition, a Corrupt and Illegal Practices Act of 1883 further reduced the amount of corruption in elections.

Another Reform Act in 1884 simplified and lessened the property qualification for the franchise so that the proportion of men able to vote after 1884 rose to two in three. As men became better off so the proportion of voters increased. The property qualification was finally abolished by another Reform Act in 1918 (which also granted the vote to women aged 30 or over).

Party organisation

The new voters were mostly from the working classes. Their vote could not now be won by threat or bribery – it had to be gained by persuasion.

Source E: Tariff reform

E1 *This poster had the caption 'A Free Trade Forecast'.*

E2 *'Flattening him out': a general election poster.*

1 *The posters were produced for a general election campaign: which one?*

2 *What is the main theme of the first poster?*

3 *Who is marching in the background? Why has the artist included them?*

4 *Which party produced the second poster? How do you know?*

5 *Which figure is Chamberlain? What part of his appearance would you expect cartoonists to have frequently used to characterise him?*

6 *What was the link between 'tariff reform' and the British Empire?*

7 *What is the main theme of this poster?*

8 *The 'free traders' got the better of the argument in the election. For what reasons do you think Britain had been and remained so keen on free trade?*

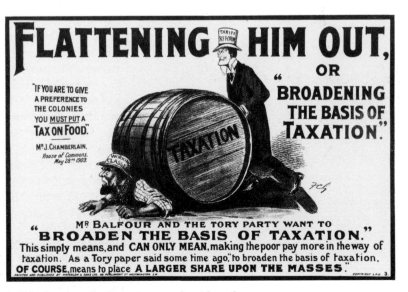

9 *Of what are these posters good evidence? How much do they actually tell you about public opinion at the time?*

Better organisation and communication were needed. Great speaking tours, like Gladstone's Midlothian campaign of 1879, were assisted by the railways. Both political parties set up national organisations. The National Union of Conservative and Constitution Associations was created in 1867. The Conservatives also had a 'Central Office' in London and clubs all over the country. The main drive for better Liberal organisation came from Birmingham. The local party there, led by Chamberlain, became famous for its success in co-ordinating its efforts both in local and national elections. The National Liberal Association was founded in 1877.

Trade unions and the origins of the Labour Party

Between 1870 and 1914 trade unions played a growing part in British life.

They were organisations that caused strong feelings in many quarters. To their members they were vitally important if better pay and working conditions were to be won. Employers and most nineteenth-century governments, whether Liberal or Conservative, believed that their powers to damage industry and the economic progress of the country were considerable and that their activities should be limited by law.

The craft unions

Unions of working people had been illegal before 1825 and between 1825 and 1850 they made slow and uncertain progress in attracting members and respectability. They made an important advance in the 1850s and 1860s with the appearance of 'craft' unions, like the Amalgamated Society of Engineers which was founded in 1851. The craft unions' members were among the most skilled of the workforce and were able to pay comparatively high subscriptions. Leaders of these unions co-

The TUC, 1868

operated to found the Trades Union Congress in 1868. Thus British trade unionism gained a national voice which, through its parliamentary committee, spoke out in favour of universal manhood suffrage (votes for all men), the secret ballot and shorter working hours laid down by law.

The problem of picketing

Union leaders knew that strikes could not always be avoided if better pay and conditions were to be won. For strikes to be effective, unions must have their own funds available to support their striking members and non-union workers be prevented from taking the place of the strikers. The protection of their funds and the right to picket were, therefore, important issues. In 1871 Gladstone's Liberal government passed a Trade Union Act which made clear that unions were legal and protected their funds. However, shocked by the violence of strikers against 'blackleg' labour (the 'Sheffield outrages' of 1867), it declared picketing to be illegal. Disraeli's government changed the law on picketing. Its Criminal Law Amendment Act of 1875 allowed picketing, as long as it was peaceful.

The 1870s were, on the whole, good years for British industry. Unions campaigned successfully for higher wages and a shorter working day (9 hours was the usual target). In contrast, British agriculture passed through a serious decline, being quite unable to compete with the cheap foreign food being brought into the country by the new refrigerated steamships. Thousands of farmers went bankrupt.

Joseph Arch

One consequence of the agricultural crisis was the formation by Joseph Arch in 1872 of the National Agricultural Labourers' Union, which was one of the earliest unions of unskilled workers. Such unions with large memberships and low subscriptions appeared in increasing numbers in

*New large
unions*

the last twenty years of the century. There were some famous and successful strikes, e.g. the Bryant & May match girls organised by Annie Besant in 1888 and the dockers led by Ben Tillett in 1889. The tension between organised labour and their employers was not lessened by the general feeling that the British economy was not advancing as confidently as before.

By now many working men were sure that their interests and those of their family and communities could not be properly looked after by the Liberals and Conservatives. Separate socialist parties already existed in Europe and the case for a British party for the labouring classes was an

The SDF

The ILP

attractive one. The Social Democratic Federation (SDF) was founded by H. M. Hyndman in 1881, but its strict Marxist ideas never proved popular. More significant was the Independent Labour Party (ILP), founded in Bradford by Keir Hardie in 1893. Hardie was a Scots miner who had already succeeded in getting himself elected to Parliament for West Ham. He called himself 'the member for the unemployed'. Quite

The Fabians

different, but influential, were the Fabians, a society of mainly middle-class socialist thinkers founded in 1883 by Sidney and Beatrice Webb. Fabius was the general of Ancient Rome who wore down his enemy, the brilliant Hannibal of Carthage, by slowly and patiently probing at his weak points. Socialism, the Fabians argued, could win victory over capitalism by such tactics, without violent revolution.

The LRC, 1900

In 1900 representatives of the SDF, ILP, Fabians and TUC set up the Labour Representation Committee (LRC) with the aim of getting Labour MPs elected to Parliament. Ramsay MacDonald of the ILP was its first secretary. It won its first by-election in 1903 and, fighting the 1906 election as the Labour Party, gained twenty-nine seats.

*The Taff Vale
and Osborne
judgements*

The LRC was indirectly given a great boost after the House of Lords (the highest lawcourt in the land) ruled that the Amalgamated Society of Railway Servants would have to pay damages to the Taff Vale Railway Company for the strike action of its members. The unions and LRC campaigned to get the law changed. Labour's influence on the Liberal government helped to pass the Trade Disputes Act of 1906 which protected union funds from employers' claims for damages.

In 1909 the House of Lords made another judgement (the so-called Osborne judgement) against the unions and the Labour Party. It declared illegal the custom of unions to use part of their members' subscriptions for political purposes like paying the salaries of Labour MPs. Once again the Liberal Party, which after the 1910 election was dependent on Labour MPs for its overall majority in the House of Commons, came to the rescue. The Trade Union Act (1913) allowed unions to use funds for political purposes as long as the majority of their members were in favour and individual members could opt out.

*Industrial
unrest, 1910–14*

Immediately before the First World War Britain experienced industrial strife of unusual bitterness. There were nasty riots in South Wales in 1910 and, during the long hot summer of 1911, four strikers were killed by troops. By 1914 the members of unions who were represented by the TUC was more than 4 million and three of the largest – the miners, dockers and railwaymen, had formed a 'Triple Industrial Alliance' to increase the co-ordination of their bargaining power and consequently strengthen it.

Education and local government

What should be the responsibilities of the State?

Nowadays we are used to the state providing services like hospitals, schools, old age pensions and unemployment pay and equally used to paying taxes to finance these services. In the middle of the nineteenth century the majority of the ruling classes took quite a different view. It would be best, they believed, if the responsibilities of the state were kept to a minimum. The government should defend the realm, keep law and order, make sure that the royal family could live in dignity and prevent the poor from dying of starvation. Otherwise people should be free to run their lives as they wished and in particular to trade freely both within Britain and internationally. The French phrase *laissez-faire* (leave be) is used to describe this approach; collectivism (where the state provides services collectively for all citizens and taxes them collectively too) is the term often used for the modern approach.

Education was an area where the government interfered more and more between 1868 and 1914.

Forster's Education Act, 1870

In 1868 education was mainly in the hands of voluntary (church) schools, which were aided by government grants. However, these shcools did not have places for all children and Britain's educational standards seemed to be lagging behind those of her industrial competitors. By the Education Act of 1870, therefore, Gladstone's government set up local school boards whose responsibility was to build board schools to fill the gaps left by the church schools. The board schools were to provide elementary education from the ages of five to twelve and to concentrate on the 3 Rs. Christian instruction had to be provided, but it was not to be biased towards a particular Christian denomination. Costs were to be met out of local rates. In 1880 elementary education was made compulsory; in 1891 it became free both in board and in voluntary schools.

Another major Education Act was passed in 1902. Control of elementary as well as secondary education passed from the school boards to the county and county borough councils, which had been created by the County Council Act of 1888. Voluntary schools were also brought into the system, since the councils paid for their running costs out of the rates.

The 1902 Education Act

The Act of 1902, which was to a large extent the work of Robert Morant, Secretary of the Board of Education, was controversial at the time because Non-conformists, especially in Wales, thought it quite wrong that voluntary schools (mainly Anglican) should get so much ratepayers' money. None the less over the years it led to real progress. Standards improved in many elementary (primary) schools. More pupils continued into secondary education. Teachers were better paid and classes became smaller. The main weakness of the 1902 Act was the damage it did to the scientific and technical education which many school boards had encouraged. The post-1902 secondary schools were strongly influenced by the independent 'public' and 'grammar' schools, whose curriculum was still dominated by classics and by 'humane' subjects.

The Local Government Board, 1871

National government gave some responsibilities to local government. In 1871 the Local Government Board was set up which supervised local boards whose main responsibilities were sanitation and health. The social reforms of Disraeli's government – the Public Health Act, the Artisans Dwellings Act, the Sale of Food and Drugs Act – added to these responsibilities and encouraged local initiative. Tremendous improvements were made by councils to the appearance and facilities of their cities.

In 1888 the County Council Act laid down that the councils of the counties and county boroughs should be elected by ratepayers. More responsibilities were given to these local councils, including some duties of the justices of the peace. The Local Government Act of 1894 replaced the local boards of 1871 with elected urban and rural district councils. Parish councils also elected by ratepayers were also introduced.

The Liberals in power, 1906–14

The new Liberal government which was led by Campbell-Bannerman from 1906 to 1908 and by Asquith from 1908 until 1916 had many talented ministers including Lloyd George, Churchill and Grey. It was an energetic reforming ministry.

'Welfare' reforms

It introduced old age pensions (5 shillings per week for everyone of seventy or older), set up labour exchanges to help the unemployed to find work more easily and trade boards to lay down minimum wages for low-paid, sweated industries like clothes making. However, its greatest social reform was the National Insurance Act of 1911. Lloyd George, Chancellor of the Exchequer, presented it to the House of Commons. It would give, he said, ninepence for fourpence. The scheme, which owed much to German experience, would safeguard insured workers against illness by providing them with sick pay and medical treatment. For this they would pay fourpence, their employer three pence and the state two pence. Approved societies and trade unions and insurance companies would act as the insuring agencies. The second part of the Act insured workers in the building and engineering trades against unemployment.

The House of Lords and the Budget of 1909

The need to raise more money to pay for these reforms helped to bring about a major constitutional crisis from 1909 to 1911. The central issue was how much power should rest with the House of Lords. Up to 1911 the Lords, who owed their position entirely to heredity, could veto any measures approved by the elected Commons except those dealing with money. In 1909 Lloyd George needed to raise more money, partly to pay for old age pensions and partly for new battleships. In his Budget, he proposed higher income tax, a supertax on the very rich, a capital gains tax on land, and extra duties on alcohol, tobacco and motor vehicles. The landowners, well represented in the Lords, considered the Budget to be not a simple money matter but an attack on their class and its place in society. In his public speeches Lloyd George, who had a sharp and witty tongue, was rude about dukes and their land deals. The Duke of Beaufort said that he would like Lloyd George in the middle of forty of his foxhounds. The House of Lords vetoed the Budget. This was a bad mistake. The Liberals had had enough. The House of Lords had a huge Conservative majority. It had blocked Irish Home Rule for nearly twenty

The Parliament Act crisis, 1909–11

years as well as other Liberal policies, passed by the Commons, which it disliked. Asquith decided that the time had come to cut back its powers. He proposed that in future the Speaker of the House of Commons should decide what was a money bill and that the Lords should have no powers to change or delay such a bill. Furthermore, they should lose the power to veto other Commons-approved bills. All they should be able to do in the future would be delay and advise changes. He then, in January 1910, called a general election. Though the Liberals only won a majority of two over the Conservatives there were another 122 MPs in favour of parliamentary reform (82 Irish Nationalists, 40 Labour). None the less many Lords were prepared to fight on 'to the last ditch' as they put it. After months of fruitless discussion between the party leaders, the death of Edward VII caused another election which left the state of the parties virtually unchanged. Asquith persuaded the new king, George V, to agree to the creation of enough Liberal lords to carry his reform proposals through the Lords if the present members continued their opposition. This was enough to make them realise that continued resistance was pointless and, in August 1911, they voted by a small majority to agree to their reduced powers which were laid down in what became known as the Parliament Act.

Ireland, 1886–1914

The question of Home Rule

After Gladstone's failure in 1886 to achieve Home Rule for Ireland, the intention of the Conservatives was to 'kill Home Rule with kindness'. They encouraged major agricultural improvements, reformed local government and, by Wyndham's Land Purchase Act of 1903, made it possible for tenants to buy their land on easy instalments. However, Home Rule would not go away. Irish nationalism became more vigorous. The Irish Nationalists were reunited in Parliament under John Redmond's leadership. In 1893, in his last ministry, Gladstone succeeded in getting a Home Rule bill through the Commons, only to have it thrown out by the Lords.

Redmond (see source F2) supported Asquith during the Parliament Act crisis and in return the Liberals agreed that once the powers of the Lords were reduced, they would immediately introduce a Home Rule bill which was bound to come into effect in the long run since the reformed Lords could only delay it. This Home Rule Act was, in fact, passed in 1912 and was intended to take effect in 1914.

Opposition in Ulster

At this stage the Ulster problem came sharply into focus. This most northerly Irish province had been settled by the Scots in the seventeenth century. In contrast to the rest of Ireland, Protestants outnumbered Catholics two to one. Dominated by the industrial city of Belfast, it was economically the most advanced region and dependent on trading links with the rest of Britain. Its Protestant inhabitants were strongly anti-Catholic and anti-Dublin. They were bitterly opposed to Home Rule which they regarded as Catholic Dublin Rule (see source F2). Supported by the Conservatives they prepared to resist it by every means at their disposal.

The Solemn League and Covenant, 1912

Led by Carson and Craig their first step was the mass signing of the 'Solemn League and Covenant' which demanded that Ulster remain part of the United Kingdom and be separated off from the rest of Ireland (see source F1). When the Liberals showed no sign of agreeing to their separation which was strongly opposed by the Irish Nationalists, an Ulster Volunteer Force was formed so that Home Rule could be resisted by force. In response the Home Rulers formed in Dublin the Irish Volunteers. Tension grew as arms were smuggled into the country and some British army officers stationed at the Curragh near Dublin indicated that they were not prepared to march against Ulster if ordered by the government (the Curragh Mutiny, 1914). Only the outbreak of the First World War which gave the government the excuse to postpone introducing Home Rule prevented Ireland from slipping into civil war.

Source F: Ulster

F1 *The Ulster Solemn League and Covenant, 28 September 1912.*

Use source F1.

1 *What was Ulster? How was it different from other parts of Ireland?*

2 *What event in Britain caused the Ulster Protestants to draw up this Covenant?*

3 *What four main reasons did they give for believing that Home Rule would be disastrous?*

4 *What did they intend to do if Home Rule was introduced?*

In source F2:

5 *What actually is happening in the picture?*

6 *Who is 'King John of Ireland'?*

7 *What is the flag on top of the building?*

8 *Explain why so many people should be going to the Protestant Emigration Office.*

9 *What other consequence of Home Rule is shown in the picture?*

10 *What were the political views of the artist? On what date do you think it was painted?*

F2 *The caption for this postcard was 'Making a site for the statue of King John of Ireland'.*

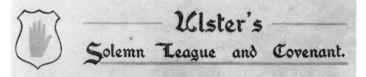

Ulster's Solemn League and Covenant.

Being convinced in our consciences that Home Rule would be disastrous to the material well-being of Ulster as well as of the whole of Ireland, subversive of our civil and religious freedom, destructive of our citizenship and perilous to the unity of the Empire, we, whose names are underwritten, men of Ulster, loyal subjects of His Gracious Majesty King George V., humbly relying on the God whom our fathers in days of stress and trial confidently trusted, do hereby pledge ourselves in solemn Covenant throughout this our time of threatened calamity to stand by one another in defending for ourselves and our children our cherished position of equal citizenship in the United Kingdom and in using all means which may be found necessary to defeat the present conspiracy to set up a Home Rule Parliament in Ireland. ¶ And in the event of such a Parliament being forced upon us we further solemnly and mutually pledge ourselves to refuse to recognise its authority. ¶ In sure confidence that God will defend the right we hereto subscribe our names. ¶ And further, we individually declare that we have not already signed this Covenant.

The above was signed by me at_____
"Ulster Day," Saturday, 28th September, 1912.

_____

God Save the King.

F3 *Protestant gunrunning at Larne during the night of 24–5 April 1914. This account is taken from* Mutiny at the Curragh *by A. P. Ryan, published in 1956.*

Read source F3.

11 *Who were the Volunteers? What did they want guns for?*

12 *Explain the sentence in italic. What should the police have done? What did they do? Why?*

13 *In Howth near Dublin three months later, an attempt at gunrunning by the National (Catholic) Volunteers was interrupted by the police and troops. When troops marched back into Dublin they were jeered by the crowd and had some stones thrown at them. The troops opened fire on the crowd, killing three and wounding thirty-eight.*

Write a short newspaper comment from the point of view of a Catholic Dubliner comparing the Larne and Howth gunrunning, the way the police and troops acted in each case and what these events suggest about the attitude of the British government.

F3

"The little seaport of Larne lies about 20 miles north of Belfast. The local Ulster Volunteers had been mobilised at 8 p.m. and a procession of motor cars and lorries almost three miles long had been formed from the direction of Belfast .... It was in theory a routine exercise of the Volunteers and, equally, *a detached historian may be forgiven for suspecting that the police were only in theory to know nothing about it.* The good work of unloading the rifles and ammunition was speedily effected and despatched to destinations as far off as Co. Tyrone and Londonderry. Here and there the local police were surrounded by a superior force. There is no record of resistance and only one casualty. The coastguard at Donaghadee, riding his bicycle vigorously to give the alarm, fell dead of a heart attack outside the post office. Had he entered he would have found the lines dead, earthed by the Volunteers.

The men and women of the Volunteer force who had been training for the past six months had the night of their lives ....

Carson in London received a telegram of one word – lion. It was the code message telling him that Ulster was now armed."

14 *What more evidence do you need to get a balanced view of the situation in Ireland in the summer of 1914?*

Votes for women

Improvements in the situation of women

The social status of women improved in the second half of the nineteenth century. Three Married Women's Property Acts passed between 1870 and 1893 gave women control over their own property. Educational opportunities for well-off girls were improved, thanks particularly to Miss Buss and Miss Beale whose Girls' Public Day School Trust was founded in 1871. The invention of the typewriter and the development of offices and high-street shops widened the job opportunities for working women.

Moreover women property owners were allowed to vote in local elections from 1894. After 1907 they could become county councillors and aldermen. Hundreds were already Poor Law guardians and members of education committees.

Mrs Fawcett

That they could not vote in parliamentary elections seemed to many women, and indeed many men, quite illogical. New Zealand had given women the vote in 1893, Australia in 1902. Why should British women be without? In 1897 Mrs Fawcett founded the National Union of Women's Suffrage Societies (NUWSS). Her members, usually know as 'suffragists', were respectable and reasonable. They were sure that eventually they would be able to win votes for women by the sheer strength of their case, clearly and firmly argued. Less respectable and noisier was the Women's Social and Political Union (WSPU) founded by Mrs Emmeline Pankhurst in 1903 and led by her and her daughters. They were known as 'suffragettes'.

Mrs Pankhurst

Asquith's opposition

Those in favour of women's suffrage had high hopes of the Liberal government of 1906. Many of its Cabinet ministers, as well as its backbench MPs, were known to be sympathetic and in 1910 a large majority of the House of Commons declared itself in favour of votes for women – in principle. But nothing happened. The main obstacle was Asquith, the Prime Minister. He did not believe that women were emotionally capable of considering major political issues properly. If they were not to fight in wars, was it fair that they should have a say in matters which could lead to war? Moreover he suspected that women might well support the Conservatives in greater numbers than the Liberals. Asquith's objections were shared by men of varied political views and social background and no other political leader was prepared to commit himself to push women's suffrage through Parliament.

Suffragette violence

In these circumstances, the suffragettes lost patience and in 1912 carried out spectacular acts of violence and disruption (see source G4). At the 1913 Derby, Emily Davison of the WSPU killed herself by rushing in front of the galloping horses. The government reacted toughly. Violent suffragettes were imprisoned, forcibly fed if they went on hunger strike and, by the so-called Cat and Mouse Act of 1913, released if they became ill in prison and immediately rearrested when they recovered.

Whether or not the violence of the suffragettes helped or hindered the women's suffrage cause is a matter of disagreement among historians (see source G5). Certainly it had achieved nothing by the time the First World War broke out.

Source G: The Liberal government and women's suffrage, 1910–14

G1 *A cartoon on women's suffrage published by the Artists Suffrage League, 1910.*

1 a) *Why is the lady fenced in?*
  b) *Explain her clothing.*
  c) *How effective a cartoon is it?*

G2 *Winston Churchill, Home Secretary, speaks in Dundee in December 1910.*

G2

"So far as I am concerned, I am still of the opinion that the sex disqualification is not a true and logical disqualification and I am therefore in favour of women being enfranchised. But I decline utterly to pledge myself to any particular bill at the present time . . ."

G3 *Churchill writes to his Cabinet colleague, Lord Grey, who with Lloyd George was a strong supporter of women's suffrage, on 20 December 1911.*

Read sources G2 and G3.

2 a) *Summarise Churchill's Dundee statement in a sentence.*
   b) *In his letter to Grey, what is it about women's suffrage that makes him anxious?*
   c) *Did Grey and Lloyd George lead 'a strong campaign' for votes for women? What evidence have you for your answer?*
   d) *What other problems did the Liberal government face between 1910 and 1914?*
   e) *Comment on Churchill's attitude as indicated by his speech and letter from the viewpoint of* (i) *a moderate suffragist,* (ii) *a militant suffragette.*

G4 *John Grigg in:* Lloyd George from Peace to War 1912–16 *(1985), quotes Ellis Davies, a friend of Lloyd George who witnessed one of his meetings in North Wales in 1912.*

G5 *A* Punch *cartoon of 13 March 1912.*

Read Source G4.

3 a) *Describe the actions taken by the suffragettes to draw attention to their cause.*
   b) *John Grigg's book is a secondary source. What primary sources do you know for sure he used? What other primary sources would you expect him to have used for his study of Lloyd George and the suffragettes?*

Study the cartoon in source G5.

4 a) *Who is the main figure?*
   b) *Who are the people in the background and what are they doing?*
   c) *Explain the caption.*
   d) *John Grigg, unlike some other historians, believes that suffragette violence turned public opinion against votes for women. Does the* Punch *cartoonist have a similar view?*

G3

"My dear Grey,

I am getting increasingly anxious about the women's suffrage situation. If you and George are going to make a strong campaign in favour of adding 6 million voters to the franchise, it will become increasingly difficult for those who do not think such a change at this juncture likely to be for the good of the country not to participate actively in some counter movement.

I do not think that the Prime Minister's position is tenable except on the basis that the question is unimportant ... [Asquith, the Prime Minister, was known to be strongly against votes for women].

This strong government on whose continuance so much depends may easily come in two."

G4

"No sooner had he appealed to the crowd in Welsh to be gentle with any suffragettes present than one of the women quite near the stage shouted 'Votes for Women' and in the attempt to lead her out – she herself fighting and kicking those who tried to protect her – the crowd pressed down and an ugly mob made for the platform. No sooner was one disposed of than other women cried out in other parts of the field. According to Press reports two women were attacked by the crowd, their hair pulled and their clothing torn ..."

"1912 was a year of mounting suffragette violence, provoking counter violence by the state. In February Mrs Pankhurst had told members of her organisation, the Women's Social and Political Union (WSPU), that the broken pane of glass was the most valuable argument in politics ... soon afterwards hammers were issued to 150 suffragettes who were sent out to smash the windows of selected shops and offices in the West End ..."

IN THE HOUSE OF HER FRIENDS.

"TO THINK THAT, AFTER ALL THESE YEARS, I SHOULD BE THE FIRST MARTYR."

3 The Russian Empire 1850–1900

The Crimean War, 1853–6

The Russian Empire had the largest army in Europe. It had had an excellent reputation since it had played a major part in the defeat of Napoleon Bonaparte between 1812 and 1815. However, this reputation was badly dented by the Crimean War of 1853–6.

Causes: the Holy Places Dispute

This war was an episode of the long-running Eastern Question (see page 26). It began with a squabble between Catholic and Orthodox priests over the case of the Holy Places in Palestine which was then part of the Turkish Empire. Napoleon III of France backed the Catholic priests, Tsar Nicholas I the Orthodox ones. Since Nicholas claimed his right to protect all Christians within the Turkish Empire, Britain feared that he was scheming to expand his power in the Eastern Mediterranean and allied herself to France in opposition to Russian plans.

Events

Clumsy diplomacy and excited public opinion turned the Holy Places crisis into war. Russia invaded Moldavia-Wallachia in 1853 (see map). Turkey then declared war and had her fleet sunk at Sinope by the Russian navy. Britain and France then declared war on Russia in the spring of 1854. Their armies invaded the Crimean peninsula, their main target being the port of Sebastopol. Having won the Battle of the Alma they slowly advanced on Sebastopol and laid seige to it. Attempts by the Russian commander Menshikov to end the seige were driven off at the battles of Balaclava, Inkerman and Chernaia. Though Todleben, in

The Crimean War, 1853–6.

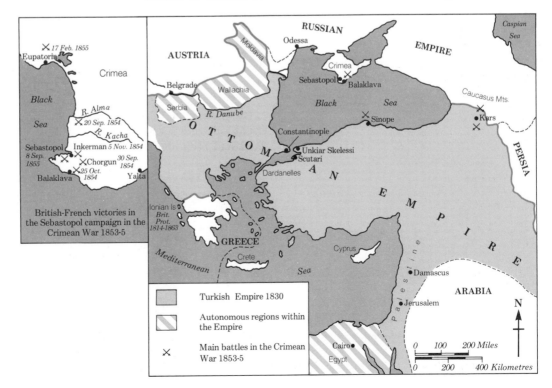

command of Sebastopol's defences, proved a skilful general, the Russians eventually evacuated the port. Tsar Nicholas died and his successor Alexander II was anxious to make peace.

Results: the Treaty of Paris, 1856

The Treaty of Paris, 1856, marked a major Russian defeat. Land was lost in the Danube basin, the claim to protect the Turkish Christians given up and no warships were to be allowed in the Black Sea in times of peace.

The French came out best from the war. Though they suffered 100,000 casualties, they fought well and Napoleon got what he wanted. The British commanders made fools of themselves. It was at the Battle of Balaklava that the Light Brigade charged the main Russian guns because of a mistaken order. British public opinion was shocked by the 60,000 casualties and Florence Nightingale became famous for her hospital work at Scutari.

The Russians suffered much the worst. They had 300,000 casualties. The government had been shaken further not just by the defeat but by the physical weakness and ignorance of the thousands of serfs who had made up the defeated army's ranks. Indeed so severely depressed was Tsar Nicholas by the setbacks in the Crimea that when he died in 1855 rumour had it that he had committed suicide.

Tsar Alexander II, 1855–81

In his place now reigned his son Alexander, who was thirty-seven. A kindly and well-meaning man, he could at times be both shrewd and determined. He was also lazy, inclined to put on weight, emotional and obstinate, as, for example, when he defied his parents and married Princess Marie of Hesse whom he had met while touring Europe. His chief interest was army parades. In many history books he is given the fine title, 'Tsar Liberator', which gives the impression that he was a keen liberal reformer. He was not. Rather he was clever enough to realise that some changes had to be made if Russia was to avoid revolution and that the time for such changes was ripe after the defeats of the Crimean War.

Alexander's main reforms

Three-quarters of Russia's population were serfs (see sources A1–3). This meant that they were peasants held by law in a position close to slavery. They could not leave their lord's estate without his permission; they had to work his land with their own tools and pay him taxes either in money or in produce. He could buy, sell or mortgage them. He could discipline them by flogging. In return for such burdens, they had land which they could cultivate for themselves and their families. For centuries this land had been divided out and supervised by the village commune or 'mir'.

Nowhere else in Europe did serfdom survive. It had been abolished in the Austrian Empire as a result of the 1848 Revolution. Some nobles, though by no means all, felt uneasy about it (see source A4). Some, again by no means all, realised that it was an inefficient method of farming and a cause of the serious financial problems which many of the landowning class were facing – and many felt widespread concern about the increasingly frequent peasant riots.

The emancipation decrees

Alexander acted swiftly. In 1856 he made a famous speech to an assembly of nobles from the Moscow area (see source B1). It would be better, he argued, that serfdom be abolished from above rather than from below, by government action rather than by peasant revolts. He then set up committees to find out what the nobles thought and to work out the

Source A: Rural Russia

These photographs were taken at the end of the nineteenth century or early in the twentieth.

A1 (**Right**) *A Russian peasant.*

A2 (**Below**) *A peasant in the fields.*

A3 (**Below right**) *Drawing water from a well.*

A4 *Count Kiselev was a Russian landowner who was often absent from his estates. He saw himself as a typical 'pomeshchik' or landlord and in this extract from his diary describes a visit to his estates. We know from other sources that his serfs found the demands he made upon them hard to bear.*

A4

"A visit to my steppe village for a day and a half does not deserve an elaborate account. My reception by the peasants on their knees, hand-kissing by my father's old servants and their children, the distribution of the presents and the cash prizes I brought, the satisfying of requests, a tour of the fields, a bad dinner and a good sleep – that is the whole story of a day's visit by a lax pomeshchik in his natural state."

1 *Describe what each of the pictures A1–3 shows. What conclusions can you draw about rural Russia in the mid nineteenth century?*

2 *What is the attitude of Count Kiselev (source A4) to his peasants?*

3 *What does he mean by the phrase 'a lax pomeshchik in his natural state'?*

4 *What appears to be the attitude of the peasants to him? Have you any reason to think that their real feelings might have been different?*

best way of freeing the serfs and at the same time adequately compensating the nobility. A genuine liberal, Rostovsteff, was responsible for the main proposals (see source B2) though conservative influences at the court made sure that in the end the nobles got a good deal.

The compensation problem

The emancipation decrees were finally published in 1861. They seemed a great step forward (see sources C1 and 2). All serfs gained their legal freedom and those who had cultivated land for themselves and their families were allowed to keep most of it, though the proportion varied from one part of the country to the next. However, the changes turned out much less well for the peasants in the long run than they had come to expect. For one thing the decrees were incredibly complicated and difficult to understand. For another compensation payments had to be paid to the landlords over a forty-nine-year period. In addition these compensation payments had to be paid through the 'mir' or village commune and freedom of movement was restricted until the compensation payments had been completed. While the serfs on the Tsar's wide estates were more generously treated, a typical noble's serf found himself after 1861 legally free but with less land than before (on average 20–15 per cent less), compensation to pay and no immediate freedom to move as he pleased. Not surprisingly there were frequent bitter land disputes and peasant risings in the 1860s and 1870s. Emancipation was to make the Russian peasantry more rather than less revolutionary.

Other reforms

The zemstvos

Russia had no representative assemblies either nationally or locally. By a decree of 1864 Alexander set up provincial and local elected councils which were called 'zemstvos'. There were zemstvo elections every three years and three classes of voter based on property qualifications defined in such a way that the rich were sure to dominate. The district zemstvos elected the provincial ones and each chose its officials. In 1870 similar arrangements were allowed in Russian cities. Zemstvo discussions centred on local matters – hospitals, roads, agriculture, poor relief and so on. With little real power of their own they had to rely on the Tsar's officials to get things done. None the less they encouraged useful work and, by their very existence, increased the general awareness of Russia's lack of a national representative assembly and of the excessive power concentrated in the hands of the Tsar and his ministers (see source E1).

The army

Another important reform was that of the army, carried out in 1874 by General D. Miliutin. Formerly the huge Russian army had been manned mainly by serfs working a long twenty-five-year service and recruited on a quota system from towns and villages. While it was easy for the noble and the rich to gain exemption from military service, this was impossible for the serfs for whom military service could be a dreadful individual burden. Miliutin reduced both the size of the permanent army and the length of service. Six-year terms replaced the twenty-five-year ones. Though every male of twenty was liable for military service exemption was possible whatever the social class of the individual as long as he could make a good case.

Law and education

Alexander also turned his attention to the law and education. He improved the legal system by trial by jury and more independent judges. Better education was provided both in schools and in universities, especially for men. It seemed for a moment as if, in the words of Prince Kropotkin, Russia really was awakening 'from the heavy slumber and terrible nightmare of Nicholas I's reign'.

Source B:
Proposals for emancipation

B1 *The speech of Alexander II to the Moscow nobles, 1856.*

B1

"It has been rumoured that I want to give liberty to the peasants. This rumour is unjust and you can say so to everyone, on all sides. But a hostile feeling between peasants and their pomeshchiki does, unfortunately, exist and this had already led to several cases of insubordination to pomeshchiki. I am convinced that sooner or later we must come to this. I think that you agree with me consequently that it is better that this [freedom] come from above, than from below."

B2

"*Proposal 2*: Along with individual freedom, the peasants must receive the full opportunity to acquire enough land of their own to provide for their everyday needs.

Proposal 8: For the lands which they give up, landowners must be remunerated and, as far as possible, without loss.

Proposal 9: The peasant's yearly repayment both of interest and redemption dues must not exceed the average amount of their present obligations, or else there will be no improvement in their living conditions."

B2 *Rostovsteff's proposals for emancipation, 1859.*

1 *What would have been the first reactions of the Russian nobility, for the most part an extremely conservative group, to the idea of freeing the serfs?*

2 *What did Alexander have in mind when he refers to the 'insubordination' of the peasantry? Why was he so worried about it?*

3 *What is the main reason which he gives for emancipation? Do you think this was the most important one in his mind or the one which he thought would most impress the nobles? Explain your answer.*

4 *Who was Rostovsteff? Sum up in twenty-five words his three proposals. Where do his sympathies lie? Explain your answer.*

5 *To what extent did the emancipation of the serfs fulfil the principles laid down by Rostovsteff?*

Source C:
The Emancipation decrees

C1 *A painting by G. G. Miasoyedor of a village group listening in a barn while one reads the decree of 19 February 1861.*

1. *What were the main points of the 1861 decree? What about it would you expect to have most pleased peasants like those in C1, and what would have most worried them?*

C2

"Russia remained quiet – more quiet than ever . . . I was in Nikolskoye in August 1861 and again in the summer of 1862 and I was struck by the quiet intelligent way in which the peasants had accepted the new conditions. They knew how difficult it would be to pay the redemption tax for the land . . . but they so much valued the abolition of personal enslavement that they accepted the ruinous charges – not without murmuring but as a hard necessity – the moment that personal freedom was obtained."

C2 *Prince Kropotkin, though of noble birth, became a well-known revolutionary writer of the late nineteenth century. In* Memoirs of a Revolutionist *published in 1930 he describes how the Emancipation decrees were received on his father's estates.*

2 *Kropotkin (C2) was not at all the average Russian noble. What are his strengths and weaknesses as a source for the emancipation of the serfs?*

3 *How does his account compare with that given in the narrative (page 48)?*

Expansion into Asia

Alaska, too far away to be defended easily, was sold to America in 1867, but thousands of square miles of Asia (i.e. east of the Ural Mountains) were conquered by Russia during Alexander's reign (see map D1). The vital strategic (and oil-rich) area between the Black Sea and Caspian Sea was secured, Turkestan was seized and Afghanistan, to the consternation of the British in India, threatened. In the Far East, China was forced to hand over the land between the Amur (see source D2) and Ussuri rivers and Vladivostok established as a port on the Pacific. The driving forces in this expansion were colonists and adventurers, often acting on their own initiative rather than on orders from Moscow. The Far East conquests were mainly the achievement of Muraviev, the ambitious governor-general of East Siberia. Later the Russian government followed a more active policy. Between 1881 and 1902 the Trans-Siberian Railway was constructed, 5,542 miles in length to link Moscow to Vladivostok on the Pacific Ocean. More Russian activity in the Far East led eventually to war with Japan in 1904 (see page 124).

Foreign policy in Europe

In 1856 Alexander had had to sign the unfavourable Peace of Paris, (see page 46). In 1870, using the chance provided by France's preoccupation with the Franco-Prussian war, Alexander ordered warships into the Black Sea. In 1877–8 Russian troops marched again against the Turks in aid of the Balkan Christians. Though they met stiff resistance at Plevna, they inflicted heavy defeats on the Turks and forced them to sign the Treaty of San Stefano. However, this treaty was regarded by the other Great Powers as too hard on the Turks and too favourable to Russia. They forced its revision at the Congress of Berlin in 1878 (see page 30).

Alexander II greatly respected Emperor William I of Germany and had valued the German alliance which was expressed in the League of the Three Emperors in 1872. Consequently he was surprised and irritated by Germany's attitude towards Russia after 1878 (see pages 87–90).

Reaction against reform

The apparent 'new dawn' of reform proved false. The Tsar had never been a wholehearted reformer and grew more conservative and repressive as he aged.

The Polish Revolt, 1863

A turning-point was the Polish revolt of 1863. Poland had lost its independence at the end of the eighteenth century when it had been carved up by its neighbours Russia, Austria and Prussia. After 1815 a central area had been allowed some limited self-government under close supervision but this it lost when a revolt in 1830, which had aimed at winning complete freedom, failed. Tsar Nicholas ruled the Poles strictly after the 1830 revolt.

At first Alexander gave them greater freedom. He allowed political exiles to return, Warsaw University to be reopened and the formation of an Agricultural Society which discussed social and political as well as farming issues. However, Count Wielopolski, whom he put in charge, upset many sections of Polish society. When he tried to remove revolutionary young people off the streets by forcing them into the Russian army, there were risings all over the country. Badly organised and ill-equipped, the revolutionaries never stood much chance of success. The peasantry refused to join them. The aid promised from France never came while the Prussians actively helped the Russians. Fighting went on for about two years but eventually the revolts were brutally suppressed. Poland lost all traces of self-government. Its educational and

Source D: Russia in Asia

D1 *Russian expansion 1815–1914.*

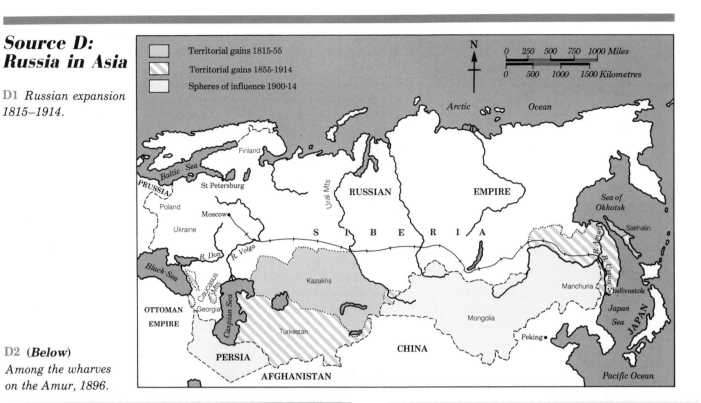

- ☐ Territorial gains 1815-55
- ▨ Territorial gains 1855-1914
- ☐ Spheres of influence 1900-14

D2 (*Below*)

Among the wharves on the Amur, 1896.

1 *Describe the Amur River scene (D2). To whom would the boats belong to and for what would they be used? How far distant is Moscow (see map D1)? Where is the nearest major Russian port?*

2 *What does source D3 show? Explain the double-headed eagle, the map and the different people on the left.*

3 *Which two nations were most worried by Russia's eastward expansion? Why were they worried and when did they sign an anti-Russian alliance?*

D3 (*Right*)

The last page of a book called Travels in the East of Nicholas II, Emperor of Russia *by E. Ukhtomsky, which was published in London in 1896. It is also the source for D2.*

legal systems were thoroughly russified. Only the peasants benefited. They gained the ownership of their land at a lower cost than their Russian counterparts.

Revolutionary ideas

In 1866 there was an attempt to assassinate the Tsar and the trend towards reaction accelerated. Count Tolstoy was appointed Minister of Education. He saw to it that university courses were checked by the police and student political activity forbidden. Believing the teaching of natural science to be dangerous to good order, he reduced the amount of science teaching in schools and replaced it by Latin and Greek. Thinking people in Russia found themselves more and more out of sympathy with the government and were attracted by revolutionary ideas. Some of these, like nihilism and anarchism, had very destructive elements such as the belief that a better society would only emerge in Russia after the breakdown of law and order and the violent sweeping away of old methods and traditions.

Populism

'Populism' was a related revolutionary movement whose supporters believed the peasantry to be the most powerful force for change within Russia. In 1873 and 1874 thousands of people, students and ex-students, went out into the countryside and tried to persuade the peasants to turn revolutionary. They had little effect. Most of the peasants were illiterate. Their unusual visitors puzzled rather than persuaded them. The government came down heavily on the populists or 'narodniks' as they were known. Hundreds were gaoled or sent into Siberian exile. As a result opposition to the government went underground. Secret terrorist societies were formed which planned to bring about revolution by assassinating leading government figures. An inspirer of such societies was Nechaev (see source E2). He taught that terror was an effective way of causing revolution and that terrorist leaders must discipline themselves ruthlessly. He led by example, personally murdering one of his followers for lack of total agreement with his plans. Also influential was Tkachev who emphasised that a successful revolution would be for the most part the work of a small group of totally dedicated leaders.

Terrorism

The most active of the secret societies of the late 1870s was 'the People's Will'. Their main target was the Tsar himself and they pursued him ingeniously, daringly and persistently. In 1879 they tried to shoot him and to mine his train. In 1880 they got into the Winter Palace in St Petersburg and blew up the dining-room ceiling, killing many diners but not Alexander who had been delayed. Every Sunday the Tsar left the Winter Palace to review an army parade. To improve security he used different routes. On Sunday 1 March 1881 the People's Will had mined one route but had also stationed two bomb-throwers on the Catherine Embankment in case the Tsar's convoy returned along that route. It did. The first bomb blew up alongside the Tsar's coach but it was specially strengthened and the Tsar was unharmed. Alexander got out of the coach to see what casualties there had been. He went over to look at the bomb-thrower who had been arrested. 'That one?' he is reported to have said, 'Why? He is quite nice looking.' The other terrorist was close by in the crowd. He hurled his bomb at the Tsar and it exploded at his feet wounding him mortally (see source E4). The five members of the People's Will responsible were arrested, tried and hanged, including their leader, Sofia Perovskaya, a noble's daughter (see source E5).

Alexander assassinated

Tsar Alexander III, 1881–94

The new Tsar was a simpler character than his father. He prided himself on his peasant-like qualities, his gruff straightforward common sense and down-to-earth way of expressing himself. He had only become heir-apparent at the age of twenty on the unexpected death of his elder brother and had had only a limited education.

Pobedonostsev – the end of reform

His tutor and most influential adviser was Pobedonostsev, one of the most extreme reactionaries of the nineteenth century (see source F1). Under his guidance the Tsar became sure that safety for Russia could only be secured by the strictest conservatism. Many of his father's difficulties had come, he believed, from his attempts at reform (see source F2). In contrast he would save Russia from disorder, he hoped, by defending the autocratic power of the Tsar, by strengthening the Russian Orthodox Church and by encouraging the Russian people to be loyal to their age-old traditions.

In practice this meant that Alexander III immediately cancelled the proposal of his father (made ironically just before he was assassinated) to set up a committee to investigate the possibility of a national assembly. The limited powers of the zemstvos were reduced, those of the secret police increased. Political opposition was ruthlessly repressed. Count Tolstoy became Minister of the Interior and redoubled the censorship of books and newspapers. Education was only allowed in so far as it did not make the lower orders discontented with their place in society. At the end of his reign, 80 per cent of the Russian population was still illiterate.

Russification

Russification was a major theme of the reign. Non-Russian minorities within the Russian Empire were forced to follow the Russian way. Poles, Finns and Asiatic peoples found themselves forced to use the Russian language at school and in official business. Individuals of the Russian Orthodox religion took precedence over Roman Catholics or Muslims. The minority which suffered worst were the country's five million Jews. Not only had they to live in a particular part of Russia, 'within the pale', but had limits placed on their opportunities in higher education and in the professions. Nor was that all. The word 'pogrom' is generally used nowadays to describe the destruction of Jewish life and property which was such a dreadful feature of European history between 1880 and 1945. It is a Russian word because some of the earliest persecutions took place in Russia early in Alexander's reign. One reason given for these vicious outbreaks was the fact that Sofia Perovskaya, leader of the 1881 assassination, was Jewish.

The French Alliance 1892

Perhaps the greatest achievement of Alexander III was to keep his country at peace. He did not trust Germany, as his father had done, and approved in 1892 an alliance with France. This was an early and important step in the formation of alliances which preceded and helped to bring about the First World War.

Source E: The growing opposition to the Tsar's government

E1

E1 The zemstvo of Tver sent a petition to the Tsar in 1879 after Russia had successfully aided the Bulgars in their struggle against the Turks.

"In his concern for the welfare of the Bulgarian people after their liberation from the Turkish yoke, the Sovereign Emperor had deemed it necessary to grant to this people [the Bulgarians] the self-government, protection of individual rights, an independent judiciary and freedom of the press. The zemstvo of Tver province dares to hope that the Russian people who bore the entire burden of the war ... with such self-sacrificing love for their Tsar Liberator will be allowed to enjoy the same blessings which alone can lead them, in the words of the sovereign, along the path of gradual, peaceful and legal development."

E2

E2 Nechaev: Catechism (Statement of Belief) of a Revolutionist, 1869.

"The revolutionary association had no aim other than the complete freedom and happiness of the people; i.e. people who live by manual labour. But convinced that this [freedom and happiness] is only possible through an all-destroying popular revolution, the association will exert all its efforts ... to further the development and extension of those misfortunes and evils which must at length exhaust the patience of the people and drive them to a general uprising."

E3

E3 The Programme of 'the People's Will', first published in 1880.

"The purpose of terrorist activity ... is to break the spell of governmental power, to give constant proof of the possibility of fighting against the government, to strengthen in this way the revolutionary spirit of the people ... and finally to create cadres [small disciplined groups] suited and accustomed to combat."

E4 The assassination of Tsar Alexander II (Illustrated London News, 2 April 1881)

1 *What were 'zemstvos' (source E1)? What sort of people would have been members? What is the main point of their petition to the Tsar? How strongly do you think that they felt about it? Explain your answers.*

2 *What was Nechaev (source E2) and what was 'the People's Will' (source E3)?*

3 *What sort of new Russia did the terrorists hope that their action would bring about? And why had they given up peaceful methods?*

An officer mortally wounded

Butcher boy killed

Tcherkess of the Emperor's Guard

Tcherkess sitting on coachman's side mortally wounded

Colonel of the Police Dvorchetski

The Emperor

Tcherkess of the suite of the Emperor killed

Colonel Dvorchetski's sledge in which the Emperor was brought to the Winter Palace

E5 *Sofia Perovskaya wrote to her mother while awaiting trial.*

E6 *The trial of the assassins of Alexander II: a painting by D. Beyer, 1881*

4 *Describe what is happening in source E4. Whom did the bomb kill, apart from the Emperor?*

5 *Describe what is happening in source E6. Of whom is the portrait? What colour would the curtains around it be? What is on the table in front of the judges?*

6 *Where is Sofia Perovskaya sitting in source E6? Who was she? If her mother had replied to her letter (source E5) and had said that having brought up her daughter to be kind and God-fearing she could not understand how she could murder the Tsar who was after all a well-meaning man, what arguments might Sofia have used to explain her actions?*

7 *Do you think terrorism is ever justified?*

E5

"I feel tormented because I do not know what has happened to you. Dear Mother, I beg you to be calm and not torture yourself because of me . . . I have lived as I felt called upon to do. I just could not go against my convictions. Therefore I await whatever fate has in store for me with a clear conscience."

Source F: The end of reform and a new policy

F1 *A letter from Pobedonostsev to Alexander III dated 6 March 1881.*

1 *How soon after the assassination was the letter written and the meeting held?*

2 *To what extent would you say that Pobedonostsev was temporarily off balance because of the recent assassination, or does the letter genuinely reflect his political attitudes (see page 53)?*

3 *Pobedonostsev recommends a new policy in his letter. What was this policy? To what extent did Alexander III follow his advice?*

F2 *Miliutin's diary of 8 March 1881 states that ministers have been discussing the proposal for a representative assembly which had been originally suggested before the assassination of Tsar Alexander II. A number of the more conservative ministers had already attacked the proposal.*

4 *Who were Pobedonostsev and Miliutin?*

5 *What do you think was Miliutin's attitude to the proposals for a representative*

F1

"If they sing you those old sirens songs – that you should remain calm, that you should continue in the liberal path . . . – oh, for God's sake, do not believe them . . . . This will mean ruin, Russia's ruin and yours.

The mad villains who killed your father will not be satisfied with any limited reforms and will only burst into a frenzy. They can be repressed, the evil seed can be uprooted, only by a battle to death with them, by blood and iron.

A new policy must be proclaimed immediately. This is the time to put an end, once and for all, to all talk about freedom of the press, freedom of assembly and a representative assembly. All this is the deceit of empty and flabby men and must be cast aside for the sake of the welfare of the people."

F2

". . . but everything they had said was pale and insignificant compared to the speech delivered by Pobedonostsev. His was no mere attack on the measure proposed but a complete condemnation of everything which had been achieved in the previous reign. He dared call the great reforms of Alexander II a criminal mistake!"

assembly? Explain your answer. Would you expect him to have remained as a minister to the new Tsar?

4 Italy and France in the second half of the nineteenth century

The unification of Italy

Of the many political ideas which had influence in nineteenth-century Europe, two, liberalism and nationalism, were particularly powerful. Liberals wanted more freedom, in trade, and of the press and ideas. They hated the custom that emperors, kings and other rulers should have power over people by the accident of birth and the belief that such power was given by God. They wished instead that political power should be held by an elected assembly. Nationalists believed that peoples with a common language and history should rule themselves and get rid of foreign domination. Between 1848 and 1880 most liberals were also nationalists but by no means were all nationalists liberals.

Italy in 1848

At the beginning of 1848, as the map in source A shows, the Italian peninsula had many different rulers, most of them foreign. A branch of the Bourbon family, originally French, ruled the Kingdom of the Two Sicilies (Sicily and Southern Italy). The Papal States were the Pope's. The Kingdom of Sardinia (Piedmont on the mainland and the island of Sardinia) had an Italian monarch. The rest of Italy was ruled by members of the Austrian Habsburg family, either as separate Duchies (Tuscany, Parma and Modena) or as part of the Austrian Empire (Lombardy and Venetia). Consequently Italian liberalism and nationalism were revolutionary forces. If they were successful Italy would be united under the rule of parliament and the foreigners would be expelled.

Mazzini

The inspiration of Italian liberals between 1830 and 1860 was Giuseppe Mazzini (1805–72). He believed passionately that only when all nations were united and free would real progress come to the world. He wrote eloquently and, having been exiled for his revolutionary activities, founded the Young Italy movement to put his ideas into practice. His personal efforts to organise revolution were almost comic in their incompetence but his ideas had great influence not just in Italy but throughout Europe.

The 1848 revolution

Hopeful liberals and hungry workers and peasants revolted all over Europe in 1848. Palermo in Sicily rose against the Bourbons in January; Rome, Milan, Florence and Venice against their rulers soon after. In March, Charles Albert of Piedmont declared war on the Austrians, stating that Italy would unite herself by her own efforts (*Italia farà da sè*). Charles was not much of a leader. His critics called him King Wobble because of his indecisiveness. He was badly defeated first at Custoza and then at Novara by the tough old Austrian general, Radetzky, and retired to a Portuguese exile leaving his son Victor Emmanuel II to make the best peace he could.

The Romans had thought Pope Pius IX (Pio Nono) to be their friend but he refused to support them against the Austrians. At the end of 1848 he fled from Rome where Mazzini and Garibaldi set up the Roman Republic. Venice too established a liberal government led by Daniele

Manin. However, the Austrian victories over Piedmont meant the end of the revolutions. The Bourbon and Habsburg princes returned to their palaces. A French army made Rome safe for the Pope and finally a combination of Austrian artillery and cholera forced the surrender of Venice in 1849.

The events of 1848 indicated to thoughtful Italians that Italy was not able to unite herself by her efforts alone. If the Austrians were to be driven out then foreign aid would be needed. Cavour, First Minister of Piedmont from 1852 to 1861, realised this and devoted his considerable skills and energy into securing that foreign aid.

Cavour and Garibaldi

Cavour

Camillo Cavour was a nobleman and a successful businessman who made his family rich by modern farming methods and clever investment

---

Source A: Italy 1815–70

A *The unification of Italy, 1859–71.*

1 *In 1858 who ruled* a) *Rome,* b) *Tuscany,* c) *Sicily? When did each become part of a united Italy?*

2 *Find* a) *Custoza,* b) *Solferino and* c) *Castelfidardo. What happened at each of these battles and when did they take place?*

3 *What gains did France make by helping Piedmont during 1859–60?*

4 *Where did Garibaldi's and Victor Emmanuel's armies meet in 1860?*

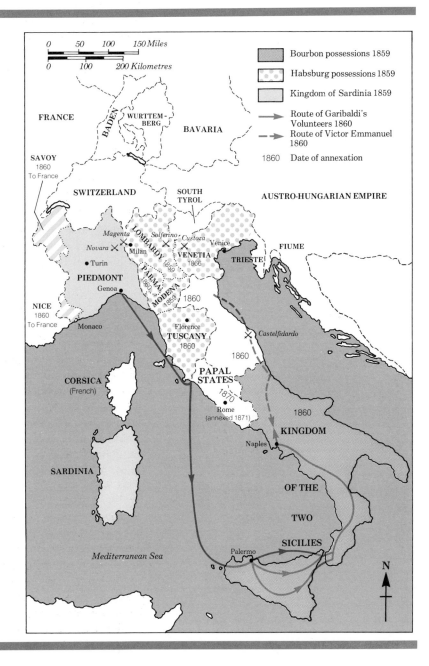

in industry. For a time he edited the nationalist journal *Il Risorgimento* (The Revival) which planned for the revival of Italy through unification. In 1850 he was elected to Piedmont's assembly which he soon controlled by his cunning and sometimes unscrupulous management of the various conflicting groups. Cavour was both a liberal and a nationalist but within limits. More individual freedom and power to parliament was all right as long as he remained in control. A united Italy was a fine idea in theory, especially if it meant the extension of the power of Piedmont over the civilised northern half of the country. He was much less keen on the unification of the whole country which would include the backward south. Idealists like Mazzini and Garibaldi who had dedicated their lives to the unification of all Italy deeply distrusted him (see source F). In their opinion he was 'piemontesissimo' – too concerned about Piedmont.

Garibaldi

Giuseppe Garibaldi was born in Nice which for most of his life was part of Piedmont. A member of Mazzini's Young Italy movement, he was condemned to death following an unsuccessful attempt at revolution in 1834 and had to flee to South America. There he made an international reputation for himself as a leader of revolutionary guerrilla bands before returning to Italy to take part in the events of 1848. He added to his reputation by his heroic defence of Rome and even more heroic escape after the surrender of the city (see source B). Somehow he dodged the Austrian armies searching for him though his wife died during the journey. After 1848 he was as keen as ever on a united Italy, but unlike Mazzini, who hoped for a republic, not a kingdom, Garibaldi was ready to accept the leadership of Victor Emmanuel, King of Piedmont.

Cavour wins the backing of Napoleon III

During the 1850s Cavour set the pace. Of the Great Powers, Britain and France seemed the most likely helpers, and Piedmontese troops fought alongside British and French ones during the Crimean War (1853–6) (see pages 45–6) in the hope of persuading them to become more active allies against Austria in Italy. However, Britain remained determinedly peaceful and, for a time, the more adventurous Napoleon III of France could not be tempted. Then in 1858 an Italian nationalist, Orsini, tried to assassinate him for not doing enough to help Italy. Oddly, Napoleon decided that this indicated that his destiny lay in helping the Italians while simultaneously making gains for France. He and Cavour met secretly at Plombières. There they agreed that Piedmont should provoke a war with Austria. France would then come to Piedmont's aid. Austria would be defeated and driven out of Italy. Lombardy and Venetia would go to Piedmont, the Duchies and parts of the Papal States would be divided between Piedmont and a relation of Napoleon's. The chief gains for France would be Nice and Savoy which were then provinces of Piedmont.

The Plombières Agreement, 1858

War and revolution, 1859–60

In 1859 Cavour managed to provoke the Austrians into war. The French intervened as planned and won two major victories at Magenta and Solferino. For Napoleon that was enough. His casualties had been heavy and the Prussian army was massing on the Rhine. Without consulting Cavour he made the truce of Villafranca with the Austrian emperor which ended the fighting and transferred only Lombardy to Piedmont. Cavour resigned in a rage.

However, the general situation in Northern Italy was much more hopeful than Cavour thought. Nationalist risings had driven the old

Source B:
With Garibaldi in 1849

B *Gustav von Hofstetter was a Swiss officer who fought with Garibaldi during the defence of the Roman Republic and marched with him after the fall of Rome in 1849. He kept a diary which was published in 1851.*

1 *What had Garibaldi been doing during the winter of 1848–9?*

2 *Where now was he marching? Who was the enemy?*

3 *What skills does he display as* a) *a soldier,* b) *a military and political leader?*

4 *This march ended with his forces melting away and his wife dying. Why then did it improve his reputation in Italy?*

5 *How important were von Hofstetter's responsibilities? Comment on his reliability as a source.*

B

"July 7th 1849 . . . During the defence of Rome I had often had occasion to admire Garibaldi's sure hand in directing a battle and his quick and sure eye for detail. Now I was able to observe his exceptional skill in matters of security and intelligence. He had acquired his ability in long years of warfare with quickly-moving light troops . . . . His energy is boundless. Whenever we left camp he first found guides and then gave instructions to those officers whose job it was to procure information about enemy movements and to provide food for the day's journey. It was my task to supervise the departure of the main column and in the meantime he and his wife rode up to the advance guard with instructions. Often he rode several miles ahead so that we would have plenty of time to . . . take evasive action against the enemy."

"July 11th . . . The failure of the enemy to comprehend our movements must have been increased all the more by the skill with which Garibaldi directed our marches. Never starting at the same hour; sudden changes in direction; one march today, two tomorrow . . . suddenly moving on to a main road only to abandon it an hour later . . . spreading false information, for example rations being ordered for as many as 60,000 men – all these were part of his game."

"July 14th . . . with the [local] people the general can behave in a way which always gets excellent results . . . . One soldier was caught stealing a chicken from a woman in a poor village and has been executed today. As the shots rang out Garibaldi rose and said to the astonished troops who did not know what had happened: 'This is the way I punish thieves. Are we fighting for freedom or are we just robbers? Are we here to protect people or to oppress them?' There were shouts from the soldiers 'Long live Garibaldi' and I am sure that the loudest shouts came from those who had just been eating the stolen chicken themselves."

Source C:
The coming of war, 1859

C *These extracts are taken from* The Political Life and Letters of Cavour 1848–61 *by A. J. Whyte.*

1 *Explain these words and phrases:* a) *Lombards, Parmanense, Modenense;* b) *Cabinet of Turin:* c) *free corps.*

2 *What was Cavour's main aim in the early spring of 1859?*

3 *What does he mean by the sentence beginning 'This fact will be . . .'*

4 *Why did Austria attack Piedmont in 1859? How sensible an action was it?*

5 *What does this source tell you about Cavour's abilities?*

C

"On February 9th 1859 Cavour introduced to Parliament his loan for 50 millions [to raise money for the war] . . . . He began to give open encouragement to deserters from the Lombards and young men of all classes to enrol in the Piedmontese army . . . .

On March 6th Cavour wrote to Paris 'The Italian emigration continues; in two months we shall have 10,000 Lombards, Parmanense, Modenense, etc. in the ranks. This fact will be the finest possible evidence of the real feeling of Italy and at the same time a provocation which Austria will not be able to tolerate'" [*At this stage, Napoleon III under pressure from Britain began to back off from the Plombières scheme but Austria lost patience with Piedmont. On 14 April the Austrian Foreign Minister sent the following note to the Austrian Ambassador in London.*]

"The Emperor, our August Majesty, owes it to his dignity and the security of his Empire to put an end to a situation so intolerable . . . by taking the question of Piedmont's disarmament in hand himself, since the good offices of England have failed to do so. With this object we are about to address directly to the Cabinet of Turin a demand to reduce her army to a peace footing and disband the free corps." [*This demand was sent. Cavour refused to accept it so Austria declared war.*]

Habsburg rulers from their duchies and their inhabitants voted overwhelmingly to be united with Piedmont. Neither Britain nor France would allow the Habsburgs back. Cavour became First Minister once more. With the active backing of the French all Northern Italy with the exception of Venetia become Piedmontese. In return France received Nice and Savoy.

Garibaldi's Redshirts, 1860

At this point Cavour would have liked the process of unification to have stopped. He tried but failed to prevent Garibaldi from organising a force to liberate Southern Italy. In the spring of 1860 a thousand redshirted guerrilla troops whose average age was only twenty landed from two paddle-steamers on the island of Sicily. Attacking with near-suicidal bravery they swept aside a Bourbon army three times their size and entered Palermo. Garibaldi's legendary personality convinced the peasantry of the south that he was invincible and, as he advanced through Sicily and then northwards up to the mainland, they rose in revolt against the hated Bourbons whose demoralised army retreated in confusion.

Cavour was not pleased by Garibaldi's success. He feared that the hero-general who had made himself dictator (sole ruler) of the areas he had freed would not hand them over to Piedmont. He therefore persuaded Victor Emmanuel, whom Garibaldi was known to respect, to march south with the Piedmontese army and meet the victorious Redshirts. This meant marching through the Papal States though Pope Pius IX was a firm opponent of unification. The Papal army was defeated at Castelfidardo and the king met Garibaldi near Naples (see source A). The dictator handed over his conquests to the king. The last Bourbon armies were defeated. The inhabitants of the south voted heavily in favour of union with Piedmont. In 1861 the first Italian parliament met at Turin and Victor Emmanuel II was declared formally to be the King of Italy.

Rome and Venice

Rome and Venice remained outside the new nation. Twice Garibaldi led attacks on the French defenders of Papal Rome but without success. Once again foreign help was needed. When Prussia and Austria went to war in 1866, Italy allied with Prussia. Venice was the reward from Prussia's decisive victory. Prussia was also crucial in the winning of Rome in 1870. The French garrison was withdrawn when the Franco-Prussian War began. When the Italians took over the city, Pius IX shut himself away in his Vatican Palace and refused to co-operate in any way with the Italian government.

After the Risorgimento

The Risorgimento or unification of Italy in 1859–60 was a marvellous achievement but one which quickly turned sour (see source F). Between 1870 and 1914 the experiences of the new country were often unhappy ones. There was a rapid economic growth but it was patchy and irregular. Parts of the north did very well but the south lagged behind. Simultaneously the population increased dramatically. Some of the ablest of the population emigrated, their favoured destination was the USA. In 1900 350,000 emigrated, in 1910 530,000.

Emigration

The weakness of Parliament

Italian parliamentary government did not work well. Cavour died in 1861. He had controlled the Piedmontese parliament by a loose agreement between the various parties of the centre. A tradition developed of forming and reforming coalition governments from deputies who were more interested in the power and influence which they could use to help

Source D: The battle of Magenta

D *This picture's title is 'The French and Sardinians win victory over the Austrians', 1859.*

1 *When and why was this battle fought?*

2 *Who are the Sardinians? How do you work out which troops in the picture are Sardinian, which French and which Austrian? (The soldier in the centre with his banner is a good clue.)*

3 *What nationality would you think the painter to have been? Explain your answer.*

4 *How accurate a reconstruction of the battle do you think this picture is likely to be?*

Source E: 'The Man in Possession'

E *Cartoon from* Punch, *6 October 1860.*

1 *Identify the two men. What clues did the cartoonist give which helped you to your answer?*

2 *What was happening in Italy at this time? Who was 'in possession' of what?*

3 *Did in fact the man on the left open the door to the King? Explain your answer.*

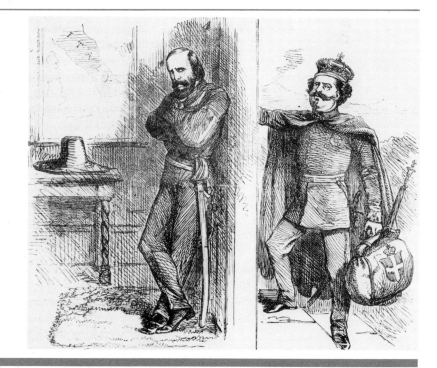

their political friends and supporters than in facing up to the main problems of the country. Only 5 per cent of the population had the vote before 1882, only 10 per cent after that. Parliament, which had never been particularly popular, became more unpopular still.

Opposition

Opposition came from various directions. Many Catholics followed the Pope's instructions and refused to take part in any Italian politics. The peasantry in the south often found that being Italian meant the replacement of a tyrannical Bourbon landlord by a tyrannical Piedmontese one. There were a number of violent peasant uprisings. In the cities revolutionary socialism became attractive to thousands. In May 1898 the government was shaken nearly to its foundations by a huge workers' protest centred on Milan which caused over five hundred casualties. In 1910 King Umberto I was assassinated by a revolutionary. Giolitti, another cunning manager of parliamentary coalitions, kept the system ticking along between 1903 and 1914. It was, however, disintegrating. The First World War hastened its collapse and the rise of Fascism (see pages 184–8).

France in 1848

The 1848 revolution

In 1848 French agriculture and industry were in a depressed state and many people were hungry. The government of King Louis Philippe was pursuing an unsuccessful foreign policy and refused to extend the franchise. Moreover, in the opinion of Lamartine, a poet and active politician, 'France was bored'. To whip up support for parliamentry reform, banquets were organised which combined good food with anti-government speeches. When in February the government tried clumsily to ban these banquets Paris rose in revolt and the king fled into exile. The new Provisional Government of which Lamartine was a member gave the vote to all adult men. It also set up the National Workshops to aid the unemployed. However, the Assembly elected by the enlarged electorate turned out to be more conservative than the Provisional Government. It disliked the National Workshops which were attracting in to Paris numerous vagabonds from the countryside.

The June Days, 1848

Suddenly early in June 1848 it closed them down. The response of the Parisian craftsmen and workers was another violent revolt, the June Days, which was crushed by General Cavaignac and 30,000 troops. Between 1,500 and 3,000 were killed in the fighting, 12,000 imprisoned and 6,000 sent into exile. In the autumn a shaken and divided country faced the task of electing a president.

Bonapartism

The most famous of the streets of Paris was dominated by a huge arch, the Arc de Triomphe, which commemorated the victories of Napoleon Bonaparte. It had been completed during the reign of Louis Philippe. For millions of French people Bonaparte stood not just for national glory but for strong intelligent rule which kept the country secure and gave opportunities to the talented.

Louis Napoleon Bonaparte

One candidate in the presidential election of December 1848 was Prince Louis Napoleon, nephew of Napoleon I. Till then he had lived as a wandering, if rich, adventurer. Twice unsuccessfully he had tried to seize power in France. The second attempt gained him a spell in Ham prison during which he was able to publish a number of books and newspaper articles. Through these he gained the reputation of being a man of progress with an interest in social and economic reform.

Source F: Garibaldi and Cavour in the Turin Parliament, 18 April 1861

F

F *D'Ideville, a French diplomat in Turin, kept a journal for the years 1859–62 which was published in Paris in 1872. (Parliament was discussing the position of Garibaldi's volunteer forces in southern Italy who had been badly treated by the Piedmontese regular army since Garibaldi had come north.)*

1 *Why were Garibaldi's volunteers and the Piedmont army having difficulty in co-operating in Southern Italy?*

2 *Why was Garibaldi so angry with Cavour?*

3 *What was D'Ideville's attitude to Garibaldi? How good a source is he for Piedmontese politics in 1861?*

4 *What were the chief differences between Cavour and Garibaldi?*

"At this point, amid profound silence, Garibaldi rose. Everyone knew perfectly well how Garibaldi hated Cavour's cabinet as everyone knew the open antagonism between his volunteers and the regular army . . . .

Conqueror of the Kingdom of The Sicilies, acclaimed by 5 million Italians as their liberator . . . he had won himself an extraordinary position and the flatterers around him had every interest in increasing it still further. His boundless pride had been over-excited by the praises of the downtrodden citizens of Naples. Arrogant towards the government, insolent to parliament, he spared the deputies no insults . . . .

With menacing voice and gesture he turned to the ministerial bench and declared 'that he could never shake hands with a man [Cavour] who had sold Nice to a foreign power nor could he support a government which had clumsily tried to stir up civil war'.

At this point the whole chamber was on its feet while the galleries broke into cheers. Cavour, leaning on the table with his eyes fixed on Garibaldi, until now had kept his temper despite these accusations . . . . He rose pale and trembling to protest . . . . Everyone was shouting 'Order, Order, it is disgraceful!' . . . every kind of insult was hurled to and fro . . .

Many Italians . . . still found it hard to believe that their hero was no more than a poor simpleton, brave no doubt but with a limitless pride that destroyed his common sense."

The Second Republic, 1848–51

Most people were unimpressed on first meeting him. Marx thought him a fool, Thiers, an experienced politician, decided that he was 'a noodle who could be easily managed'. One of his generals nicknamed him 'the melancholy parrot'. However, after the troubles earlier in 1848 the Bonaparte name was enough to allow him to run away with the presidential election. He won $5\frac{1}{2}$ million votes, his nearest rival only $1\frac{1}{2}$ million. He speedily proved himself a skilful politician, caring much more about public opinion than the Assembly which made itself most unpopular by taking away the right to vote from 3 million citizens. Since a president was only allowed to have one term of office which meant that he would have had to stand down by 1852, Louis Napoleon decided to stay in power by force. In December 1851 he prepared a *coup d'état* which was swiftly and ruthlessly carried out. Leading politicians were arrested simultaneously, half-hearted resistance in the streets of Paris was swept aside at the cost of 500 lives: 27,000 possible opponents were arrested and 10,000 exiled. He then tested public opinion with two plebiscites, the first to approve his seizure of power, the second to change his title to Emperor Napoleon III. In both he won an overwhelming majority. The Second Empire was in being (see source G).

The coup d'état 1851

The Second Empire, 1852–70

It was to last until 1870. During it most French people prospered, except the urban poor. The main railway network, 20,000 kilometres in all, was completed, canals improved and the main towns connected by electric telegraph. In the cities there was much rebuilding. The dynamic Baron Haussmann gave Paris its famous boulevards, sewers and gas lighting. Industries developed, especially in the north, though generally on a smaller scale than in Britain and Germany. Coal and iron production tripled, the number of factory workers doubled. Banks like the Credit Mobilier of the Péreire Brothers, the Credit Foncier and the Credit Lyonnais gave more support to industrial and commercial enterprises. A free trade agreement was made in 1860 with Britain (the Cobden-Chevalier Treaty) which encouraged greater competitiveness.

During the 1850s most sections of French society supported Napoleon since he seemed the best guarantee of order and progress after a period of dangerous social crisis. In the 1860s there were demands for more freedom and social reform. Napoleon took care to keep in touch with the public mood (see source H) and was ready to respond to it. In 1860 he granted the Senate and the Assembly a greater say in financial matters and, in the later 1860s, more thoroughly 'liberalised' his approach. Both the press and the trade unions were allowed greater freedom and educational reforms were begun. Finally in 1870 a new constitution ended his near-dictatorial authority by giving much greater powers to the elected Assembly. It is impossible to tell how successful the new constitution would have been since Napoleon, sick and ageing, allowed himself and his Empire to be swept away by the disaster of the Franco-Prussian War (see pages 80–1).

Foreign policy

If domestic policy was often left to able ministers like Morny, Persigny, Rouher or Haussmann, Napoleon III kept foreign policy firmly in his own hands. Instead of the peace which he had promised in 1852, he took France into four separate wars. The first was the Crimean War (1854–6).

The Crimean War, 1854–6

His aim was to defend the Catholic priests within the Turkish Empire from the Russians and to win glory for the French army and the Bonaparte name. Since the Russians were defeated, the French fought better than their British allies and the final peace negotiations took place with great publicity in Paris, the Emperor's prestige was much increased both in France and in Europe. At first the Italian War of 1859 (see pages 58–60) increased his prestige still further. His review of the victorious forces of Magenta and Solferino in Paris on 14 August 1859 was the most triumphant day of his career. In the long run, however, his double-faced Italian policies satisfied no one. French Catholics supported by the Empress (see source J5) considered that the unification of Italy had weakened the Pope too much while French liberals criticised the way in which Napoleon III had abandoned his Italian allies with the job only half done.

Colonial gains

His colonial policies were aggressive and for the most part successful. The conquest of Algeria was completed (see page 17, chapter 1). Footholds were won in West Africa, Indo-China and along the China coast. French influence in the Eastern Mediterranean grew. The Suez Canal was the idea of a Frenchman, de Lesseps, financed by French and British money and opened in 1869 by the Empress Eugénie.

The Mexican adventure, 1863–7

His next scheme, in Mexico, went badly wrong. There a civil war between Catholic conservatives and anti-clerical liberals led by Juárez had ended in victory for the latter. In 1861 Juárez stopped paying the debts owed to foreign governments. A joint French-Spanish-British force was sent with the intention of forcing repayment but in 1862 the British and Spanish pulled out. For his part Napoleon III decided that here was a splendid chance to win glory and influence for France by defeating Juárez and replacing him with a good Catholic monarch,

Source G:
The Second Empire

G *The Prince-President speaks in Bordeaux in 1852. He is campaigning for the establishment of the Second Empire. This extract is taken from* Democratic Despot *by J. A. B. Corley, 1961.*

1 *In the circumstance of 1852, how good a speech does this one sound to you?*
2 *To what extent did the reality of the Second Empire fulfil the promises of this speech?*
3 *Summarise the strengths and weaknesses of Napoleon III as a ruler.*

G

"There is one fear which I shall set at rest. A spirit of distrust leads certain people to say that the Empire means war. I say the Empire means peace, for France desires it and when France is satisfied the world is at peace."

"I grant that I, like the Emperor [Napoleon I] have many conquests to make. Like him I would try to reconcile the quarrelling parties ... I would win over to religion and morality and for the easing of their burdens that portion of the population – still so numerous – which in a land of faith knows next to nothing of the teaching of Christ and which, in the heart of the most fertile country in the world, enjoys barely the necessities of life."

"We have immense uncultivated territories to develop, rivers to make navigable, canals to finish, our network of railways to complete. In Algeria we have a vast dominion to assimilate .... We have to bring our great western ports nearer to America by those speedy communications which they yet lack. Everywhere we have ruins to build up, false gods to cast down, truths to make triumphant. That is how I see the Empire – if indeed the Empire is to be restored. I have no other conquests in mind. And you, all you round me who share my aspirations for our country's good, you are my soldiers."

Source H:
Napoleon III and the press

H *Lynn M. Case, in his book* French Opinion on War and Diplomacy during the Second Empire, *1954.*

1 *In what ways could the government control what French newspapers wanted to publish?*
2 *In what ways did it act to influence public opinion in its favour?*
3 *What light does Case's research throw on the reliability of French newspapers as historical sources during the Second Empire?*
4 *How might a government official have justified French government policy if questioned about* The Times *report?*
5 *How free from government interference are British newspapers and television news programmes nowadays? And how do they compare in this respect to the news media of other European countries and elsewhere in the world?*

H

"French newspapers at least to 1868 were subjected to stern censorship. Papers had to obtain a government permit ... and pay a special tax ... a newspaper was warned whenever it published an article that appeared ... 'excessive, dangerous or disagreeable' ... in the case of a third warning [it] would be subject to a two-month suspension, which was usually fatal to its existence."

"The ugliest aspect of press opinion during the Second Empire was the influence of outright bribery ... Bismarck allocated 5,000 francs to be used on the French press."

[*Case discovered, too, that Napoleon's government also took action to get 'news' to appear favourable to it. He gives an example from 1866. In that year Napoleon was losing a battle of wits with Bismarck in his efforts to gain some advantages for France after Prussia's swift and surprising victory over Austria in the Seven Weeks' War (see pages 78–9 and Source E, page 80). His government first issued a statement to the newspapers putting Napoleon's actions in the best possible light. It then sent out a letter to each paper praising the government's statement and Napoleon's foreign policy generally. The* Times *(of London) pointed out on 27 September 1866 that this same letter appeared in different newspapers all over France but while in the* Chartres Journal *it appeared under the signature of one A. Malteste, in the* Mayenne Echo *a C. Lemonard was the writer, while in the* Sarthe Messenger *it was a Monsieur Dufau!*]

Maximilian, an Austrian prince of the Habsburg family. Leading Catholics, including the Empress Eugénie were strongly anti-Juárez. The reinforced French army drove Juárez out of Mexico City in 1863 and Maximilian was crowned Emperor the following year. He failed, however, to win popular support and the USA which had previously been distracted by civil war demanded the withdrawal of French troops.

The last French forces left in January 1867. Within a few months Maximilian had been captured and shot by the Juarists. All Europe, but particularly Catholic Europe, was shocked. Napoleon III, whose policies appeared both bungled and treacherous, was considered to be directly responsible for the Mexican tragedy.

The Franco-Prussian War, 1870

Bismarck was contemptuous of the French Emperor. He described him as 'a sphinx without a riddle ... a great unfathomed incapacity'. Between 1865 and 1870 the Prussian Chancellor played with Napoleon, giving him false hopes of gains in the Rhineland and provoking French opinion into a warlike mood. The causes and course of the Franco-Prussian War are described in chapter 5. If Napoleon had been in good health he might have resisted the clamour for war, partly led by Gramont (Foreign Minister) and the Empress. Though his health was failing, he took personal command of the French armies and his presence only magnified the shambles of the French High Command. After Sedan (see page 81) he surrendered to the Prussians and was soon released to an English exile. He died in 1873.

The Third Republic, 1871–1914

Of all years in the history of France, 1871 must be among the worst. Not only was there the humiliation of military defeat, a harsh peace and the German Empire being ceremonially announced in the great palace of Louis XIV at Versailles, but during the months of the Paris Commune (March–May 1871), French fought against French in the streets of the capital.

Paris resists

After Napoleon's defeat at Sedan, Paris declared him abdicated and a new republic in existence. A Government of National Defence continued the war even though the Prussians had surrounded the capital. In October a young politician, Gambetta, escaped out of Paris by using a balloon. He raised an army and fought the Prussians in the Loire valley. The struggle, however, was a hopeless one and when Paris had to surrender for lack of food in January 1871, resistance to the Prussians finally ceased.

Distrust of Thiers

Paris had resisted the Prussians with great bravery. Within the city were extreme republicans and socialists who hoped to create a better and different society out of the ashes of defeat. They distrusted Thiers who had made peace with the Prussians and who intended, they believed, to restore a monarchy to France. When Thiers ordered that cannons be removed from Paris and that the National Guard (which was sympathetic to extreme republicanism) be disbanded, they rebelled and declared Paris to be a Commune, independent of and hostile to the national government of Thiers. In May Thiers sent the regular army against the barricades of the communards. A week of vicious street fighting was necessary before their resistance was finally broken (see sources I1–I5): 25,000 French people died during the fighting or from the murder of prisoners by both sides, more than in any of the battles of the Franco-Prussian War.

1871 and the Paris Commune

Source I:
The Paris Commune

I1 *Watch me, you poor amateur! – a cartoon of c. 1871. (Marat was one of the most violent of the revolutionary leaders, during the French Revolution of 1789–93. He was assassinated in his bath by Charlotte Corday.)*

I2

I2 *The Paris Commune of 24 May 1871, when the communards had taken the Archbishop of Paris hostage. These extracts are taken from A. Horne,* The Fall of Paris, *1965.*

"Between 7 and 8 p.m. that evening, the Archbishop much weakened by illness was led into an alley within the prison. With him was the ex-Empress Eugénie's seventy-five-year-old confessor and [four others]. The Archbishop evidently showed great courage and dignity, giving each of the other five hostages in turn his blessing. The National Guard's aim was as inaccurate as ever and after the first volley the Archbishop remained standing. A teenager in the firing-squad called Lolive was heard to cry out 'Nom de Dieu, he must be wearing armour!' and the rifles crashed out again. This time Monseigneur Darboy fell . . . . The National Guard ripped open his body with bayonets, then carried it off to be thrown into an open ditch at Père Lachaise cemetery."

I3

I3 *25 May 1871: the death of Delescluze, a communard leader. (Thiers' troops were tightening their grip on the city. Delescluze hastily scribbled this note to his sister.)*

25 May

"I do not wish . . . to act as the victim and the toy of the victorious reaction. Forgive me for departing before you, you have sacrificed your life for me. But I no longer feel I possess the courage to submit to another defeat after so many others . . . . Your memory will be the last that will visit my thoughts before going to rest. Adieu."

(Horne's account continues) "Lissagaray shortly before 7 p.m. saw Delescluze dressed as always like an 1848 revolutionary in a top hat, lovingly polished boots, black trousers and a frock coat, a red scarf round his waist and leaning heavily on his cane, move off . . . with some fifty men. Just before reaching the barricade across the Boulevard Voltaire, he met Vermorel (an old friend) who had been mortally wounded. After gripping his hand and saying a few words of farewell, Delescluze walked alone to the already abandoned barricade. Before the eyes of Lissagaray . . . he slowly, painfully clambered to the top of the barricade. He stood there for a moment silhouetted in the setting sun, then pitched forward on his face. Four men rushed to pick him up; three were shot down too."

1 *Who is the figure with the torch in cartoon I1? Explain the cartoon.*

2 *Write an account of the Paris Commune with special attention to the death of the Archbishop of Paris (see source I2) for a textbook to be used in Roman Catholic schools in the 1880s.*

3 *Who was Delescluze? Why does he wear a red scarf round his waist? What does he mean by 'another defeat after so many others'?*

4 *Horne is a secondary source. What kinds of primary sources would he have been able to use to write his book?*

14 *The first photographic techniques were perfected in the first half of the nineteenth century and the first ever news photograph (of a fire in Hamburg) was taken in 1842. R. Fenton took 360 photos of the Crimean War in 1855 and a team led by Brady more than 7,000 of the American Civil War (1861–5). Photographs began to be used frequently in weekly news magazines in the 1880s and in daily newspapers soon after 1900. The British and American press gave detailed attention to the events of the commune, and this photograph and engraving were done at the time.*

5 *In the photograph 14, who are standing on the barricades? How do you identify them? What enemy are they waiting for?*

6 *In the engraving 15, what is happening? What part are the women playing?*

7 *Both the photograph and the engraving attempt to show what the fighting was like. Both have their strengths and weaknesses as evidence. What are they?*

14 *A photograph of the barricade of Flanders Road, 18 March 1871.*

15 *Engraving of the barricade of White Place defended by women during 'Bloody Week'. (Published in the* Penny Illustrated Paper, *London.*)

Source J:
Women in politics –
the influence of the
Empress Eugénie

Women hardly appear in this book. Almost all the major decisions in politics are made by men, at least up to 1945. Women are noticed more often or not as victims, like the Boer women in South Africa or Nurse Cavell in Belgium in 1914. Moreover most of the evidence is written by men and all the artists including the cartoonists are male.

However, many nineteenth-century women were interested in politics and some exercised real influence through their husbands. Such influence is hard to measure and was often controversial. The Empress Eugénie, Napoleon's wife, is a good example.

She was a Spanish aristocrat who met Napoleon at a ball in Paris when he was President of the Second Republic. They were married in 1852.

J1 *December 1869: The Opening of the Suez Canal. The yacht* L'Aigle *with the Empress Eugénie of the French on board enters Port Said.*

Study source J1.
1 *How can you tell the ship is French?*
2 *To which country does the rowing boat belong? How do you know?*
3 *Why should the French make a fuss about the Suez Canal?*
4 *Can you think of any reason why Napoleon III was not present?*

J2 Encyclopaedia Britannica *entry on Eugénie, 1973 edition.*

The Encyclopaedia Britannica *is one of the world's most respected books of reference. The 1973 edition is 24 volumes long, each volume having about 1,000 pages.*

J3 *Maxime de Camp, writer and friend of the Emperor. (This extract, and Sources J5 and 6, are taken from the biography of Napoleon III by G. P. Gooch, 1960.)*

Maxime de Camp knew both Napoleon and Eugénie personally.

J2

"By her beauty, elegance and charm of manner she contributed to the brilliance of the imperial regime .... The empress acted as regent during the absence of the emperor in 1859, 1865 and 1870 – and she was generally consulted on important questions. She was brave and intelligent, but wilful and impatient. Her Catholic sympathies influenced French policy ..."

J3

"Superstitious and superficial, always preoccupied with the impression she made, parading her shoulders and bosom, her hair dyed, her face painted, her eyes shaded, her lips rouged. To be in her proper sphere she only lacked the music of the circus .... The balls at the Tuileries [palace], the soirées [receptions] at Compiègne and Fontainebleau were staged for her glory .... Frigid with no passion but vanity ... I don't believe she had a serious idea about anything."

5 *In what ways do de Camp and the* Encyclopaedia *entry disagree?*
6 *Whom do you think the* Encyclopaedia Britannica *organisers would have got to write the entry about Eugénie?*
7 *Which, J2 or J3, do you think is likely to be the more reliable about the Empress? Explain your answer.*

J4 A concert at the Tuileries Palace (the Marshal's Hall) in the presence of their Imperial Majesties and the court, 1861.

Study source J4.

8 *Where is Eugénie sitting? How have you identified her?*

9 *What sort of concert is taking place?*

10 *Of whom are the paintings on the wall?*

11 *Some of the audience would have found the music boring. Why then did they attend?*

J5 Meeting of Eugénie with Nigra, the Piedmontese representative in 1862 (as reported by Cowley, the British Ambassador).

Read source J5.

12 *Why were French troops in Rome in 1862 and why did the Italian government wish them to withdraw?*

13 *What had happened to the King of Naples in 1860? Where do Eugénie's sympathies lie?*

14 *What does this extract suggest to you about Eugénie's political ideas and influence?*

J6 Persigny, an old friend and loyal minister, writes to Napoleon in 1869 (he is worried by arguments in Council and the intrigues of the Court).

Read source J6.

15 *From Persigny's letter, what do you think had been happening at Council meetings?*

16 *What would have been the main items discussed at the Council? What policies would Eugénie have supported?*

17 *Comment on Persigny's point of view.*

J5

"Empress: What do you want, M. Nigra?

Nigra: I wish your Majesty would be a little less hostile to us and persuade the Emperor to withdraw his troops from Rome.

Empress: I would rather drown myself than lend a hand to your brigandage. You are insatiable. You call the subjects of the King of Naples who have remained loyal to him brigands. How do you describe yourselves? You are the robbers .... Wait a bit .... The day of vengeance will come. You will witness the triumph of your Mazzinis and Garibaldis .... You will be hung and I shan't come to your rescue."

J6

"The presence of the wife of the sovereign in the Council is a danger to the state, condemned by the theory and practice of all governments and contrary to the nature of things ... If she wishes to take part any differences between the Emperor and Empress should be composed before the Council meets. She gains nothing by her presence. The wife of the sovereign should remain aloof in a calm elevated sphere, inaccessible to the passions of politics ..."

18 *To what extent are women more active in politics nowadays compared with the nineteenth century?*

The Third Republic survives:

monarchism

For much of the 1870s the Third Republic looked as if it might well become a monarchy. Monarchists had a majority in the National Assembly and, from 1873 to 1877, a monarchist president, Marshal MacMahon. However, they could agree neither on their flag nor on the kind of monarchical government they wanted. More convinced republican deputies were elected to the National Assembly as time passed and the Republic survived. Its outstanding early achievement was to pay off in two years the indemnity imposed by the Treaty of Frankfurt. This meant the end of the German occupation.

Most deputies were from the middle classes and most governments were liberal ones drawn from the parties of the centre and the left. The parties, however, were numerous and loosely organised with the result that short-lived coalition governments were the rule rather than the exception. If governments changed, ministers frequently stayed in office, which allowed policies to continue. In addition a strong civil service gave effective day-to-day administration.

Economically and socially France changed more slowly than the other Great Powers of Europe. Her population increased very gently, from 36 to 39 million. There was some immigration but hardly any emigration. France remained a country of well-off peasants and numerous market towns. Cities and industries expanded but not in the spectacular manner which was commonplace in other parts of the continent.

Boulanger

The Third Republic was shaken by a number of serious crises between 1880 and 1900. A General Boulanger became Minister of War in 1886. The government was particularly unpopular because it was corrupt and was allowing itself to be bullied by Germany.

Boulanger was a handsome man who rode his black horse with style and gave the impression that he could be another Bonaparte. By 1889 his many followers were urging him to seize power by *coup détat* but his nerve failed. He fled from France and in 1891 committed suicide on the grave of his mistress in Brussels.

The Panama Scandal, 1892

Of a number of financial scandals the Panama Scandal of 1892 was the most serious. After his success at Suez, de Lesseps drew up a plan to construct a Panama Canal. The company formed to finance it was badly and fraudulently managed but it had connections with various deputies. Eventually it failed, bringing ruin to its investors but not to the politicians. There was a public outcry which forced some leading politicians, including Georges Clemenceau, a future Prime Minister, into temporary retirement. Some Jewish businessmen were involved in the fraud and the scandal encouraged anti-semitism.

The Dreyfus Affair

The greatest crisis, however, was the Dreyfus Affair (see sources K1–4). In 1894 Captain Dreyfus was court-martialled for spying for Germany. Spying was taking place, but the real villain was almost certainly another officer, Esterhazy. Dreyfus's main mistake was to have been born Jewish. He was found guilty of treason and sentenced to life imprisonment on the infamous Devil's Island, off the coast of South America. However, within the army, Colonel Picquart had doubts about the evidence used against him and a number of politicians began to question the sentence. Esterhazy was court-martialled and found not guilty. A Colonel Henry forged evidence against Dreyfus and Colonel Picquart was arrested. At this point (1898) Émile Zola wrote a letter to the President of France, accusing the army of a miscarriage of justice, which was printed in the newspaper, *L'Aurore*, under the heading 'I Accuse'. An enormous storm broke.

Senior army officers refused to admit that they were at fault and extreme nationalists and many Catholics rallied to their defence. In contrast liberals and socialists demanded justice both for Dreyfus and for Zola who had been put on trial and sentenced to a year's imprisonment.

They considered the Anti-Dreyfusards to be the old aristocracy and enemies of the Republic. Dreyfusards and Anti-Dreyfusards scuffled in the street, relatives refused to speak to each other. Eventually the case against Dreyfus collapsed when Colonel Henry admitted his guilt and committed suicide. The same year, 1898, Dreyfus was brought back from Devil's Island. None the less it took until 1906 for the army to clear him completely. He fought in the First World War as a lieutenant-colonel and died in 1935.

The main result of the affair was to harm the reputation of the army, the Catholic Church and the extreme nationalists. Tough anti-clerical laws were passed between 1902 and 1905. The influence of the Catholic Church on education was much reduced and many religious institutions closed down.

French Socialism before 1914

Despite the setback of the Paris Commune French socialism developed strongly in the years before 1914. By 1914 it polled as many as 1,400,000 votes in elections and had 103 deputies in the Assembly. However, it could not make up its mind whether it was uncompromisingly revolutionary or was ready to participate in coalition governments. Some of its leaders, like Millerand in 1899, did become ministers but the movement as a whole, including its most gifted leader, Jaurès, followed a policy of non-co-operation. Trade unions were active and inspired a number of violent strikes. However, the main trade union organisation, the Confédération Générale de Travail (CGT) had before 1914 less influence than its British and German counterparts.

Source K: The Dreyfus Affair

K1 *The headline from* L'Aurore.

K2 *Dreyfus learns the verdict of the first court-martial.*

K3 *Dreyfus on Devil's Island.*

K4 *Dreyfus's sword being broken.*

1 *The illustrations are not in the correct chronological order. List them in the correct order, dating each as accurately as possible.*
2 *Re-caption them as they might have appeared in:*
   a) *an extremely nationalistic Catholic pro-army magazine,*
   b) *a liberal or socialist anti-army magazine.*

5 Bismarck and German unification

The extraordinary monument below (see source A) was begun in Hamburg in Germany in 1891. It was in honour of Bismarck who had resigned the previous year from being Chancellor of Germany. In his twenty-eight years of power Bismarck had master-minded the unification of Germany around Prussia his homeland and by 1890 this Germany was the strongest nation in Europe. During his lifetime Bismarck was either greatly admired or hated. Since his death historians have written more about him than any other nineteenth-century person. Like his contemporaries, they cannot agree about him either.

Bismarck's early life

Otto von Bismarck was born in 1815. His father was a Junker, or Prussian landowner, his mother came from a well-known family of civil servants and professors. Their son inherited much of his father's looks and Junker attitudes but his mother's brains and ambition. She made sure that he had a good education, first in Berlin and then at the University of Göttingen. She then used her family connections to get him a civil service post in Aachen on which he might have built a respectable career. Her efforts, however, were wasted. While he was still at school his teachers remarked on his 'high spirits' and his lack of 'gravity of mind' towards his work. As a university student he spent much of his time drinking, womanising, and fighting duels (twenty-four in all) and on

Source A: Bismarck

A The Bismarck Tower, Hamburg, *designed by Hugo Lederer.*

1 *What impression of Bismarck did the designer intend to give?*

2 *What position did Bismarck hold in 1891 (see page 86)? Why should the citizens of Hamburg have erected a statue of him?*

3 *What actually are statues evidence of?*

one occasion he was imprisoned for three days by the university authorities. He hated his civil service work and, in 1840, retired into the country to manage the family estates. Though a good farmer and respected by his peasants, a normal Junker life could not satisfy his unusual nervous energy. He galloped around the countryside on his massive horse Caleb. Once he announced his arrival at a friend's house by firing his pistol at the ceiling. Another time he let loose a terrified fox in the drawing-room of a neighbour. He was known locally as 'der trolle Bismarck', the wild man Bismarck.

Source B: Bismarck on his political views before 1862

These three extracts are taken from his Reminiscences and Recollections, *written during his retirement in the 1890s and published in 1898.*

B1 *A comparison with the views of his mother.*

B1

"The views which I drank with my mother's milk were Liberal rather than reactionary; but if my mother had lived to see me in action as a minister she would scarcely have agreed with me, though she would have had great joy from my success."

B2 *First speeches at the Prussian United Diet, 1847.*

B2

"I came into conflict with the Opposition the first time I spoke longer than usual, on May 17th. I spoke against the idea that the Prussians had gone to war in 1813 [against Napoleon I] to win a constitution and gave free expression to my natural indignation that foreign rule was not thought of as an adequate reason for fighting and that the king had somehow to grant the nation a constitution as a debt to be paid for the people's efforts [against the French]. My performance produced a storm. I remained at the speaker's tribune, turning over the leaves of a newspaper which lay there, until the storm subsided."

B3

"The basic error of Prussian policy in those days was that most people believed that by journalistic, parliamentary or diplomatic double-think they could get results which in fact could only be had by war or readiness for war."

B3 *About the years 1848 to 1859.*

1 *Do you think Bismarck's mother is best described as a liberal, conservative or reactionary? Explain your thinking.*

2 *Which of these terms best describes Bismarck's political views? Quote one sentence from B2 and one from B3 to prove your point.*

3 *Which group of politicians in the Prussian Upper Diet did Bismarck upset on 17 May 1847? What had they been saying about the events of 1813?*

4 *Bismarck was and is frequently criticised for appearing to believe that 'might is right'. Can you find any sentence or phrase in these extracts which suggests such a belief? If so, where?*

5 *What are 'reminiscences' and 'recollections'? What sort of bias might be found in the reminiscences of a politician? To what other evidence would a historian turn in order to*

[*Liberals in mid-nineteenth-century Germany wished to have written constitutions which laid down which powers were held by the king and which by parliament, and to have the powers of the king clearly limited by elected parliaments. They were in favour of those political changes which would increase parliamentary power and the freedom of individuals.*

Conservatives were against change unless absolutely necessary and usually supported kings against parliaments.

Reactionaries were extreme conservatives who wished to turn the clock right back to the good old days when few dared question the right of kings to rule as they saw fit.]

check the accuracy of Bismarck's account of his 1847 speech (source B2)?

Marriage, 1847

A member of the Prussian Diet, 1851

Two events made 1847 one of the most important years of his life. He married Johanna von Puttkamer. Her strong religious sense and devoted companionship helped to settle him down. He also had his first taste of politics, as a member of the Prussian United Diet. Here he soon made a name for himself as an extreme conservative (see source B). He became the outspoken champion of the King of Prussia, arguing fiercely against the increasing number of liberals who wished for royal power to be limited by elected parliaments.

He was therefore bitterly opposed to the revolutions of 1848 which aimed, in Prussia as elsewhere in Europe, to weaken the power of the king. After the revolutions had eventually been crushed in 1849 he rose in the favour of the Prussian royal family and, in 1851, was sent as Prussia's representative to the Diet of the German Confederation.

At the German Confederation, 1851

Prussian ambassador

This Confederation had been set up in 1815 by the Treaty of Vienna. It was made up of the many independent rulers of German-speaking peoples, including the two most powerful, the King of Prussia and the Emperor of Austria (see source D). In 1851 Austria, dynamically led by Schwarzenberg, held the upper hand. Only the year before had Schwarzenberg forced Frederick William IV of Prussia to give up working, without Austria, with the princes of Northern Germany. Inside the Diet at Frankfurt no one had challenged Austrian leadership before Bismarck arrived. He challenged it on every occasion. As soon as he heard that only the Austrians smoked cigars during debates, he made a point of lighting one of his own. More seriously he became sure that Prussia must escape from Austria's shadow and build her own strength separately from and if necessary in conflict with the Austrian Empire. In 1859 he was sent as ambassador to Russia and in 1862 was transferred to Paris.

The crisis of 1862

Roon and army reform

Meanwhile a most serious political crisis had been brewing in Prussia. In 1858 King Frederick William IV had gone mad. In 1861 he died. His younger brother, who had become Regent in 1858, succeeded him as William I. The new king was a solid conservative soldier. With his minister of war, Roon, he wished to reform thoroughly the Prussian army. These reforms could not take place however until the Prussian House of Deputies (parliament) voted the money required. The Liberals had a majority in the House of Deputies and they were firmly opposed to the army reforms and refused the money. In two general elections they increased their majority so obviously had public opinion behind them. Various ministers tried and failed to find a solution. In despair William began to think seriously of abdicating in favour of his son. As a last chance Roon persuaded the king to try Bismarck.

Bismarck Minister-President, 1862

As events moved to a head in Berlin, Bismarck had managed to fall head over heels in love with a pretty twenty-two-year-old, recently married, called Katy Orlov. Roon's frantic letters to Paris remained unanswered as he toured the south of France with the Orlovs! When he got back to Paris on 18 September 1862 he found this telegram from Roon. 'Periculum in mora. Dépêchez-vous.' (Danger in delay. Get a move on.) Four days later he was back in Berlin and was summoned straight away to see the king. In his reminiscences Bismarck tells how the king showed him his letter of abdication on the table and how he was persuaded not to abdicate but rather to back Bismarck and Roon who between them would carry through the army reforms despite the opposition of the House of Deputies. A week later, as Minister-President, he

Source C: Bismarck and King William I

C

C *Bismarck could only stay in power if he kept the confidence of the king. This was something at which he had to work hard, particularly in the early days.*

A good example of the difficulties which he faced and the methods which he used to overcome them happened in October 1862. He had been Minister-President for less than a month. His 'blood and iron' speech had pleased neither his friends nor his enemies. Even Roon thought it off the point, though witty. The queen, the crown prince and his wife, all of whom were unhappy with Bismarck's appointment, thought that it proved that he was a man who stirred up trouble for the sake of it. William left Berlin to celebrate his wife's birthday at Baden. Fearing that his family might turn the king against him, Bismarck decided to go out to meet him as he journeyed back to Berlin by train.

This is how Bismarck himself continues the story in his Reminiscences.

1 *What position did Bismarck hold? How long had he held it?*

2 *What crisis was then at its height?*

3 *Why was Bismarck worried about the king's visit to Baden?*

4 *Why did the king believe that Bismarck might end up headless in front of the Opera House?*

"I waited for him in the still unfinished station [at Jüterborg] filled with third-class passengers and workmen, seated in the dark on an overturned wheelbarrow. From the curt answers of the officials I had some difficulty in discovering the carriage in an ordinary train in which the king was seated by himself in an ordinary first-class compartment. He was obviously depressed as a result of talking to his wife and when I asked for permission to tell him what had been happening in Berlin, he interrupted me with these words: 'I can perfectly well see where this will end. Over there in front of the Opera House. Under my windows they will cut off your head and mine a little while afterwards.'

'Yes,' I said, 'then we shall be dead; but we must all die sooner or later and can we perish more honourably? I fighting for the king's cause and your Majesty sealing with your own blood your rights as king by the grace of God; whether on the scaffold or on the battlefield makes no difference to the glory . . . ' As I continued to speak, the king grew more lively and began to think of himself as an officer fighting for kingdom and fatherland. In presence of personal danger, he possessed a rare and absolutely natural fearlessness, whether on the field of battle or in face of attempts on his life. The influence of our conversation in the dark railway compartment was to make him regard the part which the present situation forced upon him as if he was an officer who had orders to hold a certain position to the death if necessary . . . . In a few minutes the confidence which he had lost at Baden was restored and he had even recovered his cheerfulness."

5 *What arguments did Bismarck use to change the king's mind?*

6 *What does this incident tell you about Bismarck as a politician?*

'Blood and iron'

Nationalism and the unification of Germany

addressed the Budget Commission of the House of Deputies, the group with particular responsibility for money matters. 'Prussia', he declared, 'must increase her strength in readiness for the favourable moment which has already been missed several times. Prussia's boundaries according to the Vienna Settlement act against a healthy political life; not by means of speeches and majority verdicts will the great decisions of the time be made – that was the great mistake of 1848 and 1849 – but by 'blood and iron.'

As in Italy, nationalism and liberalism were powerful within Germany in the 1850s and 1860s. Most German liberals wanted a united Germany. Bismarck managed to gain their support for his policies because they brought about the unification of Germany, but he made sure that the German Empire which came into being in 1871 had fewer freedoms and allowed less power to the representative assemblies than the liberals wished (see page 83).

Nationalists believed that a people with a common language and history should be united and run its own affairs without interference

Austrian Germany or Prussian Germany?

from foreigners. In the 1860s German nationalists were unhappy with the situation of the German-speaking people since by the Vienna Settlement of 1815 a German Confederation had been set up which included thirty-nine independent states over whom the federal diet had no effective control. The two most powerful states were Austria and Prussia and nationalists argued whether it would be better to have a big Germany united around Austria or a smaller version united round Prussia, excluding Austria with her large empire of non-German speakers.

The Zollverein

Between 1815 and 1850 Austria carried the most political weight within the Confederation but Prussia had some significant advantages. In 1818 she had begun a customs union with her neighbours which by 1834 she had extended to include most of the German states but not Austria. This Zollverein, as it was known, helped Prussia to industrialise. Her coal, iron and railway-building industries helped her to advance much more rapidly than Austria in the 1840s and 1850s.

Bismarck therefore used every opportunity to strengthen Prussia's position at the expense of Austria by championing the cause of German unification.

He proceeded to ignore the speeches and majority verdicts of the House of Deputies, had the necessary taxes collected and the army reforms carried out. There were many protests but the taxes were paid. None the less he was acting completely illegally. He realised that he could not act so high-handedly for very long. He therefore began an aggressive foreign policy. If he was successful in increasing Prussia's power at the expense of her neighbours he believed that he would be able to win popular support for his actions in 1862, particularly if Germany became more united as a result.

The expansion of Prussia, 1864–6

Schleswig-Holstein, 1864

His first success came in 1864. The two northern duchies of Schleswig and Holstein were linked to the royal family of Denmark (see map D). However, Holstein was part of the German Confederation while Schleswig included many German speakers. A new king of Denmark tried to make both duchies more firmly part of Denmark. Simultaneously his claim to the Danish throne was challenged. Bismarck made skilful use of this complicated situation. He persuaded Austria to march with Prussia against the Danes. They said that they were acting on behalf of the German Confederation, to make sure that Schleswig and Holstein became German rather than Danish. This action won them the support of the increasing number of Germans who wanted to see themselves part of a single united nation. The Danes were soon defeated. Prussia took over Schleswig and Austria Holstein. Many disputes then took place over the running of the conquered duchies. These Bismarck used to provoke Austria into war in 1866. Europe was amazed by his recklessness. Nine out of fifteen German states were ready to fight with Austria and an Austrian victory was generally expected although Italy declared herself for Prussia.

The Seven Weeks' War, 1866

Fighting began in the middle of June 1866. It ended seven weeks later with the Austrians suffering a great defeat. The reformed Prussian army proved itself to be a superb fighting machine. Moltke, its commander-in-chief, had made sure that it was well armed with the needle gun. He had also carefully trained his officers. Most important of all he had realised more clearly than his opponents how useful the new railways could be in shifting a large number of soldiers swiftly to the key

Sadowa

battlefields. Prussian armies invaded both Hanover in the north and Austria in the south. After a fortnight the Hanoverians surrendered at Langensalza. In the same period Moltke had moved a quarter of a million men into position against the Austrians along a front 275 miles in length. Early in July three Prussian armies closed in on the main Austrian army and destroyed it at Sadowa (Königgrätz). Before the month was over, the Austrians asked for peace.

At this point Bismarck showed to the full his farsightedness and strength of personality. King William and his generals were intoxicated by their victories. They wished to make a triumphal entry into Vienna, the Austrian capital, and to strip the Austrian Emperor of many of his lands.

Bismarck argued against this. If Austria was harshly treated, he pointed out, she might turn bitter and become a permanent enemy. The important thing for Prussia was simply to make sure that Austria could never again be a rival within Germany to Prussia. After much argument

Source D: The unification of Germany

D1 *The unification of Germany, 1815–71.*

1 *When and as a result of which war did the following provinces become united with Prussia: a) Schleswig; b) Saxony; c) Bavaria; d) Lorraine?*

2 *When was the North German Confederation set up? In what ways was it different from the German Confederation?*

3 *In which modern countries are a) Warsaw; b) Prague; c) Bavaria; d) Mecklenburg?*

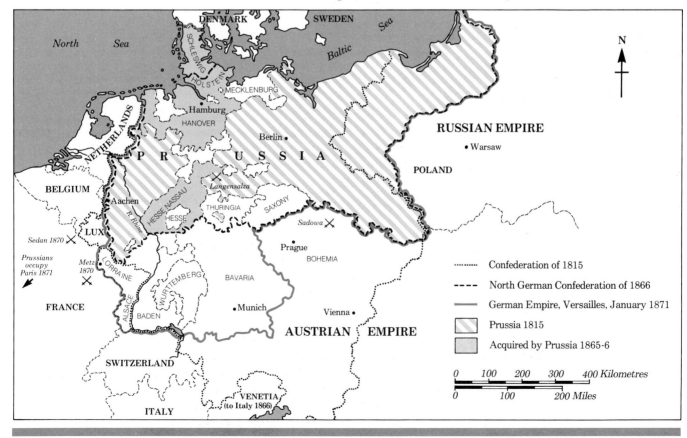

The Treaty of Prague

(and tears!) Bismarck got his way. By the Treaty of Prague the German Confederation was abolished. In its place came the North German Confederation completely dominated by Prussia, and four other independent states in the south. Austria no longer had the smallest foothold in Germany (see map D). Otherwise, though she lost land to Italy, Austria lost none to Prussia. The main gains which Prussia made were at the expense of the German states who had fought with Austria.

He then cleverly used this military success to end the conflict with the Prussian House of Deputies over the illegal collection of taxes which had continued since 1862. Many of his supporters had now won seats in the House and other members were ready to support him (see source E1). Bismarck admitted that he had been behaving illegally and the House of Deputies voted to legalise his actions. They also allowed the king and his First Minister to have much greater power in the constitution of the new North German Confederation than they would have been happy with back in 1848 or 1862.

The Franco-Prussian War, 1870–1

Although France had stayed neutral during the Seven Weeks' War, Napoleon III believed Sadowa to be a stunning setback to his country. He expected neither a Prussian victory nor the appearance in the shape of the North German Confederation of a much stronger Prussia on France's eastern border. Between 1866 and 1870 he tried to persuade Bismarck to agree to France making some gains so that the balance of power along the river Rhine would be more equal. They argued about Luxembourg in 1867, then about Bavaria, Belgium and parts of Prussia. Bismarck posed as the defender of the rights of the smaller Rhineland countries against the dangerous French and whipped up anti-French feeling in Germany and anti-German feeling in France (see source F2). He was sure that a victorious war against France would bring about the complete unification of Germany around Prussia and make this Prussian Germany the most powerful nation in Central Europe.

Spain and the Hohenzollern candidature

In 1870 he thought that his chance had come. Spain needed a king and Bismarck persuaded a reluctant William I that his distant cousin Prince Leopold of Hohenzollern-Sigmaringen should be allowed to be put to the

Source E: The effect of the victories of 1866 on Prussian opinion

E *Gustav Mevissen had been a leader of the Prussian liberals for many years and a firm opponent of Bismarck since 1862. However, when the troops returning victorious from Sadowa marched in triumph down the Unter den Linden in Berlin he joined the crowds to watch. He wrote down his feelings that day.*

1 *In what ways would you expect Mevissen and Bismarck to have disagreed a) in 1848; b) in 1862; c) on broad political issues?*

2 *What does Mevissen mean when he says 'I am no admirer of Mars'?*

E

"I cannot shake off the impressions of that hour. I am no admirer of Mars; I am more attached to the goddess of beauty and the mother of graces than to the powerful god of war, but the prizes of war exercise a magic charm upon the child of peace. One's usual attitudes are forgotten and one's spirit goes along with the boundless rows of men who acclaim the god of the moment – success."

3 *Explain in your own words his feelings as he watched the military march past.*

4 *What effect did the successes of Bismarck's foreign policy have on German liberal opinion?*

5 *Why was it important for Bismarck that this change of opinion did take place?*

**The Ems
Telegram**

Spanish as a candidate. The French government protested angrily. This would mean Prussian influence south of the Pyrenees as well as along the Rhine. To Bismarck's dismay William took notice of these protests and made Prince Leopold withdraw as a candidate. The French however were not prepared to let the matter rest there. An influential group in the French Assembly and at the imperial court (led by the Empress Eugénie) wanted war with Prussia. They knew that the Emperor's popularity was waning and thought that a glorious victory over Prussia was the best way of regaining general support. As far as the Hohenzollern candidature was concerned, the French ambassador was sent to meet William I at the health resort of Ems (see source F3) and requested that the king promise that members of his Hohenzollern family should never again seek the Spanish throne. This William was not prepared to do since he already regarded the affair as closed and he decided not to meet the French ambassador again. Then, as was his custom, he telegraphed Bismarck in Berlin with an account of the day's events. Bismarck saw his chance. He produced a shortened version of the Ems telegram which gave the impression that the meeting between the king and the French ambassador had been a bad-tempered one and had it published in the Berlin newspapers. The result was exactly as he had hoped. Both sides demanded war and on 19 July 1870 France declared war (see sources F4–6).

**The rival
armies**

The French generals were confident of victory. They had an excellent new rifle, the 'chassepot', and an early type of machine gun. They had thoroughly reformed their military methods in the light of the Seven Weeks' War. However, their confidence was misplaced. Moltke moved his armies much more skilfully than his rivals Bazaine and MacMahon, whose task was made more difficult by the presence of the sick Emperor at the front. Though they inflicted heavy casualties on the Prussians, one French army under Bazaine took refuge in the fortress town of Metz while another led by MacMahon and Napoleon III was surrounded and forced to surrender at Sedan.

Metz and Sedan

Sedan was the effective end of the war though Paris and the French provinces fought bravely on into 1871. As the Prussian armies laid siege to Paris, the German princes assembled in the palace of Louis XIV at Versailles. At the beginning of the war the four independent states of South Germany, Baden, Württemberg, Hesse-Darmstadt and Bavaria had agreed to fight with Prussia. Now united by military victory they were ready to become part of one German nation. On 18 January 1871, in the huge Hall of Mirrors at Versailles, William was proclaimed German Emperor.

**Germany
unified, 1871**

**The results of
the War**

The Treaty of Frankfurt (1871) ended the Franco-Prussian War. The French were harshly treated. They lost the provinces of Alsace and Lorraine, had to pay an indemnity of 5,000 million francs and suffer an army of occupation until the indemnity was paid. Bismarck agreed with this harshness. He thought France would seek a war of revenge however she was treated in 1871. So she should be weakened as much as possible to prevent her ever getting her revenge. Many historians believe that this was his greatest mistake for which Germany and Europe would eventually have to pay most dearly. Such thoughts would have seemed astonishing to Germans in 1871. Bismarck was the hero of the hour. By his skill, cunning and strength of will he had made a nation which was feared or respected throughout Europe.

Source F: Causes of the Franco-Prussian War

F1 Tomahawk *cartoon, 18 May 1867.* Tomahawk *was an English magazine, a rival to*
Punch.

1 *Who is the figure on the left and who on the
  right?*
2 *What part of Europe were they discussing
  in 1867?*
3 *Explain why the one gives the appearance of
  praying while the other looks both sad and
  thoughtful.*
4 *How fair a comment on the 1867 situation
  is this cartoon?*
5 *Why do newspapers have cartoons? How
  much can historians learn from them?*

F2 *This is what* Le Temps, *one of the main
Parisian newspapers, had to say on Monday
11 July 1870 during the 'Hohenzollern candidature' crisis.*

F3 *The meeting at Ems 13 July 1870.*

6 *Who are the two central figures? Why is one
  wearing his hat and the other not? Who do
  you think the two people in the front left
  and the two in the doorway are?*
7 *Where and when did this meeting take
  place? What exactly are the two central
  figures talking about?*

F4 *William met Benedetti the French
ambassador on Wednesday 13 July and his
secretary sent the famous telegram to
Bismarck that same evening. This is what he
sent.*

F2

"France has nothing to gain from war since Liberty has everything to
lose. That is why we are against the policy [of the French government]
which is continuously placing peace in danger and has thrown Europe
into the crisis through which we are now passing."

F4

"Count Benedetti ... persistently asked me to allow him to send a
telegram immediately saying that I would not agree to the Hohenzollern
candidature should it recur in the future; this I refused to do, eventually
rather sternly .... Since then his Majesty has received a letter from
Prince Karl Anton [Prince Leopold's father]. His Majesty had informed
Count Benedetti that he was expecting to hear from the Prince, but
having regard to the above unreasonable demand, his Majesty decided
... not to receive Count Benedetti again but to send a message ... to
the effect that his Majesty had learnt from the Prince the same news that
Benedetti had already received from Paris, and that his Majesty had
nothing further to say to the Ambassador ... "

F5 *This is Bismarck's shortened version which was printed in the Berlin newspapers.*

F5

"After the news of the withdrawal (from the Spanish throne) of the Prince of Hohenzollern had been officially communicated by the Spanish Government to the French Government, the French Ambassador in Ems none the less demanded that his Majesty should allow him to telegraph Paris that his Majesty had promised that never again would he agree to a Hohenzollern candidature. His Majesty has therefore decided not to receive the Ambassador again and has informed him by adjutant that he has nothing further to communicate to the Ambassador."

F6 *Here is what* Le Temps *had to say on Saturday 16 July.*

F6

"The king of Prussia has refused to receive France's representative and TOLD HIM THROUGH A HOUSEHOLD ADJUTANT that he had nothing further to communicate to him. This fact was published in the Official Berlin Gazette and brought to the notice of foreign governments by M. de Bismarck. To such insolence there is only one answer. WAR."

Read carefully sources F2–6.

8 *What did* Le Temps *want on 11 July and then on 16 July?*

9 *What aspects of the events at Ems particularly upset the French?*

10 *In what ways was Bismarck's version of the telegram from the king different from the original, apart from being shorter?*

11 *Bismarck claimed that his use of the Ems telegram was the main cause of the Franco-Prussian War. In what ways does the evidence here support that claim?*

12 *If you wished to check how important a cause of war the Ems telegram actually was, how helpful would you expect to find each of the following:*

    a) *other Parisian newspapers?*
    b) *Berlin newspapers?*
    c) *the views of King William of Prussia?*
    d) *the views of the Emperor Napoleon III?*
    e) *the views of de Gramont, the French Minister of foreign affairs?*
    f) *the views of Prince Leopold of Hohenzollern-Sigmaringen?*

13 *Could it be that Bismarck was exaggerating the importance of the Ems telegram? Explain your answer.*

The German Empire, 1871–90

The Reichstag and Bundesrat

The new German Empire had two representative assemblies. The Bundesrat or upper house was made up of delegates from the former independent states which had united to form the Empire. The Reichstag or lower house was elected by universal suffrage by all men over twenty-five. However, neither assembly had much power. The Bundesrat was dominated by the Prussian delegates who would do as they were told by the Emperor. The Reichstag could only discuss matters referred to it by the government and could neither appoint nor dismiss ministers. Its main influence came from its ability to reflect public opinion. Bismarck saw to it that these assemblies had much less power than the French Assembly or the British Parliament. Power in Germany rested with the Emperor, the Chancellor and his officials, and the army. The dominant social group was the Prussian landowning class.

Bismarck and the Catholics

One in every three Germans was Catholic. In 1870 the head of the Roman Catholic Church, Pope Pius IX, had announced the principle of Papal Infallibility which held that since the Pope was assisted by God when he decided what was correct in matters of faith and morals, he could not be mistaken. Moreover the Pope was very critical of many modern developments including the growing power of the new nation-states like Italy and Germany. He wished Catholics to keep education firmly under their own control and to resist interference from the state.

Source G:
The results of
the war

G1 *The proclamation of the German Empire 18 January 1871.*

G2 *(Right) Murdered Alsace: this engraving of 1874 shows a scene in 1871. Under cover of night young Alsatians bid a tearful farewell to their parents and slip away from their former homes. They wish to avoid being called up to the German army.*

Study source G1.

1 *Who is being cheered and why?*

2 *Why is this event taking place in Versailles rather than in Berlin?*

3 *Which figure is Bismarck? Immediately on Bismarck's left is the Prussian Chief of General Staff. What was his name?*

4 *Who do you think are the figures beside the one being cheered? Why should they be positioned there?*

Study source G2.

5 *Where is Alsace? When, and in what way, was it 'murdered'?*

6 *Who are the dark figures in the background?*

7 *What nationality do you think the artist was? Explain your answer.*

8 *Comment on the view that the attitudes of the Alsatians and the French shown in this picture suggest that the treatment of Alsace by Bismarck was a great mistake.*

9 *Comment on the treatment of Alsace as Bismarck might have done to an English newspaper reporter.*

The Kulturkampf

Some Catholics were upset by Pius IX and most Protestants thought his ideas stupidly backward-looking. Bismarck tried to use the Pope's unpopularity to bring the Catholic Church in Germany more under government control. In 1872 he began what became known as the 'Kulturkampf' (civilisation struggle) by trying to weaken Catholic schools and influence church appointments.

The Jesuit Order was expelled and thousands of Catholics who protested against these policies imprisoned or driven abroad. On balance, however, Bismarck's anti-Catholic policies failed. The Catholic leadership was not impressed by his bullying. Within the Reichstag the Catholic Centre Party grew in strength. When a new Pope, Leo XIII, succeeded the difficult Pius in 1878, Bismarck began to look for a compromise. By 1887 he had allowed back to the Church much of its independence though the Jesuits were forbidden to return. He could console himself with the thought that by being harsh on the Catholics he had kept the support of the national liberals when he needed it and by later being kind to the Catholics he won the support of the Centre Party at a time when he needed that for new policies concerning tariffs and the army.

German socialism

The trend which most disturbed him in the 1870s and 1880s was the rise of German socialism. In the Reichstag elections of 1877 the German Social Democractic Party, which was strongly influenced by the ideas of Marx and Engels, polled nearly 500,000 votes. Bismarck's instincts were those of an aristocratic, conservative landowner. He could see no good in socialism and feared that it could soon inspire an international revolution. He therefore attempted to destroy it. In 1878 he had socialist newspapers banned, then their political meetings. Their political leaders were harassed, some being forced abroad, and trade unions were driven

Social reforms

underground. He also gave his support to some major 'welfare' reforms, hoping to 'kill socialism with kindness'. In 1883 all industrial workers were compulsorily insured against sickness and in 1884 against accidents. In 1889 lower-paid workers were granted old-age pensions. In these three cases employers had to make a substantial contribution to the costs and the state helped with the pensions too.

Though these welfare reforms were better than any others in Europe they did not impress the socialists nor lessen their popularity with the voters. Despite his persecution of them, they campaigned for lower working hours and more trade union rights. In the 1890 election they won 1,500,000 votes and by 1914 were the largest party in the Reichstag with 4,500,000 votes.

Tariffs

If Bismarck failed with the socialists, he succeeded with tariffs. As in other European countries German farmers were threatened by cheap food from overseas. The Chancellor gained the support of conservative and centre groups to impose tariffs to protect farmers and certain industries. The German economy benefited and so did the finances of the imperial government since it collected customs duties without the supervision of the local or national assemblies.

The Emperor William II

The Emperor William I, Bismarck's staunch ally throughout his career as Chancellor, died in 1888. His successor, his son Frederick, survived him by only three months. Frederick's son then succeeded as Emperor William II. The new ruler was twenty-eight, intelligent, well-meaning

***Bismarck
resigns, 1890***

and keen to impress, but impulsive, indecisive and without persistence. He and Bismarck soon quarrelled. The Emperor wished to make his mark. The elderly arrogant Chancellor was set in his ways and unused to interference. The Emperor wanted policies kinder to the socialists, less friendly towards the Russians and more adventurous towards the colonies. He forced Bismarck to resign in 1890 (see source H1).

The German Empire which Bismarck, backed by William I, had created and had ruled for more than two decades was designed to be run by a strong Emperor or Chancellor or both. After 1890 it had an inadequate Emperor and no Chancellor with Bismarck's authority or staying power. The dominant Prussian ruling class was narrow-minded and increasingly aggressive. Aware of its military and economic strength the German nation lurched around like a bad-tempered bear in a cage and finally broke loose in 1914.

Source H: Bismarck and the Kaiser

H 'Dropping the Pilot' (Punch, *29 March 1890*).

1 *Who are the figures in the cartoon? What event is being shown? What is the general attitude of the cartoonist towards the pilot?*

DROPPING THE PILOT.

6 International relations (1871–1914) and the causes of the First World War

France and Germany

The Treaty of Frankfurt signed in May 1871 ended the Franco-Prussian War (see page 80). Although it would have been wiser not to, Germany also took the provinces of Alsace and Lorraine, tempting both strategically and for their rich iron and coalfields. Neither the Alsatians nor the Lorrainers, nor the French people as a whole, came to accept the loss (see sources A1 and A3). However much Bismarck might claim that Germany was 'a satiated state' which had no quarrel with any of her neighbours, France had been made a permanent enemy. Consequently, for his remaining nineteen years as Chancellor, Bismarck concentrated on making and maintaining anti-French alliances and, above all, on preventing a French alliance with Russia which might force Germany into a war on two fronts.

The League of the Three Emperors, 1873

Bismarck's first step was the League of the Three Emperors (Dreikaiserbund) of 1873. The Emperors of Germany, Austria-Hungary and Russia agreed to co-operate internationally, especially against revolutionary movements. Their agreement was, however, more a vague statement of attitudes than an alliance. Germany's isolation soon became clear. In 1875 France had not only paid off her war debt more quickly than expected but was thoroughly reforming her army. Bismarck thought about attacking her to prevent her recovering her strength but both Britain and Russia would not tolerate such action.

The Eastern Question crisis, 1875–8

Another international crisis blew up in 1875. Russia gave support to widespread Slav revolts in the Balkans and forced the Turks to sign the Treaty of San Stefano (see map, source F). This treaty reorganised the Balkans much as Russia wanted, with a new 'Big' Bulgaria. Neither Britain nor Austria-Hungary wanted Russia to control the Balkans so, at a Great Power conference chaired by Bismarck, the Treaty of Berlin (1878) replaced that of San Stefano. Big Bulgaria became smaller and Austria-Hungary became responsible for the day-to-day running of Bosnia.

The Dual Alliance, 1879

The 1875–8 Balkan crisis made clear the bitterness of the rivalry between Russia and Austria-Hungary in south-east Europe. None the less, Bismarck tried to stay friendly with both. In 1879 the Dual Alliance of Germany and Austria-Hungary was signed in secret. It was a defensive alliance, each country promising to come to the other's aid if attacked by Russia. The Dreikaiserbund was renewed in 1881.

The Reinsurance Treaty, 1887

Then in 1887 Germany signed another secret treaty, the so-called Reinsurance Treaty, this time with Russia, by which Germany agreed not to support an Austrian attack on Russia nor Russia a French attack on Germany. Meanwhile Bismarck had persuaded Italy to join the Dual Alliance (which therefore, in 1882, became the Triple Alliance) and encouraged French and British rivalry over colonies (see source B1).

Source A: Alsace-Lorraine and French public opinion

A1 *A picture by the artist Hansi. The quotation is from Victor Hugo, a famous French author, and reads: 'This heaven is our blue sky, this field is our land. This Lorraine and this Alsace is ours!' Hansi was born at Colmar in Alsace in 1873. He wrote and illustrated books and articles critical of the Germans in Alsace. Eventually, in 1914, he was put on trial by the German authorities for treason and fled to a Swiss exile.*

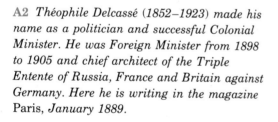

...Ce ciel est notre azur Ce champ est notre terre! Cette Lorraine et cette Alsace, c'est à Nous!
Victor Hugo.

A2 *Théophile Delcassé (1852–1923) made his name as a politician and successful Colonial Minister. He was Foreign Minister from 1898 to 1905 and chief architect of the Triple Entente of Russia, France and Britain against Germany. Here he is writing in the magazine* Paris, *January 1889.*

A2

"It has been eighteen years since Alsace-Lorraine was taken from France. Has France become less dear to her and Germany less odious? The persistence of the Alsace-Lorrainers in electing candidates of the party of protest, the desertion of their young men 'en masse' at the moment of conscription, declare well enough that their feelings have not changed."

A3 *A public opinion survey was carried out by the French magazine* The White Review *in the spring of 1895. A questionnaire about whether Alsace-Lorraine should be won back by war was sent out and 130 replies received.*

A3

a) *From Alsace itself:*
"The general public gives less and less attention to [the] Alsace-Lorraine [issue] and then vaguely on special occasions like Christmas and July 14th ... it preoccupies the superior mind, the thinkers, the historians, the politicians."

b) *A young person:*
"These things do not interest me."

c) *Another in his twenties:*
"This is the first time I've heard of the Treaty of Frankfurt ... I don't think that this question interests the youth of the day or the country, nor does it interest me ..."

1 *Who are the soldiers in the foreground (source A1)? In which direction are they looking? Explain a) the posts and wires, b) the building in the distance and the flag on it.*

2 *What evidence does Delcassé give (source A2) for his belief that the population of Alsace and Lorraine was still as anti-German in 1889 as it had been in 1871?*

3 *What other evidence contradicts this view?*

4 *How reliable is the evidence of* The White Review *public opinion survey (source A3) for French public opinion generally in the 1890s?*

Source B: Bismarck and overseas expansion

B1 *Bismarck did not believe in colonies. However in the 1880s he strongly supported colonial expansion. His aim was to anger Britain and to persuade France, Britain's main colonial rival, to be more friendly towards Germany. This is a Punch view of Bismarck, 1884.*

THE " IRREPRESSIBLE " TOURIST.

B-sm-rck. "H'm!—Ha!—where shall i go next?"

B2

"A reliable man, well-informed about Russia said to me: 'if Prince Bismarck wants to create an impression on the Russians, he must deal them such a blow that they sink on their knees. If he can't or won't, he should leave them in peace; these pinpricks [restrictions on Russian trade] goad them further'. Bismarck however, drunk with his sense of power, continued the system of harassing and worrying them which corresponded to his temperament. The last pinprick . . . was the order forbidding the German Reichsbank [to loan money to Russian businesses]. This insulting vote of no confidence occurred at a time when Alexander II was staying in Berlin as a guest."

B2 *Friedrich von Holstein (1837–1909) was promoted to high rank in the German Foreign Office by Bismarck in the 1870s. They fell out during the 1880s and, after Bismarck's resignation in 1890, Holstein was highly influential in foreign affairs until his own resignation in 1906. Bismarck, in his retirement, strongly criticised Holstein and his Emperor. This extract from Holstein's memoirs was written in 1898 and refers to the years 1886–90.*

1 *List the main alliances Bismarck made for Germany between 1875 and 1890.*

2 *What alliance against Germany did he want to prevent if he possibly could?*

3 *Look in detail at source B1. Explain Margate, Wight, South Africa. What is the attitude of the Punch cartoonist?*

4 *Study source B2. In what ways does Holstein believe that Bismarck's treatment of the Russians was unwise?*

5 *Why is Holstein an important source for German foreign policy in this period?*

6 *Is there any indication in the source that he might be biased against Bismarck? If so, what is it?*

7 *Comment on the view that Bismarck was a brilliant statesman and in the long run his policies caused much more good than harm both to Germany and to Europe.*

Emperor William II

Bismarck's alliances were typically complicated and secretive. They worked while he was in power but after he was sacked in 1890 soon came apart. He told the world that this was because his successors had none of his skill. This was only partly true. He himself put his policies at risk by failing to give adequate training to his successors and he weakened the alliance with Russia by refusing to allow German investment in Russian industry (see source B2).

A more aggressive policy

Moreover the younger generation in Germany wanted a more aggressive worldwide foreign policy. The Emperor (Kaiser) William II had this more aggressive international approach but he possessed neither the calm firmness nor the skill in appointing able enough ministers to use Germany's great strengths to her permanent international advantage. The general effect of the Kaiser's foreign policy was to alarm his neighbours and to increase the influence of Germany's military leaders.

He allowed the Reinsurance Treaty with Russia to lapse since it got in the way of better understandings with Austria-Hungary and Britain. Instead Russia turned to France, who had already been generous with financial loans and, in January 1894, a Franco-Russian defensive alliance against Germany and Austria-Hungary was signed.

The Schlieffen Plan

The German General Staff had already worked out how they would win victory in a two-front war against such an alliance. By the 1892 plan of Count Schlieffen, France had to be smashed first by a swift attack from the main German armies. The Russians would be fended off until the surrender of France. Then they would be overwhelmed by the full weight of Germany's forces.

Nationalism

In 1895 Europe had not seen a general war since the Crimean War forty years earlier. Though Germany and Austria were now teamed up against France and Russia, there was no obvious reason why a European war could not be avoided for at least as long again. However, the popular mood was changing. Nationalism had been a powerful force throughout the century. It had helped to create first Italy and then Germany. It was a lively cause of unrest in the Balkans where South Slavs, Bulgars, Greeks and Romanians struggled to turn themselves into independent nations at the expense of the Turks and of each other. As chapter 1 showed, nationalism in Western Europe took on new shape in imperial rivalries. The size of one's overseas empire became an important measure of one's national power (see source C). The spread of mass education encouraged rather than discouraged nationalistic ways of thinking. Social Darwinists argued that conflict between nations was as natural and as unavoidable as the struggle for survival among biological species.

Nietzsche

Of great influence in 1900 was the German writer Nietzsche. He was very critical of the values of the average middle-class Europeans of his time. They seemed to him stuffy and self-satisfied. He called for the complete rethinking of all values and expected that a race of supermen would be needed who would not hesitate to use violence if required to create a nobler world. He argued that violence and therefore war could be a purifying step towards this better world.

National honour

In the twenty years leading up to 1914, public opinion became more excitable where national honour was concerned. When disputes took

Source C:
Nationalism and war

C *The most popular lectures at the University of Berlin in the 1880s were those on politics by Heinrich von Treitschke. Treitschke also wrote a best-selling German history, was a successful journalist and, for a time, a member of the Reichstag. Even those who disliked his ideas regarded him as a powerful influence on German thought before the First World War. These extracts are from his 'Politics' lectures.*

1 *What had Treitschke in common with Nietzsche and the Social Darwinists as outlined on the opposite page?*

2 *Between 1900 and 1914 Germany was badly divided by party political differences and by social strife. If her political leaders had turned to their copies of Treitschke's lectures about politics for guidance and had heeded his advice, what might they have done?*

3 *Treitschke was extremely anti-British. At a time when there was much mutual respect*

C

"Again and again there will be confirmation of the truth that only in war will a nation truly become a nation. Only common great deeds for the idea of the fatherland will hold a nation together . . . . Social selfishness must yield and party hatred quieten down . . . the individual must forget himself and feel part of the whole."

"At the end of the next victorious war we must try to acquire some colonies."

"We want and ought to claim our share in the domination of the earth by the white race . . . . Ultimately the importance of a nation will depend upon its share in the domination of the transatlantic world."

between the British and the Germans, why do you think that this was so?

4 *What recent events in German history convinced Treitschke of the truth of his first sentence? Can you suggest examples which disprove it?*

5 *Most modern university students in Berlin and elsewhere would regard these views as dangerous rubbish. How could such a change in attitudes take place in barely a century?*

Britain and Europe

Fashoda, 1898

The German navy

place, war, which was expected to be a short, sharp and glorious affair fought by professional soldiers, was seen as an increasingly acceptable solution.

In the ten years between 1897 and 1907, Britain's relationship to Europe changed greatly. Before 1897 her industrial and naval strength had allowed her to follow a policy of apparent isolation staying clear of formal alliances with European powers.

However, in 1898 she nearly went to war with France over the Fashoda incident (see page 12). Then from 1899 to 1902 she found herself fighting a difficult war against the Boers in South Africa with all the world hostile. Worst of all, Germany, who had already overtaken her economically and had the most powerful army in Europe, began building a fleet which was intended to rival Britain's in the North Sea.

In the view of Admiral von Tirpitz, the creator of the German fleet, Germany would never be the genuine world power which she deserved to be until Britain was persuaded by a challenge to her naval power to make more 'places in the sun' available to the Germans. He was keenly supported by the Kaiser. They did not expect their navy to drive Britain into an alliance hostile to Germany; on the contrary they thought it would make an Anglo-German alliance more likely. They miscalculated. Though there were a number of attempts to build such an alliance, one as late as 1912, none came to anything. The German government did not understand how serious a threat their fleet was to Britain. For centuries the British navy had been the island's main defence and the British army was tiny by European standards. By challenging the navy, Germany was in fact threatening Britain's independence and pushing her into the arms of Germany's enemies (see source E3).

The 'Ententes' of 1904 and 1907

The German naval-building programme began in earnest in 1898. In 1902 Britain agreed to co-operate with Japan in the Far East. The Japanese navy would keep an eye on the Russians so some Royal Navy squadrons were moved from the Far East to home waters. Then in 1904 the skilful diplomacy of Delcassé, the French Foreign Minister, brought about the signing by France and Britain of the Entente Cordiale (friendly agreement). The main points dealt with colonial matters. France accepted that Britain would be the chief influence in Egypt and in return Britain agreed to support the French in Morocco. In 1907 Britain came to a similar agreement with Russia over disputed areas of Asia, notably Tibet, Afghanistan and Persia. Germany had believed that colonial differences would make it impossible for Britain to work at all closely with either France or Russia. Now these difference had been sorted out and Britain was able to forge closer links particularly with France.

Morocco

Two serious crises over Morocco helped to push France and Britain still closer. The Kaiser was irritated by the Entente Cordiale of 1904, which seemed to him to be a Franco-British scheme to keep Germany from gaining any part of North Africa.

The 1905 crisis

The following year he sailed into Tangier and made a fierce speech demanding that an international conference be called to discuss the situation in Morocco and that Germany's interests must be respected. At first the French wavered and Delcassé resigned. Then, sure of Britain's support, they steadied. At the Algeciras Conference of 1906 Germany was left empty-handed and France stayed the dominating European power in Morocco.

The Agadir crisis, 1911

The second crisis began in 1911 when the Sultan of Morocco was trapped in his capital, Fez, by rebel tribesmen. France sent 20,000 troops to his aid. The German government then took action in a clumsy, angry and muddled way. It sent a gunboat to the South Moroccan port of Agadir (see source D1). It claimed to be defending German business interests but also aimed to scare the French either into giving to Germany a share of Morocco or some other part of Africa. Once again Britain strongly supported France, answering Germany's threats with counter-threats. After months of difficult negotiation Germany settled for 100,000 square miles of the French Congo, much of which was swamp or jungle. Once again Germany had failed to weaken France's position in Morocco and had strengthened the Franco-British Entente. After the first Morocco crisis French and British military leaders had joint discussions; after the second their naval chiefs agreed that the British fleet would defend the North Sea, the French fleet the Mediterranean.

The arms race

An arms race was now under way which added greatly to the tension between European nations. Between 1890 and 1914 the military expenditure of the major powers of Europe soared (see source E).

The dreadnought

In 1906 Britain accelerated the naval arms race by launching the first 'dreadnought' type of battleship. It was the brainchild of Fisher, Admiral of the Fleet. It was faster, better armed with guns that could fire further and more accurately than any ship in the world. It could sink any rival before coming into range of their guns. Consequently it made all other warships, including Britain's, obsolete. Fisher argued that the dread-

Source D:
A problem in Morocco

D1 *A German cartoon of the Agadir crisis, 1911.*

Study the cartoon D1 and the map D2.

1 a) *Identify from left to right the three boys with the boats.*
   b) *Who is the old man in the top hat?*
   c) *Name the toy boat in the middle of the pond and the toy town.*
   d) *Whose side did the old man take?*

2 *For what reasons were the four European powers shown in the cartoon interested in Morocco?*

3 *In what years did the crisis happen? How did it end and what were its long-term consequences?*

D2 *North Africa, 1880–1914.*

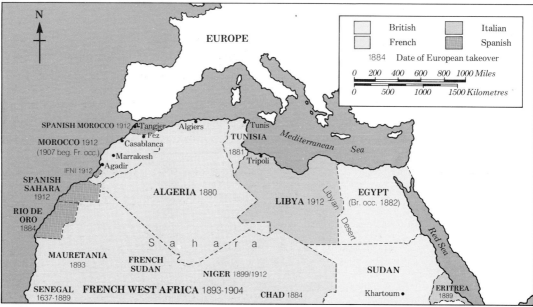

nought would give Britain such a lead in the naval race that Germany would either give up altogether or be left far behind, since to have her own dreadnought fleet would require deepening the Kiel Canal.

The German reply

The Germans, however, responded energetically to Fisher's challenge. They built their own dreadnoughts and completed the deepening of the Kiel Canal in 1914. Fisher had calculated badly. Instead of ending the naval race, the building of dreadnoughts speeded it up at colossal expense (see source E2).

Disarmament talks

At the suggestion of Russia a disarmament conference was held at the Hague in the Netherlands in 1899 in an attempt to slow down the arms race. Another was held in 1907. These achieved little since the major powers were too suspicious of each other to risk what they called their vital interests. When Britain suggested that the naval race be ended, Germany, not without reason, considered that that would simply give Britain a permanent advantage over her. In 1912 Haldane, a British Minister, visited Germany to see if the naval race could be slowed and the increasing enmity between Britain and Germany be lessened. However, for Germany Tirpitz was only ready to consider slowing down his naval building programme if Britain agreed to stay out of a Franco-German war. This was a much higher price than Britain was ready to pay.

Source E: The arms race

E1

Some military and economic statistics for 1900

	Austria-Hungary	France	Germany	Britain	Italy	Russia
Population (millions)	45	39	56	42	32	133
Men in regular army	400,000	600,000	600,000	280,000	200,000	860,000
Annual iron-steel production (million tonnes)	2.5	3.25	14	14	$\frac{1}{2}$	5
1st class battleships	–	13	14	38	9	13
2nd class battleships	6	10	–	11	5	10

E2

Expenditure on arms per head of population, $

	1800	1900	1910	1914
Britain	3.84	12.60	7.19	8.23
France	4.66	5.21	6.47	7.07
Russia	1.26	1.44	2.32	3.44
Germany	2.80	3.48	4.06	8.19
Austria-Hungary	1.50	1.46	1.68	3.10
Italy	2.52	2.34	3.36	3.16

These figures are in dollars and are taken from *Europe 1815–1914* by Gordon A. Craig (1972).

E3 *The* Daily Mail, *5 February 1903, comments on the rapid increase of the German fleet under Tirpitz leadership.*

The Daily Mail *began in 1896 as a halfpenny daily newspaper and was aimed by its owners, the Harmsworth brothers, to have a much bigger readership than established 'quality' newspapers like* The Times. *It had short simple paragraphs and lively, often sensational reports. By 1900 it sold more than a million copies per day, a huge number for that period.*

E4 *The English captain of* HMS Albemarle, *who visited the German fleet at Swinemunde in 1904, reported that:*

E5 *The Kaiser watching battlefleet manoeuvres. Painted by Willy Stower, 1912.*

E3

"While great naval power in the hands of Britain cannot constitute a menace, in the hands of Germany it will be a great peril to the world, the more so as the recent history of German policy is one of daring aggression and as the want of space at home compels Germany to conquer the colonies of others or perish."

E4

"the junior [German] officers never appeared to have thought it worth their while to conceal the fact that the mission of the German fleet was to wipe out the English fleet."

Study sources E1 and E2.

1 *Compare the strengths of the Germany/Austria-Hungary partnership with that of the Franco-Russian partnership in 1900. What would Britain add to France and Russia? Why was Germany not too bothered about Britain in the event of a continental war?*

2 *Which of the major powers had most increased its spending per head of population between 1900 and 1914? (Assume the populations in 1914 were the same as in 1900.)*

Which country was spending the most, in absolute terms, on arms in 1914? How much was this in dollars?

3 *Explain the thinking behind the* Daily Mail *comment (source E3). Reply to it as if writing for a German newspaper of the time.*

Study sources E4 and E5.

4 a) *What impression is Willy Stower aiming to give in his painting?*
  b) *How reliable is the report of the captain of* HMS Albemarle *as evidence of the intentions of the German government?*

The Balkans

The most dangerous area of Europe was the Balkans (sources F1 and 2). The Turkish Empire continued to weaken. The Balkan peoples were as determined as ever to win their independence; Russia and Austria-Hungary were each equally determined that, whatever happened, the other would not gain too much influence.

The Slavs within the Austrian Empire

Austria-Hungary had a particular worry. If the Slavs of the Balkans successfully won independence from Turkey with Russia's help then the millions of Slavs within the Austrian Empire might wish to join them rather than be ruled by Austria-Hungary. Serbia, to the south, was a particular threat. The existence of Austria-Hungary would be at risk.

Russia's ambitions

Moreover, after her defeat by Japan in the Far East, Russia became more active in the Balkans. Her Slav language and Orthodox religion made her the natural champion of the Slavs of south-east Europe in a period of enthusiastic nationalism. She also hoped to achieve her centuries-old ambition of driving the Turks completely out of Europe and taking possession of their capital Constantinople.

The retreat of Turkey, 1878–1913

The Treaty of Berlin which ended the crisis of 1875–8 (see page 87) had greatly weakened Turkish power in Europe. While Serbia, Romania and Montenegro won complete independence, Bulgaria virtually did and Bosnia and Herzegovina were occupied by the Austrian army though remaining Turkish in name. Turkey lost more land in the 1880s, Thessaly to Greece in 1881 and Eastern Rumelia to Bulgaria in 1885. The Turkish Sultan Abdul Hamid II was a bad ruler, cruel and out of touch. Christians were savagely persecuted. In Armenia in 1895, 300,000 were massacred, in Constantinople in 1896, 6,000. Eventually in 1908 the Young Turk movement, determined to modernise Turkey by western methods, led a successful revolution which led eventually to Abdul Hamid being deposed.

The weaker Turkey became, the greater the rivalry and ill-feeling between Russia and Austria and between the Balkan states.

Bosnia-Herzegovina annexed, 1908

In 1908 Austria-Hungary took the opportunity provided by the revolution in Constantinople to annex the provinces of Bosnia and Herzegovina into her empire. Since 1878 she had run the provinces but they were still formally part of the Turkish Empire. Russia and Serbia were furious. Russia claimed to have been double-crossed; Serbia, a Slav nation, believed that the mainly Slav provinces should belong to her. However, Germany aggressively supported the Austrian action so Russia and Serbia accepted the situation with bad grace and waited for their chance of revenge.

Italy conquers Tripolitania, 1911

Italy took advantage of Turkey's weakness in 1911 when she invaded Tripolitania in North Africa. This was the signal for the Balkan countries to sink their differences and attempt to drive the Turks from Europe.

The First Balkan War, 1912

In 1912 Serbia, Bulgaria, Greece and Montenegro formed the Balkan League and declared war on the Turks. They won a number of victories and pushed them back to a narrow strip of land about sixty miles wide defending Constantinople (see map F). The First Balkan War was ended by the Treaty of London but the task of settling the new frontiers in the Balkans proved very difficult. Austria-Hungary interfered to make sure that Albania appeared on the map as an independent country in order to prevent Serbia from having a port on the Adriatic, but the country most dissatisfied was Bulgaria.

The Second Balkan War, 1913

In 1913 Bulgaria fought against the rest, who were joined by Romania and Turkey, in the Second Balkan War and was totally defeated. She lost land to everyone, particularly to Serbia. The main result of the Balkan wars was a successful and confident Serbia looking forward to another battle, this time with Austria-Hungary.

Source F: The Balkans 1908–14

F1 *The Balkans 1912–13.*

1 *At the end of 1913 what land in Europe was still Turkish?*

2 *Why was Bulgaria so keen to win Thrace? In which country is Thrace today?*

3 *By approximately how much did Serbia increase in size as a result of the Balkan Wars? Which two neighbouring countries particularly objected to this increase? Why?*

F2 Impressions of Bosnia, 1908 and 1913.
J. H. Baernreither was an Austrian lawyer who had also been a member of the Imperial Diet (Assembly) in Vienna. He became particularly interested in the 'South Slav' problem, travelled in the Balkans, had articles published in the Austrian newspapers and advised government ministers. The extracts are all from his Fragments of a Political Diary, *published in Vienna.*

Bosnian Journey, 1908.
"There was no love for Austria-Hungary in the Balkans; it was to blame for everything and said to have spies everywhere .... In Serbia in particular systematic agitation against Austria was going on ..."

Pamphlet on Bosnia, 1913.
"I pointed out [in this] that political interest and national consciousness was much more active than is imagined in Vienna and demand more careful handling, in view of the Greater Serbia agitation ..."

Conversation with Aehrenthal, the Austrian foreign minister 1909.
"I [Baernreither] pressed him to give Serbia some gleam of positive hope [for a trade agreement] and an end to the ban on meat imports. 'Bulgaria is more important than Serbia,' he replied ... He spoke of the Serbs in the tone that used to be employed in Vienna before 1866 about the Prussians who 'needed a good thrashing'. The awful error of his policy was that he did not thereupon destroy the Serbs or actually thrash them. Which might have produced some results."

Sarajevo during the First Balkan War, 1912.
"There is an enormous interest in the war. The Muslims are depressed, silent and keep themselves to themselves. The Catholics [mainly Croats] are divided ... the Serbs are naturally in high spirits ... cases are reported of men in good positions going into Serbia to join up .... A course in nursing the wounded was arranged at the hospital attended by Serbian ladies .... The old heroic days are coming to life again and breeding unmeasured hopes for the future."

Study the extracts of Baernreither's political diary (Source F2) and pages 96, 97 and 99.

4 *What happened to Bosnia* a) *in 1878,* b) *in 1908? Why were the Serbs angry about what happened in 1908?*

5 *Explain the phrase 'Greater Serbia agitation'. Why were the Austrians so against it?*

6 *Who was Aehrenthal? What was his policy in 1909 towards Serbia?*

7 a) *In 1912 why were* (i) *the Muslims depressed,* (ii) *the Croats divided, and* (iii) *the Serbs in high spirits?*
  b) *What were 'the unmeasured hopes for the future'?*

8 *Comment on the value of Baernreither as a source for 1908–14.*

9 *Where is Sarajevo? Why did the assassination there lead to war* a) *between Austria and Serbia,* b) *between Austria and Russia and* c) *between Russia and Germany?*

Crisis – summer 1914

Sarajevo

On Sunday, 28 June 1914, the Archduke Ferdinand, heir to the Austrian throne, was in Sarajevo, capital of Bosnia, with his wife. He had come to inspect the army which was on manoeuvres. Bosnian revolutionaries, armed and aided by Serbia, planned to assassinate him on that day. In the morning they threw a bomb but it bounced off the Archduke's car and only wounded an officer. In the afternoon the Archduke went to visit the officer. His driver got lost and stopped for a moment in a crowded street. Nearby was Princip, one of the revolutionaries. He had time to shoot and kill both the Archduke and his wife before being overpowered.

To much of Europe here was just another Balkan crisis which the politicians would soon sort out. The British newspapers were much more interested in Irish problems, the French in a juicy political scandal. However, the Sarajevo crisis was different. Austria-Hungary was out to smash Serbia just as long as Germany would support her against Russia. Germany was ready to do so even though they were risking a major European war. Their generals and most of their politicians were sure that a major war was going to come anyway. Since France had begun army reforms which would be fully effective in 1916 and Russia ones which would be completed in 1917, the sooner this war came the better would be Germany's chances.

The Austrian ultimatum to Serbia

On 23 July Austria-Hungary issued Serbia with a tough ultimatum which Serbia was intended to reject. Sure of Russian support, Serbia rejected some of its demands. Austria-Hungary declared war on Serbia on 28 July. At this crucial point the politicians began to lose control of their generals.

The mobilisation question

A major war would be won, the generals believed, by the nations who by careful use of their railways and timetables were the quickest to shift the largest number of troops to the main battlefields. Once the troop trains were running in one direction days if not weeks would be needed to move them in another. Consequently the Tsar of Russia and his generals had a very difficult decision. Their quarrel was with Austria-Hungary. Should they mobilise their troops just against her or should they order a general mobilisation since there was a possibility of a German attack?

Russia mobilises

On 30 July Tsar Nicholas ordered a general mobilisation. By this time the German generals were straining at the leash. If Russian troops were on the move, the sooner they got going too, the better. On 31 July the Kaiser allowed German mobilisation to begin and after some uncertainty declared war on Russia on 1 August. That same day he heard that Britain would stay neutral as long as Germany did not attack France.

Germany puts the Schlieffen Plan into action

However, the German army was mobilising according to the Schlieffen Plan. Trains carrying the bulk of the army were steaming towards France. When the Kaiser suggested to Moltke, his Chief of Staff, that the advance westwards be stopped, Moltke pointed out that to stop now would throw the German forces into complete confusion and place them in the greatest danger from a French attack, since the French army had mobilised that day. The German troop trains steamed on.

The invasion of Belgium

On 3 August German troops entered France and Belgium. Up to this point the British government had wavered (see source G). Only a few senior politicians knew how much joint military planning had been done with the French and an important section of public opinion wanted to stay out of what seemed to them an irresponsible continental war.

Britain joins in

The invasion of neutral Belgium united public opinion in favour of war. Britain declared war on Germany on 4 August (see source G1).

Who was to blame?

An enormous amount of historians' time has been spent arguing about who was to blame for the calamity of the First World War. At the end of it Germany and Austria-Hungary were saddled with war guilt. Did not Austria-Hungary actually want a war with Serbia and did not Germany want a major war sooner rather than later? Then other historians pointed out that before 1914 things were not that simple. In the Balkans Russia and Serbia were both aggressive, while Britain, France and Russia had by their alliances locked Germany in Europe and prevented her overseas expansion. Moreover they had been fully committed to the arms race. In the 1960s the German historian Fischer swung the pendulum back when he argued that the German political and military leadership welcomed the 1914 war and intended to use it to conquer much of Central Europe. Indeed they actively encouraged Austria-Hungary to use the Sarajevo assassination to provoke Serbia into war in the hope that this would cause the European war which they wanted. Most historians now agree that the German government, egged on by its generals, deliberately provoked the war of 1914.

Source G: Britain wavers as Europe goes to war

G1 *At dawn on 1 August the British Foreign Office knew that Austria-Hungary and Serbia were already at war. Russia had ordered a general mobilisation but was still talking to Austria-Hungary. Germany had sent an ultimatum to Russia and an enquiry about French intentions. Sir Edward Grey, Foreign Secretary, had to advise the Liberal Cabinet and Parliament as to what Britain should do. The Cabinet was split and public opinion unready for war. Moreover Asquith his Prime Minister had kept secret even from the Cabinet the joint military planning which had taken place with the French. Taking advice from the senior civil servant at the Foreign Office, Sir Arthur Nicolson, Grey kept in close hourly touch with the British Ambassadors in Berlin (Goschen), Paris (Bertie), St Petersburg (Buchanan), and Belgium (Villiers) before the final decision was taken. These telegrams passed between the British Foreign Office and the main cities of Europe.*

Goschen (Berlin), to Grey 1 August
"Military Attaché reports that . . . almost the entire general staff have left Berlin . . . supreme confidence in military circles . . . M.A. confident in the event of war Germany will pass part of her forces through Belgium."

Sir Arthur Nicolson, Permanent Under-Secretary at the Foreign Office, personal note to Grey, 1 August
"M. Cambon (the French Ambassador) pointed out to me this afternoon that it was at our request that France had moved her fleets to the Mediterranean on the understanding that we undertook the protection of her Northern and Western coasts . . . it would be as well to remind the Cabinet of this fact."

Grey to Bertie (Ambassador in Paris)
"August 1st 8.20 p.m. After the Cabinet today I told M. Cambon . . . that France must take her own decision without reckoning on an assistance which we were not in a position to promise . . ."

Buchanan (Ambassador in St Petersburg) to Grey
"August 1st 11.45 p.m. German Ambassador handed to Minister of Foreign Affairs formal declaration of war this evening at 7 p.m."

Grey to Goschen (Berlin), 1 August
"The German Ambassador asked whether if Germany gave a promise not to violate Belgian neutrality we would engage to remain neutral. I replied that I could not say that: our hands were still free . . . our attitude would be determined largely by public opinion here and that the neutrality of Belgium would appeal very strongly to public opinion."

Goschen (Berlin) to Grey, 2 August
"Orders were sent last night to allow British ships [forcibly held in the port Hamburg] to proceed on their way . . . this must be regarded as a special favour . . . no other foreign ships have been allowed to leave."

Villiers (Ambassador in Brussels) to Grey
"August 2nd 11.45 a.m. Belgium government now have official confirmation that a German force entered the Grand Duchy of Luxembourg."

Goschen (Berlin) to Grey
"August 2nd received 3.30 p.m. Minister of Foreign Affairs tells me that it seems probable that the French have already commenced hostilities by dropping bombs from airship in the vicinity of Nuremberg."

Grey to Bertie (Paris)
"August 2nd 4.45 p.m. If the German fleet come into the Channel . . . to undertake hostile action against the French coasts or shipping the British Fleet will give it all the protection in its power . . . . The Government felt that they could not bind themselves to declare war upon Germany necessarily if war broke out between France and Germany tomorrow."
[*3 August:* Germany declares war on France.]

Study the telegrams closely.

1 *What are the responsibilities of a) ambassadors, b) consuls? Who was the French ambassador in London?*

2 a) *Who was the British Foreign Secretary in 1914? What party did he belong to?*
b) *When did he know for sure a) that Germany would (i) probably (ii) definitely attack France; b) (i) probably (ii) definitely invade Belgium?*

3 a) *M. Cambon spent much of 1 and 2 August in a state of alarm and exasperation. Why was this? To what extent was his exasperation justified?*
b) *When were the French sure that the British would fight with them?*

4 *Note each piece of evidence which suggests that the German government was anxious to keep Britain neutral if at all possible. Why then did it allow the generals to invade Belgium?*

The British Consul in Antwerp (Belgium) to Grey
"August 3rd 1.30 p.m. Received reliable information that advance guard of German troops crossed Belgian frontier."

Grey to the German Ambassador, 4 August
"I have the honour to inform Your Excellency that in accordance with the terms of the notification made to the German government today Her Majesty's Government considers that a state of war exists between the two countries as from today, 11 p.m."

G2 *The 'Scrap of Paper'. A British anti-German propaganda poster, December 1914, published by the Government Recruitment Committee in the* Daily Graphic.

5 *What is the piece of paper shown on the poster?*

6 *Does it prove that the Germans had broken an important promise?*

7 *Why was the German invasion of Belgium so important to the Liberal politicians who wanted to declare war?*

8 *The Foreign Office telegrams do not tell us about the actual decision to declare war on Germany. Who would have made that decision and whom would he have consulted before making it? What would be the best sources for finding out when and why he reached that decision?*

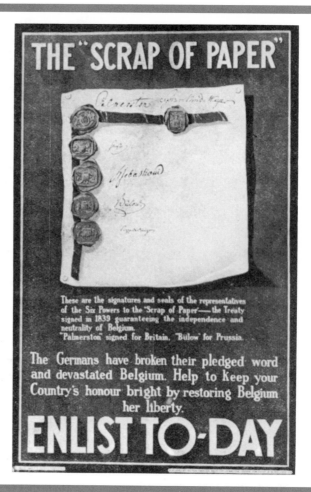

7 The First World War

September 1914

In September 1914, the war was greeted with delight in the cities of Europe (see source A). 'It will be over by Christmas' thought the young men as they hurried along to the recruiting centres so as not to miss the fun. One of the few gloomy comments came from Lord Grey, Britain's Foreign Secretary. 'The lamps are going out all over Europe;' he said, 'we shall not see them lit again in our lifetime.' Yet even Grey in his gloomiest moments could not have foreseen the appalling effects of the war.

The end of an era

It lasted longer than anyone expected. Its military casualties, civilian suffering and damage to land and property made it much the most destructive war in history. It changed the map of Europe and the nature of European society, but out of the slaughter and destruction no obviously better world appeared. Nor after 1918 was it possible to turn the clock back in any important way. Consequently the war also destroyed the confidence which most Europeans had in progress, civilisation and the power of human reason. It was in every sense the end of an era, and a dreadful one.

Source A: Declaration of war

A *The reaction to the news of the declaration of the war in St Petersburg as recalled by Rodzianko, chairman of the Duma (National Assembly) in his memoirs.*

1 *Who were the Tsar and Tsarina of Russia in 1914? How popular were they before the outbreak of war?*

2 *Explain a) why the crowd should have fallen to its knees, and b) why the placards would have had 'Long live Slavdom' written on them.*

3 *What kinds of economic and political demands would the workers have been presenting? (See pages 120–2.)*

4 *What does this extract tell you about the comparative popularity of nationalism and socialism in Russia in 1914? How much success would you expect those European socialist leaders to have had when they urged working people to oppose the war?*

A

"The huge crowd filled the square [in front of the Winter Palace] and the nearby streets and when the Tsar appeared ... an enormous hurrah filled the air. Flags and placards with the inscription 'Long live Russia and Slavdom' bowed to the ground and the entire crowd fell to its knees as one man ...

Coming out of the palace into the square we mingled with the crowd. Some workers came by. I stopped them and asked them how they happened to be there when not long before they had been striking and presenting economic and political demands almost with weapons in their hands.

The workers answered 'that was our private affair. We found that reform was going too slowly through the Duma. But now all Russia is concerned. We came to our Tsar as to our banner and we shall go with him in the name of victory over Germany.'"

Out-of-date generals

An important cause of its long-drawn-out dreadfulness was the failure of military men to foresee what kind of war it would be (see source B). On land they expected quick, decisive victories by their huge rapidly mobilised armies, which would back up swift cavalry breakthroughs with massed infantry advances. At sea a 'dreadnought' version of the Battle of Trafalgar would be equally decisive. They were certain that a long war was impossible. In order to pay for it governments would have to raise taxes so much that they would have a revolution on their hands.

A war of attrition

None of these predictions turned out to be true and neither generals nor politicians knew what to do except go on fighting since peace without victory was unthinkable. Instead of being a glorious adventure for a few weeks the war became an endless slog. Victory would go to those nations which economically, socially and militarily were the most durable.

Source B: The theory and practice of war

B *Captain Sir Basil Liddell Hart is one of the best-known writers on the history and nature of modern warfare. The following extracts are taken from an article which he wrote in 1968 summing up his views about military thinking in the First World War.*

Liddell Hart goes on to argue that the trench stalemate on the Western Front could have been foreseen. Bloch, a Polish banker, Mayer and Grouard, French military writers, and Repington the military journalist of The Times *newspaper made much more accurate predictions but were ignored.*

1 *How did von der Goltz, Foch, Haig and Sukhomlinov believe before 1914 that the war would be won? For how long did the generals go on believing this after the outbreak of war?*

2 *What new weapons had in fact given greater advantage to the defenders? Explain why this was so. What two other developments also added to the advantage of the defenders?*

3 *Liddell Hart thinks that the generals had no excuse for failing to foresee what would happen to their mass attacks. What arguments does he use to show their short-sightedness? How well do you think he makes his case?*

4 *Once the trenches were dug, what else could the generals have done besides the mass attacks?*

B

"If there was one feature of the half-century preceding 1914, it was the increasing advantage of the defensive, due to the growing power of infantry firearms – first the magazine rifle and then the machine-gun .... The American Civil War made these factors plain. It was not to be expected that European generals would profit from this second-hand experience, since the great Field Marshal von Moltke (the Elder) dismissed it as no more than 'two mobs chasing each other round the country ...'

... The Franco-Prussian War ... demonstrated the same change in conditions .... Nevertheless we find the future Field Marshal von der Goltz declaring that 'the idea of the greater strength of the defensive is mere delusion' ... in 1903 the future Marshal Foch confidently predicted that 'any improvement in firearms is bound to strengthen the offensive' .... The future Field Marshal Haig, fresh from the South African battle-fields (1899–1902), [advised a Royal Commission] that 'cavalry will have a larger sphere of action in future wars' ... General Sukhomlinov, the Russian War Minister, warned 'that he could not hear the term "modern war" without a feeling of annoyance. As war was, so it remained'....

Then came the Russo-Japanese War (1904–5) which foreshadowed nearly all the factors which upset military calculations in 1914 – the paralysing power of machine-guns, the hopelessness of frontal attacks, and the consequent relapse of the armies into trenches .... To ardent soldiers war was unthinkable without successful attack so they were able to persuade themselves the attacks could succeed....

The German machine-guns had paralysed movement on the battlefield for months in 1914 when Haig (now commanding the British First Army) remarked that 'the machine-gun was a much overrated weapon and two per battalion were more than sufficient' .... Long before the war ended, there would be ... more than forty per battalion .... In 1916 when the first tank performed before Lord Kitchener (Britain's Secretary of War) his comment was 'a pretty mechanical toy. The war would never be won by such machines.'

[During] the British summer offensive of 1916 ... Haig impressed on all at conferences and other times, that the infantry would only have to walk over and take possession of the enemy trenches .... In 1917 Nivelle declared 'We shall break the German front when we wish ...'"

The Western Front, 1914

The failure of the Schlieffen Plan

True to the Schlieffen Plan the main German thrust was westwards against France (see map below). Striking through Belgium, Moltke, chief of the German General Staff, aimed to envelop Paris from the west and east. The French army, which had invaded Alsace-Lorraine, had to turn back to meet the main German attack, and the small British force had to retreat from Belgium into France to link up with its French ally. After a month's fighting the Germans were across the Marne, Paris was threatened and the French government moved to Bordeaux.

However, Moltke was worried. In the east the Russians had mobilised much faster than expected and the German generals in East Prussia (see map on page 106) were shouting for reinforcements. In the west his advance had got badly out of line. The army which should have come between Paris and the sea had been driven further to the east and was open to a counterattack from Paris. On 15 August, well behind his advancing armies and plagued by unreliable communications, an anxious Moltke made what was probably the most serious mistake of the war. He sent two army corps from the western front to reinforce the east. Thus weakened the Germans were unable to hold the Allied counterattack across the Marne which began in early September. They retreated and dug themselves into a line of trenches which ran from the Belgian coast through northern France to Switzerland.

The Western Front 1914.

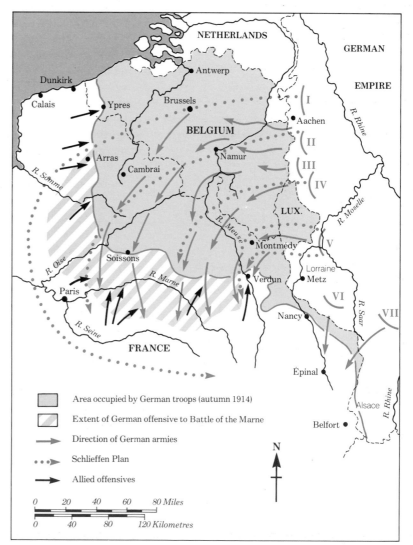

The Eastern Front, 1914

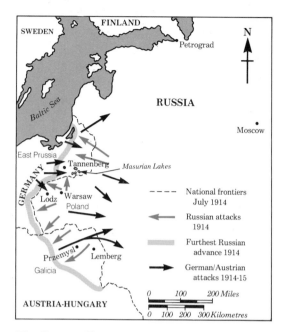

The Eastern Front 1914–15.

The Western Front, 1915–17

Costly offensives

Verdun, 1916

The Somme, 1916

In the east (see map left) the Russian invasion was soon halted. Hindenburg and Ludendorff for Germany out-generalled their Russian rivals Samsonov and Rennenkampf.

Samsonov committed suicide after his army had been trapped and destroyed near Tannenberg, while Rennenkampf lost his command, having been defeated first at the Masurian Lakes (September) and then near Lodz (November). In contrast, the Russians were too strong for the Austrians whom they heavily defeated at Lemberg (September). In the autumn Austria appeared to be gaining compensation at the expense of the Serbs, whose capital Belgrade they occupied. However, in December Peter, the seventy-year-old Serbian king, led in person a remarkable counterattack which in twelve days' fighting drove them out. At the end of 1914 the armies both in the west and the east had ground to a halt.

Christmas 1914 passed. The war was far from over. On the contrary its end seemed to be getting further away rather than nearer. Against the pre-war predictions of the experts the defending rather than the attacking armies held the advantage. The theory had been that any defensive position could be weakened by heavy artillery firing shrapnel (exploding shells), and then overwhelmed by massed infantry. In practice the defenders dug deep trenches and underground shelters, reinforced their positions with barbed wire and added machine gunners to their riflemen. When, in 1915, massed infantry attacked the trenches, they were driven back with terrible losses. The generals, however, were too old to learn new tricks. For the next three years massed offensives were sent again and again against ever stronger trench defences. The result was slaughter on a scale previously unknown.

In 1915 the Allies (France and Britain) took the initiative. Four great offensives were begun, at Neuve Chapelle, Aubers, Ypres and Loos. Each gained a few acres of mud churned up by high explosives and then petered out with hundreds of thousands of casualties.

In 1916 it was the turn of the Germans. Falkenhayn, who had taken over from Moltke, intended to 'bleed France white'. To do this he focussed his attacks on the famous fortress city of Verdun which stood near the centre of a large salient (or bulge) in the line of trenches in north-east France. Falkenhayn's attacks began well. His troops got close to Verdun and the French, who poured in reinforcements along the one main road left open (christened the Sacred Way), suffered heavy losses. However, the city held out. To take the pressure off the French, the British and the Russians attacked the Germans also. Eventually Falkenhayn had to order the retreat from Verdun. German casualties were about 340,000, the French 380,000.

Meanwhile the British attacks in the Somme valley were getting nowhere at enormous cost. Though his five-day bombardment of the German trenches had done little real damage, General Haig ordered a wide uphill advance. Day One saw 60,000 casualties. None the less the Somme offensive continued from the end of June to early November. In September an Australian officer commented: 'We have just come out of a place so terrible that a raving lunatic could never imagine the horror of the last thirteen days.' The Somme battles cost the British 420,000 casualties, the French 200,000 and the Germans 450,000.

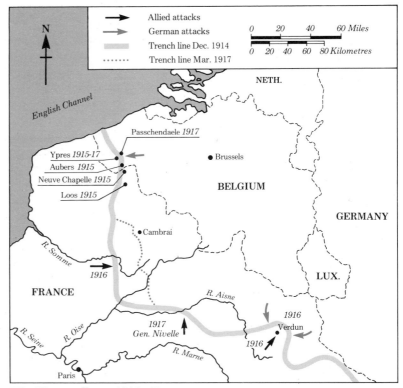

The Western Front 1914–17.

The French Army mutinies, 1917

A new commander of the French was appointed, Nivelle; and another offensive began, this time between Laon and Rheims. It was a re-run of the Somme; nothing gained for 200,000 casualties. But now the French army mutinied. Some of their finest regiments refused to obey their officers' further orders to attack. During the six weeks it took General Pétain to restore discipline the Germans, by some stroke of fate, remained ignorant of the mutiny. Also that year another British attack, with horrific casualties, got nowhere in the mud of Passchendaele.

Other fronts, 1915–17

There was much more movement on the Eastern Front. While the Germans could outfight the Russians, the Russians usually got the better of the Austrians. Though the German and Austrian generals did not find working together easy they managed a combined offensive in Galicia (see map opposite) in the summer of 1915 which forced the Russians to retreat 300 miles with the loss of 300,000 men.

The Defeat of Serbia

Following this success a combined German-Austrian-Bulgarian army conquered Serbia. King Peter and many of his followers preferred exile to surrender.

Brusilov's breakthrough, 1916

Despite the defeats which it had already suffered, the poor supplies it received and the weakening of the Tsar's government, the Russian army was not yet finished. In the summer of 1916 General Brusilov answered an appeal from the French who were near breaking-point at Verdun by launching a furious attack against the Austrians. He broke through the Austrian lines near Lutsk, captured a whole army 250,000 strong and only halted when German reinforcements arrived. There is no doubt that this remarkable Russian effort helped the French and British armies survive through 1916.

Source C: Weapons of the First World War

C1 *Siege Battery Royal Garrison Artillery in action in 1917 near Ypres. They are firing 8 inch howitzers.*

C2 *A German dug-out which has been smashed by artillery on the Somme battlefield, 1916.*

1 In source C1 where are the German and where the Allied trenches?

2 At what are these guns aiming?

3 If everything went to plan, what would happen when they stopped firing?

4 How can you tell that source C2 is a German dug-out and that the living soldier is British?

5 How would the soldiers have been killed?

6 In source C3 why is there a sort of raised step made out of sacks in the foreground? Why are there slats of wood in the background?

7 Why did the armies in the First World War dig trenches?

8 Look at source C4. What is a machine-gun?

9 How did it give such an advantage to the defenders in a battle?

10 Why are these gunners wearing masks?

11 Look at source C5. What is a tank?

12 What made it such an effective weapon on the Western Front?

C3 (**Right**) *French trench at Noyers, 1916.*

C4 (**Below**) *British machine-gunners at the battle of the Somme, July 1916.*

C5 (**Below right**) *One of the tanks used at Cambrai, 1917. Here it is breaking down the German belts of barbed wire.*

Source D:
As the soldiers saw it

D1 *Captain Naegelaen of the French Army, in Champagne in 1916, waiting to 'go over the top' at 6 a.m.*

D2 *Captain Delvert, defending Verdun in 1916, describes a German attack.*

D3 *This is what a Russian, B. V. Mirey, on the Galician Front, December 1915, has to say.*

1 *Which of the authors of these extracts were a) attacking, b) defending?*

2 *How are the attackers armed? How far do they get in their attacks? What are the main causes of death and injury among them?*

3 *What are the main forms of defence? How are the defenders most likely to be killed or injured?*

4 *To what extent do these extracts support or conflict with Liddell Hart's comments (source B)?*

5 *What impression does Mirey suggest that his artillery colonels intend to make in their reports? In what ways is he critical of them? In what ways may eye-witness reports from the front line be unreliable?*

D4 *British troops bury their dead near Ypres, September 1917.*

6 *Imagine you are the soldier on the far right of the picture and write home to your wife about the twenty-four hours which led up to this burial service.*

D1

"The hours went by, slowly and inexorably; we couldn't even swallow for tension: there was always the thought – in a few hours where shall I be, here or one of those vile corpses torn to bits by shells. The moment comes – thirty, twenty, ten minutes more, the hand goes round and I go on counting the seconds. Gradually I got to my knees, my pocket bulging with cartridges and a dead man's rifle in my hands – 5.58, 5.59, 6 o'clock. I shouted 'Forward!' and then a red explosion blinded me and threw me to the ground. My right knee was pierced and I was wounded in the stomach and the cheek. Near by were other wounded and dead."

D2

"At 4 o'clock the bombardment lifted and the attack began. An officer came out of the ground 200 yards away, followed by a column-of-four, their rifles at the slope, and it looked like a parade. We were all taken aback, which no doubt the Germans intended, but after a few seconds we began to fire madly, and the surviving machine-gun came in too. The officer dropped dead fifty yards off, his right arm stretched out towards us, his men piling up and dropping next to him. It was not to be believed."

D3

"After artillery preparation we went about a mile forward under heavy enemy gunfire. Once we were within 500 yards we were hit suddenly by devastating machine-gun and rifle fire . . . . There was the enemy in solid trenches with great parapets and dug-outs; sitting behind 10 to 15 rows of uncut wire waiting for us. We lay on the frozen ground for hours as the snow drifted down; if we were wounded there was no help because we were so close to the wire. But behind us our artillery colonels . . . were drinking rum tea and writing their reports – 'After brilliant artillery preparation our glorious forces rushed forward to occupy the enemy trenches but were held up by counter-attacks of strong reserves.'"

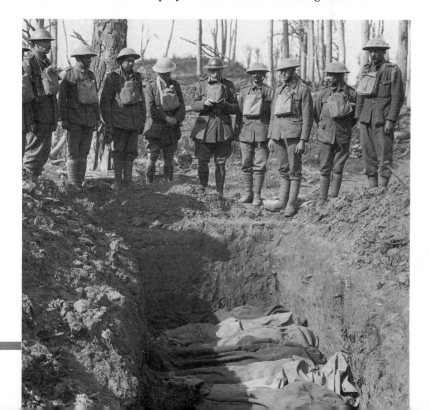

The Russian revolutions

However, this attack finally drained the Russian armies of its last energies. When the March revolution took place in Petrograd (see pages 129–30) the soldiers refused to march against the revolutionaries. They also refused to fight again against the Germans when the new Provisional Government tried to continue the war. Lenin, who won power by the October revolution, was ready to make peace with Germany at almost any price. The war on the Eastern Front was effectively over. The main question remaining was how much Germany would demand as the price of peace.

By the Treaty of Brest-Litovsk (1918) the Germans demanded a very high price. They took a wide band of western Russia which included nearly a third of her population. It also contained some of her best farmland and most of her coalmines. Even the Bolshevik leaders of Russia, who wanted peace at any price, hesitated before signing, so harsh were the German terms. The rest of Europe was given clear warning of what a German victory would mean.

The war against Turkey

German influence within Turkey had been strong before the war so it was not surprising that Turkey joined the Central Powers in November 1914, especially since they were fighting Russia, traditionally her worst enemy (see map E1).

Gallipoli, 1915 – Churchill's plan

With deadlock on the Western Front and Russia in trouble in the east, Winston Churchill, First Lord of the Admiralty, came up with an attractive plan. Why not invade Turkey and capture Constantinople? From there a strong attack could be directed against Austria-Hungary through the Balkans. Austria would collapse and Germany would not be able to continue the war alone.

Its failure

A good plan in theory came to grief in practice. The British forces (including a large contingent from Australia and New Zealand – the ANZACS) landed on the Gallipoli peninsula with the aim of winning control of first the Dardanelles, then of Constantinople. However, the Turkish defences were far stronger than expected. The British forces hardly got off the beaches and had eventually to withdraw with heavy losses (see source E). It was a major defeat for the Allies and encouraged Bulgaria to join the Central Powers and to carry out their successful invasion of Serbia.

Kut, 1916

The British suffered another humiliating defeat at Turkish hands in 1916. The Turkish Empire reached down to the Persian Gulf. A British Indian army invaded from the south and advanced too far and fast up the valley to the River Tigris (see map E1) to Kut where it was cut off and forced to surrender.

Lawrence of Arabia

This however was the last major success of the Turks. They were defeated by the Russians in Armenia and by the British in Persia. The Arabs rose in revolt, and, as General Allenby's army advanced from Egypt into Palestine in 1917, provided useful assistance by raids and sabotage. T. E. Lawrence (Lawrence of Arabia), who had been an archaeologist in the area before the war, encouraged the Arab leaders to revolt and played a remarkably heroic part in the fighting against the Turks.

Africa

In Africa all the German colonies were conquered by the Allies except German East Africa. There the German commander, Lettow-Vorbeck, skilfully defended the colony and, though greatly outnumbered, kept fighting until the war ended.

Source E:
The war against Turkey

E1 (**Right**) *South East Europe and the Middle East.*

E2 (**Below**) *Troops landing at Suvla, 7 August 1915; painting by Norman Wilkinson. (Suvla Bay is at the top of the Gallipoli Peninsula.)*

1 *How far is Gallipoli from Constantinople?*

2 *From this map work out the advantages of Gallipoli as a place for an invasion. From the painting work out its disadvantages.*

3 *Why did the British fleet not sail up to and bombard Constantinople?*

4 *How much of the Ottoman Empire was in British hands in the summer of 1916? How much in September 1918?*

5 *Between which two cities did most of Lawrence of Arabia's activities take place?*

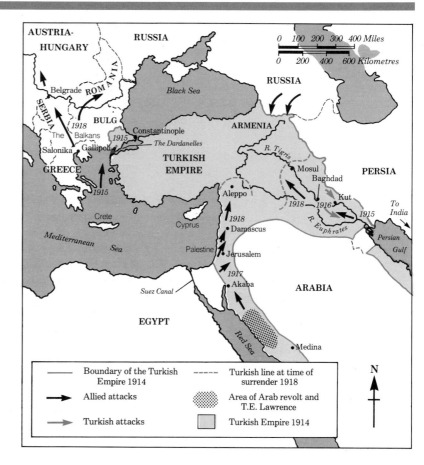

The war at sea, 1914–17
Coronel, 1914

In the first months of the war the sea battles went the way the experts had predicted. Off the coast of Chile near Coronel a small German fleet met an equally small British one. The German ships, more modern and better armed, blew the British out of the water.

The Falkland Islands, 1914

This same German fleet was then intercepted by a bigger and better-armed British fleet near the Falkland Islands and annihilated in its turn.

Coronel and the Falkland Islands were however minor affairs. The big decisive battle of the dreadnoughts never took place. New weapons like the submarine, the torpedo and the mine kept the famous expensive battleships penned in harbour behind their torpedo nets. From time to time the smaller German High Seas Fleet tried to lure the British Grand Fleet out into the North Sea to split it up and defeat it bit by bit.

Jutland, 1916

In 1915 there was an indecisive battle-cruiser engagement near the Dogger Bank and in 1916 the biggest naval battle of the war, off Jutland. Jellicoe, commander of the British fleet, fought at Jutland with the greatest caution. He knew that if he lost the Grand Fleet Britain had lost the war. At one point in the battle the Germans were in danger of complete destruction but they slipped away to safety. Once back home they claimed victory since they had caused more destruction than they had suffered themselves. The British for their part claimed victory since the German Fleet never again left port.

The U-boat threat

The chief task of the navies turned out to be economic warfare. Much the most effective weapon was the German U-boat. In 1914 there were only thirty of them and little more than a hundred when the war ended. None the less so much destruction did they cause to the merchant ships bringing food and other essential war supplies to Britain that early in 1917 Britain's defeat by economic strangulation seemed likely.

Convoys

However, Lloyd George, who had become Prime Minister in 1916, forced his reluctant admirals to provide destroyers to escort convoys of merchant ships. The convoy system and better mines lessened the U-boat danger. For its part, the British navy mounted an increasingly effective economic blockade against the Central Powers which by 1917 was really hurting.

Total war

So the war became a total war demanding economic and social as well as military sacrifices from its participants. Governments interfered more and more in the lives of ordinary people in order to avoid defeat.

In Britain

The British, who were used to the greatest freedom, noticed the greatest change. Though 2½ million men had volunteered for the army by the end of 1915, they were not enough, and conscription, hitherto unknown in Britain, was introduced in 1916. All men aged between 18 and 41 not in essential occupations like coalmining or munitions work were called up. In the desperate spring of 1918 the age-limit was raised to 50. The Defence of the Realm Act (DORA) gave the government powers to take action (like imprisoning people who were opposing the war effort) without consulting Parliament.

Source F: Propaganda

During the war the British Department of Information published a leaflet which described 'a Corpse-Conversion Factory' close behind the German lines: 'Attila's Huns were guilty of atrocious crimes', it read, 'but they even desecrated the bodies of dead soldiers – their own flesh as well as the fallen of the enemy – by improvising a factory for the conversion of human corpses into fat and oils and fodder for pigs.' There was no doubting the existence of the factory, the pamphlet continued, and quoted from an article in the German press which described it.

This story was spread round the world as an example of German barbarism. It was a lie and admitted to be so in the British Parliament in 1925. The German article referred to the conversion of horse and other animal remains.

The Sunday Chronicle of 2 May 1915 published news told to them by a 'charitable great lady' of the little Belgian refugee girl unable to blow her nose because the Germans had cut off her hands.

One of Germany's main news agencies, the Wolff Bureau, was 'reliably informed' that a French doctor, helped by two French officers in disguise, tried to infect the Metz water supplies with plague and cholera germs.

The Weser Zeitung of Bremen told of a ward full of German wounded whose eyes had been gouged out by Belgian nurses.

None of these 'news' stories was true.

F1 'No hands', an American poster.

1 How could atrocity stories begin? Who spread them? For what reasons?

2 What does the picture show? What does it suggest to you about the influence of such stories?

3 There is much reliable evidence that the German occupation of Belgium was harsh. Edith Cavell, a fine nurse, was shot for aiding the escape of Allied prisoners. The citizens of Louvain and their property were badly knocked about for 'unfriendly acts' towards the invading forces. Why then did the Allies feel the need to make up fictional atrocities? Would it not have been better simply to tell the truth?

4 How would you set about discovering whether or not the story of the Belgian refugee with no hands was true?

5 To what extent is the use of propaganda by governments justified a) during wars, b) in peacetime?

In 1916 Lloyd George, who had proved an outstanding Minister of Munitions, replaced the overcautious Asquith as Prime Minister. Lloyd George streamlined the government and set up five new government departments to organise industry to ensure a steady supply of war materials. Women became essential to the war economy (see source G). By 1917, 60 per cent of all munition workers were female.

In France

Some of France's richest industrial and wheat-growing areas were occupied by the Germans for most of the war so the economic struggle which the French faced was a hard one. Agriculture was kept going by women and old men. There were serious food shortages. In 1917 not only did some troops mutiny at the front but there were strikes and defeatist talk back home. Georges Clemenceau was appointed Prime Minister with near dictatorial powers. Nicknamed 'Tiger', he brought new vigour to the war effort and raised morale gradually. In order to cope with the shortage of food, rationing was introduced in 1918, the cities having three meatless days each week. Industry, with government encouragement, was eventually able to meet military needs quite well. New factories were built and run both by refugees from the occupied areas and by women.

In Germany

From the start of the war the German army had had the power to take the raw materials which it needed. Under Rathenau, a brilliant organiser, military needs were carefully calculated and supplies strictly controlled to meet these needs. Germany's scientists were used to find substitutes for vital items affected by the British blockade. Ersatz (substitute) foods were commonplace during the second half of the war. At first the army, trade unions and civilians worked well together but as military needs increased the army became more dictatorial. Workers were shifted from factory to factory, food was rationed and prices controlled. By 1918 Ludendorff and his generals were the real rulers of Germany, not the Kaiser and his ministers.

In Austria-Hungary

Like Russia, Austria-Hungary found that the economic burdens of a long war were eventually too great to bear. Austria depended on Hungary for food, which the Hungarians were increasingly unready to supply. The Austrian government had therefore to impose food rationing and other economic controls. These created bad feeling between the various nationalities of the Empire. The Hungarians and Croats for instance felt that the war was being fought mainly in the interests of the German-speaking Austrians. Such tensions helped to cause the collapse of Austrian resistance in 1918.

Financing the war

To pay for the war, all governments raised indirect taxes and Britain increased income tax a little. Most of the money came however from government loans. The Allies borrowed heavily from the USA and from their own people, the Central Powers mainly from their own people. When these loans were not enough, governments printed money and caused serious inflation.

Censorship

All governments strictly controlled the news. The best source of war news were the newspapers of neutral Switzerland.

Source G: Women during the war

G1

G1 *In Britain there were 1,300,000 more women in work in 1918 than in 1914, 700,000 directly replacing men. By 1918, 25 per cent of the French armaments industry depended on female labour. 'If the women in the war factories stopped work for twenty minutes,' declared General Joffre, 'we should lose the war.' In this extract Mrs H. A. Felstead remembers 1914.*

"I was in domestic service and 'hated every minute of it' . . . earning £2 per month and working from 6 a.m. to 9 p.m. so when the need came for 'women war-workers' my chance came to 'out'. I started hand-cutting fuse shells at the converted war works at the ACs Thames Ditton, Surrey. It entailed the finishing off by hand . . . the machine-cut thread on the fuse had to be very accurate so that the cap fitted perfectly. Believe me we were very ready for bed in those days and as for wages I thought I was very well off earning £5 per week. I left ACs in 1916 for a much lighter, cleaner job at the 'Wireless' Teddington where they made wireless boxes for the signallers. They were some of the first to be used in warfare . . ."

G2 (**Below**) *Women making gas masks.*

G3 (**Right**) *French poster.*

LA FEMME FRANÇAISE PENDANT LA GUERRE

SECTION CINEMATOGRAPHIQUE de l'ARMÉE FRANÇAISE

G4

G4 The New Statesman (*a weekly political magazine*) *23 June 1917.*

"[Working women] appear more alert, more critical of the conditions under which they work, more ready to make a stand against injustice than their pre-war selves . . . . They have a keener appetite for experience and pleasure and a tendency quite new to their class to protest against wrongs even before they become intolerable."

1 *Why were women so much more important to the 1914–18 war effort than in previous wars?*

2 *What sort of war work did Mrs Felstead undertake? Did she see her new employment as a change for the better? What would you expect the women making gas masks (source G2) to have liked and disliked about the job?*

3 *What female work does the French poster artist emphasise? Do you think the artist was male or female?*

The final drama, 1917–18

1917: enter the USA – exit Russia

In this year the course of the war changed drastically. Russia made peace as a result of its revolutions while the USA joined the Allies. There were a number of reasons for America's decision. Huge sums of money had been invested in Britain and France which would be lost if they were defeated. Moreover, thanks to the British secret service, Zimmermann, the German Foreign Minister, was discovered trying to bribe Mexico into an alliance by the offer of the American state of New Mexico.

The Lusitania – unrestricted U-boat warfare

Most serious of all was Germany's campaign of unrestricted U-boat warfare. Already in 1915 US public opinion had been deeply shocked when the British liner *Lusitania* had been sunk off the coast of Ireland with the loss of more than a thousand people of whom 128 were Americans. Though the German government understood that such U-boat tactics were likely to bring the USA into the war, it believed that they would bring complete victory in Europe before the American war effort could be fully mounted.

President Wilson of the USA declared war on Germany in April 1917. American troops were not to arrive on the Western Front for another year. Though peace was not finally agreed between Communist Russia and Germany until the Treaty of Brest-Litovsk (March 1918) the Germans were able to move substantial numbers of troops from the Eastern to the Western Front from November 1917. At the beginning of 1918 the German armies in the West outnumbered the Allies. They were fresher and their morale was higher. Could they win victory before the Americans arrived?

1918: The Ludendorff offensives

They very nearly did. Ludendorff began a series of tremendous attacks on 21 March 1918 (see map H2). He had specially-trained troops who took advantage of the holes smashed through the Allied lines by concentrated artillery fire. A successful breakthrough on one section was followed by another swift attack further along the line. The Allies were forced back further than at any time since 1914.

Marshal Foch appointed Allied C-in-C

The Germans once more crossed the Marne. But the Allies, though retreating, were not broken. Lloyd George for Britain and Clemenceau, France's fiery new Prime Minister, agreed that the French Marshal Foch should in this great crisis take command of the whole front. Foch met Ludendorff's attacks with great skill and calm. American troops were now pouring into France and, on 1 June, went into action for the first time. German morale began to crumble. Military police had to be used to keep some regiments going forward.

Counter-attack

In July Foch ordered the Allied counter-attack (see map H2). Massed tanks (which had been used for the first time in 1916 by the British) were used most effectively. Everywhere the Germans were driven back and day by day the superiority of the Allies became clearer. On 8 August the British army won a major and striking victory near Amiens. For Ludendorff this was 'the black day of the German army'. Though it was still retreating in good order, he knew that defeat could not now be avoided.

Salonika, 1918

The final collapse of the Central Powers was brought about by an attack from an unexpected direction (see map E1). In 1915 a joint French-British army had landed near Salonika in Greece to defend Allied interests in the Balkans. In three years it had done little except persuade the Greeks to join the Allies. Early in September 1918 this

Source H: 1918

H1 (*Above*) *An artist's reconstruction of 'The Great Battle on the Western Front', 6 April 1918. The caption read 'Advancing German hordes mown down by British artillery. Gunners with fuse O – firing with open sights into masses of German infantry: our gas-masked gunners inflict terrific casualties on the enemy. (Illustrated London News.)*

H2 (*Right*) *The Western Front, 1918.*

Study picture H1 carefully.

1 a) *What does the picture show?*
  b) *What impression does it give to the readers of the* Illustrated London News?

2 *What actually was happening on the Western Front in 1918?*

3 *What evidence does this picture provide of censorship at work?*

Study the map.

4 *How far south did the German army get in 1918? How much of a) Belgium, b) Germany did the Allied troops occupy before the war ended?*

English Channel

British

R. Somme

April 1918

March 1918

May-June 1918

French

R. Seine

Paris

R. Marne

Verdun

Americans

St Mihiel

FRANCE

Brussels

BELGIUM

GERMAN EMPIRE

LUX.

Ardennes

N

National frontiers 1914

Trench line March 1918

Ludendorff's offensives

Line of furthest German advance

Allied counter-attacks Aug.-Sep. 1918

German line when the war ended

0 20 40 60 80 Miles

0 40 80 120 Kilometres

army, strengthened with Serbs, advanced against the Bulgars. Before the month was ended Serbia had been reconquered and Bulgaria knocked out of the war.

The Austrian Empire collapses

The victory of the Salonika army signalled the end of the Austrian Empire. There were revolutions in Czechoslovakia, Hungary and Austria. At Vittoria Veneto the Italians drove a mutinous Austrian army back across the Piave river and revenged their 1917 defeat of Caporetto.

The end of Germany

In Germany the army chiefs told the government that further resistance was useless. Early in October Prince Max of Baden, who was widely respected internationally, became Chancellor. He contacted President Wilson asking for an armistice according to the Fourteen Points which Wilson had offered in January as a basis for peace but which had been rejected by Germany, then confident of victory. The Allies insisted on unconditional surrender and the abdication of the Kaiser. Revolution spread through Germany. Ludendorff resigned on 16 October. Two days later the High Seas Fleet mutinied. Berlin was paralysed by strikes and demonstrations. Finally, on 9 November the Kaiser abdicated and moved away into a Dutch exile. Ebert, a Socialist, became the new German Chancellor. The Allies then agreed an armistice with the government based on an altered version of the Fourteen Points. Fighting ceased at 11 a.m. on 11 November 1918.

The costs of the war

The costs of the war were so great that they are difficult to put into meaningful figures: $8\frac{1}{2}$ million soldiers were killed, 21 million wounded, many mutilated for life, and $7\frac{1}{2}$ million taken prisoner. Five million civilians died as a direct result of the war. An influenza epidemic killed another six million in the winter of 1918–19. Many of these 'flu' victims had been weakened by the hardships of the war. Other destruction was on a similarly huge scale. Thirteen million tons of shipping lay on the sea-bed. In Northern France nearly 250,000 buildings had been destroyed, in Eastern Europe many more. The financial costs were well-nigh incalculable though one expert has suggested the figure of 138 billion dollars. Even more incalculable was the amount of personal suffering and sorrow within these statistics. A generation of young men was missing from Europe in the 1920s. Few from their families and loved ones were prepared to forgive or forget. The war ended not in a spirit of reconciliation but in bitterness and desire for revenge.

Source I: The costs of war

In his book Death's Men *Denis Winter provides vivid descriptions of the experiences of the war of many ordinary people based on their own memories. Here are three examples.*

I1

I1 *Harry Lauder, the famous music-hall comedian who often entertained the troops on the Western Front received news of the death of his son on New Year's Day, 1917.*

"and we shall come some day his mother and I to the place where he is waiting. 'Hello, Dad' he will call. I will feel the grip of his young strong arms about me just as in the happy days before that day which is of all the days of my life the most terrible and hateful in my memory."

I2 *Sergeant Cook went to see the mother of his friend Gibson who lived in one of the poorest part of Leeds.*

I3 *Leicester people recalled a local mother who lost all three sons in the Somme battle.*

I4 *Henri Barbusse, the French novelist, wrote* Under Fire *in 1916, a terrifying description of life in the trenches which he had himself experienced. It ends with the soldiers arguing about what they were fighting for and came to this conclusion.*

I5 *Subaltern J. S. Engall, killed in 1918, wrote to his parents not long before his death.*

I6 *A poster for the National Exhibition of War-Relief, Pozsony (Hungary, July–August 1917) by Pat Sujan.*

1 *What does Barbusse mean by 'the entente between the multitudes'? Could he really believe that this was something that the Allies were fighting for which the Central Powers were not?*
2 *What is Subaltern Engall fighting for? How do his ideals compare with those of Barbusse?*
3 *In 1916 Barbusse's soldiers believed that the slaughter and miseries would count for little if progress was advanced one step. What signs of 'progress' could French soldiers returning home in 1919 point to?*
4 *In Britain in 1919 how might people like the Engall parents, Harry Lauder and the Leicester mother be persuaded that their boys had not died in vain? Are you persuaded by such arguments?*
5 *In the poster (I6) who is the figure? Would there have been many like him? What probably would have been their experiences in the 1920s and 1930s?*

I2

"'I've lost my only boy,' she said, and then became mute with grief."

I3

"Each night she would call them in from their uncomprehending play on an empty road."

I4

"The understanding between democracies, the entente between the multitudes, the uplifting of the people of the world ... all the rest matters nothing at all. And a soldier ventures to add this sentence though he begins it with a lowered voice 'If this present war has advanced progress by one step, its miseries and slaughter will count for little'."

I5

"should it be God's holy will to call me away, I am quite prepared to go ... I could not wish for a finer death; and you my dear Mother and Dad will know that I died doing my duty to my God, my Country and my King ..."

LANDES-
KRIEGSFÜRSORGE-AUSSTELLUNG
POZSONY JULI-AUGUST 1917
Eröffnung am 18. Juli

8 Revolutionary Russia 1894–1924

Economic change, 1890–1914

In 1910 Russia overtook France to become the fourth largest industrial power in the world – after the USA, Germany and Britain. The previous twenty years had seen rapid industrial expansion. During the reign of Tsar Alexander II there had been railway building which had encouraged the coal, iron and construction industries. In 1892 Count Witte had been appointed Minister of Finance by Alexander III. He was to hold this position for the next ten years. Witte was an exceptionally able financier and very successful in attracting foreign loans to invest in Russian industry. The country's average annual growth rate in the 1890s was about 8 per cent. Between 1908 and 1914 it rose to nearly 9 per cent. In the ten years from 1895 to 1905 the railway network doubled in length and most of the famous Trans-Siberian line was constructed. In 1880 foreign investment was estimated at about 100 million roubles. By 1900 it had risen to 900 million. Between 1908 and 1913 the number of banks doubled. As industry expanded the population, which was growing rapidly anyway, shifted into urban areas. Villages and towns mushroomed into cities as between 1880 and 1914 the urban population trebled (see source A3). Some boom towns, like the Black Sea port of Odessa and the oil centre of Baku beside the Caspian, grew faster still.

Industry

Industry came to Russia later and faster than elsewhere in Europe and it had special characteristics. The factories were either small or gigantic, as in St Petersburg where the Putilov engineering works (see source A1) employed 30,000 men. Many were owned by foreigners, like the world's largest textile factory, in Narva, owned by a German, or the infamous Lena goldmines, the joint owners of which were British. For industrial workers, whose numbers in 1914 are estimated to have been about 15 million, working conditions were, for the most part, worse and wages lower than anywhere in Europe (see source A3).

Population changes

Because the population was growing fast – 73 million in 1861, 125 million in 1897 and 170 million in 1917 – there was a land shortage in the countryside and overcrowding and high rents in the cities. The steady decline in the wealth of the nobility, noticeable in the 1850s, continued. Whereas in 1877 they had owned 197 million acres this had dropped by 1911 to 116 million. Some adjusted to new conditions and became very rich, the majority did not and grew poorer.

As the cities and industries grew and educational standards improved, the numbers of the Russian middle class increased. However, it was proportionally smaller than in any other European country.

Peasantry

The land shortage pressed hardest on the peasantry even though they now held a larger share of the farmland as a result of the 1861 emancipation decree (see page 48). Modern Russian historians estimate that whereas in 1861 about three peasants in ten might have had difficulty in supporting themselves, by 1911 this had risen to one in two. Many

Source A: Industrial and social conditions in Russia before 1914

A1 *The Putilov Engineering Works: strikers facing the factory guard. A strike on 22 January 1913 led to a massacre of workmen (Illustrated London News).*

A2 *Victims of the Lena shooting. In 1912 protesting strikers at the Lena goldfields were shot at by the police. More than 500 were killed or wounded.*

A3 *Housing conditions in St Petersburg (1910) are described here by Norman Stone in Europe Transformed, 1983.*

A3

"Prince Vyazemski's tenements were filled with 6,000 people, many living in a corner . . . in St Petersburg, with the lowest wages in industrial Europe, rents were higher than in any other capital city. Only a third of the metal-workers kept their families in the city; drunks were everywhere; there was an almost uncountable illegitimacy rate. In flats the average per room was 1.7 people, in cellar rooms 3.9 and in the 'night houses' there were 5 men to a single board bed separated by chalk marks."

1 *Who are the figures on the far left of source A1? How do you identify them? Who do you think is the figure with his back towards you? Explain your answer. How are the factory guards armed?*

2 *What does source A2 show? How long after the shooting do you think the photograph was taken? Explain your answer.*

3 *What do these visual sources tell you about Russian industry before 1914? In what ways can photographs give a distorted idea of a situation?*

4 a) *Who gained from the high rents in St Petersburg (see source A3)?*
b) *Give four reasons why most metal workers kept their families out of the city.*
c) *What primary sources might Professor Stone have used to find out about St Petersburg housing?*

made ends meet by taking temporary work in urban areas, but others starved. There was a terrible famine in 1891 and another in 1901–2.

Revolutionary activity
Social Revolutionary Party

During the 1890s there was a revival of revolutionary activities. The Social Revolutionary Party (the SRs) led by Chernov was formed in 1898. Like the Narodniks of the 1870s (see page 52) the SRs' main hope was the peasantry. They believed that Tsarist society should be overthrown and replaced by one based on co-operative peasant communities. The assassination of government officials was one of their tactics.

Social Democrats

Another revolutionary party, the Social Democrats (SDs), was also founded in 1898. For many years the SDs attracted less attention than the SRs. There were many fewer of them, and their leaders, notably Plekhanov and Ulyanov (better known as Lenin), lived in exile. However, though both the SRs and SDs in their various ways helped to bring about a successful revolution in Russia in 1917 it was Lenin and his party which emerged masters of Russia at the end of it.

Marxism

The Social Democrats were Marxist. Karl Marx was a German who did most of his writing and research in London where he was exiled in 1849 because of his revolutionary ideas. His most influential works were the *Communist Manifesto* and *Capital*. He believed that there was a pattern in history formed by the struggle between social classes. He taught that before the French Revolution of 1789 the society of Europe was feudal, with the aristocracy or landowning class holding economic and political power. The development of modern industry and commerce in Western Europe had strengthened, he believed, the economic power of the middle classes (bourgeoisie) and in 1789 they had won political power from the aristocracy. This post-1789 society he called 'capitalist' since capital or wealth was for the most part concentrated in the hands of the bourgeoisie. Marx was sure that capitalism contained within it the seeds of its own destruction. In order to make the greatest profits factory owners and businessmen needed to keep as low as possible the wages of their workers (the proletariat). Just as in 1789 the bourgeoisie had risen to overthrow the aristocracy so a revolution of working people would overthrow the bourgeoisie.

The communist ideal

This communist revolution, Marx insisted, should lead first to 'the dictatorship of the proletariat' and eventually to a genuine communist society where wealth and property were used for the common good and where the brotherhood of man was a reality.

To Marx's ideas Lenin added two important points relevant to Russia. Firstly, the Russian peasants, unlike those of Western Europe, were a revolutionary force alongside the factory workers. Secondly, a successful revolution should be led by a small group of dedicated party workers.

Lenin (1870–1924)
Early life

Lenin was born Vladimir Ulyanov at Simbirsk 800 kilometres to the east of Moscow where Europe meets Asia. His father was the local inspector of schools, devoted to his work and slightly suspect to local officials because of his liberal sympathies. His mother's family were landowners, so the Ulyanovs, though by no means rich, moved on the fringes of noble society. Like his elder brother Alexander, Vladimir excelled at school. In 1886 his father died and the following year tragedy struck. Alexander was proving an outstanding university student in St Petersburg but became involved in the plot to assassinate Tsar Alexander III. He and

Source B: Russian society in 1900

B *The 'Class Pyramid' as shown in a Russian political poster of 1900. The words mean (clockwise from top): We rule over you; We deceive you; We eat for you; We feed you; We work for you; We shoot you; We govern you.*

1 *Which section of Russian society is shown at each of the.six levels?*
2 *Explain the captions 'we deceive you' and 'we eat for you'.*
3 *Which political party do you think produced this poster? Explain your answer.*
4 *How fair a comment on Russian society in 1900 do you think it is?*

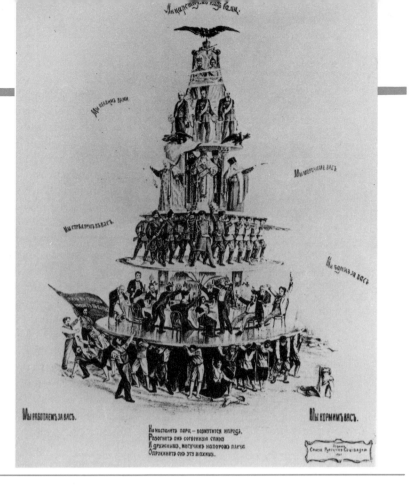

Source C: The young Lenin

C1 *This extract comes from David Shub, Lenin, 1948. Shub was born in Russia in 1887. He became a member of the Social Democratic party in 1903. He escaped from political exile in Siberia to the USA where he lived for the rest of his life.*

1 *Who was Alexander Ulyanov? Why was he hanged?*
2 *How old was Vladimir Ulyanov in 1887? Who did he become?*
3 *How significant do you consider the death of Alexander in Vladimir's life?*

C2 *A serious famine affected the province of Samara where the Ulyanov family including Lenin were still living. Unlike the rest of his friends, he refused to help in famine relief work.*

5 *How could Lenin argue that a famine was in some ways a good thing?*
6 *What does this extract tell you about Lenin's character?*

C1

"In the early morning of 8 May 1887, Alexander [Ulyanov] and four of his comrades were hanged in the courtyard of the Schlusselburg fortress.

When the St Petersburg newspaper carrying the news of Alexander's execution reached Vladimir in Simbirsk, he threw the paper to the floor and cried:

'I'll make them pay for this! I swear it!'

'You'll make who pay?' asked a neighbour, Maria Savenko.

'Never mind, I know,' Vladimir replied."

4 *Shub takes this conversation from a biography of Lenin published in Moscow immediately after Lenin's death. How likely do you think it is that such a conversation really took place?*

C2

"'The famine', he said, 'is the direct consequence of a particular social order. So long as that order exists, famines are inevitable .... It [the famine] will cause the peasant to reflect on the fundamental facts of capitalist society. It will destroy his faith in the Tsar and Tsarism and will in time speed the victory of the revolution.'"

7 *What evidence of Marxist influence is there in this source?*

some other students were betrayed to the police, tried and hanged. In later years Lenin spoke little of his brother but he had been close to him and must have been hurt deeply by his death (see source C1). His own life was immediately affected. Despite his outstanding intellect and capacity for hard work, he had great difficulty completing his university studies since he was a marked man where the police were concerned. He was expelled from Kazan University for taking part in a student protest. Before long he moved to St Petersburg where he got to know leading Marxists like Plekhanov. In 1895 he was arrested for working on an underground newspaper. Years of exile followed, first in Siberia, then in Europe. Despite continual police harassment he kept and improved his contacts with Marxists both inside and outside Russia.

Split in the Social Democratic Party

Iskra (the Spark), a newspaper first published in Munich, Germany, in 1900, was a major focus of social democratic activity. It was smuggled into Russia and circulated widely to party members. In 1903 a serious dispute occurred with the party in exile over aspects of policy and control of *Iskra*. The policy issue was about membership. Lenin argued that it must be limited to those who were absolutely committed to party policies and active in revolutionary work. Martov wished for a widening of membership to all those sympathetic to their aims. The party split, the majority (the Bolsheviks) following Lenin, the minority (the Mensheviks) siding with Martov.

Tsar Nicholas II

Enemy number one of both the SRs and the SDs was Tsar Nicholas II. He could hardly have been less suited to his enormous task. The only kind thing that can be said about him was that he was a loving husband and father. Tutored by Pobedonostsev, he was a convinced reactionary and intended to continue his father's represssive policies. However, unlike his father, he was neither decisive nor determined. He allowed his strong-willed but hysterical German wife Alexandra too much influence and usually appointed ministers of bumbling incompetence even though he was unable to give a clear lead himself (see source D1). The government's policies were often vague and sometimes contradictory.

Early problems for Nicholas

The reign began badly. The coronation celebrations were chaotic. Poor crowd control of a rush for free beer led to hundreds of deaths. Disasters followed. There were serious strikes in 1895–6. Attempts to russify Finland drove the Finns close to revolt. The governor-general of Finland was assassinated in 1904. The Jews continued to be persecuted, a terrible pogrom taking place at Kishinev in 1903. Despite all this, the Tsar was carried away by the empty-headed nationalism of the court and allowed a war with Japan to start in 1904 (see source D2).

The Russo-Japanese War, 1904–5

Causes of the war

His Minister of the Interior remarked that 'it would be a merry little war'. It was nothing of the kind. Its cause was rivalry between the two countries over Manchuria and Korea, parts of the decaying Chinese Empire. Japan had already fought and defeated China in 1895–6 and had intended to occupy Korea and Port Arthur. However, Britain, France and Russia combined to prevent this and Russia added insult to injury by taking Port Arthur for herself in 1898 and sending troops and adventurers in search of business into Manchuria and Korea. The Tsar knew that such actions might well lead to war and that Japan had secured the backing of both Britain and the USA in 1902.

The war began with a Japanese attack on Port Arthur in 1904 and it immediately became clear that Russia had completely misjudged the

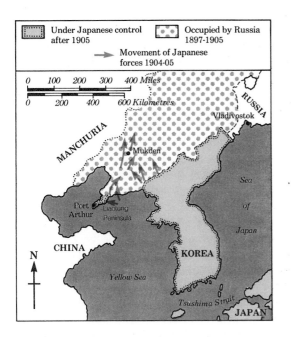

Under Japanese control after 1905 | Occupied by Russia 1897-1905
Movement of Japanese forces 1904-05

fighting capacity of westernised Japan. Her armies were defeated first at Port Arthur, then at Mukden, and her Far East navy was badly damaged. The Baltic Fleet was then sent halfway round the world only to be annihilated as it arrived in Japanese waters in the Battle of Tsushima Straits (May 1905).

Count Witte, who had warned against the war, was sent to negotiate its end. At Portsmouth (USA) he gained what in the circumstances was a reasonable peace. Though Japan's power in Korea and the Liaotung Peninsula was accepted, Manchuria was returned to China.

Defeat brought revolution. Not only was the war humiliating but it had cost 1,000 million roubles, caused prices to rise rapidly and demonstrated with dramatic clarity the incompetence of the government. In January 1905 a huge, hymn-singing demonstration led by a priest, Father Gapon, met in the square outside the Winter Palace in St Petersburg. The Tsar was elsewhere. The police, attempting to disperse the crowd, opened fire killing hundreds, women and children among them.

Source D: Inside the Russian government

D1 *From Polovstev's Diary for 22 September 1901. The writer was a member of the State Council which advised the Tsar, so he was able to observe the Russian government at first hand.*

D1

"Because of the unrestrained abuse of power by officialdom ... regulations bordering on the ridiculous, the absence of any sound policy discussed in advance, capricious [thoughtless] interference in affairs, especially appointments by the empress, the grand dukes and duchesses and the crowds of scoundrels surrounding them, the Russian people are sinking deeper and deeper into misery and oppression."

1 *Give a modern example of 'officialdom'. In what ways was Polovstev critical of Russian officialdom?*

2 *What are the most important criticisms that Polovstev is making here of the Empress?*

3 *How good a source is he for Nicholas's methods of governing?*

4 *What actions would Tsar Nicholas II have had to take to be a better ruler in Polovstev's eyes?*

D2

"From that time onward, and still more in 1903, the dispatches sent to his Majesty's vice-gerent [commander] in the Far East repeatedly expressed the sovereign's desire that Russia acquire a dominant influence in the Pacific Ocean."

[On 8 February 1904 the Tsar appointed Kuropatkin commander of the army in Manchuria.]
"This appointment followed the wishes of public opinion .... It was none the less rather absurd for it turned out that the Russian army now had two commanders. Such a combination was obviously incompatible with [did not follow] the most elementary rules of military science which always requires single leadership, particularly in time of war. Therefore it was natural that this appointment would result in nothing but confusion."

D2 *From the Memoirs of Count Witte. Witte was Minister of Finance from 1892 to 1903. Despite his ability Nicholas disliked him and sacked him in 1903 because of his opposition to an aggressive policy in the Far East. He was Prime Minister again during the crisis of 1905–6. Then he was dismissed again. He wrote his memoirs in France after his dismissal, about which he was bitter. Witte remembered how in 1902, at the end of a naval review, Emperor William II of Germany, having saluted himself as 'Admiral of the Atlantic Ocean' saluted Emperor Nicholas as 'Admiral of the Pacific Ocean'.*

5 *What evidence does Witte provide that the Tsar was personally responsible – to a certain extent at least – for the outbreak of the Russo-Japanese War?*

6 *To what extent did the Tsar contribute to Russia's defeat?*

7 *What does this source tell you about the Tsar's abilities as a ruler?*

The 1905 revolution

Russia exploded. There were widespread peasant riots and a wave of strikes. In June 1905 sailors on the battleship *Potemkin* mutinied and in October a mammoth ten-day general strike paralysed the major cities.

October Manifesto

Acting on Witte's advice, the Tsar gave in to many of the opposition's demands (see source E1) and by so doing saved the Russian monarchy for another twelve years. His October Manifesto created a representative national assembly (Duma) and reduced the powers of the police. The October Manifesto (see source E2) was enough to win back the support of the nobility and middle-class moderates who were frightened by the more extreme demands of the striking workers, among whom the SRs and SDs were active, and by the disorder in the countryside. In December the government arrested the leaders of the St Petersburg Soviet. When Moscow workers rose in revolt in their support they were smashed by the army after a week of street fighting.

The failure of the Moscow revolt was effectively the end of the 1905 revolution. Regaining his confidence, the Tsar sacked Witte who was recommending further reforms and replaced him by the more conservative Stolypin.

1905–14

Repression under Stolypin

Nicholas had summoned the Duma so that he would survive. He did not intend to co-operate with it unless he had to. Stolypin was intelligent, capable and ruthless. He undertook the task of repression with vigour (see source E3). Between 1905 and 1908 4,000 people were executed and ten times that number exiled to Siberia. In reply the SRs assassinated thousands of government officials.

Land reforms

Stolypin also tried to win the support of the peasantry by land reforms. He aimed to lessen the influence of the village communes and to encourage more individual farming which he believed would prove more efficient and profitable. How successful he was is hard to estimate. The statistics are complex and unreliable. It seems that by 1916 about a quarter of the peasants were farming outside the communes but they were not noticeably more loyal to the government.

Ineffective Dumas

The first Duma met in 1906, upset the Tsar by its demands and was dissolved after three months. The second, to which many ex-revolutionaries were elected, lasted the same length of time in 1907 and was dissolved by Stolypin (see sources F1–2). The government then changed the electoral law so that the deputies of the Duma would be more upper class. The third Duma, 1907–12, and the fourth 1912–17, were more co-operative and saw out their full terms. They had little effect on policies.

Assassination of Stolypin

Stolypin was assassinated in 1911 and Nicholas returned to his old failing of appointing ministers who were not only reactionary but stupid. Demonstrations and strikes became more frequent; a revolt of miners in the Lena goldfields ended with 270 dead and 250 injured.

Unrest in St Petersburg

In July 1914 St Petersburg was disrupted by major strikes which began at the Putilov factory. None the less, barely a fortnight later, carried along by a patriotic fever which was particularly contagious at court, the Tsar ordered a general mobilisation of his army against Austria-Hungary and Germany.

Source E: The 1905 revolution

E1 *Memo of 9 October 1905 from Witte to the Tsar.*

E1

"The government should give a real rather than fictitious leadership to the country . . . . Leadership demands above all else a clearly formulated [stated] goal . . . accepted by everyone. The public has set such a goal, a goal of great and invincible significance for justice and truth are on its side. The watchword of freedom should become the watchword of all governmental activity. There is no other way to save the state."

E2

"We impose upon the government the duty of executing our inflexible will . . .
3) to establish as an unshakeable principle that no law can be put into effect without the consent of the State Duma and that the elected representatives of the people should be guaranteed the opportunities of real participation in control of the legality of the action of the authorities appointed by us."

E2 *The October Manifesto 17 October 1905.*

E3 *A punitive expedition shoots a revolutionary, 1905.*

E4 *A Russian cartoon of Witte and Dubasov 31 December 1905.*

1 *What was the situation in Russia at the beginning of October 1905?*

2 *Sum up in not more than twenty-five words the advice which Witte is offering to the Tsar (source E1). Did the Tsar follow it? Explain your answer.*

3 *Sum up in not more than twenty-five words Clause 3 of the October Manifesto (source E2). How big a change in Russia's method of government did this clause mean?*

4 *What is happening in source E3? Why did the government take such action?*

5 *In source E4 Dubasov (facing) was Governor-General of Moscow. Witte (with beard) was Prime Minister. Whose skulls are the snooker balls?*

6 *What would you expect to be the political views of the cartoonist?*

Source F: The Duma

F1 *The Tsar dissolved the Second Duma in 1907. He went on to announce a change in the electoral law for electing the next Duma.*

F2 *A Russian view of the State Duma, 1906.*

1 *What was the Duma?*

2 *What powers had Tsar Nicholas II given to it in 1905? Had he been happy to do so? Explain your answer.*

3 *What were the main reasons for closing it down?*

4 *In source F2 who is the gagged man? Whom do the soldiers represent?*

5 *What attitudes has the cartoonist towards the Duma in 1906?*

6 *How might Stolypin have commented in private about the closing down of the Duma? (The Duma members actually arrived to find the building locked against them with Stolypin's order pinned on the door!)*

F1

"To our sorrow a substantial portion of the representatives of the Second Duma has not justified our expectations. Many of the delegates sent by the people approached their work – not with sincerity, not with a desire to strengthen Russia . . . but with an obvious desire to increase sedition [revolutionary activity] and to further the disintegration of the state."

The First World War

The effects of war

The war ended Romanov rule in Russia. Fifteen million men were mobilised into the armies. The generals could not make good use of them. The administration could not meet their needs. Their absence at war caused factory and farm production to fall when in other countries the effect of the war was to boost production. Five hundred factories stopped work. The railway system was quite inadequate. Vital military supplies were delayed for months. Equally vital food supplies for the cities rotted in sidings. In 1915 there were serious food shortages and dangerous inflation.

Russian defeats

At the front, though some victories were won against the Austrian armies, the Germans inflicted severe defeats and heavy loss of life. By the end of 1915 there had been more than 3.5 million Russian casualties. The great 1916 offensive of General Brusilov temporarily lightened the gloom but then he too had to retreat. By 1917 defeats and lack of equipment – some units were facing the enemy without even enough rifles to go round – had demoralised the troops.

Within Russia the government was barely functioning (see sources G1 and G2). The Tsar went to the front to take personal command of the generals, leaving his wife in charge in Petrograd (St Petersburg, with a more Russian, less German-sounding name).

Rasputin's influence

The Tsarina was now under the influence of Rasputin, the 'Mad Monk', an illiterate, drunken, lustful rogue who could however control by hypnosis the haemophiliac condition of the Tsarina's son. Minister followed minister in quick succession until December 1916. Then some nobles, appalled by the situation at court, clubbed Rasputin to death and pushed his body through the ice of the River Neva. His death came too late to make any difference.

The revolutions of 1917

There were two revolutions in Russia in 1917. The first towards the end of February overthrew the Romanovs; the second at the end of October brought the Bolsheviks to power. (At this time Russia used the Julian calendar which was eleven days behind the rest of Europe. The 'February' revolution took place when the rest of Europe had already got to March and the 'October' one was in Europe's November.)

Riots in Petrograd

Food and fuel shortages caused riots in Petrograd in January and February 1917. Troops sent to quell the riots mutinied. The Duma warned the Tsar that the riots would soon turn to revolution.

Source G: The Tsar and Tsarina during the war

G1 *Letter from Tsar Nicholas to his wife, Alexandra, 9 September 1916. The Tsar was at the front with the army. He is replying to a letter from his wife about appointing Protopopov as Minister of Internal Affairs.*

G1

"Thank you for your long letter, in which you pass on our Friend's [Rasputin's] instructions. It seems to be that this Protopopov is a good man but he has had much to do with factories . . . . I must consider this question, as it has taken me completely by surprise. Our Friend's opinions of people are sometimes very strange, as you yourself know – therefore one must be very careful, especially to appointments to high office . . . . All the changes make my head spin. In my opinion they are too frequent. In any case they are not good for the internal situation of the country as each new man brings with him alterations to the administration."

G2

"Forgive me dearie; believe me – I entreat you don't go and change Protopopov now, he will be all right, give him the chance to get the food supply matter into his hands and I assure you . . . all will go . . . Protopopov is honestly for us. Oh lovey, you can trust me. I may not be clever enough – but I have a strong feeling and that helps me more than the brain often. Don't change anyone until we meet . . . let's speak it over quietly together. You don't know how hard it is now – so much to live through and such hatred of the 'rotten upper sets'. The food supply must be in Protopopov's hands – he venerates our Friend and will be blessed."

G2 *Letter from the Tsarina Alexandra to the Tsar, 11 November 1916, sent from Tsarskoe Selo, the Imperial Palace outside Petrograd.*

1 *What part did the Tsarina play in the internal government of Russia in 1916?*

2 *Who was Rasputin?*

3 *In both letters the question of Protopopov is discussed. What post did the Tsarina want him to have? In November she wished his powers to be increased: in what way? How important were these decisions about Protopopov for the people of Russia? Explain your answer.*

4 *In September Nicholas was not at all sure about Protopopov's suitability. Summarise his comments. How sensible do they seem to you? What decision would you expect him to make?*

5 *What decision did he in fact make? How do you know this?*

6 *What arguments does Alexandra put forward in support of Protopopov? Comment on the soundness of these arguments.*

7 *What does she mean by the 'hatred of the rotten upper sets'? What action did some of these 'sets' take the following month?*

8 *Discuss the characters of the Tsar and Tsarina as shown by these letters. To what extent does this evidence back up or conflict with the comments made about them on page 124?*

The Provisional Government

When its warnings were ignored it formed a Provisional Government with Prince Lvov, a liberal, as Prime Minister and Kerensky, a socialist, as Minister of Justice. Tsar Nicholas abdicated in favour of his brother the Grand Duke Michael, who in turn abdicated the following day.

Though the Provisional Government was widely recognised both outside and inside the country it faced enormous difficulties which quickly proved too much for it. It took over a nation in chaos. In the army, the factories, the main towns and cities it faced hostile 'soviets' which were councils of workers and soldiers dominated by the SRs and SDs. The Provisional Government also tried to keep the war going against Germany but by so doing made probably its greatest mistake since it lost the loyalty of too many troops and made economic recovery impossible.

Lenin returns from exile

The Germans calculated that Lenin might well cause conflict within Russia and thus weaken her ability to continue fighting, so they arranged for him to be moved by rail from his Swiss exile. He arrived in Petrograd in April. Under his leadership the Bolsheviks emerged as the party with the clearest policy. 'End the War', 'Land to the Peasants', 'All Power to the Soviets' read their banners. In the summer they tried to seize power but failed. Lenin had to go into hiding again, but close by, in Finland. The Provisional Government struggled on but its authority was ebbing away. In the war there were more defeats and more casualties. In rural areas the peasants began to take over the land by force.

Kerensky, Prime Minister

In July Alexander Kerensky, the most able member of the Provisional Government, became Prime Minister but he could not turn the tide.

Military Order No. 1

Within the army discipline was breaking down. Little enthusiasm remained for the war with Germany. The Petrograd Soviet had, by its Military Order No. 1, instructed soldiers only to take orders from revolutionary committees, not from their officers.

Kornilov conspiracy

In an attempt to restore order within the army and to destroy the soviets General Kornilov tried to capture Petrograd. His attempt failed when a railway strike held up his troops whom he was moving by train and when they refused to continue because of the strength of popular resistance. The effect of what became known as the 'Kornilov conspiracy' was to help the Bolsheviks and to damage Kerensky.

In October Lenin slipped back into Petrograd. He was sure that the time was ripe for the Bolsheviks to seize power. After lengthy argument he won his colleagues round.

Military Revolutionary Committee

Trotsky headed the 'Military Revolutionary Committee' which made its headquarters the Smolny Institute, formerly a famous girls' school. On 7 November units of Red Guards took possession of the key strongpoints.

Winter Palace stormed

While Kerensky left the city to seek loyal troops the remaining ministers took refuge in the Winter Palace. There on 8 November they were assaulted by the Red Guards and bombarded from the river by the cruiser *Aurora* which was under Bolshevik command. To prevent bloodshed they quickly surrendered (see sources H1–3). Kerensky, returning with about 700 loyal troops, was beaten off. He then fled into exile. Moscow, after a week's fighting, was also secured for the Bolsheviks.

Source H: The October Revolution

H1 (*Right*) *The origin of the Red Guards. The national militia demonstrate their solidarity. They have refused to give up the arms which they have seized from the Arsenal.*

H2 (*Below*) *A painting by S. Lukin called 'The Inevitable' – something which is bound to happen.*

H3 (*Below right*) *A Bolshevik patrol in Petrograd during the fighting between Lenin's and Kerensky's followers, 1917.*

H4 *Lenin addresses the Bolsheviks in the hall of the Smolny Institute having just received news that the Winter Palace has fallen. This speech was published the following day in the newspaper* Pravda (*Truth*).

1 *To which political groups is the colour red usually given?*

2 *What was the name of the government which Kerensky led?*

3 *Why is the revolution which took place on 7/8 November described as the October Revolution?*

4 *Who would have ordered the Red Guards to give up their weapons?*

5 *Describe as precisely as you can what source H2 shows and explain its title.*

6 *Does anything strike you as odd about the photograph in source H3?*

H4

"'Comrades, the workers' and peasants' revolution, whose need the Bolsheviks have emphasised many times, has come to pass.

What is the significance of this revolution? Its significance is, in the first place, that we shall have a Soviet Government, without the participation of a bourgeoisie of any kind. The oppressed masses will themselves form a government. The old state machinery shall be smashed to bits and in its place will be created a new machinery of government of Soviet organisations. From now on there is a new page in the history of Russia, and the present Third Russian Revolution shall in its final result lead to the victory of Socialism."

7 *Put as accurate dates as you can on each piece of evidence, H1, H2 and H3.*

8 *What did Lenin mean by a Soviet Government? What does he mean by the bourgeoisie and why is he so against them? Why did he describe this latest revolution as the Third Russian Revolution?*

The Bolsheviks take power

An 'All Russian Congress of Commissars' was now the government (see source H4). This Soviet was the Bolshevik leadership, chaired by Lenin.

Bolshevik success

There were a number of reasons for the success of the Bolsheviks. Their plans were presented in a clear and forceful manner so that they had plenty of support among soldiers, workers and peasants. They were well organised and armed so that they could quickly take advantage of their opponents' weaknesses. And their leaders, especially Lenin and Trotsky, were intelligent, decisive and always acted with energy and resourcefulness.

Constituent Assembly closed

To stay in power the Bolsheviks were utterly ruthless. Freedom of the press and of speech was restricted to a greater extent than during the worst Tsarist repressions. When the elections of the Constituent Assembly took place the SRs gained a clear majority with 370 seats to the Bolsheviks' 175. Throughout 1917 the Bolsheviks had been arguing for a Constituent Assembly. Now the popular vote had gone against them they first upset the Assembly's proceedings with catcalls and drunken soldiers, then in January 1918 closed it down. Most of the SR leaders were arrested and many shot supposedly 'resisting arrest'. A force of secret police, more efficient and more sinister than that of the Tsar, was created. Headed by Dzerzhinsky, it was known as Cheka.

Peace with Germany

The Bolsheviks wanted peace with Germany, but so harsh were the terms demanded that Trotsky, negotiating for Russia, refused to accept them. Lenin however insisted that he should. If peace was not quickly gained, Lenin argued, then the Bolsheviks might find themselves swept away just as the Provisional Government had been.

Treaty of Brest-Litovsk

By the Treaty of Brest-Litovsk (March 1918) Russia had to give Poland and the Baltic Province to Germany and Austria-Hungary, smaller areas to Turkey and independence to Georgia, the Ukraine and Finland. All in all 62 million people and some of Russia's best farmland and industry were lost.

Communist measures

Among the earliest acts of the new Communist (Bolshevik) government were to allow the peasants to take possession of the land, to nationalise without compensation factories and banks, to end private trading, to force people to work on public projects and to forbid peasants to hoard food.

Civil war

Each of these acts turned parts of the population against the government and the country slipped into civil war (see map I1). Anti-Communist (White) armies were formed (see source I2). A Czech regiment which had been fighting with the Russians against the Germans seized a long section of the Trans-Siberian railway and joined the Whites to whom Britain, France, America and Japan also sent aid. In 1918 it looked as if the Communists (Reds) would be overwhelmed but a year later they had the upper hand. The Whites were fighting on a wide front and were disunited. The Reds (see source I3), operating from the heart of Russia, fought with determination and increasing skill under Trotsky's inspiring leadership.

Threat from Poland

Even before the civil war was finally over, the Communists found themselves fighting Poland. By the end of 1918 Germany and Austria-

Hungary had been defeated by the Allies, and Poland, revived again as an independent nation, intended to use Russia's weakness to her advantage. The Polish army invaded Russia in April 1920. At first it was successful but a Red army counterattack drove it back almost to Warsaw. French aid then swung the balance in Poland's favour and by the Treaty of Riga (March 1921) Russia gave up much of the land which the Poles had sought.

Mutiny at Kronstadt

For ordinary Russians 1918–21 had been even worse than the dreadful war years 1914–18. There had been no economic recovery. On the contrary Bolshevik rule appeared to be turning disaster into catastrophe. In 1921 the sailors of the Kronstadt naval base mutinied. Previously they had been amongst the most loyal supporters of the Bolsheviks. Now they said that the government had betrayed the 1917 Revolution and demanded new elections and greater freedom for trade unions and the press. In response Lenin and Trotsky did not hesitate. Though the sailors

Source I: The Civil War

I1 *The Civil War.*

1 *Study map I1. From where did the main White attacks come? What was the strength of the Red situation geographically?*

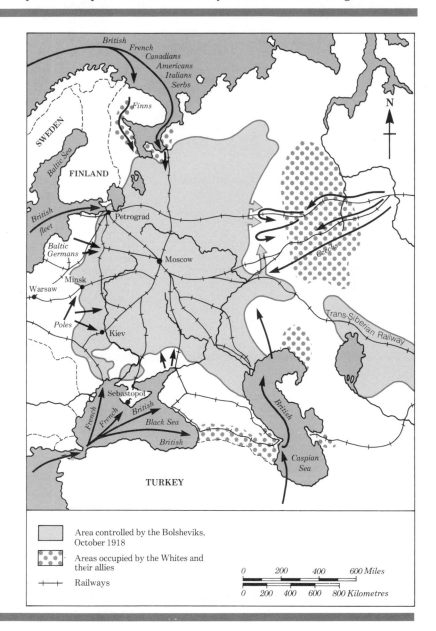

Area controlled by the Bolsheviks, October 1918

Areas occupied by the Whites and their allies

┼─┼─┼ Railways

I2 *An Anti-Bolshevik Civil War poster issued in Omsk, 1919. It is called 'Federal Soviet Monarchy'.*

I3 *A pro-Communist poster, 1920: the Red Army soldier proclaims the message 'Glory to the victor'.*

2 *The poster I2 shows Trotsky and Lenin as 'the Federal Soviet Monarchy'. Which is which? What do they hold as sceptre and orb? Explain the significance of these. 'They promised Bread, Peace and Freedom', reads the caption; 'they have brought Hunger . . . . and . . . .'. Fill in the gaps to fit the mood of the poster.*

3 *In poster I3 what is happening in the three sections above the soldier's head? Who is under his feet and who behind him?*

were well armed the Red Army attacked their base across the ice and, after a day's hard fighting, ended the revolt. The leaders of the mutiny were made out to be noble and middle-class counter-revolutionaries, sympathetic to the Whites – virtually the opposite of the truth – and shot.

NEP, 1921

For Lenin the Kronstadt mutiny came as a timely warning. He realised that the government was changing too much too fast. Despite opposition from within his party, he put communist economic policies into reverse. By the New Economic Policy (NEP) of 1921 the peasants had to give to party officials a percentage of their harvest and private trading was allowed once more. The local merchant, a figure much persecuted since 1917, was able to resume business. The NEP was a success. Though there were famines in 1922 and 1923, a real recovery was clearly evident by 1925. The nightmare years had passed and a Communist government was firmly in control.

Lenin's achievement

By this time Lenin was dead. He did not recover fully from a stroke in 1922 and died in 1924. His achievement is one of the most considerable in recent history. Because of him, more than any other individual, communism became the political, economic and social system of one of the world's most powerful nations. From Russia it has spread to many other parts of the world. As Marx and Lenin explained them, communist ideas have held out hopes of a better future to the poor and oppressed everywhere. And Lenin was more than a writer and thinker. He was a skilful and practical politician. By his powers of argument and strength of personality he dominated his colleagues whom he welded into a committed revolutionary élite. He had a grip on essentials and an acute sense of timing. He never doubted that he was correct and was coldly ruthless in the pursuit of his ideals.

Source J: A communist version of communist history

The writings of all historians are affected to some extent by who they are, the country in which they live and their political beliefs. This is especially true of recent history since it influences modern politics so directly. For most of the twentieth century communist Russia has viewed the capitalist West as a dangerous enemy and vice-versa. There has been a tendency for many western non-Marxist historians to underestimate the Communists' achievements and to exaggerate their faults while Russian Marxist historians have gone to the opposite extreme. These extracts come from An Illustrated History of the USSR *published in Moscow in 1977 by the Novosti Press Agency. Since this book is written in English and published by the Soviet government's publisher, it is reasonable to regard it as the 'official' government history for the outside world.*

J1 On the first months of Bolshevik government, 1918.

J1

"Thus began the triumphal march of Soviet power all over the country. By March 1918 it had become firmly established everywhere .... The masses, who had been oppressed for centuries, became masters of their country. The first thing that the Communist Party and the Soviet government did upon embarking on the building of socialism was to replace the old state apparatus by a new state machinery with entirely different functions – to protect the interests of all working people and to administer the country's economic and cultural affairs."

J2

J2 The only points which this communist Illustrated History *makes about 1921, except that the Red Army liberated various areas from White control, are these.*

"A decisive role in rehabilitating [making more healthy] the national economy was played by the New Economic Policy (NEP) which replaced the economic policy of 'war communism' practised during the Civil War to ensure victory over the interventionists and internal counter-revolution. Under the NEP the alliance of the proletariat and of the peasantry rested on a mutually advantageous economic basis. The peasant delivered a fixed amount of produce to the state and could sell the remainder on the market. The New Economic Policy drew the peasants into economic construction. The food situation in the towns improved."

1 *Compare source J1 with the account given on pages 132–3. List the differences which you find between them. Then compare J2 with the account of 1921 on the page opposite. Note any event which could be important which is left out in the Russian version. Why do you think that it has been omitted?*

2 *How might a communist historian criticise pages 132–5?*

9 The Treaty of Versailles and the League of Nations

The Big Four (Three)

The vast palace built by Louis XIV to the south west of Paris at Versailles was the centre of the peace negotiations which were intended to settle the serious and numerous problems caused by the Great War. The key figure was Woodrow Wilson, President of the USA, who crossed the Atlantic in order to play an active part in the discussions. He was determined that the war should prove to be the war which ended wars and that the Versailles Settlement should begin a new era of international harmony. He also had clear ideas about the nature of the final settlement. In January 1918 he had drawn up 'Fourteen Points' which should be the foundation of any peace negotiations. These Fourteen Points were important to the Germans since they had agreed to an armistice in November 1918 on the understanding that the Fourteen Points would be the basis of the peace settlement – with two exceptions; firstly the point about the freedom of the seas was not included because of Britain's objections, and secondly, compensation would have to be paid for damage done to the civilian population and property.

Orlando, the Italian representative, intended to expand Italy's frontiers at the expense of the Austro-Hungarian Empire. After a sharp disagreement with Wilson over the port of Fiume he returned angrily to Rome. All in all, Italy was most unhappy with the final terms of the Treaty. The other two main leaders were Clemenceau for France and Lloyd George for Britain. Clemenceau had one simple aim: lasting security for France, since twice he had seen his homeland invaded by the Germans. He demanded harsh terms which would permanently weaken Germany and make another attack impossible. While Lloyd George personally might have preferred a moderate peace, he had just won an election by promising to treat Germany toughly. Consequently the demands of the other Allied powers and the practical problems arising led to a final settlement significantly different from the Fourteen Points and harsher towards the defeated.

The Fourteen Points

These were the Fourteen Points:
1 the end of secret diplomacy and secret treaties;
2 freedom of the seas both in peace and war;
3 international free trade;
4 international disarmament;
5 a fair consideration of all colonial claims;
6 the evacuation of Russia by German troops;
7 Belgium independence to be restored;
8 Alsace and Lorraine to be returned to France;
9 Italy's frontiers to be re-drawn on the basis of nationality;
10 the peoples of Austria-Hungary to become self-governing;
11 Serbia, Montenegro and Romania to be restored;
12 Turkey to become a nation rather than an empire and the subject peoples of the old Ottoman Empire to gain independence;

Source A: Working towards the peace settlement

A1 *The Big Four taking the air during their discussions. Left to right: Lloyd George, Orlando, Clemenceau, Wilson.*

1 *Name the countries which each of the four leaders represented (source A1).*
2 *Who left the conference in a huff and why?*
3 *Sum up in a sentence the chief aim of each of the four.*

A2 *Watching the handing over of the treaty terms to the German delegation, 7 May 1919.*

4 *In which building in which town was photograph A2 taken?*
5 *In which famous room was the treaty finally signed?*
6 *What sort of people (in photograph A2) are looking into the main hall? Who would have been in the main hall?*
7 *Why was there a delay between handing over the treaty to the German delegation and their signing it?*

A3 *The German delegation leaving their hotel on their way to sign the treaty, 28 June 1919.*

8 *In source A3 the German delegation are looking rather depressed. Why was this?*

13 Poland to be given back its independence;

14 'a general association of nations' to keep international peace to be created (the League of Nations).

The peace settlement

They appeared in the peace settlement in the following ways: Points 1, 2, 3 and 4 were general statements of principle which were ignored on the whole in future years. Point 5 turned out to mean that Germany lost all her colonies. Point 6 happened, though much of Russia occupied by the German army went to Poland. Points 7, 8 and 9 were carried out. With 10 the subject peoples of the Austrian Empire gained full independence rather than self-government. Serbia and Montenegro (11) became part of the new independent Yugoslavia, and Romania (11) was restored. Though Turkey became a nation rather than an empire (12), few of its subject people gained independence. Poland (13) did reappear and the League of Nations (14) was set up.

The settlement was harsher than the Fourteen Points in three main ways: a) the losses of Germany in Europe b) the size of the reparations bill, and c) the war-guilt clause which justified the reparations claim.

Views of the settlement

Wilson believed that he had done his best and the shortcomings of the peace treaties could be put right in time.

The final terms were an uncomfortable compromise, too harsh for Wilson and harsh enough to keep the Germans bitter, but not harsh enough for French security, nor to keep Germany permanently weak.

Details of the treaties

In all there were five separate treaties all signed in towns near Paris and sneeringly called by the Germans 'suburban treaties'. The major one, Versailles (1919), was with Germany; St Germain (1920) with Austria; Trianon (1920) with Hungary; Neuilly (1919) with Bulgaria; and Sèvres (1920) with Turkey. A war between Greece and Turkey quickly made the Sèvres Treaty meaningless and it was replaced by the Treaty of Lausanne in 1923.

European frontiers

There were many changes to the frontiers of Europe (see map opposite). Germany lost Memel to Lithuania; Posen, the Polish Corridor and part of Upper Silesia to Poland; part of Upper Silesia to Czechoslovakia; North Schleswig to Denmark; Eupen and Malmédy to Belgium; and Alsace and Lorraine to France. The Saar coalfield was to be under the economic control of France and administered by the League of Nations.

The Austrian Empire of the Habsburg dynasty disappeared. Austria turned into a small republic with 6.5 million inhabitants. The mainly Slav provinces of Bosnia-Herzegovina, Croatia and Slovenia were merged with Serbia and Montenegro to create a new nation, Yugoslavia. Hungary became independent but lost land to Romania. Another new country was made from the mainly Czech and Slovak provinces, Czechoslovakia. Galicia went to Poland; Istria, South Tyrol and Trentino to Italy. Though the new small Austria was almost entirely German-speaking she was forbidden to unite with Germany.

Poland reappeared on the map after an absence of a century. Since her neighbour Russia was not represented at Versailles – the Bolshevik government was fighting for its life in the Civil War and was then to fight another war with Poland almost immediately – the Russo-Polish frontier was not fixed until the Treaty of Riga (1921). Estonia, Latvia, Lithuania and Finland, former Russian provinces, became independent.

Bulgaria lost some land to Yugoslavia and some to Greece. Most of the

Europe according to the Versailles settlement.

gains which Greece made from Turkey by the Treaty of Sèvres, including Smyrna in Asia Minor, were won back by the Turkish army under the inspiring leadership of Kemal.

The colonies

The former possessions of Germany and Turkey outside Europe were divided up among the victors. Britain gained Palestine, Iraq and Trans-jordan in the Middle East, and Tanganyika in Africa; South Africa was given South West Africa; Belgium was given Ruanda-Urundi which bordered the Belgian Congo; France gained Syria in the Middle East, Kamerun and the other half of Togo in Africa; Japan won the Shantung area of China and a number of Pacific islands. The other island possessions of Germany were divided among the other victors.

Mandates

The interests of native inhabitants were to be safeguarded, in theory at least, by the mandate system. The European powers in control were expected to prepare these colonies for eventual independence and had to report regularly to the League of Nations the progress being made.

Germany's armed forces

Strict limits were placed on Germany's armed forces. She was forbidden conscription, tanks, aircraft, submarines, warships over 10,000 tonnes and an army of more than 100,000. A wide area of the Rhineland bordering on France (the Demilitarised Zone) had to be empty of troops.

War guilt

The Central Powers were held responsible for causing the war and required to pay for the damage done (reparations). Germany had to hand over all merchant ships over 1,600 tonnes, coal, horses, sheep and cattle. Then in 1921 £6,600 million was fixed as the amount to be paid. This sum was mainly the result of the British insistence that war pensions should be included. France would have settled for a smaller sum.

The League of Nations

Finally the League of Nations, which Wilson had included in the original Fourteen Points and which he believed would, over the years, put right any weaknesses in the settlement, was established.

Weaknesses of Versailles

Weaknesses soon appeared in the Versailles Settlement. As far as the new frontiers were concerned, the Germans were especially bitter about their losses to Poland and Czechoslovakia. President Wilson had made much of the principle of self-determination: that peoples with a common language, culture and sense of identity had the right to national independence. But this right was denied to millions of Germans under Czech or Polish rule and to Austrians who wanted to be united within Germany. In fact such was the mixture of nationalities in Eastern Europe that it was impossible to create nations with defensible frontiers and a balanced economy which did not include large 'minorities' with a different language and culture (see sources C1–4). The Versailles peacemakers created an Eastern Europe of small nations with dissatisfied minorities squashed between two dangerous giants, Russia and Germany, though Russia and Germany were in such difficulties in 1919 that they seemed unlikely to be a danger for many years to come.

Self-determination and the minorities

The German army

The military limits on Germany did not work out as intended. The army of 100,000 allowed was trained to a high standard to be the core of a much larger force. A secret agreement was made with Russia so that German troops could train in Russia with modern weapons.

Reparations

Nor were reparations ever satisfactorily paid. The Germans did their utmost to avoid paying. At first they argued that they simply could not afford to pay, so badly were they suffering from the effects of defeat and internal chaos. They fell behind with their repayments. In 1923 the French lost patience and occupied the Ruhr industrial area to extract reparations by force. The Germans resisted passively. The consequences were disastrous for Germany – runaway inflation in 1923 (see page 200) – and serious for France whose government eventually withdrew the occupying troops (see page 164). In 1924 a committee of international financial experts headed by Dawes, an American banker, worked out a new plan for the repayment of reparations and for reviving the German economy with foreign, mainly American, loans. The German government, led now by Stresemann, agreed to the Dawes Plan but requested changes to the terms of the reparations payments so that they were less of a burden. New terms were agreed by the Young Plan of 1929 which, if it had been carried out, could have had reparations ending in 1988. However, almost immediately first the USA and then Europe, and especially Germany, were struck down by the Great Depression. So badly affected was the whole industrial world that the question of reparations became irrelevant.

Source B: Central Europe 1918–19

While the discussions were taking place at Versailles, Europe was in chaos. Events were taking place over which the peacemakers had little or no control.

B1 *Otto Bauer (1881–1938) was an Austrian Socialist who played an active part in the revolution of October 1918 which brought Habsburg rule to an end. During October the Poles, Czechs, Slovaks, Slavs and Hungarians all declared themselves independent of Austria, while the Germans within Austria tried to create a new state of German-Austria. In this extract from his book* The Austrian Revolution, *published in 1923, Bauer described the economic and political conditions in Austria during the period of peace negotiations in Paris.*

B2 *J. M. Keynes (1883–1946), one of the greatest modern economists, was at the Paris conference as financial adviser to the British delegation. On 14 May 1919 he wrote to his friend Duncan Grant:*

B3 *This is the* Encyclopaedia Britannica *(1973 edition) entry on Poland.*

1 *What had happened to Austria-Hungary in the autumn of 1918 (see page 118)? Name three subject peoples of the Habsburg Empire who were now determined to win their independence.*

2 *Why were the Austrian workers so unsettled and excited (source B1)?*

3 *What would a) the French, and b) the Russian governments have felt about Austrians shouting 'Dictatorship of the Proletariat' in the streets?*

4 *What was both surprising and depressing Keynes in May 1919?*

5 *How would the French government have justified its sales of arms to Poland and the Polish government its purchase of arms from France?*

6 *Lloyd George opposed a really harsh peace for Germany since he feared the spread of Communism in Central Europe. Had he much evidence for this fear early in 1919?*

B1

"As labour discipline in the factories had been based on military power, it dissolved when the latter collapsed .... The factories were transformed into debating forums. General industry was not able to absorb the workers who streamed out of the munitions factories or returned home from the Front. The number of unemployed mounted month by month. It reached its highest point in May 1919. At that date there were 186,080 workless of which 131,500 were in Vienna alone.

Wild excitement prevailed in the barracks of the Volkswehr [the People's Militia – the socialist street army] ... conscious of being the chief support of the Revolution .... Every edition of the newspapers brought news of the struggle of the Spartacists [Communist revolutionaries – see page 198] in Germany ... 'Glory to the Great Russian Revolution', 'Dictatorship of the Proletariat', 'All power to the Communists' – these were the cries which now resounded through the strees."

B2

"there is no food or employment anywhere and the French and Italians are pouring munitions into Central Europe to arm everyone against everyone else. I sit in my room hour after hour receiving deputations from the new nations. All ask, not for food or raw materials, but ... for instruments of war against their neighbours ..."

B3

"Poland's position after World War I was most difficult. The state was coming into being through the unification of three parts (German, Austrian and Russian). These lands had different levels of political and cultural development ... the former Russian and Austrian parts had suffered serious devastation ... industrial plant had been carried off ... to Russia or Germany; where it remained a lack of raw materials caused widespread unemployment. Agriculture was ruined ... famine reigned and epidemic diseases spread. In various parts of the country there were different currencies ... all were of low and uncertain value

. . . .

On January 23rd 1919 ... Czech forces fell unexpectedly on insignificant Polish forces and occupied the greater part of the province [of Teschen] ....

The Soviet Army was advancing westwards. In November 1918 it was still on the Dnieper, but by February 1919 it had moved forward to the Bug."

7 *What were the chief problems facing Austria and Poland in 1919? Which of these problems were beyond the control of the Versailles peacemakers? Which should they have concentrated on solving?*

8 *Comment on the reliability of each of the three sources.*

Source C: The minorities problem, 1919–39

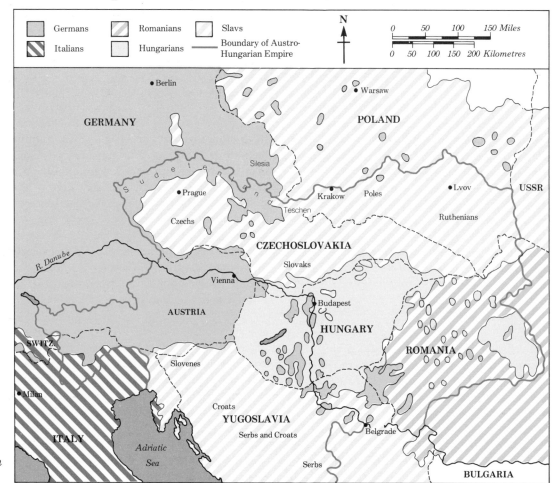

C1 *Racial settlement of Central and Eastern Europe.*

C2 *Jules Cambon (1845–1935) had been French ambassador in Berlin before the war (his brother Pierre was ambassador in London) and was a leading member of the French delegation at Versailles. This is what he said during the negotiations.*

C2

"President Wilson is claiming to inaugurate [give] justice ... and we have to be content to do our best. *In those parts of Eastern Europe where nationalities are mixed and frontiers uncertain it is like trying to square the circle to seek for a frontier which does not offend some feeling or interest.* We are seeking to accomplish an act of good faith but with how many injustices will it be weighted? And what seeds of hatred are we sowing in a devastated soil?"

1 *Study map C1. In which parts of Europe were people (a minority) still living in a country where the majority were of a different race?*

2 *Why was this a problem between 1919 and 1939? Are there any 'minorities' problems in today's world? If so, where?*

3 *Put into your own words the sentence in italics in source C2 and make its meaning clear. How good a source for the Versailles negotiations is Jules Cambon?*

C3 *Otto Bauer was angry about the treatment of Austria.*

4 *Who was Otto Bauer? What has upset him? From the map work out under whose alien rule 3 million German-Austrians had fallen.*

C4 *During the negotiations at Versailles a Special Commission was set up to investigate and make recommendations about the frontiers of Czechoslovakia. The Commission had this to say about the German minority. Bohemia is the western part of Czechoslovakia.*

5 *The Versailles peacemakers knew that to include a large German minority within Czechoslovakia would cause problems. What were their reasons for doing so?*

6 *What was the Special Commission (source C4)? What sort of arguments might a German like Otto Bauer have used to try to persuade the Commission to change its mind?*

C3

"The Peace Treaties robbed the [Austrian] Republic even of its name. In the October Days [1918], in the days of the triumph of the right of peoples to self-determination we adopted the name German-Austria. The name was intended to convey our desire to unite the districts of the Habsburg Monarchy into a free community. The Peace Treaties robbed our republic of districts inhabited by more than 3 million Germans; a third of German-Austrians fell under alien [foreign] rule."

C4

"The Commission fully acknowledged the fact that the incorporation of so large a number of Germans into Czechoslovakia may involve certain disadvantages for the future of the new state . . . . [However it is sure that] the only practicable solution was to incorporate [the German Bohemians] into Czechoslovakia . . . . The Commission was guided by the following considerations . . . a) Economically: the whole Bohemian terri-tory inhabited by Germans is industrially and economically much more dependent on Bohemia than on Germany; b) Geographically: Bohemia surrounded by mountains forms a natural geographical unit . . .; c) Political Reasons: politically German-Bohemia has always belonged to Bohemia; d) Reasons of National Security: . . . the mountain chain forms the country's defensive wall . . . to withdraw the defensive system behind the line created by the mountains would mean the surrender of the country to Germany."

Criticisms of the settlement

Keynes

Two of the cleverest men at the Versailles negotiations, the South African politician Smuts and the British economist Keynes, predicted that the settlement would eventually prove disastrous. Smuts was critical of its harsh spirit. In his opinion merciful peaces worked out better in the long run than merciless ones. Keynes, who resigned in disgust from the British delegation, agreed with Smuts. He also was sure that economically the settlement was a nonsense. Reparations could never work and the prosperity of all Europe depended on free trade between economic partners. A poor Germany would mean a poor Europe. Keynes quickly published a powerful criticism of the peace terms called *The Economic Consequences of the Peace.* It was very controversial and influential. Many young Britons growing up during the next twenty years believed that the Versailles settlement was unfair and therefore not worth defending.

The USA fails to ratify the treaty of Versailles

The most serious blow to the effectiveness of the peace settlement and the new League of Nations was the failure of the US Congress to agree to support the peace terms which President Wilson brought back from Versailles. Wilson had underestimated the opposition, which had been building up during his absence in Europe, to America becoming closely involved in European affairs. He started a lengthy tour of the country to swing public opinion in favour of the Treaty and League, but had a serious stroke which paralysed him. So the United States, the world's most powerful nation, did not agree to the peace settlement nor would it join the League.

Source D: Criticism of the Treaty

D1 *This cartoon by Dyson appeared in the* Daily Herald *on 17 May 1919 with the title* Peace and Future Cannon Fodder. *'The 'Tiger' is Clemenceau.*

PEACE AND FUTURE CANNON FODDER

The Tiger: "Curious! I seem to hear a child weeping!"

D2 *Keynes threatened to resign in a letter to Austen Chamberlain, Chancellor of the Exchequer (and, in Paris, his immediate boss) dated 1 June 1919. (Keynes resigned on 5 June.)*

1 *In source D1 explain what the cartoonist meant by the '1940 class' and 'cannon fodder'.*

2 *How much discussion was there with the German representatives?*

3 *What had Keynes in mind when he argued that the Treaty would disrupt Europe economically? How right did he prove to be?*

4 *Why did he believe that the New States could not survive nor the League of Nations live? How right did he prove to be?*

D2

"If the decision is taken to discuss the Treaty with the Germans with a view to substantial changes . . . I am ready to stay for another two or three weeks. But if the decision is otherwise, I fear that I must resign immediately. I cannot express how strongly I feel about the gravity of what is in front of us . . . . The Prime Minister is leading us all into a morass of destruction. The settlement which he is proposing for Europe disrupts it economically and must depopulate it by millions of persons. The New States which we are setting up cannot survive in such surroundings. Nor can peace be kept or the League of Nations live. How can you expect me to assist at this tragic farce any longer . . .?"

5 *Keynes was a very clever man. Why did neither Chamberlain nor Lloyd George take any notice of him?*

France feels betrayed

For France, President Wilson's failure was a terrible shock. She had only agreed to the settlement because Wilson had promised American aid should German military power revive. Moreover, Britain made matters worse by saying that she now was unready to act alone with France since American support was withdrawn. Not surprisingly the French believed themselves to have been badly betrayed by their former allies (see sources E1–3). They took direct action when the Germans showed signs of not co-operating with the peace terms; in Frankfurt in 1920, the Saar in 1922, as well as in the Ruhr in 1923. They also formed an alliance in the 1920s (the so-called Little Entente) with Poland, Czechoslovakia, Romania and Yugoslavia against Germany and Russia.

Source E: The safety of France

E1 Jules Cambon comments on the meeting of 14 February 1919 at the Hotel Crillon in Paris at which President Wilson outlined his plans for a League of Nations.

E1

"[Wilson] had asked for a Bible to be placed on the table and he began to read his paper with his hand on the book .... The scheme has been worked out ... by Mr Wilson who knows that the Senate in Washington does not intend to be dragged into a war willy-nilly and consequently everything has been omitted which might involve automatic action on the part of the Associated Powers [League members]. Very well: but there will be plenty of time for Belgium and France to be swallowed up before the mere decision that the League of Nations should intervene."

E2 This suggestion from the French government was put by Clemenceau to Britain and the USA early in the negotiations:

E2

"A) The common security of the democracies of the west ... demands that Germany should not be able to attack again as in 1870 and 1914.
B) To prevent another such attack German forces must be forbidden access to the Left Bank of the Rhine and the river should be her western frontier.
C) To prevent such access, the river bridges must be occupied. By this means and this means only will Germany be deprived of her offensive base and the western democracies secure good defensive protection."

E3 Lloyd George and Wilson refused to agree to the Rhine frontier suggestion though Clemenceau and Marshal Foch argued forcefully for it. Instead Britain signed a treaty with France on 28 June 1919 which contained these clauses:

E3

"Whereas there is a danger that the stipulation relating to [the arrangements made about] the Left Bank of the Rhine contained in the Treaty of Peace ... signed at Versailles may not at first provide adequate security and protection for the French Republic; and

Whereas His Britannic Majesty is willing subject to the consent of His Parliament and provided that a similar obligation is entered into by the United States of America to undertake to support the French Government in the case of unprovoked aggression being made against France by Germany ...

Great Britain agrees to come immediately to France's assistance in [such an] event."

Key:

▨ Ruhr basin under French occupation 1923-5

▦ Zone of Allied occupation

▨ Ceded by Germany

▧ Demilitarized Zone

0 25 50 75 100 Miles

0 50 100 150 Kilometres

N

E4 (Left) France and the Rhineland 1919–30.

1 *What does the Bible on the table (source E1) tell you about President Wilson?*

2 *What, in Cambon's opinion (source E1), was the main weakness of the League?*

3 *From which directions and with what success did the Germans attack France a) in 1870 (see page 81), and b) in 1914 (see page 105)?*

4 *What did Clemenceau suggest would give France decent security against Germany? What arguments would Lloyd George and Wilson have used against him?*

5 *What eventually was decided at Versailles about the Rhineland? What happened a) in 1936 (see page 216) and b) in 1940 (see page 221)?*

6 *For what reasons was Britain able to argue that she was never bound by the Treaty of 28 June 1919?*

7 *'France alone had a clear and sensible policy towards Germany in 1919 as the events of the next twenty-one years was to prove. She was badly betrayed by Britain and the USA.' Comment on this statement.*

It was, and is, easy to criticise the Versailles peacemakers. It is also easy to forget how enormous were the problems which they faced. Not only was there the destruction of the war years to be made good but revolution and social and economic chaos existed in 1919 from the Rhine to the Urals.

Emerging from chaos, 1924–9

None the less after four anxious years from 1919 to 1923 Europe moved into a period of some prosperity and hope. The Dawes Plan of 1924 helped an economic recovery along and Stresemann, Germany's Foreign Minister, won the confidence of Briand, his French counterpart. In 1925 French troops withdrew from the Ruhr and there was a major conference of European statesmen at Locarno in Switzerland. By the Locarno Pact a number of agreements were signed of which the joint guarantee by Britain, France, Germany and Italy of the frontiers of Belgium was the most important. During the following year the first stage of the withdrawal of Allied troops from German soil was completed and Germany was allowed into the League of Nations.

Locarno, 1925

The League in action, 1920–33

Simultaneously during the 1920s the League was doing some useful work. Its main aims were to provide collective security, to defend weaker nations from the aggression of the stronger by joint action (see source F) and above all to solve international disputes by peaceful discussion. Its headquarters were at Geneva, in Switzerland. It had an Assembly made up of representatives from each member-state and a Council of eight members, four permanent and four non-permanent. The four permanent members were Britain, France, Italy and Japan; the four non-permanent were elected by the Assembly. The Council was set up to deal swiftly and decisively with international crises. Its decisiveness was limited, however, by the fact that all its decisions, and indeed those of the Assembly, had to be unanimous. There was also an International Court of Justice at the Hague in the Netherlands and various Special Commissions for issues such as Minorities and Mandates. Aid was given to refugees, relief to famine victims and medical measures taken against epidemics. The International Labour Organisation (ILO), in which workers, employers and governments were represented, proved influential in improving working conditions.

Soon after the war ended the League got Danzig and the Saar running again satisfactorily. It kept the Germans and Poles of Upper Silesia co-operating together. In 1922 it provided vital economic assistance to Austria. The previous year it had solved a dispute between Sweden and Finland over the Aaland islands and in 1923 helped settle a dangerous disagreement between Italy and Greece over Corfu. In 1925 it ended a Greek invasion of Bulgaria. Its Special Commissions did valuable work. Germany joined in 1926.

Weaknesses of the League

However, the League's weaknesses were real. Its successes were entirely with small nations. The most powerful nation in the world, the USA, was never a member, Germany only belonged for the seven years 1926–33, and the USSR did not join until 1934. Should a major international crisis blow up it depended too much on Britain and France, who could not agree on its future. Neither were fully committed to its ideals. While France wanted it to have more teeth in the shape of a guarantee by members that they would be ready to take up arms to prevent aggression, Britain vetoed this believing it to be a French scheme to involve Britain in Eastern European entanglements.

The end of the fourteenth point

The good years ended in 1929, the year of Stresemann's death and the Great Crash. Economic disaster spread from the USA to Europe in 1931 and the Nazis came to power in Germany two years later. An important cause of Hitler's popularity was his promise to destroy the Versailles settlement, a promise which he kept. Soon after winning power in 1933 he took Germany out of the League. His main reason, he said, was that few of the member states were fulfilling a major aim of the League by disarming. In 1935 he began openly to rearm Germany, increasing the army to 600,000 and introducing conscription.

Japan and Manchuria, 1931–2

The League could not meet the Nazi challenge effectively, for two main reasons. Firstly, one of the leading members, Japan, had invaded and conquered the Manchurian province of China. When China had appealed to the League it investigated the conflict (see source F) and decided that Japan was in the wrong. Japan then invaded the rest of Manchuria and, in 1933, left the League, which took no further action. Its weakness was therefore only too clear. Secondly, Britain, whose leadership was vital to the League, not only refused to recommend any action against Japan but, in 1935, signed a naval agreement with Hitler. Britain's aim was to avoid a naval race similar to that of 1900 to 1914, but it was recognising Germany's right to a navy which had been forbidden by the Versailles settlement. France and other League members were appalled.

Italy and Abyssinia (Ethiopia) 1935–6

The death-blow to the League was struck by Italy, which invaded and conquered Abyssinia in 1935–6. Mussolini, Italy's Fascist dictator, desired a glorious foreign policy and revenge for the Italian defeat in 1896 at Adowa by the soldiers of the Ethiopian emperor Menelek. To begin with the League responded firmly to the Italian invasion. The action was not only condemned but also, for the first time in the League's history, its members voted for economic sanctions against Italy. However, oil, without which Italian industry could not have survived for very long, was not included in the sanctions. Mussolini was able to continue his invasion and, in 1936, Hitler marched his troops into the Rhineland. By this time Britain and France were more worried about Germany than Italy. They refused to support any further action against Mussolini who successfully completed the conquest of Abyssinia and took Italy out of the League.

After 1936 no one could believe in the League any longer. It played no part in the international crises which led up to the start of the Second World War in 1939. Its last fruitless gesture was to expel the USSR for its attack on Finland in 1940. During the war some of its economic and social functions were continued in North America and, in 1946, it was absorbed into the new United Nations. The melancholy lesson of its twenty-seven years of existence, which began with such high hopes and ended in such failure, was that the major world powers had much to learn before genuine and lasting international peace and co-operation would be possible.

Source F: The failure of the League of Nations: Japan and Manchuria 1931–2

F1 *Article XVI of the Covenant of the League of Nations.*

F1

"Should any Member of the League resort to war in disregard of its convenants . . . it shall . . . be deemed to have committed an act of war against all other Members of the League, which hereby undertake immediately to subject it to the severance of all trade or financial relations . . . .

It shall be the duty of the Council in such cases to recommend to the several governments concerned what effective military, naval or air force the Members of the League shall severally contribute . . . to be used to protect the Convenant of the League . . ."

F2 *In 1931 China was in a state of near civil war. A Japanese army guarding the South Manchurian Railway was frequently quarrelling with the local Chinese officials. On the night of 18/19 September Japan suddenly occupied Mukden and then advanced deep into Manchuria. This map shows Japanese expansion in the Far East, 1928–39.*

F3 *Statement by the Japanese government, 24 September 1931.*

F3

"The Japanese government has constantly been exercising honest endeavour in pursuance of its settled policy to foster friendly relations between Japan and China . . . . Unfortunately the conduct of officials and individuals of China . . . have been such that our national sentiment has been irritated . . . .

A detachment of Chinese troops destroyed the tracks of the South Manchurian Railway in the vicinity of Mukden and attacked our railway guards at midnight on 18 September. In order to forestall imminent disaster the Japanese army had to act swiftly . . . . These measures having been taken our soldiers were mostly withdrawn within the railway zone. The Japanese Government harbours no territorial designs on Manchuria. What we desire is that Japanese subjects be enabled to engage in various peaceful pursuits and be given the opportunity for participating in the development of that land . . ."

F4 *In fact the Japanese troops did not withdraw. Instead they drove the Chinese out of Manchuria which changed its name and reappeared in 1932 as a supposedly independent nation, Manchukuo. The Japanese government issued the* Japan-Manchukuo Protocol *which contained this clause.*

F5 *In response to the protests of the Chinese government, the League of Nations formed a Commission headed by Lord Lytton to investigate. The Lytton Commission visited China, Manchuria and Japan and published its findings on 1 October 1932.*

F6 *This memorandum circulated among British defence chiefs in February 1932. (The source for this and source G6 is Sir Maurice Hankey, secretary of both the British Cabinet and the Committee of Imperial Defence.)*

F7 *Minutes of the meeting of the Far East Committee of the Cabinet, March 1933.*

1 *What did the Japanese do in Manchuria in 1931–2 which so upset the Chinese? The Japanese strongly defended their actions in Manchuria at the League of Nations (sources F3 and F4). Summarise their case.*

2 *The Lytton Commission (source F5) maintained that the Japanese case was weak in at least two important respects. What were these?*

3 *What difficulties would you expect the Lytton Commission to have faced as it gathered evidence in the Far East in 1932?*

4 *On the basis of the Lytton Commission's findings the League put forward a number of proposals for the future of Manchuria and instructed Japan to withdraw her troops.*

F4

"Whereas Japan has recognised the fact that Manchukuo, in accordance with the free will of its inhabitants, has organised and established itself as an independent state . . ."

F5

On the events of 18 September 1931:
"An explosion undoubtedly occurred on or near the railroad between 10 and 10.30 p.m. . . . but the damage . . . was not sufficient to justify military action. The military operations of the Japanese troops during this night . . . cannot be regarded as . . . legitimate self-defence."
On Manchukuo:
"The new State of Manchukuo could not have been formed [without] the presence of Japanese troops and activities of Japanese officials, both civil and military . . . the present government [of Manchukuo] cannot be considered to have been called into existence by a genuine and spontaneous independence movement."

F6

"Hong Kong was virtually defenceless and Singapore not in much better case . . . the principal units of the China fleet were moored in the Whangpo River off Shanghai . . . incapable of resistance to the Japanese fleet or of escape . . . . Military reinforcements would have to come from India, and communal disturbances, combined with trouble on the north-west frontier made the reduction [of our Indian forces] inopportune."

F7

"[It was] agreed that sanctions against Japan were out of the question . . . . The Chief of the Imperial General Staff recommended that Britain should act in a manner to regain Japanese confidence so that she could once again influence Japanese policies and so maintain her own position in the world and her possessions in the Far East."

Japan refused and left the League in 1933. What then according to Article XVI (source F1) of the Covenant should the League have done?

5 *Why was Britain's attitude so important to this Manchurian crisis?*

6 *What did the top British generals and admirals recommend to the British government (source F7)?*

7 *What were their reasons for such advice (source F6)?*

8 *What action did a) Britain, and b) the League take against Japan? Comment on their wisdom.*

10 Britain, France and Spain between the wars

The Right and Left in European politics

'Right' and 'Left' are used frequently as a shorthand way of describing the major division of political opinion in twentieth-century Europe.

The Right

Parties of the Right (of which Fascism, including Nazism, was an extreme example) usually supported the church and army. They tended to be strongly nationalist. In their moderate form they were conservative and would protect institutions against too rapid change. They usually encouraged free trade and appealed to businessmen and landowners.

The Left

Parties of the Left, in contrast, believed that their first responsibility was to working people who should have greater equality and political power. They were socialist or communist and had close links with trade unions. The most extreme parties of the Left were Communists, who were Marxists and different from other socialists in their beliefs that real advances of the working class could not take place without a revolution and that private businesses should be taken over by the state. Other Socialists disagreed strongly with such views.

Between the two world wars extreme political parties did well. The Fascists considered the Communists their most dangerous rivals, and vice versa.

Right and Left in Britain, France and Spain

In Britain socialism developed in the moderate shape of the Labour Party, while the Conservatives, who were also very moderate by European standards, represented the Right. Neither Communism or Fascism, despite Mosley's efforts (see source F), gained much support. In France the division of opinion between Right and Left was much sharper, especially in the 1930s. Fascism and Communism attracted lively support and civil war was avoided only narrowly. In Spain the divisions were sharper still. The Spanish Civil War (1936–9) had the Right supporting General Franco's Nationalists, while the Left rallied to the Republicans. Hitler and Mussolini, champions of the extreme Right, actively aided Franco; Stalin, champion of the extreme Left, sent help to the Republicans (see page 168).

Britain between the wars

The inter-war years have often been regarded as a dreary period in British history, a time of missed opportunities when dangerous problems in economics and international affairs could have been dealt with more resolutely and effectively. In economics the most serious problem, unemployment, could, argued J. M. Keynes and later economists, have been lessened by a different approach, while Hitler, the most serious international problem, might have been stopped earlier and at far less tragic cost by a stronger foreign policy instead of appeasement.

Sometimes it has been argued that the brightest and best of Britain's youth had died on the Western Front so that the political leadership of the 1920s and 1930s was second-rate. Whatever the quality of the leaders, the British electorate appears to have wished to avoid any excitement. Baldwin, the most successful vote-winner of the period, stood for a return to normal, for calm, security and peace.

British party politics, 1918–22

From 1868 to 1906 and then again from 1945 to 1974 Britain had a two-party system; in the former period Conservatives against Liberals, in the latter Conservatives against Labour. Between the two world wars the situation was more complicated, as the tables in sources A1 and A2 show. The most significant trend was the decline of the Liberal Party (see source B).

Lloyd George and Asquith

In 1906 the Liberal Party had won the most convincing election victory in its history (L. 399 seats, C. 256, Lab. 29). While Asquith was Prime Minister and Lloyd George his Chancellor of the Exchequer an impressive number of reforms had been passed. Less than twenty years later, when Asquith, ennobled as the Earl of Asquith and Oxford, was still alive and Lloyd George had many years of active politics ahead of him, the Liberals were finished. In the 1924 election they were a poor third (C. 412, Lab. 151, L. 40).

A political crisis during the war was an important cause of this astonishing Liberal decline. Asquith was not a good war leader. He lacked a sense of urgency and had too much confidence in his military experts, whose expertise in 1915 and 1916 led only to defeats and heavy losses. Conservative leaders had been invited to join the Liberals in a coalition government in 1915, and the following year a complicated and in some ways underhand plot between Lloyd George and the Conservatives replaced Asquith by Lloyd George. Though the latter was unquestionably the better leader Asquith and many Liberals never forgave him for the plot. In 1918, when the Ludendorff offensives were at their most dangerous, Asquith led a strong personal attack on Lloyd George – the Maurice debate – which was unsuccessful but widened the split further.

Lloyd George Prime Minister, 1916

The coupon election, 1918

The coalition of Lloyd George Liberals and the Conservatives, led by Bonar Law, stayed together to fight the 1918 election. Lloyd George and Bonar Law sent out a joint letter to approved coalition candidates; a coupon was how Asquith sneeringly described it, comparing it to the coupons for wartime rationed goods. However, in this 'coupon' election the coalition gained a huge majority, so Lloyd George continued as Prime Minister with Conservative and Liberal support.

When this support was withdrawn in 1922 (see source B4) Lloyd George found himself without significant party support. He and Asquith never really made things up. While they squabbled, too many of their supporters drifted away to the two other parties.

The coalition government The economic background

The four years when Lloyd George was Prime Minister of the coalition government (1918–22) were difficult. Peace had to be negotiated. Britain's basic economic position was less sound than in pre-war years. International competition was much stronger, particularly from the USA and Japan, and long-established industries like coal, iron and textiles faced an uphill struggle. While many British companies did not help themselves by their slowness in adapting to these changing circumstances, the government of the 1920s made their task more difficult by keeping the exchange rate of the pound too high. They argued that a high exchange rate increased international confidence in Britain as a world trading power. However, it made exporting an even tougher task.

Source A: Party politics in Britain, 1922–35

A1

Date of general election	The main parties, MPs elected and percentage of vote won			Name of government formed
	Conservative	Labour	Liberal	
1922	344 (39%)	142 (30%)	Libs (Asquith) 62 (19%) Nat. Libs (Lloyd George) 53 (10%)	Conservative
1923 (Dec.)	258 (38)	191 (31)	158 (30)	Labour
1924	412 (47)	151 (33)	40 (18)	Conservative
1929	260 (38)	287 (37)	59 (24)	Labour
1931	National (made up from all 3 parties) 521 (67)	Opposition (Lab and Lib) 85 (24)		National
1935	432 (54)	154 (38)	20 (7)	National

A2

The senior government ministers 1918–39

Date	Party in power	Prime Minister	Foreign Secretary	Chancellor of the Exchequer
1918	Coalition	Lloyd George (Lib)	Lord Curzon (Cons)	A. Chamberlain (Cons)
1922 (Jan.)	Conservatives	Bonar Law	Lord Curzon	Baldwin
1924	Labour	MacDonald	MacDonald	Snowden
1924	Conservatives	Baldwin	A. Chamberlain	Churchill
1929	Labour	MacDonald	Henderson	Snowden
1931	National	MacDonald (Lab)	Simon (Lib)	N. Chamberlain (Cons)
1935	National	Baldwin (Cons)	Hoare (Cons)	N. Chamberlain (Cons)
1937	National	N. Chamberlain (Cons)	Eden (Cons)	Simon (Lib)

This information is taken from Keith Robbins, *The Eclipse of a Great Power, Great Britain 1870–1975*, Longman, 1983

Study tables A1 and A2.

1 *What are the main responsibilities of* a) *the Prime Minister,* b) *the Foreign Secretary,* c) *the Chancellor of the Exchequer?*

2 *In which election did the Conservatives win* a) *their highest,* b) *their lowest proportion of the votes? What were the proportions?*

3 *Which party formed a government after the 1923 election? Who were its chief ministers? How did it get majorities in Parliament to be able to govern?*

4 *Which party dominated the National Government after 1935? What was the National Government (see page 160)? Who was its first Prime Minister?*

5 *For how many years after the First World War were Labour and Liberal more or less equal in terms of numbers of votes cast? Which 1920s election was the most serious setback for the Liberals? Why did they complain about the way the British electoral system worked?*

Source B: The decline of the Liberals

B1 *Lloyd George said this about Asquith in 1923.*

B1

"He could never lead a government. There is no life in him. He is like a great boulder blocking the way."

B2 *Asquith wrote this confidential letter to a ministerial colleague in November 1916, just before the crisis which led to Lloyd George replacing him as Prime Minister.*

B2

"As to Mr Lloyd George, you know as well as I do his qualities and his defects. He had many qualities which would fit him for the first place but he lacks the one thing needful. He does not inspire trust."

B3 *A poem which used to be recited by Asquithian Liberals.*

B3

Lloyd George no doubt, when his life ebbs out,
will ride in a flaming chariot,
Seated in state on a red hot plate
Twixt Satan and Judas Iscariot.

B4 *The Conservatives in the post-war coalition deserted Lloyd George after a special meeting at the Carlton Club in 1922. At that meeting, one of the most effective speeches against him was made by Baldwin.*

B4

"The Prime Minister was described this morning in *The Times* as a live wire. He was described to me in more stately language as a dynamic force, and I accept those words. He is a dynamic force and it is from that very fact that our troubles arise. A dynamic force is a very frightening thing, it may crush you but it is not necessarily right.

It is owing to the dynamic force and that remarkable personality that the Liberal Party has been smashed to pieces and it is my firm conviction that the same thing will happen to our party."

B5 *Philip Snowden, a leading member of the Labour Party, writes of the years 1918–22 in his* Autobiography *(1934).*

B5

"In a very short time the popularity of the Coalition Government began to decline . . . the by-elections began to go against them . . . the most significant fact emerging from these by-elections was the growing strength of the Labour Party . . . .

These successes were not only due to the unpopularity of the government but to the reorganisation of the constitution of the Labour Party [which] made provision for the formation of constituency Labour parties . . . . These changes greatly improved the organisation of the constituencies . . . and led to the adoption of a different class of candidate who was responsible to the constituency and not to a national Trade Union.

The Liberals had entered upon this election (1922) as a divided party. Mr Lloyd George kept his National Coalition Liberals and Mr Asquith's group fought as an independent party . . . . The platform recriminations [insults] showed the bitterness of feelings with which they regarded each other. Mr Lloyd George's election speeches indicated that he did not desire reunion of the Liberal Party on the old lines."

1 *For how long was Asquith Prime Minister and for how long Lloyd George? What happened in 1916?*
2 *What was Lloyd George's main criticism of Asquith (source B1)?*
3 *What were the main criticisms made by Asquithian liberals of Lloyd George (sources B2 and B3)?*
4 *What was Baldwin advising the Conservatives at the Carlton Club meeting of 1922? What were his main reasons for this advice? Why was this meeting such an important one?*
5 *Why did the Liberals do badly in the election of 1922 (source B5)? What other reasons does Snowden give for Labour's greater success? Comment on the value of Snowden as a source for the 1922 election.*

Industrial unrest

After a short economic boom there was a bad depression, rising unemployment and industrial unrest. The miners' union had been hoping that the coalmines, which had been nationalised during the war, would be nationalised permanently. When Lloyd George refused, the miners looked once more to what became known as the 'triple alliance' of miners, dockers and railwaymen, and planned joint industrial action to force the government's hand. However, the plans came to nothing. The miners struck in 1921 but the other two unions failed to join them. Union leaders described the day of failure, 15 April, as Black Friday. Eventually the miners went back to work with nothing gained.

Black Friday, 1921

Social reforms

The government made some important reforms. At the end of the war Lloyd George had promised 'homes fit for heroes' and an ambitious house-building programme was carried out between 1919 and 1922. National insurance was extended; some relief, which became known as 'the dole', being given to those who were unemployed for long periods and their dependents.

However, just as had been the case before the war, the main problem was Ireland.

Ireland, 1914–23

When war had begun in 1914, Asquith had postponed the introduction of Irish Home Rule. Many Irishmen joined the British army and fought bravely against Germany. However, in 1905 a new political party, Sinn Fein, had been founded. It was more extreme than Redmond's Nationalist Party and believed that Home Rule, which would keep defence and foreign policies in British hands, was too little, too late. Complete independence was its goal. The Sinn Fein leaders believed the Great War was a fine opportunity to win independence while Britain's energies were concentrated elsewhere. It backed an ill-planned uprising in Dublin in 1916, the Easter Rising, which, though having little chance of success, cost the lives of hundreds of people, many of whom were innocent Dubliners, before it was crushed by British forces. The British government showed no mercy. All the Rising's leaders were executed except Eamon de Valera, who held an American passport. The executions were a mistake. Previously lukewarm Irish opinion now swung towards Sinn Fein which in the 1918 election won most of the Irish seats except those in and around Protestant Belfast.

Sinn Fein

The Easter Rising, 1916

The Sinn Fein MPs did not come to London. Instead they formed their own Assembly in Dublin. They demanded that Ulster should remain part of Ireland and the whole country be granted independence. By 1919 a vicious guerrilla war had broken out with the Irish Republican Army (IRA) ambushing British officials and army units. For its part the British government employed recently demobilised soldiers, the 'Black and Tans', against the IRA and against the families providing them with supplies and shelter. In 1920 Lloyd George proposed that Ireland be divided in two. He suggested splitting Ulster from the rest of Ireland and giving each part its own parliament. A Council for the whole of Ireland should also be set up which would work out over the years how a united Ireland could one day be achieved. The Protestant majority in Ulster accepted his plan, which became the Government of Ireland Act (1920).

The IRA against the 'Black and Tans'

Sinn Fein did not accept it and continued violent non-co-operation. Lloyd George would not budge on partition but he was prepared to agree to an Irish Free State which would be almost completely independent, except that it would stay part of the Empire and allow the British navy

The Irish Free State

Partition and civil war

to keep some bases. Most Sinn Fein leaders were prepared to sign a treaty on these terms. A few, who hated the idea of a separate Ulster and of staying in the British Empire, were not. The treaty was signed. As far as Britain was concerned the Irish Question had at last been satisfactorily answered – or so it seemed for the next forty-five years. Another year's fighting, this time a civil war within the Free State, was needed before the anti-treaty Irish were ready to accept the partition of Ireland.

Party politics, 1922–31

The fall of Lloyd George, 1922

In 1922 Lloyd George seemed ready to risk leading the whole of the British Empire in support of the Greeks against the Turks during the so-called 'Chanak' crisis. The Conservative members of the coalition held a special meeting at the Carlton Club during which the most influential speech was made by Stanley Baldwin (see source B4). He criticised the Prime Minister as a 'dynamic force' who might soon damage the Conservatives as he had already damaged the Liberals. By a large majority the Conservatives decided to withdraw from the coalition. Lloyd George had no choice but to resign. Bonar Law became Prime Minister for a few months. When he retired in 1923, for health reasons, Stanley Baldwin succeeded him.

Baldwin Prime Minister

Baldwin was the most influential British politician of the inter-war years. His father was a Midlands iron manufacturer and Conservative MP for Bewdley. Son Stanley inherited both the business and the Bewdley constituency. Once in Parliament he was rapidly promoted within the party and was a Cabinet minister in the coalition.

Baldwin was a fascinating character. He gave the impression of being an ordinary down-to-earth Englishman, an unflappable pipe-smoking lover of the countryside. Behind this image, which he presented well both on the radio and on film newsreels, lay a cunning politician whose skill and sense of timing in promoting and demoting his colleagues kept the Conservatives united under his leadership. In contrast to Lloyd George's dynamism he offered tranquility, to Labour's new experiments the old tried and tested ways. He was in fact rather lazy but the electorate found him very reassuring.

The 1923 election

Soon after he became Prime Minister in 1923 Baldwin called a general election. He had decided that to ease the nation's economic difficulties, major industries needed to be protected from foreign competition by tariffs or customs duties. But he also knew that protection and the end of free trade were controversial. He remembered how 'tariff reform' had split the Conservatives before 1914. He therefore thought that the issue should be put to the electors and was confident that he could win their support.

Ramsay MacDonald Prime Minister

He was wrong. Though the Conservatives were still the largest party after the election, with 258 seats, Labour with 191 could outvote them with the support of the Liberals (158). Consequently Labour, led by Ramsay MacDonald, governed the country for the first time.

MacDonald was born in Scotland, the son of a maidservant. Having impressed his teachers at his board school he became a pupil-teacher there until he was eighteen. He travelled south to England and ended up in London, where he earned a living as a secretary and as a journalist. He joined both the ILP and the Fabians (see page 37), became a Labour county councillor and campaigned energetically for a separate Labour

Party to fight national elections. When the LRC (see page 37) was founded in 1900 he was its first secretary and entered Parliament in 1906 as MP for Leicester. MacDonald proved to be one of the most effective speakers among the Labour MPs and when Keir Hardie retired in 1911, he succeeded him as chairman of the parliamentary group until 1914. He was elected to this post again in 1922 and became Prime Minister the following year as a result of the general election (see source C1).

His main aim during his short time in office (he took office in January 1924 and resigned in October the same year) was to convince the electorate that Labour did not mean revolution and would obtain desirable social change through Parliament. Acting as his own foreign minister he had some success in achieving friendlier relations with Germany and with the USSR. Home affairs ran less smoothly. At the request of Labour MPs he interfered to prevent Campbell, the editor of a communist magazine, from being prosecuted, but in such a clumsy way that the

Source C: The 1923 election

C1 (*Below, left and middle*) Labour election poster of 1923.

C2 (*Below, far right*) Poster published by the Labour party in 1923.

YESTERDAY - THE TRENCHES

TO-DAY - UNEMPLOYED

LABOUR'S LEADER

The Rt. Hon. J. Ramsay MacDonald

1 What is the main idea of source C1? Was this a good subject for election posters in 1923? Explain your answer.

2 What idea of MacDonald is the poster (source C2) trying to give?

Liberals decided to vote with the Conservatives against him. The Labour government had to resign.

The 1924 election

In the election campaign of 1924, during which the central issue was whether the Labour government should continue, Baldwin played down the protection issue and emphasised how the experienced Conservatives would provide calm and orderly government of the traditional kind. He was helped by the appearance in the press of the 'Zinoviev letter', a forgery which suggested widespread communist revolutionary plotting all over the country. The Conservatives triumphed (C. 412, Lab. 151, L. 40).

The Conservative government, 1924–9
Crisis in the coalmines, 1925

Baldwin's greatest quality was in defusing crises by the tactful handling of people. His most severe test came with the General Strike in 1926 (see sources D1–6). The miners, who had felt badly let down in 1921 (see page 154), were in no mood to be pushed around, but in 1925 the coal-owners, who were finding overseas competition tough, demanded that the miners should work longer hours for lower pay. A miners' strike, supported by a general strike led by the TUC, was threatened. On Friday 31 July 1925 the government gave way. This was Red Friday, a workers' victory in contrast to Black Friday in 1921 (see page 154). Baldwin bought time by setting up a Commission of Inquiry into the coal dispute and subsidising miners' wages for nine months. In the meantime preparations were made to meet the emergencies of a General Strike. The subsidies ended in April 1926. The Commission of Inquiry suggested a compromise, but neither side would accept it. The miners went on strike and the TUC called out all the unions in their support (see source D1) on 3 May.

The miners' strike, 1926

General Strike, 1926

Baldwin refused to give way to any of the union demands but took care not to inflame a dangerous situation by angry words or thoughtless actions. He insisted that the miners' strike was one thing, the General Strike quite another (see source D4). If the TUC forced the elected government to act in a manner which the government believed to be against the national interest, then the TUC would be running the country and a revolution would have taken place. The government could not therefore give way. The strike was solid for nine days. Emergency measures and strikebreaking by non-unionists kept essential services running (see sources D2–3). The country remained for the most part peaceful and good-humoured. The TUC came to see the logic of Baldwin's argument. Its leaders were not in the least revolutionary. Having tried and failed to get the miners to accept a compromise they called off the General Strike on 12 May. The miners held out until November but had then to return to work for less pay and longer hours.

Anti-union legislation

Clearly 1926 was a bad year for the unions. Before long, in 1927 Baldwin's government made general strikes illegal, by the Trades Disputes Act. By the Trade Union Act of the same year, trade union members who wished to pay a political levy to their union to help the Labour Party had to opt in by stating in writing that they wished to. This reversed the 1913 rule following the Osborne Judgement (see page 37) that it was up to those who did not want to pay the political levy to opt out. The government's intervention aimed to lessen the political activity of the unions and, not surprisingly, angered them and the Labour Party.

Source D: The General Strike, 1926

D1 *Harry Watson, who worked on Tyneside, remembers the call from the TUC for the strike.*

D1

"In the branch everyone present welcomed the decision to support the miners .... They were an important section of the community and we depended on them for everything .... Take the river alone, we used to transport hundreds and thousands of tons of coal each week to the power stations .... Also it was in the minds of the older more experienced men that the implications of the coal-owners' behaviour supported as it was by the government was that if they got away with it with the miners, then everyone else in the working class would feel the backwash of events .... And when it was reported that the owners were asking them to accept not only a reduced rate of pay but a longer working day as well ... there was no question or doubt in anybody's mind."

D2 *Armoured cars and troops at Hyde Park in London prepare to escort food convoy, 10 May 1926.*

D3 *A volunteer bus conductor on one of the London General Omnibus Company's buses, 6 May 1936.*

D4 *Baldwin made a radio broadcast to the nation on 9 May 1926.*

(Thanks above all to the work of G. Marconi, communication by radio over a distance of hundreds of miles was possible by 1900. In the early 1920s commercial broadcasting began both in the USA and Britain. In 1922 the British Broadcasting Company had been set up with John Reith as its first general manager. It became a Corporation with a monopoly of public broadcasting in 1926, with a Board of Governors appointed by the Crown. Though the BBC was from the first fiercely proud of its freedom from government interference, it did not give the strikers air space to explain their position. It did however give listeners a thorough, accurate and balanced account of events.)

D5 *Abe Moffatt, one of the leaders of the Scots striking miners, said this on victimisation after the strike ended.*

D6 *(Below right) Cartoon in* Punch *26 May 1926.*

1 *What were the main reasons for Harry Watson's union branch supporting the General Strike? What information really made up their minds for them?*

2 *In his broadcast*
(a) what promise did Baldwin make about the coal dispute;
(b) what seems to him to be wrong about the General Strike;
(c) what was the government's policy towards the General Strike?

3 *Write captions for the two photographs (sources D2 and D3), as if you were writing*
a) For the British Worker, *which strongly supported the strike;*
b) for the British Gazette, *the official government newspaper during the strike.*

4 *Quite apart from its content, what do you think of the 'tone' of Baldwin's broadcast? Nowadays politicians take advice from advertising agencies before they appear on television. Do you think Baldwin got the tone right for the 1926 crisis?*

5 *What is meant by victimisation (source D5)? How reliable a source would you consider Abe Moffatt to be?*

6 *Explain the* Punch *cartoon of 26 May. Does the cartoonist approve or disapprove of Baldwin's handling of the crisis?*

D4

"The General Strike has now been in progress for nearly a week and I think it right as Prime Minister I should tell the nation once more what is at stake in the lamentable struggle that is going on. There are two distinct issues – the stoppage in the coal industry . . . and the general strike.

The stoppage in the coal industry has followed nine months' inquiry and negotiation . . . I shall continue my efforts to see that in any settlement justice is done both to the miners and to the mine-owners.

What then is the issue for which the government is fighting?

It is fighting because while negotiations were still in progress the Trade Union Council ordered a general strike, presumably to force Parliament and the community to bend to its will . . .

Can there be a more direct attack on the community than a body not elected by the voters of the country . . . should dislocate the life of the nation and try to starve us into submission . . .

This is the government position – the general strike must be called off absolutely and without reserve. The mining industry dispute can then be settled . . .

I am a man of peace. I am longing, working and praying for peace. But I will not surrender the safety and security of the British constitution."

D5

"My father, two younger brothers and I were all victimised. My father was getting near retirement and he never got back. Eventually Alex got back in another combine and David got back but I never got back, bar when I got into a small private mine in 1938. The Fife Coal Co. was a big combine and a vicious one."

THE MAN IN CONTROL.

JOHN BULL *(to the Pilot).* "YOU'VE GOT US THROUGH THAT FOG SPLENDIDLY."
MR. BALDWIN *(sticking quietly to his job).* "TELL ME ALL ABOUT THAT WHEN WE'RE PAST THESE ROCKS."

Other measures

The government also came into conflict with local Labour councils which spent more on unemployment relief and health benefits than the government allowed. The borough of Poplar in London made a habit of overspending. Neville Chamberlain, then Minister of Health, took a strong line, and on three occasions himself took over the responsibility of councils which had broken the rules.

More positively, the Government simplified local government by the Local Government Act of 1929 which abolished the separate boards which had been responsible for poor relief and public health, giving their work to the county councils and county boroughs. A Central Electricity Board was set up to extend the major new technological advance, electricity, across the country. By 1940 two-thirds of British homes were linked to the central electricity grid. In 1928 the vote was given to all women aged twenty-one or over.

1929 election

In the 1929 election Baldwin's campaign slogan was 'Safety First', while Labour again concentrated on the need to lessen unemployment. The electorate proved ready to give Labour a second chance, though, as in 1924, keeping them dependent on the Liberals. Labour gained 288 seats, the Conservatives 260 and the Liberals 59.

The Wall Street crash and its effects, 1929–31

MacDonald was unlucky in the timing of his victory. In 1929 came the Wall Street crash and the worst economic crisis in modern history. It was a particularly difficult crisis for an inexperienced Labour government to deal with. The financial experts of the Treasury and Bank of England all warned that the only way to avoid financial disaster was to cut government spending. The crunch came in 1931 when what was held by the experts to be an essential loan from New York banks would only be made if unemployment pay was included in the cuts.

National government, 1931

Many of the Labour Cabinet could not agree to such cuts and the government seemed about to resign. MacDonald went to Buckingham Palace but to the amazement and anger of most Labour MPs came out Prime Minister, not of a Labour government but of a National one. His new coalition included Conservative and Liberal ministers and was appointed to push the cuts through. Only a handful of MacDonald's former Labour Cabinet colleagues were invited to join the new Cabinet. For this act of 'betrayal' MacDonald was expelled from the Labour Party, which turned first to Lansbury and later to Attlee as its leader. However, when MacDonald called a general election in 1931 the National Government won an overwhelming majority.

The Labour split

MacDonald's last years were not happy ones. Labour never forgave him. The measures for which he split his party did not have the effects for which he had hoped. The Conservatives did not respect him and his health failed. He handed over to Baldwin in 1935.

MacDonald had many qualities. He looked impressive and spoke well. He preached a sincere if woolly brand of idealism and persuaded many ordinary Britons that socialism was not dangerous. He was, however, a vain man. Labour colleagues believed that he despised them and was something of a snob. He had no grasp of economics and his handling of the 1931 crisis scarred his party badly without clearly benefiting the wider national interest.

Rising unemployment

The worldwide depression following the Wall Street crash in New York in 1929 raised the level of unemployment in Britain. In 1932, the worst of the inter-war years, 13 per cent of the workforce was unemployed. By 1938 the figure had fallen to 8 per cent. The social and political effects were less startling than in the USA or Germany, since Britain's unemployment level in the 1920s (about 6.5 per cent on average) had been already unusually high. The worst affected areas were those of traditional heavy industry like shipbuilding (Jarrow on Tyneside) and mining (South Wales). Hunger marches (see source E1) attracted attention, but the outbreak of the Second World War was necessary before these areas revived economically.

Jarrow

New industries

However, some industries expanded. House-building boomed. Many new private estates and urban developments appeared, especially in the south-east. New industries – motor vehicles, electrical (see source E2), radios, chemical – appeared, again chiefly in the south-east. If Newcastle and Bradford were comparatively depressed, Oxford, Slough and Coventry were comparatively prosperous.

Source E: Labour conditions

E1 *Jarrow Marchers near Luton in Bedfordshire, 28 October 1936, on their way to London.*

1 *Where is Jarrow? In which industry are these marchers likely to have worked? For what reasons and with what success did they march to London in 1936?*

E2 *The Hoover Factory, West London: an example of modern factory building.*

2 *What sort of goods would this factory have produced? For what reasons would it have been sited near London rather than in the north?*

*Improving
living standards*

Even in areas of acute depression people did not starve. A family on unemployment benefit in the 1930s was no worse off than a family in 1900 whose father earned an average wage. For the majority of Britons the standard of living rose and, with developments like electricity, the radio and the spread of high-street shops like Marks & Spencer, the quality of life improved too.

Nevertheless unemployment was the cause of great misery as well as being an awful waste of human resources. The Chancellor of the Exchequer from 1931 to 1937 was Neville Chamberlain. He got through Parliament in 1934 the Unemployed Insurance Act. This was a tidy piece of administration which made central government responsible for the unemployed rather than local government which had provided relief through the Poor Law regulations. However, the Act was extremely unpopular since, in order to be paid the dole, the long-term unemployed had to agree to a 'means test'. If they had built up their own savings and had wage-earning children living at home, their benefit was reduced. The Act had the effect of discouraging thrift and of driving young people from their parents' homes.

*The Unemployed
Insurance Act,
1934*

Means tests

Immigration

Other trends helped to keep unemployment high. The depression was world-wide so there were many fewer jobs to emigrate to. Moreover, many immigrants came to Britain in the 1930s, particularly Jews fleeing from Nazi Germany. Unemployment and immigration fuelled Mosley's Fascist movement and its anti-semitism (see sources F1–2).

*Baldwin Prime
Minister,
1935–7*

On MacDonald's retirement in 1935, Baldwin became Prime Minister once again. He was now sixty-seven and not in search of excitement. Despite the rearming of Germany and Italy and the threatening behaviour of their dictators he was slow to order Britain's rearmament. His excuse was that public opinion, which was anti-war and keen on collective security through the League of Nations, would not tolerate it.

*Abdication
crisis, 1936*

His main achievement was during the 'abdication' crisis of 1936. Early that year King George V had died. His heir Edward VIII loved and intended to marry Wallis Simpson, an American woman who was soon to be divorced. However, the king of England was also head of the Church of England. By the standards of Baldwin and most of the religious and political leaders of that generation, it was unthinkable that the king should marry a divorcee. Since Edward refused to give up Mrs Simpson, Baldwin persuaded him to abdicate in favour of his younger brother George. He then convinced Parliament and the British people that there was no alternative. George VI and his young family were soon very popular. It was generally felt that Baldwin had dealt with a most delicate issue with tact, skill and firmness.

*Chamberlain
Prime Minister,
1937–40*

Baldwin retired in 1937 to be succeeded by Neville Chamberlain. The latter's three years as premier were dominated by his unsuccessful efforts to appease Hitler (see page 219). What is all too easily forgotten was that he was a strong and effective minister, responsible, during the Conservative Government of 1924–9, for major improvements in the benefits to widows, orphans and the unemployed, and for the Local Government Act of 1929.

Source F: The British Fascist experience

F1 *During the political crisis of 1931 which led to MacDonald's National government, a Labour cabinet minister, Sir Oswald Mosley, resigned from the party and founded his New Party which failed utterly in the 1931 election. He then, in 1932, founded the British Union of Fascists (BUF) which in its uniform and ideas owed much to Mussolini and Hitler. During the 1930s the BUF gained a lot of attention and aroused fear. How important a movement was it?*

Its most active year was 1936 when Mosley organised a number of marches in working-class districts with a large Jewish population. One of these was intended to go through the East End of London and ended in the so-called 'Battle of Cable Street'. This is how Skidelsky, Mosley's biographer (1975), describes what happened.

1 *Who was the leader of the British Fascists? What was he doing in the East End of London on 4 October 1936 (see source F1)?*

F2 *The Battle of Cable Street. Police chase demonstrators, 4 October 1936, following a clash between Fascists and Communists during a giant march by Fascists in the East End of London.*

2 *Study source F2 and check it against source F1. In which street are the police? Against whom are they charging? Explain the slogan painted on the wall. What political group do you think painted it? Explain your answers.*

F1

"On Sunday, 4th October 1936 . . . the fascists planned to march from the Royal Mint near Tower Bridge through Shoreditch, Limehouse, Bow and Bethnal Green, halting at each place for speeches by Mosley. Moderate Labour leaders had tried to get the procession prohibited or diverted. However the Communist Party . . . planned to prevent it by force. 'They shall not pass' was their motto. When Mosley arrived at the Royal Mint 3,000 fascists had assembled. However, much larger crowds had gathered in its path. No doubt many had come only to watch but the activists erected barriers in Cable Street . . . . The foot and mounted police charged repeatedly in an attempt to clear a passage for Mosley's men but without success. Meanwhile Jack Spot 'King of the Underworld' armed with a chair leg full of lead headed a group which broke through the police ranks in an effort to reach Mosley, standing tense . . . surrounded by his bodyguards. A pitched battle developed in which many blackshirts were injured . . . . Eventually Sir Philip Game [who was in charge of the police] sent for Mosley. He said 'As you can see for yourself if you fellows go ahead from here there will be a shambles. I am not going to have that. You must call it off.' Mosley asked 'Is that an order?' 'Yes,' replied Game. Mosley complied. The fascists marched off and soon dispersed. They had not passed. In the fighting between anti-fascists and the police, 83 demonstrators were arrested and about 100 people (including police) injured."

France between the wars

France appeared to be a major world power in the 1920s. Her foreign policy was decisive and generally successful. The franc was strong. When the economic crash came in 1929, France at first weathered it more easily than her neighbours. However, during the 1930s she was hit by a series of economic and political crises which made clear the existence of deep divisions within French society and such serious weaknesses that she was quite unable to stand up to the Nazi onslaught of 1940.

Problems after the First World War

Some of these weaknesses could be found in the 1920s. The First World War had seriously damaged France. Her northern provinces, where most of the war on the western front had been fought, were devastated. Worse than that, 10 per cent of her men had been killed. Between the wars her population hardly grew. Despite 3 million immigrants it was much the same size in 1939 as in 1913 but had a higher proportion of old people and widows. Economically the country stagnated. Most French governments between the wars believed inflation to be the greatest economic evil and kept the value of the franc high to prevent wages and prices rising too fast. However, as in Britain, the strong currency made exporting difficult.

French public opinion was bitterly disappointed with the Versailles settlement. It believed that France, despite her colossal sacrifices, had been betrayed by Britain and the USA. To make up for this betrayal, France signed defensive alliances with Belgium (1920), Poland (1921), Czechoslovakia, Yugoslavia and Romania (1924). These were aimed against Germany, Hungary and Bulgaria.

Poincaré Prime Minister

The first post-war government, the Bloc National, was a right-wing coalition and fiercely anti-German and anti-communist. It turned against 'Tiger' Clemenceau who had negotiated the settlement and forced the resignation of Briand who did not want to press the Germans too hard about reparations. Poincaré, a clever, humourless lawyer, whose aim was to make the Germans pay reparations exactly as had been agreed, became Prime Minister in 1922.

Occupation of the Ruhr, 1923

That year Germany fell behind in paying. In January 1923 French and Belgium troops occupied the Ruhr industrial area in an attempt to force payment. The attempt, though at first appearing successful, eventually backfired badly. The Germans were driven to passive resistance. 'Only two men have managed to unite the German people', commented an American diplomat, 'Bismarck and Poincaré!' There were also acts of sabotage and some civilian deaths. The extraordinary inflationary crisis within Germany (see page 200) had international effects which harmed the French economy, already in difficulties because of the costs of the occupation. France suffered inflation too. In 1924 the occupation ended but not soon enough to prevent a serious financial crisis which saw the franc drop sharply in value against both the dollar and the pound. This crisis forced Poincaré to resign in May 1924.

Cartel des Gauches

Poincaré recalled

The new government was a coalition of the left, the 'Cartel des Gauches'. Its common bond was dislike of the Catholic Church, and it was unable to agree on policies to deal with the enormous crisis. The pace of inflation accelerated and Poincaré was recalled in 1925 to head a coalition government of the right. It won the confidence of the business community, ended the financial crisis and set in motion an economic recovery. Meanwhile Briand, now Foreign Minister, was developing an effective working relationship with Stresemann, his German counter-part, and 1926–9 were years of hope for France. The war damage had been repaired; the economy was growing surely if slowly; she was the strongest power on the continent of Europe and was now on better terms with her old German enemy. Though she experienced many changes of government because of the numerous parties within the Assembly and their readiness to vote coalitions down in the hope of winning immediate advantage for themselves, this did not necessarily mean weak government. The French civil service was efficient and accustomed to keeping the country running while the politicians and electorate worked out who was to be in charge.

Depression

Poincaré resigned because of ill-health in 1929. That same year Briand lost office, Stresemann died and the Wall Street crash began the Great Depression. France survived better than most until 1933. Then both prices and unemployment rose sharply. In 1933 1,300,000 were out of work. Depression brought into the open deep divisions within French society which the coalition governments of the Third Republic were increasingly unable to close. The parties of the moderate left, the Radicals and the Socialists, had enough support in elections to have been able to govern, but they never found a way of co-operating for any length of time.

Extremist parties

French Communism

Meanwhile the extreme parties of the Left and of the Right flourished in the depressed conditions. The French Communist Party had been founded in 1920 when it broke away from the Socialists and insisted on working closely with Moscow and the Comintern (see page 178). It gained votes at elections (800,000 in the election of 1933 against the Socialists' 2,000,000) and had deputies in the Assembly, but refused to join any coalition government. It also set up its own trade union organisation. Its CGTU had 300,000 members in the early 1930s while the socialist CGT had 900,000.

French Fascism

On the Right were the so-called 'Leagues', like the Croix de Feu (Fiery Cross), which had begun as ex-servicemen's clubs and then were transformed into Fascist street armies seeking to stamp out socialism and communism. They found the examples of the Nazi brownshirts and Fascist blackshirts worth copying.

A Left coalition government faced the economic crisis of 1933 and, like MacDonald's Labour government in 1931, could not agree what economic policies it should follow. Governments came and went rapidly.

The Stavisky Affair, 1934

In January 1934 a shady financier and night-club owner named Stavisky was found shot through the head. He probably committed suicide because he was about to be arrested for fraud. However, he was the acquaintance of members of the government who tried to hush things up. The rumour spread that the police had shot him. The Fascist Leagues used the Stavisky Affair to whip up anti-government feeling and on 6 February 1934 organised a huge demonstration in Paris which marched towards the Chamber of Deputies. When the police barred the way, a street battle took place which lasted for hours killing one policeman, fourteen demonstrators and wounding more than a thousand. The country seemed on the edge of civil war and a government of national unity was hurriedly formed.

The main effect of the 1934 crisis was to convince the parties of the

Left that a Fascist takeover was a real possibility. Hitler's successes in Germany worried Moscow enough to instruct the French Communists to co-operate with rather than oppose the Socialists. Eventually in 1936 the Radicals, Socialists and Communists formed the Popular Front (Rassemblement Populaire) to fight the general election. They won an overwhelming victory, 380 seats against 237 for the right. The Communists made the largest gains, 62 seats. Blum, the Socialist leader, became Premier.

The Popular Front, 1936

The Popular Front had promised major social reforms. The so-called Matignon agreements caused wages of industrial workers to be raised by between 7 and 15 per cent. The working week was reduced to forty hours and holidays with pay introduced. The arms industry was nationalised and the Bank of France reformed. Simultaneously the rearmament programme was accelerated to meet the Nazi threat. However, the depressed French economy could not meet all these demands and Blum found himself confronted by a worsening economic and political crisis. When he tried to introduce a pause in the reform programme, all he got was sharp criticism from his Popular Front colleagues and his policy of neutrality towards the Spanish Civil War also angered many of his supporters on the left. The economic crisis continued and French businessmen made matters worse by exporting capital. When Blum attempted to make capital exports illegal he was forced to resign (1937).

Demoralisation in the government

The failure of the Popular Front left France without an effective government when she faced the greatest danger in her history, Nazi Germany. Her politicians were demoralised. They seemed to prefer opposition to government. On the extreme Left, the Communists ended their co-operation with the Socialists and followed a strict Moscow line. For the extreme Right, which had the support of many French businessmen, the experience of the Popular Front had been nerve racking. 'Might not Hitler be better than Blum?' some right-wing politicans asked. As the events of 1938–40 were to show (see pages 218–22) French resistance to the Nazi onslaught was feeble.

The Spanish Civil War

In Britain democracy was never in danger during the inter-war years. In France it survived by the skin of its teeth. In Spain it came and went with a cruel civil war which lasted from 1936 to 1939.

Spain in the early twentieth century

Nineteenth-century Spain had been an economically backward country. Its kings were weak, the powerful institutions being the Catholic Church, the army and the landowning nobility. In the twentieth century, as new industries appeared and cities grew, liberal and socialist politicians demanded major reforms and communists and anarchists talked of violent revolution. Some provinces, notably Catalonia and the Basque country wanted their own self-government.

From 1923 to 1930, though Alfonso XIII was king in name, Spain had a virtual dictator, General Primo de Rivera. An army plot forced him to resign and in 1931 a moderate socialist government was elected. Since Alfonso had already gone into exile because of the widespread opposition to the monarchy, the new socialist government declared Spain to be a republic.

Spain a republic

Source G: France during the Popular Front

H1 *Leading article in the Left-wing newspaper,* Le Populaire, *June 1936.*

H1

"Don't sing us lullabies. An entire people is now on the march, with a determined stride towards a magnificent future. In the atmosphere of victory, confidence and discipline which is spreading through the country, yes, EVERYTHING IS POSSIBLE for the bold."

H2 *Editorial in the right-wing* L'Écho de Paris, *12 June 1936.*

H2

"The striking building workers were able to walk through the streets of Paris under the folds of the red flag. Strikers from cafés and restaurants did the same. Yesterday morning they organised a great march along the boulevards. A truck carrying young men brandishing their fists and shouting led the procession which created a traffic jam in the boulevards. All revolutions begin in this way. Paris has the distinct feeling that a revolution has begun."

H3 (**Below**) *An election poster of 1937.*

H4 (**Right**) *A cartoon published in June 1936.*

1 *What is meant in twentieth-century politics by the terms 'left' and 'right'? To which side do the following six political groups belong: a) socialist, b) Croix de Feu, c) Bloc National, d) Cartel des Gauches, e) Popular Front, f) Radicals?*
In what ways did communists and socialists disagree?

2 *What was the mood of left-wing voters in the summer of 1936?*

3 *The Right feared a revolution in 1936. What kind of revolution did they expect it to be?*

4 *Which party produced poster H3? What people in particular are being attacked? Why?*

5 *What is the message of cartoon H4? What were the political views of the person who drew it?*

Reforms

Reforms were then attempted. The powers of the church were lessened, particularly in education. New land laws benefited the peasants at the expense of the landowners. Catalonia was given self-government.

Revolt in the Asturias

However, in 1932 the republican government was threatened both by a right-wing plot and by a communist rebellion. In 1933 a more right-wing government attempted to restore order but the Asturias miners rose in revolt and set up their own communist government. General Franco was called in to end the revolt, which he did without mercy.

The Popular Front in power

Franco's actions against the Asturias miners helped unite the communists and socialists into a Popular Front in 1936. In response the church leaders, the army generals and Spain's Fascist Party, the Falange, co-operated more closely. The Popular Front won the 1936 general election easily and set in motion its anti-clerical policies which intended to reduce further the power of the Catholic Church. In some areas however its extreme supporters took to attacking priests and burning churches. Law and order broke down and there were many political murders.

Civil war

The civil war began with an army revolt in Spanish Morocco and in Andalusia. It was led by General Franco, whose Nationalist forces were soon in control of two large sections of the country. Though given enthusiastic backing by Mussolini and Hitler, and though working with the Falange, Franco was not himself a Fascist. He was rather a conservative Catholic Spaniard who believed that the army and his own dictatorship were necessary if the traditional Spain which he valued was to be saved from revolution and anarchy.

The Nationalists held much of south and central Spain. They had most of the country's trained troops. They were well supplied and supported by Germany and Italy. The Republicans for their part controlled the two great cities of Madrid and Barcelona and the Basque industrial coast. Most of their forces were untrained, though they had some help from the Soviet Union and from left-wing enthusiasts from all over the world.

Nationalist successes

In a war full of atrocities the Nationalists almost always held the advantage. In August 1936 they captured Badajoz and linked up their two main areas. By the end of 1937 they had conquered all the Basque country. Their task was helped by conflict within the Republican forces, since there was an anarchist revolt against the Republican government in Barcelona in May 1937 (see source I3). None the less the war was far from over.

The end of civil war

A surprise Republican attack captured Teruel in January 1938, though it was lost again a month later. Through the summer and autumn of 1938 the advances of the Nationalist army down the Ebro valley towards Barcelona were checked but another attack in December broke through. Barcelona surrendered in January 1939, Madrid in March. The unconditional surrender which Franco demanded was signed the day after the capital fell. A million Spaniards are estimated to have died in the civil war, of whom 600,000 were soldiers.

Franco's dictatorship

Franco's dictatorship continued to his death in 1975. Before he died he had arranged that the monarchy should be restored. Prince Juan Carlos became king and democracy returned to Spain. Forty years after the civil war began, free elections were held once again.

Source I: The Spanish Civil War

I1 *The Spanish Civil War 1936–9.*

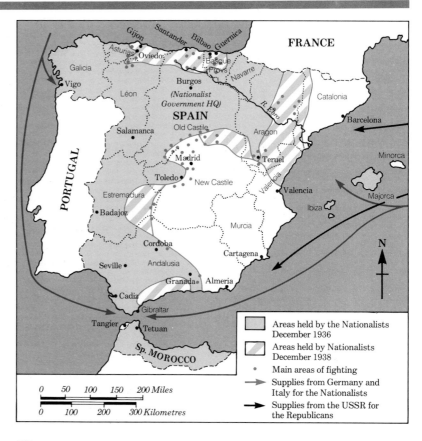

I2 *In 1937, Orwell, political writer and committed socialist, arrived in Spain to fight for the Republicans against Franco. He joined a section of the POUM militia. The POUM was the United Marxist Workers' Party, separate from both the larger Communist and Anarchist militias which also fought for the Republican cause. Orwell first saw active service up in the hills about 320 kilometres west of Barcelona. This extract is from* George Orwell: A Life *by Bernard Crick, 1980, and describes the POUM militia in action.*

I3 *Anarchists versus Communists in Barcelona, 1937. Orwell was in Barcelona during the Anarchist revolt. This extract comes from his book about the Spanish Civil War,* Homage to Catalonia, *which was published in 1938.*

1 *Which of sources I1–3 is a) primary, b) secondary and c) a combination of the two? Explain your answer.*

2 *In Source I2 what was POUM and who were the Fascists? How accurately can General Franco be described as a Fascist?*

3 *Orwell was in Barcelona in 1937. Why did he regard his time there as 'one of the most unbearable periods in his life'? During the Anarchists' revolt where did his sympathies lie? Explain your answer.*

4 *Using page 168 and sources I1–3 describe the main weakness of the Republicans. What advantages did Franco have?*

I2

"It was a quiet part of the line, as he wrote: boredom and cold were the main enemies . . . It was as well that the Fascists were not active in that part of the line, for the POUM had little with which to resist them beyond enthusiasm and fifteen rounds of ammunition each . . . Every cartridge had to be separately tested in the breech to see if it would fit for three different types of rifle were in use . . . Food, wine, candles, cigarettes and matches were in reasonable supply . . . but 'we had no tin hats, no bayonets, hardly any revolvers or pistols, and not more than one bomb between five or ten men . . .' They [the POUM soldiers] were left in the line, in badly constructed trenches, for debilitatingly long periods until their leave was due. No regular alternation of line or reserve was ever organised. In eighty days he was able to get his clothes off only three times . . ."

I3

"I was in no danger. I suffered from nothing worse than hunger and boredom, yet it was one of the most unbearable periods of my life. I think few experiences could be more sickening, more disillusioning or finally more nerve-racking than those evil days of street warfare . . . Sometimes I was merely bored with the whole affair, paid no attention to the hellish noise and spent hours reading . . . sometimes I was very conscious of the armed men watching me fifty yards away. It was like being in the trenches again; several times I caught myself, from force of habit, speaking of the Civil Guards [Republican forces] as 'the Fascists'."

11 The Soviet Union 1924–53

Joseph Stalin

Stalin's reputation

The truth about Stalin is particularly hard to discover (see sources A1–3). While he lived he had the history of his own times written and rewritten to exaggerate his abilities. After his death his successors produced their own versions to magnify his faults. Stalin had many of his closest colleagues murdered, so their evidence is lacking. Moreover the Soviet government does not allow historians to research freely into the Stalinist period. Consequently many episodes in his career remain mysterious. None the less there is evidence enough to be sure that by any measure Stalin was an extraordinary person. He led the Russian people to quite remarkable achievements, but at an equally remarkable cost in human misery.

Stalin's early life

Stalin, which means Man of Steel, was his Bolshevik name. He was born Joseph Djugashvili near Tiflis in Georgia in 1879. Both his parents were from serf families. His father worked in a shoe factory, his mother took in washing. Unlike most of the Bolshevik leaders he grew up in extreme poverty. None the less his mother was ambitious for her son, and religious. Though widowed when he was only eleven, she made sure that he had a good education. While at elementary school he impressed his teachers by his intelligence and his classmates by his surly determination to come top. His mother wanted him to become a priest and he won a scholarship to the Seminary at Tiflis. His teachers there were not impressed (see source B2). They found him too argumentative and too often reading banned books. After four years he was expelled.

Political activity

Even before his expulsion he had met Marxist revolutionaries and soon became involved in their activities in Georgia. According the local police records (see source B3) he published anti-government pamphlets and encouraged strikes. During the 1905 revolution he led demonstrations in Georgia and met Lenin for the first time. In the year immediately after the failed revolution he organised bank raids for party funds, stirred up strikes, attended Bolshevik conferences or sat in gaol. By 1913, when he was arrested once again and exiled to Siberia, he was well-known and respected among the Bolsheviks.

The 1917 revolution

Freed by the February revolution of 1917, Stalin returned at once to Petrograd and led the Bolsheviks until Lenin's arrival from Switzerland. Throughout the eventful summer and autumn of 1917 he stayed in the background, editing the party newspaper and sitting on committees. His most bitter enemy, Trotsky, commented that 'the greater the sweep of events, the smaller was Stalin's part in it'. Yet somehow he managed to be in the right place at the right time. Though he did little during the October Revolution Lenin gave him the important post of Commissar for Nationalities in his new government. During the Civil War Stalin led the defence of the strategically important city of Tsaritsyn and was used by Lenin as a reliable and ruthless troubleshooter.

Source A: Stalin: for and against

A1 *This painting by V.P. Yefanov was entered for the 'Socialist Industry' exhibition held in Moscow in 1937. According to the catalogue 'it depicts the enthusiastic reception accorded J.V. Stalin ... at the conference of wives of engineers and technicians engaged in heavy industry', which was held in Moscow in May 1936.*

A2 Landmarks in the life of Stalin *by Yaroslavsky, first published by the Foreign Languages House, Moscow, and then in London in 1942.*

A2

"Stalin is a gifted organiser ... has written many splendid books ... loves children and young people, has an extraordinary capacity for work, teaches us the art of government and of war ... is fearless in battle, merciless towards the enemies of the people, wise and deliberate, upright and honest ... At the helm of the great Soviet ship of state ... stands the great pilot, Stalin, the teacher and leader of nations. The children of the Soviet Union say, 'Thank you, Comrade Stalin, for our happy life'."

A3 *This French poster of around 1950 suggests that France may be Stalin's next target.*

1 *In source A1 what idea of Stalin does the painter aim to give?*
2 *What does the setting which he chooses for Stalin suggest to you about official Soviet values in 1937?*
3 *In what form does the French cartoonist show the Soviet leader? What idea does he aim to give?*
4 *Comment on the Yaroslavsky extract (source A2). What would you think if someone wrote about the present British Prime Minister in such a way?*
5 *Yaroslavsky knew Stalin quite well. How reliable would you expect his book to be?*

Increasing power

General Secretary of the Communist Party

Lenin's doubts

Stalin gave the impression of being one of the least brilliant and ambitious of the leading Bolsheviks. He neither wrote nor spoke particularly well. He usually agreed with Lenin or the prevailing opinion on policy matters. Much of his time was spent on day-to-day administration. 'A grey blur' was how he seemed to other party leaders. They welcomed his appointment as General Secretary of the Communist Party in 1922. He would do the job well in a quiet, unassuming way.

In fact they badly underestimated his ambition and his cunning. As General Secretary he controlled the only political party in the USSR and appointed to its senior posts only people loyal to him. Consequently he had great powers which he was ready to use to his personal advantage. He was fortunate that Lenin had a severe stroke in 1922 from which he never fully recovered. The Bolshevik leader was considering dismissing Stalin (see source C1) when in 1924 he had a second stroke and died.

During the next three years, Stalin completely outwitted the other

Source B: The young Stalin

B1 *Stalin wrote this on his youth.*

B1

"I became a Marxist because of my social position (my father was a worker in a shoe factory and my mother was also a working woman) . . . but also because of the harsh intolerance and . . . discipline which crushed me so mercilessly at the Seminary . . . . The atmosphere in which I lived was saturated with hatred against Tsarist oppression."

B2 *Entries in the Conduct Book of the Seminary.*

B2

September 1898:

"At 9 p.m. a group of students gathered in the dining hall around Joseph Djugashvili, who read them books not sanctioned by the Seminary authorities, in view of which the students were searched."

October 1898:

"In the course of a search of students . . . Joseph Djugashvili tried several times to enter into an argument . . . expressing dissatisfaction with the repeated searches . . . and declaring that such searches were never made in other seminaries. Djugashvili is generally disrespectful and rude towards persons in authority."

B3 *This is a confidential report of the Tsarist secret police.*

B3

"In the autumn of 1901 the [Marxist] Social Democratic Committee of Tiflis sent one of its members, J. V. Djugashvili, formerly a pupil of Tiflis Seminary, to Batum for the purpose of carrying out propaganda among factory workers . . . Social Democratic organisations began to spring up in all the factories of Batum as a result of Djugashvili's activities. The results of the Social Democratic propaganda could already be seen in 1902, in the prolonged strike in the Rothschild factory and in street demonstrations."

1 *Seminaries are training centres rather than schools. For what career do they train?*

2 *Write a school report on Joseph Djugashvili noting both his strengths and weaknesses. Why was the Seminary bothered about the books he was reading?*

3 *Who were the Social Democrats (see source B3), their leader in 1895 and their main beliefs?*

4 *Why should the Tsarist police be interested in Djugashvili (Stalin)? How reliable would the report be?*

5 *What reasons does Stalin give for becoming a Marxist? Why were so many young Russians attracted by Marxist ideals at that time?*

Increases his power

Bolshevik leaders. Trotsky was his most dangerous rival so Stalin allied himself with Zinoviev and Kamenev. A major difference of opinion arose over the USSR's international position. Trotsky argued that the Russian government should actively encourage communist revolutions all over the world. Stalin, Zinoviev and Kamenev took a contrary view. The USSR should first build up her own strength (Socialism in one country) before getting involved in foreign adventures. While Trotsky angered party members by his arrogance, Stalin impressed them by his apparent readiness to listen and to accept the majority view. In 1925 Trotsky was dismissed from the Central Committee and in 1927 from the Party. In 1929 he was expelled from the USSR and in 1940, an exile in Mexico, murdered on Stalin's orders. As soon as he was sure that Trotsky was beaten, Stalin swung the Party first against Zinoviev and Kamenev, then against other possible rivals. In 1927 Zinoviev and Kamenev were expelled from the Party and by 1928 Stalin was effectively dictator of the USSR.

Trotsky disgraced

Master of the USSR, 1928

Source C: Lenin on Stalin

C1 *This memorandum was dictated by Lenin to his secretary in December 1922 and January 1923, after his second stroke from which he never properly recovered. It was effectively his last advice to the Communist Party and dealt mainly with the characters of 'the two most able leaders' on the Central Committee of the Party, Trotsky and Stalin.*

This memorandum was not published before Lenin died and was only brought before the Central Committee on the insistence of Lenin's wife, Krupskaya, who deeply distrusted Stalin.

C2 *Isaac Deutscher in* Stalin *(1966) quotes an eyewitness of the Central Committee discussion in May 1924.*

1 *Why in January 1923 was Lenin particularly concerned about who should take over from him?*
2 *What, in Lenin's opinion, were Stalin's major faults (see source C1)?*
3 *What action did he recommend that the Central Committee should take?*
4 *Who saw to it that the memorandum was considered by the Central Committee (see source C1). Why do you think Zinoviev and Kamenev supported Stalin? Had they any reason later to regret this action (see above)? Why did Trotsky say nothing?*
5 *What does Deutscher use for his primary evidence about the Central Committee meeting (see source C2)? Comment on its reliability.*

C1

"Comrade Stalin, having become General Secretary, has concentrated an enormous power in his hands; and I am not sure that he always knows how to use that power with sufficient caution ... He is too rude and this fault ... becomes unbearable in the office of General Secretary. Therefore, I propose to the comrades that they find a way of removing Stalin from his present position and appoint to it another man ... more patient, loyal, polite and attentive to colleagues, less capricious, etc."

C2

"Terrible embarrassment paralysed all those present. Stalin sitting on the steps of the rostrum looked small and miserable. I studied him closely; in spite of his self-control and show of calm, it was clearly evident that his fate was at stake."

[*He was saved by Zinoviev.*]

"'Comrades', declared Zinoviev, 'every word of Ilyich [Lenin] is law to us .... We have sworn to fulfil anything the dying Ilyich ordered us to do. You know perfectly well that we shall keep that vow. But we are happy to say that in one point Lenin's fears have proved baseless. I have in mind the point about our General Secretary. You will have all witnessed our harmonious cooperation in the last few months; and, like myself, you will be happy to say that Lenin's fears have proved baseless."

[*Kamenev supported Zinoviev. Trotsky remained silent since Lenin had commented on his strengths and weaknesses in the same memorandum. Despite the protests of Krupskaya, the Central Committee decided that the memorandum should not be published and that Stalin should remain General Secretary.*]

Collectivisation of agriculture

The Russian people soon discovered that their new master was coldly and terrifyingly ruthless. The towns faced starvation in 1928 because the farmers failed to send them enough grain. There was some hoarding as the richer peasants, the kulaks, tried to push up prices. Stalin used this crisis to collectivise Russian agriculture, in other words to ban private farming and to concentrate farming in larger units, the 'kolkhoz' and the 'sovkhoz'. The kolkhoz was owned collectively by its members. The government laid down how much it should produce and the prices which would be paid. Separate machine tractor stations provided mechanised assistance. The 'sovkhoz' was a state farm with an official manager who hired peasant labour.

The kulaks

The 'kulaks', whose name means 'tight-fisted', were peasants who had done well out of the land reforms of the late nineteenth century. They produced surplus food which they sold to the towns and sometimes for export. In some areas they were disliked by the less-well-off peasants. Stalin's particular aim was to destroy the kulaks as a class, but their resistance, and that of the middling peasantry, was much greater than he had expected. Collectivisation had to be enforced by the army and the secret police. Villages were burnt, villagers killed or transported to Siberia. In desperation the peasants burnt their crops, smashed their tools and slaughtered their animals. Stalin was not deterred. Between 1929 and 1933 Russian agriculture was collectivised but at a dreadful price. In 1929 there were about 34 million horses in the USSR, in 1933 only 17 million. During the same period 45 per cent of the cattle and about 60 per cent of the sheep and goats were destroyed. Fertile land was left uncultivated and there was still starvation in the urban areas. Not until 1937 did agricultural production return to pre-collectivisation levels.

Source D: Collectivisation: different views

D1 *The* Manchester Guardian, *25 March 1933, printed this report from Malcolm Muggeridge in the Caucasus region of Russia:*

D1

"'How are things with you?' I asked one man. He looked about anxiously to see that no soldiers were about. 'We have nothing, absolutely nothing. They have taken everything away,' he said and hurried on .... It was true. They had nothing. It was also true that everything had been taken away. The famine is an organised one ....

It is literally true that whole villages have been exiled. I saw myself a group of some twenty peasants being marched off under escort."

D2 *Red Army soldiers arrive on a collective farm, ready to help the workers, 1934.*

D3 *Isaac Deutscher was a member of the Polish Communist Party until 1932 and travelled in Russia during the period of collectivisation. In his biography of Stalin he describes a railway journey when he met a police colonel who was:*

D4 *A kolkhoz worker finds grain hidden by a peasant.*

D3

"completely broken in spirit by his recent experiences in the countryside. 'I am an old Bolshevik,' he said, almost sobbing, 'I worked in the underground against the Tsar and then I fought in the civil war. Did I do all that in order that I should now surround villages with machine-guns and order my men to fire indiscriminately into crowds of peasants? Oh no, no!'"

D5

"The plan to collectivise agriculture was charted by Lenin .... He pointed out that the peasants should be persuaded, not forced .... In 1929–30 the peasants began to unite voluntarily in ... collective farms. The Communist Party and the state came to the help of the farmers ..... Soon the collective farm members found it much easier to work and to sell their produce .... By the end of 1931 more than 60 per cent of all peasant families had become collective farm members."

D5 *From* An Illustrated History of the USSR, *Moscow, 1977.*

D6 (***Below right***) *Tractors arriving at a kolkhoz, 1930.*

1 *What were the soldiers doing in the market towns and villages of South Russia (source D1)? Why should villagers be nervous of talking to an English journalist in front of them?*

2 *What did the colonel in source D3 mean when he said 'I am an old Bolshevik and worked in the underground'? On whose instructions and for what reasons was he having to order his men to fire on peasants? Why did this upset him?*

3 *In source D2 how can you tell the soldiers from the workers?*

4 *What impressions do the photographs D2 and D6 give? To what extent are they natural rather than posed photographs?*

5 *In what ways do sources D2, 4, 5 and 6 differ from sources D1 and D3? What seems to you the most striking difference? Which account seems the most reliable? Explain your answer.*

6 *Write a letter to the* Manchester Guardian *of 30 March 1933, in answer to Malcolm Muggeridge's article (source D1), as from the Russian Embassy in London, defending the policy of collectivisation.*

The Five-Year Plans

Simultaneously Russian industry was expanded by the Five-Year Plans. The first of these ran from 1929 to 1932. It was declared a success and ended a year early (see sources E1–2). The second was launched in 1933 and ended in 1937. In both plans every section of heavy industry and individual plants within each section were set targets to be reached by the end of the five-year period. Stalin's aim was to increase industrial production as fast as possible so that the Soviet Union would have the economic and military power to defend herself against any enemy. Heavy industry took priority over consumer goods. Though his economists exaggerated the success of the plans there is little doubt that considerable economic growth took placed at a time when the rest of the world was in the grip of the Great Slump. The annual average growth rate seems to have been between 12 and 14 per cent and towards the end of the 1930s Germany had been overtaken so that the USSR was second only to the USA in heavy industry, though lagging far behind in living standards.

Economic achievements

The landscape was transformed in many places by dams, power stations, canals, railways and even new cities like Dneiprostroy and Magnitogorsk. Many, perhaps most, Russians enthusiastically supported the plans and were proud of their achievements. The government made a hero of Stakhanov, a coalminer who set productivity records, to encourage hard work. Equally a source of popular pride were the great improvements in education and in the medical and social services which were also taking place.

Source E: The Five-Year Plans

E1 *A Soviet propaganda poster about the Five-Year Plans, 1933.*

E2 (**Far right**) *A German Communist Party poster of 1932 which spells out the achievements of the USSR's first Five-Year Plan.*

1 *The man in the top hat (source E1) is a capitalist businessman (American, British, French or German). What is the 1928 book and what is he saying about it? What does the bottom half of the cartoon show? Explain the '5 in 4' flag fixed to the chimney.*

2 *You do not have to understand German to get the message in source E2. To what industries does the poster draw particular attention? What do the various figures indicate?*

3 *How accurate would you expect the figures to be? Explain your answer.*

4 *In what sort of condition was German industry at this time? Why should a German political party boast about a Russian achievement?*

The purges

Dealing with opposition

Since the government completely controlled the newspapers and the radio, ordinary Russians had only the haziest idea about the incredible purges which Stalin ordered between 1934 and 1939. He struck at anyone who might be his rival and plot against him. Between 1930 and 1933 some party leaders and generals had criticised his collectivisation policies. In 1934 one of his closest and most able associates, Kirov, was assassinated in Leningrad by a student. Stalin used Kirov's murder to begin the first great purge and many historians believe that he ordered the assassination. The secret police were ordered to root out all traitors and show-trials were staged of some of the most famous Bolsheviks, heroes of the 1917 revolution and former colleagues of both Lenin and Stalin. The Sixteen (Zinoviev, Kamenev and fourteen others) were accused of plotting with Trotsky to murder Kirov. They were found guilty and shot in August 1936. Another group (the Seventeen) met the same fate in January 1937 and a third (the Twenty-One) in March 1938. Continual interrogation, brutality and threats against their families caused most of the accused to make grovelling public confessions of their guilt which could not possibly have been true. Meanwhile, in 1937 Stalin learnt that some of the most senior officers of the Russian army were plotting against him. They too were thoroughly but secretly purged, including Marshal Tukhashevsky, hero of the civil war and commander-in-chief.

Extent of the purges

At last in 1939 Stalin announced the end of the purges. How many died is not known for certain: 800,000 members of the Communist Party is a recent calculation. The more senior you were the greater the risk. Of the 13 members of the top political committee (the Politburo) 6 died, 98 out of 138 members of the Central Committee, 14 out of 18 People's Commissars. In the army half the officer corps (35,000 in all) were shot or imprisoned, 3 out of 5 marshals and 14 out of 16 army commanders. The purgers were purged too. One of the last victims was Yezhov, head of the secret police, who only two years earlier had purged Yagoda his former boss. In addition millions of political opponents real or imagined were imprisoned in labour camps. From this destruction, which was so extreme and unnatural that it must raise the question whether Stalin was completely sane, he emerged stronger than ever. Into the thousands of vacancies created by the purged stepped men and women who not only owed him everything but were terrified of him.

The 1936 constitution

Meanwhile in 1936 a new constitution had been introduced. All adults over the age of eighteen could vote in elections by secret ballot. The Supreme Soviet, which met twice a year, replaced the All-Union Congress of Soviets and appointed the 'presidium' or senior ruling group. The local responsibilities of the various Soviet Socialist Republics, which together made up the Union of Soviet Socialist Republics, and the central powers of the state were made clearer. Stalin claimed that the USSR was the most democratic country in the world. The snag was that there was only one party for whom you could vote and the party leader had control of Russian society.

Soviet foreign policy, 1917–41

The West's view of the USSR

The capitalist West viewed the communist USSR with deep suspicion and vice versa. This was hardly surprising since the communists wished to destroy capitalism throughout the world and set themselves up as champions of all oppressed workers. For their part the Russian Communists believed that capitalist countries would work together to try to destroy them and had vivid memories of the British, French, Americans and the Japanese helping the Whites against them during the civil war.

Comintern

From 1917 to 1920 the Bolshevik leaders hoped that communist revolutions would spread like wildfire through the chaos of post-war Europe and they set up the Comintern (the Communist International) to help such revolutions along. After 1920 they became more ready to live and let live. The revolutions had not happened and an alliance of France, Poland, Romania and Czechoslovakia had been formed, which was anti-Russian as well as anti-German. Chicherin was appointed Commissar of Foreign Affairs. At Genoa in 1922 he headed off an attempt by the major powers to force the Soviet Union to pay debts owed by the Tsar's government. He also had some success in persuading the smaller European nations to see the USSR as a possible ally rather than an enemy.

Allies in Europe

His greatest achievement however was to sign the Treaty of Rapallo with Germany. The two countries publically agreed to be allies and secretly to collaborate on military matters. By 1925 the USSR was much less isolated since she was diplomatically recognised by Britain, France, Italy and Japan as well as by Germany.

Stalin's foreign policy

These friendlier relations did not last. The continuing pro-revolutionary activities of the Comintern upset Britain and France while the

Source F: The purges

F1 *This is from* Joseph Stalin: A Short Biography, *compiled by G. F. Alexandrov and others and published in the USSR in 1947.*

F1

"The Socialist victories achieved by the Party served still more to infuriate the enemies of the people. In 1937 new facts were brought to light regarding the fiendish crimes of the Trotsky-Bukharin gang of spies, wreckers and assassins, linking the espionage service of the capitalist states. The trials which followed revealed that these dregs of humanity had been conspiring against Lenin whom they had intended to arrest, and against the Party and the Soviet State from the very first days of the October Revolution . . . .

The Soviet courts disclosed the crimes of the Trotsky-Bukharin fiends and sentenced them to be shot. *The Soviet people approved the annihilation of the Trotsky-Bukharin gang.*"

F2 *And here is the official report on the 1938 'Trial of the Twenty-One'.*

F2

"Bukharin: 'I consider myself responsible both politically and legally for wrecking activities, although personally I do not remember having given directions for such activities. I have degenerated into an enemy of society, am guilty of treason . . . of organising "kulak" uprisings and preparing terrorist acts . . . . Mine is a perfectly voluntary confession . . . . My execution will be a severe lesson to those disloyal to the Soviet Union and its leadership.'"

F3 *Bukharin was an able Communist economist who made the mistake of having a mind of his own. He was imprisoned by the Tsar for his revolutionary activities in 1911, escaped and went into exile until 1917. He edited* Pravda, *the Bolshevik newspaper, became a leading member of the Communist International, and was elected to the Politburo in 1924. He never trusted Stalin and criticised his collectivisation policies. He was expelled from the Politburo (ruling group) in 1929. Robert Conquest writes of him in* The Great Terror *(1973).*

F3

"Bukharin had not been tortured . . . . After three months of interrogation and threats to his young wife and child, he agreed to confess all charges including that of having planned to assassinate Lenin. But when two days later his confession, amended and corrected by Stalin personally, had been given him to sign he was so shocked that he withdrew his whole confession. The examination then began all over again . . . . His [eventual] confession avoided admitting direct complicity in any of the worst acts but accepted general responsibility. Anything less would have probably meant his omission from the trial and the execution of his wife."

1 *Who were Bukharin and Trotsky? How close had they been to Lenin and to Stalin? When did they fall out with Stalin and for what reasons? Where was Trotsky during the purges? Why are his ideas singled out as being particularly fiendish? How did he die?*

2 *Comment on the Alexandrov extract (source F1), particularly the sentence in italic and its use of words like 'wreckers', 'fiendish', 'gang' and 'dregs'. Of what is it good evidence?*

3 *Bukharin could never have been remotely responsible for the crimes which he publicly confessed. Conquest in source F3 gives three methods used by the NKVD, Stalin's secret police. What were these? Which would you expect to have been most effective on a experienced Bolshevik like Bukharin who had braved much danger already in his revolutionary struggles against the Tsar's secret police?*

4 *What evidence is there that Stalin took a close personal interest (see source F3) in the progress of the interrogations and trials? Do these purges seem to you to provide sufficient evidence that Stalin could be described as mad?*

USSR's muddled policy towards China made General Chiang Kai-shek firmly anti-communist while failing to remove him for power. Once Stalin was in power the Comintern's revolutionary activities were reduced. True to 'Socialism in one country' he turned against Troskyite foreign adventures and aimed to present Russia as a peace-loving country in order to buy the time needed to make her strong enough to resist attack. He quickly realised how dangerous Hitler was and from 1934 looked for allies against him. The USSR joined the League of Nations in 1934 and was both amazed and appalled by the appeasement policies being pursued by Britian and France. So suspicious were these Western European powers of the USSR and, despite their fear of Hitler, so unready to discuss an anti-Nazi alliance that Stalin suspected that they were really hoping for a German attack on the USSR. During the Spanish Civil War, though he sent some aid to the Republicans (among whom were the Spanish Communists) in order to counter the support given to Franco by Hitler and Mussolini, he was reluctant to support them too openly for fear of upsetting Britain and France.

The threat of Nazism

The search for an alliance

As Hitler's successes continued Stalin grew even more anxious about the intentions of Britain and France. It seems likely that he would have been ready to go to war in defence in Czechoslovakia if Britain and France had joined him. Consequently he regarded the Munich agreement as further evidence that an anti-Nazi alliance was impossible and that the USSR's interests might be best taken care of by a defensive alliance with Hitler. While he was sure that in the long run the Nazis were the USSR's greatest threat, a temporary alliance while they fought against the Poles would buy time, during which the Soviet armed forces would be strengthened.

Source G: Soviet foreign policy

G1 *Stalin writes to the Central Committee in 1925.*

G1

"War may become inevitable, of course not tomorrow nor the next day, but in a few years . . . the banner of peace remains our banner as of old. But, if war begins, we shall hardly have to sit with folded arms. We shall have to come out but we ought to be the last to come out. And we should come out in order to throw the decisive weight on the scales, the weight that should tip the scales."

G2 *Lord Cushendun, British representative at a disarmament conference in Switzerland in 1928 reports.*

G2

"There are two kinds of war and where there are two kinds of war, there are two kinds of peace. There are international and civil wars and of these the civil is the more horrible. It is a fair question to ask whether the Soviet Government sets its face against civil as resolutely as against international war . . . . For years past the whole basis of the Soviet world policy has been to produce armed insurrection amounting to civil war in every country where they can exercise influence . . . . We ought to be told whether the Soviets have decided no longer to interfere in the affairs of other nations."

1 *Sum up in a sentence Stalin's thinking about peace and war (source G1).*
2 *When Lord Cushendun (source G2) talks of 'armed insurrection amounting to civil war' what does he have in mind? To what extent had the West and the Soviet Union become more friendly by the beginning of 1929?*

The Nazi-Soviet Pact

This was the thinking behind the Nazi-Soviet Pact of August 1939 which so surprised the world. While it gave Hitler the chance to invade Poland without fear of a Russian counterattack, it allowed Stalin to occupy the 'buffer zone' of eastern Poland. Latvia, Lithuania and Estonia were also conquered without difficulty, but the invasion of Finland to secure land to strengthen the defences of Leningrad had different results. The small Finnish army inflicted some embarrassing defeats on the Russians before it was eventually worn down by sheer weight of numbers. Though the war against Finland (1939–40) ended in complete victory for the USSR it convinced Hitler, among others, that the Soviet army was in a poor state. It also caused the USSR to be expelled from the League of Nations.

Stalin badly overestimated the strength of first the Polish and then the French resistance to Germany. He must have hoped that the Nazi-Soviet Pact would buy more time than the mere two years 1939–41. He also obstinately refused to believe how speedily Hitler would turn on the USSR after the conquest of France, even though British intelligence warned him that the German armies were poised to attack. All in all, the Nazi-Soviet Pact was a major mistake. It handed Poland to the Nazis on a plate and eased their conquest of Western Europe. Instead of giving the Soviet army plenty of time to increase its strength, it meant that in next to no time it had to face alone the victorious German armies which were battle-hardened and supremely confident.

The Great Patriotic War, 1941–5

In contrast to the years 1939–41, Stalin's leadership during the Great Patriotic War, from the catastrophic defeats of 1941–2 through to the victories of 1943–5, were outstanding. Somehow he managed to concentrate the major decisions of war and of government in his own hands, yet allow his generals, once he trusted them, considerable freedom of

Source H: A soviet nightmare, 1936

H *This Soviet cartoon was published in 1936.*

1 *Who is the baby in the cradle?*

2 *Who is the large white figure behind the cradle? How did you identify him?*

3 a) *Who are the figures on the left of the cradle? How did you identify them?*
b) *What happened in 1936 (see page 216) which could have caused the Soviet Union to think that these two figures wanted to be friends with Hitler?*

4 *Why did the Russians worry so greatly about Nazism? Was this worry justified (see pages 224 and 227–30)?*

5 *What is the main message of this cartoon?*

action. When the Germans seemed to be closing in on Moscow and most government officials were evacuated, he stayed in the Kremlin and from there supervised the successful winter counterattack which saved the capital. In his radio broadcasts he reminded the people of their history and called on them as patriots to make the great sacrifices necessary to drive the invader from the USSR's sacred soil. For his part he gave tireless, decisive, intelligent and above all resolute leadership.

On 24 June 1945 he reviewed the victory parade of the Red Army. The following day he was proclaimed 'Hero of the Soviet Union'. For once this was not the hollow title of a cruel tyrant but a genuine tribute from a proud and grateful nation.

Stalin's last years, 1945–53

Some rulers mellow as they grow older; not Stalin. If anything he grew more coldly ruthless and more unnaturally suspicious. He used the USSR's military triumphs and her immense army to make sure that she was in a dominating position in Eastern Europe during the peace negotiations which ended the Second World War. He made this position stronger still by forcing communist governments into office in Eastern European countries with men who thought like him at the top. Never had Russia been so feared in Europe since 1812–15 when Russian armies had defeated Napoleon.

Conditions of the people

Within the USSR the lives of ordinary people were grim. Their apparently inhuman master allowed them no relaxation. The new Five-Year Plans still concentrated on the expansion of heavy industry and military technology, not on improving living standards which lagged way behind the West. All political criticism continued to be sternly repressed. Ex-prisoners of war from Germany found themselves transported into Siberian labour camps for fear that they had been infected by Western opinions. Zhdanov, the Minister of Propaganda, controlled the work of artists and writers more strictly than ever (see sources J1–2).

Zhdanov and censorship

More purges

Then the purges began again. Early victims were communist leaders in Eastern Europe, who were too nationalist in their thinking and suspected of being sympathetic to the Yugoslav leader Tito, who had successfully defended his independence from Stalin's threats. Then in the USSR senior officials started to disappear in mysterious circumstances. In 1953 nine well-known doctors were accused of murdering Zhdanov, who had died in 1948, and another set of show trials was expected. Instead Stalin himself died of a stroke aged seventy-three.

Death of Stalin, 1953

Isaac Deutscher, among the best of Stalin's many biographers, ends his book by noting how Stalin's successors first put his embalmed body in a place of honour beside Lenin's in Moscow's Red Square. Then they removed it and all other memorials to him. They did not know what to make of his complicated personality and life. Later generations inside and outside the USSR have shared their puzzlement (see sources I1–3). Neither the greatness of his achievements for the Russian people nor the evils which he inflicted upon them can possibly be ignored.

Stalin's reputation since his death

Stalin died in 1953. In February 1956 Khrushchev, First Secretary of the Communist Party, bitterly attacked Stalin's rule. He accused him of 'flagrant abuses of power and of brutality', for 'the mass arrests [of the purges] which caused tremendous harm to our country and to the cause of socialist progress'. Seven thousand victims of the purges, many of whom had been executed, were declared innocent. The famous city of

Stalingrad had its name changed to Volgograd. Stalin's mummified body was removed from the mausoleum in Red Square where it had been placed in 1953 beside Lenin's.

Khrushchev's attack has caused Soviet historians considerable difficulties when writing about the period 1914–1953. For example, Novosti, the official Soviet information agency, published in 1977 an *Illustrated History of the USSR*. Written in English and attractively produced, about half of its 190 pages are about the twentieth century. Yet Stalin is mentioned only once (see source I2). What will his reputation be in the USSR and the West in the twenty-first century?

Source I: *Stalin's reputation since his death*

I1 *This is from* A History of Russia *by N. Riasanovsky, published in 1969.*

I1

"As in the case of Ivan the Terrible, there was madness in Stalin's method. That madness, formerly a matter of suspicion and controversy, received convincing documentation in Khrushchev's celebrated speech ... in 1956 .... In addition to fighting real battles and struggling against actual opponents, Stalin lived in the paranoiac world of constant threat and wholesale conspiracy. Fact and fantasy were blended together ..."

I2

"A State Committee of defence was formed, headed by Stalin."

I2 *From an* Illustrated History of the USSR, *page 134, in the section on the German invasion of Russia in 1941. Stalin also appears in a photograph of Allied peace negotiations in 1945, but he is not identified in the caption.*

I3 *Stalin's statue in the centre of Budapest, Hungary, is toppled by rebels, 23 October 1956.*

1 What does Riasanovsky (source I1) mean when he says that 'Stalin lived in the paranoiac world of constant threat and wholesale conspiracy'?

2 What was, for Riasanovsky, the crucial evidence of Stalin's madness? Who provided it and when?

3 Why were there many statues of Stalin in Hungary and so many of them destroyed in 1956?

4 Why did so many Russians also become critical of Stalin in 1956? What in particular did they criticise about his rule?

5 What does the Novosti treatment of Stalin in the 1977 Illustrated History *suggest to you a) about Stalin's reputation in Russia in 1977, and b) about the Soviet attitude towards 'official' history?*

Source J: Stalinist views on the arts

J1 *Anna Akhmatova wrote this poem in the 1920s.*

J2 *Zhdanov talks about poetry in 1946.*

1 *Who is Zhdanov (source J2)? For what reasons does he object to Akhmatova's poems? Why does he go on about the black cat?*

2 *Had there been much bloodshed in Russia between 1914 and 1924? Does the mood of the poem (Source J1) seem to you in any way objectionable? What might Zhdanov have disliked about it?*

3 *What sort of literature do Stalin and Zhdanov wish to be written in Russia? What will be the consequences for those writers who do not produce works along the desired lines (see source J2)?*

4 *Such an approach to art and literature is quite different from ours. Write a report, as Zhdanov might have done, having visited a British Council exhibition in Moscow of modern British painting and sculpture. If artists are, as Stalin said, the 'engineers of the soul', what might he make of the state of the contemporary British soul?*

5 *Should an artist be able to produce and exhibit in public anything he or she likes? Make out a case for government censorship and another against.*

J1

"You will never be alive again,
Never rise from the snow;
Twenty-eight bayonets,
Five fire wounds.
A bitter new garment
I sewed for my friend.
It does love blood–
The Russian earth."

J2

"The magazine *Leningrad*, in one of its numbers, has published a number of poems of Akhmatova written between 1909 and 1944. Among them . . . is a poem written while she was being evacuated during the Great Patriotic War. She describes her loneliness when she is forced to part from her black cat. The black cat looks at her like the eye of the century. This is not a new theme. Akhmatova was already talking about her black cat in 1909. The emotion of loneliness and of despair, foreign to Soviet literature, is central to Akhmatova's work.

Is there anything in common between such poetry and the interests of our people and our state? No, absolutely nothing. Her work belongs to the distant past . . . and cannot be tolerated in the pages of our magazines.

Comrade Stalin has called our writers 'engineers of the soul'. This definition is profoundly significant. It indicates the enormous responsibility which Soviet writers have for the education of adults and for the education of Soviet youth. They must be vigilant against tolerating the wrong standards in their literary work."

12 Mussolini and Italy

Source A: *The public Mussolini*

A1 (**Right**) *The violinist.*

A2 (**Far right**) *Due aquile (two eagles), 1923.*

A3 (**Below left**) *With his lion cub Ras, 1924.*

A4 (**Below right**) *Daily morning exercise.*

Read the narrative on pages 186–7.

1 *These photographs were specially taken for publication. What impressions does Mussolini wish to give to the Italian people and to the world?*

2 *What do they tell you a) about Mussolini, b) about Fascism?*

In old photographs Mussolini (see sources A1–4) and Hitler can seem comic to us now. It also appears laughable that they saw themselves as supermen brought by destiny to save their countries. Nor was there anything in their early careers to suggest their future success. In 1919 Mussolini was a Milanese journalist best known for the violence both of his temper and his writing, and for sudden changes in his political beliefs. At that same date Hitler was a failed artist whom the First World War had pulled out of the gutter and whose chief political instinct was a deep hatred of Jews. Neither had had a particularly distinguished war. Mussolini had an accident when training and returned to journalism in 1917. Hitler endured the Western Front and ended up a corporal. In normal times neither could have expected a successful career in national politics.

Conditions between the wars favour dictators

The 1920s and 1930s were not normal however. As Europeans tried uncertainly to convince themselves that the sacrifices of the war were not in vain, they were overwhelmed by unmanageable economic problems. There was anger, bewilderment, despair and bitter social conflict. Such abnormal times provided men like Mussolini and Hitler with their opportunity. They gave the appearance of strength and of confidence. They knew whom to blame. They promised national recovery to patriotic citizens who felt humiliated and demoralised. Not only did they manage to impress millions of their fellow countrymen but many foreigners as well.

Fascism

Fascism is the name given to their political ideas which in the 1930s were shared by other European groups, for example Codreanu's Iron Guards in Romania and the Falangists in Spain. It comes from the Italian word 'fascio' which means group. The Fascio di Combattimento (Fighting Group) which Mussolini founded in 1919 was the first Fascist group. Fascists were clearer about what they were against than what they were for.

Negative beliefs

They were against Liberals because they valued individual freedom too much. Such freedom Fascists argued weakened the state. They were also against democracy. According to them, 'one man one vote' meant the rule of the second-rate, low standards and inefficiency. They were against foreigners and international co-operation. Communism they considered their greatest enemy, since it was an international movement which aimed to turn workers against their fellow citizens and to destroy the nation-state.

Positive beliefs

On the subject of what they positively favoured, they tended to be vague and wordy. They believed in a one-party state headed by a leader with dictatorial powers. The state, which was much more than the sum of all its citizens and whose interests the leader knew best, should have total control over the lives of its citizens and should increase its power at the expense of other nation-states. Fascists valued action more than thought, glory and violence more than peace.

Mussolini's early life

Benito Mussolini was born in 1883 (see sources B1 and 2). His father was a blacksmith and a socialist, his mother a schoolteacher. He too qualified as a teacher but soon gave up because, said his enemies, he could not keep the pupils in order. He spent some years in Switzerland involved in revolutionary socialist activities. Eventually the Swiss expelled him and he took to writing novels and to journalism. In 1910 he became secretary of the Forli branch of the Socialist Party and, within a year, had made a reputation for himself by his outspoken opposition to the Italian invasion of Tripolitania. He was sentenced to five months in gaol for leading a protest demonstration. In 1912 he was in Milan, leader of the quarrelsome Socialist Party and editor of its newspaper *Avanti* (Forward).

Quarrels with socialists

The First World War split him from his socialist colleagues. They wished Italy to stay at peace while Mussolini wanted to fight with France and Britain. War, he argued, would help to cause social revolution. Having lost the argument he was expelled from the party, founded a new paper, *Il Popolo d'Italia* ('the Italian People'), and was arrested for the violence of his speeches in favour of the war. Until his accident while training he had had fifteen months as a soldier. When the war ended he was back at his editor's desk in Milan. Already in 1913 he had stood as a Socialist for parliament but failed to get elected. In 1919 he tried again, as a Fascist, and failed again winning only a handful of votes.

The start of Fascism, 1919

None the less he had founded his Fascist Party at a good time. In 1919 Italy was a chaotic, hysterical place. The war had been very costly in

Source B: Mussolini at school

The following two school comments were printed in The Life Of Mussolini *by De Begnac, published in Italy in 1936.*

B1 *First his last report from the Salesian School in Faenza when he was twelve.*

B1

"[Benito Mussolini] has a lively intelligence, an unusual memory but a character quite out of the ordinary . . . passionate and unruly he cannot adapt himself to the life of the school . . . . He places himself in opposition to every rule of the school . . . . One personal motive guides him and this is the principal streak in his character . . . . He cannot support an injury; he wants revenge . . . he rebels against every punishment to a point which obliges the Headmaster reluctantly to ask his parents to withdraw him."

B2 *When he was sixteen he was suspended from the Royal Normal School at Forlimpopoli. This is an extract from a letter from the Principal to his parents.*

B2

"Since the History master was absent, the Italian master instructed the pupils to write an essay on 'Time is Money'. Shortly afterwards your son handed up to the master a scrap of paper on which was written 'Because time is money, I am going home to study geometry in view of the imminence of the examinations. Does this not seem more logical? Benito Mussolini.' The Council of Masters, having held an emergency meeting to maintain the prestige of the school and the respect of those who frequent it, has suspended your son for ten days."

1 What did Mussolini do to get himself
   a) *expelled from the Faenza school,*
   b) *suspended from the Forlimpopoli one? How old was he on each occasion?*

2 *What characteristics of the adult Mussolini can be observed in the school pupil?*

3 *What sort of future would his teachers have predicted for him?*

4 *This evidence was published in Italy when Mussolini was at the height of his power and his government believed in the strict censorship of all political books. What conclusions can you draw from these facts?*

Fiume – d'Annunzio

both men and money, yet Italy seemed to have gained little. Her representative at the Versailles peace negotiations made out that she had been betrayed and humiliated by her former allies. The port of Fiume, claimed by both Italy and Yugoslavia, was occupied by d'Annunzio, poet, war hero and extreme nationalist, in defiance of both the world and the Italian government. Though d'Annunzio had to withdraw after fifteen months, the popularity of his extreme nationalism and his ability to defy the government by the use of a private army of volunteers was noted by Mussolini.

Post-war economic problems

Another great worry for Italians in 1919 was the economic situation. Many young people could not find jobs. Nor could soldiers returning from the battlefields. Prices were rising. There were many strikes led by socialists and communists who, encouraged by the success of the Bolsheviks in Russia, hoped for a similar revolution in Italy. For a while Mussolini thought of including socialists within the Fascist movement but the other leaders persuaded him that their best chances of success lay in openly anti-socialist policies. Before long they were turning the economic crisis to their advantage. The blackshirted Fascist squads took violent and illegal action to break strikes and to disrupt socialist and communist demonstrations (see source C). Often they had the active co-operation of factory owners and police chiefs. In 1920 and 1921 law and order broke down as blackshirts and reds fought it out in the streets.

Breakdown of law and order

The politicians

Meanwhile the elected politicians by squabbling played into Mussolini's hands. The governments were weak coalitions and the leaders of the political parties continued to play the pre-war political game of trying to outwit each other and of 'waiting and seeing' in the hope that time would bring them the advantage. In 1920 Giolitti, one of the most successful pre-war coalition leaders but now seventy-eight, became Prime Minister once again. He thought that he could use the Fascists to his advantage and helped them to win thirty-five seats in the 1921 election. However, his coalition collapsed almost at once and the next lasted only eight months.

Giolitti

The General Strike, 1922

In July 1922 the socialists called a general strike. The Fascists organised huge counter-demonstrations and, proclaiming that they were acting in the public interest to keep normal services going, seized control of the cities of Milan, Genoa, Livorno and Ancona. With the government still inactive and the socialists (the largest political party) divided, the Fascists maintained the initiative. The blackshirt squads were got ready for a march on Rome, and, though Mussolini stayed close to the Swiss frontier in case things went wrong, four Fascists leaders told the government that unless Mussolini was made Prime Minister the Fascists would take power by force.

The March on Rome

As they spoke, the squads were marching on the capital. The government had more than enough troops at its command to have crushed the poorly armed and rain-drenched blackshirts. Some ministers were keen to take firm action against them. However, the Prime Minister dithered and when he had finally steeled himself to use force, King Victor Emmanuel III lost his nerve and refused to sign the necessary decree. It may be that he feared that he might be overthrown by his younger brother the Duke of Aosta. Whatever the reason he left himself no

Source C: Fascist threats and violence, 1921–2

C1 *Chiurco's* History of the Fascist Revolution (*the official history*) *was first published with a preface by Mussolini in 1929.*

C1

"The lorry-load of fascists arrives in a given district and they announce themselves to the head of the League [Association of Agricultural Workers]. They begin with a discussion, then either the head of the League gives way or persuasion is followed by violence. He generally does give way. If not the revolvers have their say."

C2 *The Marquis Dino Perrone Compagni, a Fascist landowner, writes to the mayor of a local village early in April 1921.*

C2

"Sir, Since Italy belongs to the Italians and cannot permit herself to be governed by people of your sort, speaking for your fellow citizens who are under your administration I advise you to resign before Sunday April 17th. If you refuse you alone are responsible for the consequences. If you take it upon yourself to draw the attention of the authorities to this generous, kindly and humane advice, your time allowance will expire before Wednesday the 13th, a lucky number!"

C3 *Italo Balbo was one of Mussolini's most able and daring lieutenants. His* Diary *was published in 1922. It includes 'Thoughts of a Returning Soldier 1919'.*

C3

"When I came back from the war, I, like so many others, hated politics and politicians, who it seemed to me had betrayed the hope of fighting men and inflicted on Italy a shameful peace . . . . Struggle, fight to return the country to Giolitti who had bartered every ideal? No. Better to deny everything, destroy everything in order to build everything up again from the bottom. Many at that time, even the most generous souls, turned towards Communism which offered a ready and more revolutionary programme and was engaged on two fronts in a struggle against the bourgeoisie and against Socialism. It is certain . . . that without Mussolini three-quarters of Italian youth coming home from the trenches would have become Bolsheviks. They wanted revolution at any cost!"

C4

"[In Ravenna] I went to the Chief of Police, leaving Dino Grandi in command of the thousands of Fascists who had collected in the suburb of San Roch. I announced that I would set fire to the houses of all the socialists in Ravenna if within half an hour he did not place at my disposal the necessary means of getting them away. It was a dramatic moment. I demanded an entire fleet of lorries. His officials completely lost their heads; but half an hour later they showed me where I could find the lorries, ready filled with petrol.

I was organising a column of fire . . . I took my place in a car at the end of the long column of lorries and we set out . . . nearly twenty-four hours of driving during which no one rested for a moment or touched food. We went through all the centres and towns of the provinces of Forli and Ravenna and destroyed all the red buildings . . . . It has been a terrible night. Our passage was marked by columns of fire and smoke."

C4 *An extract from Balbo's* Diary, *30 July 1922, on 'Fascist Terror and the General Strike July–August 1922'.*

1 *What was happening in Italy in 1921? Whom did the Fascists regard as their chief opponents?*

2 *What methods did the Fascists use to get control of country districts (see source C1 and C2)?*

3 *Who was Giolitti (see opposite)? Why did Balbo hate him and other politicians (see source C3)? If Mussolini had not founded the Fascist movement, what does Balbo believe would have happened to Italian youth?*

4 *What does Balbo mean by 'red buildings' (source C4)? How did he get the lorries he wanted?*

5 *What else might the Chief of Police have done? What conclusions would the average citizen of Ravenna and Forli have drawn from the events of 30 July?*

The king makes
Mussolini Prime
Minister

alternative but to make Mussolini Prime Minister. The latter arrived in Rome by sleeper. The following day the blackshirts entered Rome without a shot being fired.

The road to dictatorship

Mussolini had a tiny party in parliament and only limited support in the country. None the less within four years he had made himself dictator. He was able to do this partly because of the co-operation which he received from the king and from senior politicians, partly by thuggery, and partly through the mistakes of his opponents.

Though he started with only a few Fascist ministers in his government, he straight away had the Fascist squads reorganised as state militia. He persuaded parliament that the party which got the most votes in an election should automatically receive two-thirds of the seats and, in the 1924 election, the Fascist terror tactics of cudgels and forcible feeding with castor oil made sure of a huge majority.

Matteotti

In 1924 Matteotti, a leading Socialist and fearless critic of Fascist policies and methods, was kidnapped in broad daylight. Eventually his body was discovered in a ditch. His murderers were definitely Fascists; whether they were acting on Mussolini's orders or not is unclear. Such was the shock caused by this outrage that Mussolini's position seemed at risk. However, instead of staying in parliament and attacking the Fascists from there, his opponents made the critical mistake of withdrawing in protest. Mussolini went on to the attack. He sacked the non-Fascist members of his government, arrested the main opposition leaders, banned their parties and took over the national newspapers. By 1926 Italy was a dictatorship.

Mussolini's rule

Mussolini was a great showman and for the next fourteen years put on an impressive act. He was also an endless phrase-maker. The 'corporate state' was one of his favourites. With the stated aim of ending the strife between employers and workers first thirteen and then twenty-two corporations were set up for the main sections of the Italian economy. The corporations were supposed to represent the interests of the workers and to solve disputes. Between them they nominated a thousand candidates for parliament, from whom the Fascist Grand Council (itself selected by Mussolini) chose four hundred. Simultaneously strikes and lock-outs were made illegal.

As *Il Duce* (the Leader), Mussolini always gave the appearance of bustling, purposeful activity. He led a 'battle for wheat' to boost the agricultural economy, announced educational reforms to end illiteracy and reforms of the criminal law to destroy the Mafia. He demanded greater efficiency in every walk of life and his supporters boasted that at last the trains ran on time. He began major public works, for example motorways, railway electrification and the draining of the Pontine marshes.

Home policy

Most of the Fascist show was an illusion. The corporations were an excuse to destroy genuine trade unions. They increased the economic power of big businesses and landowners at the expense of workers and small businesses. Moreover they created a new and corrupt bureaucracy. Though there was some increase in literacy, educational standards remained low. The Mafia was weakened but not destroyed. If some mainline trains ran on time, the branch lines continued as before. In economic matters Mussolini had no clear policies. The 'battle for wheat' did more harm than good since it upset the balance of the agricultural economy.

Source D: The General Strike, 1922

D *On 31 June 1922 the Socialists declared a general strike in protest against Fascist violence and the failure of the government to do anything about it. Less than a fortnight later, on 12 August,* Justice, *the main Socialist newspaper, carried this editorial:*

1 *Explain the phrase 'our Caporetto' (see page 118) and 'the Fascist hurricane'.*
2 *Who had called the general strike? For what reasons? How had the Fascists reacted to it?*
3 *How reliable a source do you consider* Justice *to be for the events it describes? Explain your thinking.*
4 *If in mid August the Fascists were 'masters of the field' how much longer did it take Mussolini to win power and what still stood in his way?*

Source E: The March on Rome

E *This photograph shows Mussolini celebrating the March on Rome in 1923, on the anniversary of the real event.*

1 *Did Mussolini actually march on Rome in 1922? Did his blackshirts have to fight their way into Rome in 1922?*
2 *Why did Mussolini insist on celebrating the 'march' in such style?*

Source F: Dictatorship

F *'Bandi' cartoon by Guiseppe Scalariri of 1923. Bandi led a Fascist 'squad'. Procura del Re means Law Courts; Prefettura means local government; Questura means Police; Olio di ricino means castor oil.*

1 *What does this cartoon tell you about the Fascist methods of keeping Italy under control?*
2 *What do you think are the political views of the cartoonist? Explain your answer.*

D

"We must have the courage to admit that the general strike . . . has been our Caporetto. We emerged from this test well beaten. We have played our last card and lost Milan and Genoa, which seemed the strongest part of our defence . . . . [In Milan] the party newspaper has once more gone up in flames, the administration of the town snatched from its lawful representatives . . . . It is the same everywhere. Every important centre bears the mark of the Fascist hurricane. We must face facts. The Fascists are masters of the field. Nothing is to prevent them dealing more heavy blows in the certainty of winning fresh victories."

The country was overpopulated and the pre-war safety-valve of emigration had been blocked by American immigration controls. However, *Il Duce* demanded an increased population. The Great Slump increased unemployment and lowered wages when land shortages were biting. An important cause of Mussolini's aggressive foreign policy of the 1930s was his need to distract attention from the growing economic problems at home.

Concordat with Rome

His major achievement was the 1929 Concordat (understanding) with Pope Pius XI. By the so-called Lateran treaties Mussolini agreed that the Vatican City should be independent and paid compensation for the land taken from the church during unification. In return the Pope recognised the Italian state and agreed that Catholic priests, who were paid by the state, should take an oath of loyalty to it. This Concordat worked reasonably well. It was welcomed by the majority of the Italians and survived Mussolini's fall.

Foreign policy

For someone who so glorified violence and national honour, Mussolini was surprisingly peaceful in the 1920s. In 1923, having occupied the Greek island of Corfu after an Italian general had been murdered by Balkan brigands, he was persuaded by international pressure to withdraw. He also came to a peaceful settlement with Yugoslavia over Fiume (1924). The port itself came to Italy while the suburbs went to Yugoslavia.

Abyssinia

The 1930s were different. Economic difficulties and his sense that Fascism was getting stale made him seek to give reality to his warlike boasts. Abyssinia (Ethiopia) was an obvious target, since there was the humiliating defeat of Adowa (1896) to revenge. He began planning the invasion in 1932 and incidents on the Abyssinia borders with Eritrea and Italian Somaliland provided the excuse for its launch.

In October 1935 the Italian army invaded Abyssinia. Against its modern weapons, which included poison gas, the Abyssinians had no chance. The main concern of Britain and France was to prevent Italy allying with Nazi Germany and in December 1935 their foreign ministers came up with a plan of giving two-thirds of Abyssinia (see map H1) to Italy (the Hoare-Laval pact). Public outcry in Britain caused Hoare to resign. Mussolini rejected the plan anyway.

Emperor Haile Selassie

Emperor Haile Selassie fled to Europe and the capital Addis Ababa fell in May 1936. The feeble efforts of the League of Nations to help the Abyssinians are described on page 147. The economic sanctions of the League pushed Mussolini towards an alliance with Hitler. Their failure increased his popularity within Italy and his own already excessive confidence in his own abilities.

In the long run the conquest of Abyssinia did Italy harm. The wild country areas took years to tame. Fascist rule was corrupt as well as cruel. The new colony proved very expensive and the Italian economy was in no fit state to support it.

None the less Mussolini was triumphant. Looking back, near the end of his life, he believed 1937 to have been his best year.

Source G: How Il Duce appeared to others

G1 *F. von Papen, German politician and Nazi diplomat, had this to say in 1933.*

G1

"His massive head conveyed an impression of great strength of character. He handled people like a man who was accustomed to having his orders obeyed but displayed immense charm . . . . [He] was calm and dignified and appeared the complete master of whatever was being discussed."

G2 *Don Sturzo, leader of the Catholic Action party and opponent of Mussolini, who left Italy in 1924, gave his views in 1927.*

G2

"[Mussolini] can pass from theory to theory, from position to position, rapidly, inconsistently with neither remorse nor regret. In this game he has one constant aim – to lay hold of the elements of imagination and sentiment which make for success. Hence his speeches are attuned to the state of mind of the public to which he is speaking, if the public were other he would use other language "

G3 (**Below**) *Mussolini the orator.*

G4 *D. Mack Smith's biography of Mussolini was published in 1981.*

G4

"He could charm whenever he wished . . . he could always impress a visitor when he tried, and all the fascist leaders remembered how they had fallen under a real spell, especially in the early days before his faults become more obvious. They were thrilled by his immense vitality, intelligence and quickness of mind and everyone agreed that his practice of journalism had given him an excellent memory for facts."

G5

"Surrounding himself with nobodies, he less and less saw politics as the art of finding agreement or composing differences but liked to hit out to stop others taking initiatives, to act as though he could take the world by assault on his own . . . . Any minister who dared suggest that Britain was still a power to be reckoned with might be angrily told to hold his tongue. The other fascists had given up trying to speak honestly and openly to someone who had such a need to believe that he was always in the right. Luckily he changed his mind so often that if they wanted anything they could often just wait for the wind to change."

G5 *G. Bastianini, a Fascist ambassador returning to Italy in 1936, notes the change in the Duce.*

1 *Using sources G1–5 list a) Mussolini's strengths as a political leader, b) his weaknesses, and c) characteristics which were helpful to him in winning power but unhelpful if he were to use his power wisely.*

2 *What are the main changes Bastianini (G5) notices in Mussolini in 1936? How reliable a source would you expect him to be?*

3 *Divide the sources into four groups; a) secondary, b) primary and likely to be neutral, c) primary and likely to be hostile, and d) primary and likely to be friendly. Explain why you put each source into a particular group.*

Source H: The conquest of Abyssinia

H1 *The Hoare-Laval proposals for Abyssinia.*

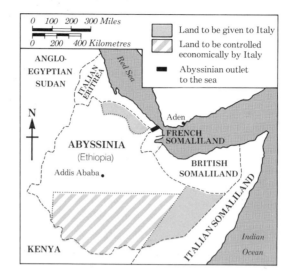

H2

This is a dictation exercise in an Italian primary school, winter 1936–7.

"One year has passed since November 18th, 1935. We have showed the world that we are the strong ones, the just ones, the best ones. The fifty-two sanctionist nations denied us bread, iron, gold and cloth. We have found it all anyway; bread from the fields of Italy, iron from the houses of Italy; gold from the women of Italy; white coal from the waters of Italy. They wanted to humiliate us but our riches and sacrifices have raised us above them."

H3 *'A compassionate Italian soldier releases Ethiopian slaves'. This picture from an Italian magazine of 1936 shows how the Abyssinian conquest was seen in Italy.*

1 *Who were Hoare and Laval? What did they propose? What was their chief reason for proposing their plan? What results did it have?*

2 *Read source H2 and say what happened in the autumn of 1935.*

3 *Explain the phrase 'the fifty-two sanctionist nations'.*

4 *What important import did the 'sanctionist nations' not deny to Italy?*

5 *Comment on the sentence 'we are the strong ones, the just ones, the best ones'.*

6 *What was the aim of the artist of H3? What kind of arguments does it indicate that the Fascists used to justify their actions in Ethiopia both to Italians and to the world?*

H4 *D. Mack Smith also wrote* Mussolini's Roman Empire, *which was published in 1976.*

H4

"Despite the fascist declaration that they never used the odious methods employed by other colonising nations ... the instructions [of Mussolini] were not only to execute prisoners but to continue to use poison gas and a systematic policy of terror and extermination .... One Italian journalist, unable at that time to refer to such matters publicly, noted in his diary what was happening, how mock trials were held where the accused understood nothing and how petrol would sometimes be poured over prisoners to burn them alive. Some prominent citizens surrendered on the promise of a pardon only to be shot out of hand ....

Haile Selassie later recalled that the first generation of Ethiopian elementary schoolteachers were systematically exterminated and the development of the country consequently set back decades."

H5 *How the Abyssinian conquest appeared outside Italy: a cartoon by the British cartoonist, David Low.*

BARBARISM   **CIVILIZATION**

7 *Who is Mack Smith's main source? Why was he unable to speak in public about what he had seen?*

8 *How might David Low have got the information on which he based his cartoon?*

9 *What are sources H4 and H5 saying about the Italian occupation of Ethiopia?*

10 *Compare cartoon H5 with picture H3.*

11 *What problems would a historian like Mack Smith face in checking the accuracy of 'atrocity stories'?*

12 *What do these sources tell you about the nature of Fascist rule?*

Alliances

From 1937 it was downhill all the way as Mussolini became more dependent on Hitler. Formerly he had been independent and as ready to co-operate with France and Britain as with Germany. Indeed in 1934 he had prevented a Nazi takeover of Austria. However first the Ethiopian adventure and then his support of Franco in the Spanish Civil War ended any chance of an alliance with France and Britain. In 1936 Italy signed with Germany and Japan the Anti-Comintern Pact, withdrew from the League of Nations the following year, and supported the Nazi takeover of first Austria and then Czechoslovakia. In the spring of 1939 Mussolini sent 100,000 Italian troops into Albania and deposed his former ally King Zog. In May 1939, the Pact of Steel was signed with Germany.

Pact of Steel with Germany

The German alliance was not popular and Mussolini was warned by his military advisers that Italy would not be ready for a major war for another three years. This Mussolini told Hitler when he signed the Pact of Steel. Consequently he was annoyed and worried when Germany invaded Poland only three months later. His military advisers were able to keep him from going to war in 1939 but in 1940, as German troops smashed through Northern France, he insisted on declaring war against France and Great Britain believing that Italy could not fail to win some speedy and impressive victories.

War declared

It was a disastrous mistake. The attack on the South of France was inglorious. The Italian army in North Africa and the Italian navy at its Taranto base were crippled by British attacks. Worse followed in the Balkans. What was expected to be a triumphant march from Albania to Athens became a humiliating retreat which was only ended by the arrival of German reinforcements. In 1941 Italian East Africa, including Ethiopia, was conquered by the British and so low was Hitler's opinion of his ally that he did not even bother to consult him before invading Russia.

The war was very much Mussolini's war and he could not survive in defeat. In June 1943 the Allies, victorious in North Africa, invaded Sicily, Italian soil. Within a month the Fascist Grand Council had voted him out of power. Hardly a protest was heard as the king had him arrested and replaced him as Prime Minister by Marshal Badoglio.

Mussolini arrested

German rescue

Only the Germans supported him now. They organised a daring raid which freed him from prison and set him up as head of their puppet state of Salò in Northern Italy. But Mussolini had had the stuffing knocked out of him. He hardly appeared in public and his most significant act was to order the execution of those Fascist leaders whom he considered traitors, including his own son-in-law. In the last days of the war he was captured with his mistress by Italian partisans. They were shot and their bodies hung up head downwards for public display in one of Milan's main squares.

Death of Mussolini, 1945

The obvious cause of Mussolini's downfall was the failure of his absurdly overambitious foreign policy and military schemes. His fall was so rapid because his approach to the Fascist party had been 'to divide and rule'. In contrast to Hitler he would not allow the Fascist Party to develop a strong organisation nor did he win the loyalty of his chief lieutenants. His rule sat comparatively lightly on the back of Italian society and was blown to oblivion by the gales of war.

Source I: Italy and the Second World War

I1 *A Soviet cartoon of 1943.*

1 *What is represented as a striped animal? What sort of animal is it and why?*
2 *What does the trap represent (see page 228)?*
3 *Who is sinking with a stone round his neck?*
4 *What is the main message of the cartoon?*

I2 *Here Adolf Hitler is quoted, speaking in 1944.*

5 *In what parts of the world and with what success did the Italian armed forces see action during the Second World War? What successes had they?*
6 *What truth if any is there in Hitler's statement? Explain the reasoning.*
7 *If Mussolini was ever able to 'pass judgement without emotion on events' during the last months of his life how should he have regarded the consequence for a) Italy, and b) himself, of his unshakeable friendship with Hitler and Nazi Germany?*

I2

"When I pass judgement . . . without emotion on events, I must admit that my unshakeable friendship for Italy and the Duce may well be held to be an error on my part. It is quite obvious that our Italian alliance has been more of service to our enemies than to ourselves."

13 Germany 1918–45

A defeated and bitter nation

Defeat made Germany a bitter and violently divided land. Many Germans, including many ex-soldiers, refused to believe that they had been fairly beaten on the battlefield. They preferred to believe that 'the November criminals' (Jews, Communists and politicians generally) had somehow stabbed them in the back. They also convinced themselves that the Allies had double-crossed them by getting them to stop fighting by promising them a moderate peace and then at Versailles forcing a harsh one on them. Moreover the collapse of the Kaiser's government left a political vacuum which no single political party was able to fill. Since the Allies kept their blockade going through the winter of 1918–19 the economic situation was grim. Communists plotted violent revolution (see source A1), and nationalists threatened violent counter-revolution.

The Spartacists, 1919

Bolshevik-style revolution seemed near. In Berlin in January 1919 Karl Liebknecht and Rosa Luxemburg led a Spartacist (Communist) revolt. Chancellor Ebert who was leader of the Socialist Party (SPD) sent Noske, a colleague, to deal with it. Unable to get much assistance from other Socialists and trade unionists, he used ex-army volunteers, the Free Corps, to restore order. The Spartacist leaders and a thousand of their followers were brutally murdered without a trial.

The Weimar Republic

Also in January 1919 elections were held for a new parliament (Reichstag). The SPD won the largest share of the votes (38 per cent) and formed a co-alition government with two other moderate parties. Because of the un-rest in Berlin the new assembly met in the city of Weimar (hence the name Weimar Republic given to the republican parliamentary democracy which lasted from 1919 to 1933).

The constitution

The constitution of the Weimar Republic made the parliament (Reichstag) supreme in Germany. It was elected by proportional repre-sentation, which made possible a number of small parties. The three major ones in the 1920s were the SPD on the left, the German National-ists on the right and the Catholic Centre party. No one party dominated, so Weimar governments were coalitions.

Ebert

The President, who was also elected, selected the Chancellor (Prime Minister) and in emergencies could take power personally. The first President from 1919 until his death in 1925 was Friedrich Ebert, a Bremen saddle-maker by trade and for many years a leader of the SPD. The army chiefs had supported his becoming Chancellor in the last weeks of the war, since they hoped that as a moderate rather than extreme socialist he could prevent social revolution and get the best poss-ible peace terms from the Allies.

The Treaty of Versailles

The first great crisis of the new republic was the Treaty of Versailles (see pages 136–40). The Allies presented the Treaty to the German

Source A: The Spartacist rising January–March 1919

A1 *An election poster of the Bavarian People's Party, 1919 (Bavaria is a province of Germany). The caption reads: 'The Bolshevik is loose'.*

1 *How does the Bavarian People's Party see 'the Bolshevik' (source A1)? Who were the Bolsheviks (see page 124)? Why were they feared? Was the Bavarian People's Party left- or right-wing? Explain your answer.*

A2 *The Spartacists were a Communist group named after Spartacus, the gladiator leader of a slave revolt against Ancient Rome, and they planned a revolution similar to that of the Bolsheviks in Russia. Rosa Luxemburg was one of their leaders and this is her view.*

A3 *General Groener, who succeeded Ludendorff in October 1918 and was effectively in control of the German army until the end of 1919, writes to his wife on 17 November 1918.*

A4 *The Vorwarts building after the fighting between Spartacists and Free Corps, Berlin 1919.*

2 *Rosa Luxemburg was a communist, Ebert was a socialist. What important political principles would they have agreed about (see page 150)? About what did they disagree in the winter of 1918–19 (see source A2)?*

3 *Most army generals disliked the socialists. Why were they ready to support Ebert in the winter of 1918–19 (see source A3)?*

4 *The Vorwarts building (source A4) was the home of the Communist newspaper. What does the photograph tell you about the revolt? What happened to the leaders? How many Spartacists died?*

5 *How did German Communists feel about the Weimar Republic between 1919 and 1933?*

A2
"the role of the working class is to be realised only through the path of an armed workers' revolution".

A3
"I intend to support Ebert, whom I estimate as a straightforward, honest and decent character, for as long as possible so that the cart does not slide further to the left."

government in June 1919 without any previous consultation. Scheidemann, the Prime Minister, resigned rather than sign it, so harsh and humiliating did it appear. With the Allies threatening to take military action, a new government headed by Erzberger was formed, which did sign, but under protest. Millions of Germans never forgave it for doing so.

Threats to the government

The Weimar coalition governments faced constant threats from both the Left and the Right. In 1920 there were communist-led risings in the Ruhr and a right-wing revolt, the 'Kapp putsch' (attempt to seize power), in Berlin. The army helped put down the former; a general strike organised in support of the government by the Berlin trade unions dealt with Kapp. However, disorder and political terrorism continued. Erzberger, who had signed the Versailles Treaty, was assassinated in 1921. In 1922, it was the turn of Rathenau the Foreign Minister, because he was a Jew and had made a treaty of co-operation with the Soviet Union.

The inflationary crisis, 1923

In 1923 came the French occupation of the Ruhr (see page 164). The Germans replied with passive resistance. Unemployment rose rapidly and the German government started to pay its debts by simply printing money. The result was catastrophic inflation (Source B). Prices rose so fast that money lost almost all its value. Barter took the place of money and there were food riots. While everyone dependent on their savings (mainly the middle classes) was ruined, a few businessmen and landowners increased their fortunes. More communist revolts took place and an extreme nationalist party, the National Socialists (Nazis), tried to seize power in Munich (Source C). The government however stood firm.

State of emergency

Led by Stresemann and backed by the army it declared a state of emergency and suppressed all the revolts. Stresemann also called off the passive resistance to the French occupation and introduced a new currency (the rentenmark) with the aim of ending the runaway inflation. Both political and economic stability slowly returned. In 1924 the state of emergency was ended, the French withdrew from the Ruhr and, helped by the Dawes Plan for the payment of reparations, the economy improved.

Support for the government

Somehow in Germany, unlike in Italy, parliamentary democracy had survived. This was partly because of the courage and determination of the political leaders of the Weimar Republic and partly because the army chiefs and civil servants who stayed on from the imperial government supported it, though they despised it, as the least of the possible evils. However, the Republic had dangerous enemies. On the left, the communists hated it for its caution, its refusal to carry through far-reaching social changes and for the murder of the Spartacist leaders; on the right, the nationalists never forgave it for signing the Versailles Treaty.

Ebert died in 1925 and was succeeded as President by Hindenburg. The next four years were comparatively good ones. Stresemann, now Foreign Minister, managed to get on to better terms with Britain and France, loans from the USA helped the economic recovery and the Young Plan further lessened the burden of reparations. Though the nationalists strongly attacked Stresemann's policies they had only limited popular support. Hitler's Nazi Party won just 3 per cent of the vote in the 1928 elections.

The Great Slump

However, 1929 was the year of the Wall Street crash and the Great Slump which followed created circumstances which were fatal for the

Source B: Inflation

B1 *A waste-disposal yard in 1923 during hyper-inflation. Mark notes are for sale as waste paper. (The price-list reads: paper money 20,000 marks; old rags 50,000 marks; old bones 5,000 marks.)*

B2 *One woman's experience in the 1923 inflation is reported by Dr Frieda Wunderlich who edited a weekly magazine in Berlin.*

B2

"As soon as I received a salary I rushed out to buy the daily necessities .... My salary ... was just enough to buy one loaf of bread and a small piece of cheese or some oatmeal. On one occasion I had to refuse to give a lecture at a Berlin city college because I could not be assured that my fee would cover the subway fare to the classroom and it was too far to walk. On another occasion, a private lesson I gave to the wife of a farmer was paid somewhat better – by one loaf of bread for the hour. An acquaintance of mine, a clergyman, came to Berlin from a suburb with his monthly salary to buy a pair of shoes for his baby; he could buy only a cup of coffee."

B3 Mark exchange rates 1921–23.

B3

January 1921	64.9 marks to the dollar
January 1922	191.8
January 1923	17,791
July 1923	353,412
September 1923	98,860,000
November 1923	4,200,000,000,000
November 1923	New currency introduced

1 *What had happened in January 1923 to cause a financial crisis?*

2 *If you had had 400,000 marks in the bank in January 1922, how many dollars was that worth in* a) *January 1922,* b) *January 1923,* c) *July 1923,* d) *November 1923?*

3 *In the waste-disposal yard how did a box of money notes compare in value with* a) *old bones,* b) *old rags?*

4 *What problems did* a) *Dr Wunderlich and* b) *her clergyman friend face as a result of the 1923 inflation? What sort of people were able to survive better (see source B2)?*

5 *Things got better in 1924 and 1925, but what lasting damage did the 1923 inflation do?*

Weimar Republic. The depression hit Germany harder than any other European country because the American loans which had fuelled the recent economic recovery were withdrawn. As businessmen went bankrupt unemployment rose. In 1931 there were serious banking failures, including the large Darmstadt and National Bank. By the start of 1932 6 million Germans were out of work. This was an economic crisis greater than the country had ever experienced. Following so soon after the inflationary disaster of 1923–4 it caused millions to despair. As in Italy between 1920 and 1922, the extreme parties benefited most from such conditions. In 1928 the moderate SPD, Centre and People's Party had won between them 54 per cent of the vote. By November 1932 this had fallen to 34 per cent. On the left the Communist share rose from 11 per cent in 1928 to 17 per cent in November 1932, while the Nazi improvement was even more spectacular: from 3 per cent to 33 per cent.

Growing Nazi support

Adolf Hitler

Adolf Hitler, leader of the rising Nazi party, was born in Austria in 1889, the only child of a customs official. He did poorly at school and drifted to Vienna where he tried without much success to make a living painting postcards and advertisements. The 1914 war saved him from becoming a vagabond. Although turned down on medical grounds by the Austrian army, he was accepted by the Germans and fought uncomplainingly on the Western Front. He was awarded the Iron Cross for bravery and was promoted to the rank of corporal. During the disorders of 1919–20 he worked as a political agent for the army and joined, in Munich, the tiny and extremely nationalistic German Workers' Party. This he made his own and in 1920 left the army to devote himself full-time to politics. His party was renamed the National Socialist German Workers' Parts (NSDAP) or Nazi for short. It had its own newspaper, its private army of brown-shirted thugs (the Storm Section or SA) and by 1923 some popular support in Bavaria. Then, associating himself with General Ludendorff, Hitler tried to seize power in Munich, the capital of the province of Bavaria. This 'beer-hall putsch' was a fiasco (source C1) and brought him eight months' imprisonment. None the less it was not a completely wasted experience. He used the publicity of his trial to spread his ideas (source C2) and during his comparatively comfortable stay in prison wrote *Mein Kampf* (My Struggle) which was both an autobiography and political manifesto.

Munich putsch

Hitler's political philosophy

Mein Kampf shows that Hitler's political philosophy was thoroughly fascist. To Mussolini's ideas he added two particular twists. Nazism was much more racist than Italian Fascism. It held that racial types were quite distinct, that some were clearly superior to others and that interbreeding was wrong. Nazism decreed that the most superior race was the Aryan which included most Germans and was destined to rule the world. Definitely inferior were the Slavs of Eastern Europe and the Negroes. Especially inferior and dangerous were the Jews (see source D3) who were constantly plotting to infect and to weaken other races, since they were determined to dominate the world if they possibly could. The second twist was Hitler's plan for expanding Germany (see sources D1 and 2). The Aryans did not have the space in Central Europe which they deserved. Once the Treaty of Versailles had been scrapped and all Germans united in a single country, 'Lebensraum', or extra living space, would be won from the inferior Slavs in the East.

Source C: 9 November 1923 – The so-called Munich putsch

C1 *This extract is from W. Shirer's* The Rise and Fall of the Third Reich *published in 1960.*

C1

"a detachment of police blocked the way . . . the Nazis tried to talk their way through . . . a shot was fired and in the next instance a volley of shots rang out from both sides . . . . Within 60 seconds the firing stopped but the street was already littered with fallen bodies – sixteen Nazis and three police dead or dying, many more wounded and the rest, including Hitler, clutching the pavement to save their lives [Hitler then fled and was arrested two days later]. . . . Ludendorff did not fling himself to the ground. Standing erect and proud in the best soldierly tradition . . . he marched calmly on between the muzzles of the police rifles . . . and was arrested on the spot."

C2 *Hitler speaks from the dock. (The sentence of the court was the acquittal of Ludendorff and five years' imprisonment for Hitler, which was reduced to nine months.)*

C2

"the eternal court of history will judge us, the Quarter-Master General of the old army, his officers and soldiers, as Germans who wanted only the good of their own people and Fatherland, who wanted to fight and die. You may pronounce us guilty a thousand times over, but the goddess of the eternal court of history will smile and tear to tatters . . . the sentence of the court. For she acquits us."

1 *Why did November 1923 seem a good time to try to seize power by force?*

2 *Who was 'the Quarter-Master General of the old army' and why was Hitler so pleased to have him as an accomplice?*

3 *Why, despite Ludendorff's bravery, did the 'putsch' (attempt to seize power) fail (see source C1)?*

4 *What was Hitler's aim during his trial?*

5 *What does the decision of the court suggest to you about the political attitudes of the Munich judges? Explain your answer.*

Source D: Selections from *Mein Kampf*

1 *What was* Mein Kampf?

2 *It is not written particularly clearly: summarise sources D2 and 3 and make their meaning clear.*

3 *What would you expect Hitler's attitude to the League of Nations to be (see page 146)? Quote the sentence(s) from* Mein Kampf *which support your argument.*

4 *From this evidence what would you expect to be Hitler's main aims: a) in foreign policy, b) in home affairs?*

5 *What arguments would you use against Hitler's extraordinary anti-semitism (criticisms of the Jews)?*

6 Mein Kampf *was published in Germany in the 1920s and was translated into English in the 1930s. How reliable is it as evidence of Hitler's aims? Comment on these aims. Why do you think so many people ignored them for so long?*

D1

"we National Socialists consciously draw a line beneath the foreign policy of our pre-war period. We take up where we broke off six hundred years ago. We stop the endless German movement to the south and west and turn our gaze on the land to the east."

D2

"What is refused to amicable [friendly] methods must be taken by force . . . . If land is desired in Europe, it could be obtained by and large only at the expense of Russia . . ."

D3

"Just as the Jew systematically ruins women and girls, he does not shrink from pulling down the blood barriers of others . . . . It was and is the Jew who brings Negroes into the Rhineland, always with the same secret thought and clear aim of ruining the hated white race by the necessarily resulting bastardisation of other nations . . . . The folkish ideology [Hitlers's ideas] must at last succeed in bringing about that nobler age in which men no longer see it as their concern to breed superior dogs, horses and cats but in raising man himself."

Hitler increases his political power

Enemy of parliamentary democracy though he was, Hitler decided after the failure of his revolt in 1923 that his best chance of winning power was legally through elections. Having got to power through democratic means he could then destroy democracy. From 1924 to 1929 he could do little else but pull together the party, which had split during his imprisonment, and wait. When after 1929 circumstances changed to favour extremists like himself, he used them with great skill. By allying himself with Hugenberg's Nationalist Party he won not only a stronger position in the Reichstag but greater publicity through Hugenberg's newspaper network. He obtained generous funds from industrialists like Kirdorf and Thyssen. From 1930 to 1933 he and his lieutenants campaigned energetically all over the country. Hitler himself was a brilliant speaker at mass rallies (see source E1) and in Goebbels he had a colleague who had a genius for propaganda and for giving the party an image of power and purpose through uniformed demonstrations and carefully staged ceremonies. Meanwhile Rohm's SA brownshirts increased their numbers and skill in street brawls against communists and socialists.

Hitler's appeal to the electorate

Moreover Hitler cunningly presented Nazism in different ways to different sections of the German people (see sources E1–6). To industrialists and landowners he would be a crusader against communism, to the middle classes (see source E1) a defence against both big business and revolutionary workers. To farmers (see source E2) he would give subsidies against falling prices, and to workers the hope of steady employment (see source E4). To all Germans he promised a revival of national power. He himself appeared a simple man without airs and graces, an honest patriot devoting his life to Germany's recovery. That he also preached a message of hate against the Jews and the communists – 'the November criminals', – did not harm his cause. His audiences between 1930 and 1933 needed people to blame. That he and his brownshirts (see source E6) obviously were ready to use violence to get their way and could possibly misuse power once they gained it was generally ignored. Hitler was a master of deception. He could appear to be the most reasonable and moderate of men when it suited him. He convinced not only ordinary people but many experienced German and foreign politicians that he was a statesman who could be trusted.

Electoral successes

The Nazis went from electoral success to electoral success. In the 1930 elections they won 18 per cent of the votes and 107 seats, in July 1932 37 per cent and 230 seats. This made them much the largest single party in the Reichstag. Hitler also challenged Hindenburg in the presidential elections of 1932. Though he lost, he gained 13 million votes against Hindenburg's 19 million. He was clearly a politician with a future.

Weak government

Chancellor from 1930 to 1932 was Bruning of the moderate Centre Party. With the extremist parties growing in strength in the Reichstag and brawling in the streets, he was unable to maintain an effective coalition government and often had to rule, as the Weimar constitution allowed, by presidential decree. However, in 1932 he fell out with President Hindenburg who replaced him as Chancellor first with Papen (May–December 1932) and then General Schleicher (December 1932–January 1933). Neither could create a strong government against

Hitler becomes Chancellor

Nazi opposition and Papen persuaded Hindenburg to invite Hitler to become Chancellor. The President viewed the idea with reluctance, because he disliked Hitler and his party's violence. Papen went back to Hitler and got him to agree that in the new government of eleven ministers only three would be Nazis. Papen and other experienced politicians persuaded themselves and Hindenburg that they could control Hitler, particularly since the Nazi share of the popular vote had fallen back in the last election (November 1932) from 37 per cent to 33 per cent.

New elections

They could not have been more wrong. Hitler's moment had come. As the new Chancellor, Hitler immediately requested another election. The brownshirts terrorised the cities and Goebbels made good use of the state radio. Then on the night of 27 February 1933 the Reichstag building went up in flames. Perhaps the half-crazy Dutch revolutionary, van der Lubbe, who was arrested, tried, and found guilty, was the criminal; perhaps the Nazis were responsible and framed him. Whatever the truth may be, the Nazis blamed the Communists and redoubled their hate campaign against them. In the March elections of 1933 the Nazi vote rose to 44 per cent. With the support of the 8 per cent won by Hugenberg's Nationalists, they had an absolute majority in the Reichstag. This they used to expel the eighty-three Communist deputies. By a huge

Enabling Law

majority the Reichstag then voted an Enabling Law which allowed Hitler to rule for the next four years without interference from parliament.

Hitler in power

As he had planned, Hitler had come to power legally according to the rules of the Weimar Republic. Armed by the Enabling Law he now set to work to destroy this parliamentary democracy and replace it by a totalitarian dictatorship. All political parties, except the Nazis, were banned by the end of 1933. Trade unions were replaced by the Nazi Labour Front. Local government was also nazified. The only serious

Dealing with the opposition

opposition remaining was within the Nazi Party and in the army. The first he eliminated with cold-blooded ruthlessness by the so-called 'Night of the Long Knives' in 1934. Röhm, leader of the SA, wished to bring the army under his control. He was also critical of Hitler whom he considered was treating the old ruling classes of Germany too gently. Hitler did a deal with the army chiefs who hated Röhm and his ambitions. He would destroy the SA leader if they promised complete loyalty to him personally. Röhm was summoned to a party conference where he was murdered by members of the SS, Hitler's personal bodyguard. Thousands of other SA leaders, and others against whom Hitler had a grudge, were also killed. When Hindenburg died a month later, Hitler took over as Head of State as well as Chancellor and every member of the armed services took an oath of personal obedience to him as their 'Führer' (Leader). The military chiefs were kept content by rapid rearmament and the success of Nazi foreign policy. They were also carefully watched. If, like Generals Fritsch and Blomberg in 1938, they showed signs of independence, they were sacked and disgraced.

Loyalty to Hitler

Once war broke out, Hitler took direct and detailed control of all military operations. Even when he had led them to catastrophic defeat most of the armed forces continued to serve him loyally to the end. This was partly because of the oath which they had taken and partly because the SS had been expanded under Himmler into an army within the army, 600,000 strong. The SS were responsible for some of the worst Nazi atrocities. Since they could expect little mercy from Hitler's enemies they remained fanatically loyal to him and were always on the watch for plotters.

Source E: The appeal of Hitler and Nazism

E1 Inside the Third Reich *by Albert Speer,
1970. These are the memoirs written during
his imprisonment after the Second World War
by one of Hitler's closest associates. Speer, who
was an architect, designed buildings for
Hitler, became a personal friend, and from
1942 to 1945 was Minister of Armaments. His
father was a prosperous architect, his mother
the daughter of a businessman. Both were
liberals politically. He first heard Hitler speak
in 1930 at Berlin University.*

1 *What surprised Speer when he first saw
Hitler?*

2 *How did Hitler win over the students? What
does his success at Berlin University tell
you about Hitler as a political leader?*

3 *What was Speer's chief reason for joining
the Nazi Party?*

4 *What were the main reasons for his mother
joining the Nazi Party?*

5 *Both Speer and his mother were intelligent,
well-educated, artistic and civilised people.
What would have been the main 'rough
spots' for them in Hitler's ideas? Why was
Speer not too bothered about these rough
spots?*

E2 *This comes from a Nazi leaflet for the
presidential election, 1932.*

E3 *Another Nazi leaflet, this time for the
Reichstag elections of July 1932.*

6 *What was the economic situation in
Germany in 1932 and 1933?*

7 *How strong was the Nazi Party in 1932?
Who did it see as its main rivals
politically?*

8 *What does the Nazi Party offer* a) *to
German farmers,* b) *to German women
(sources E2 and 3)? Where, in the Nazi
view of things, do the main threats to
Germany come from?*

E1

"His appearance surprised me. On posters and in caricatures I had seen
him in military tunic, with shoulder straps, swastika armbands and hair
flapping over his forehead. But here he was wearing a well-fitted blue
suit and looking markedly respectable . . . . Then in a low voice, hesi-
tantly and somewhat shyly, he began a kind of historical lecture rather
than a speech . . . . His initial shyness soon disappeared . . . . He spoke
urgently with hypnotic persuasiveness . . . I was carried along on the
wave of enthusiasm which one could almost feel physically bore the
speaker along from sentence to sentence. It swept away . . . any reser-
vations. Finally Hitler no longer seemed to be speaking to convince. . . .
It was as if it were the most natural thing in the world to lead students
of . . . the greatest university in Germany submissively by a leash.

I applied for membership in the National Socialist Party and in
January 1931 became Member Number 474,481.

It must have been during these months that my mother saw an SA
parade in Heidelberg. The sight of discipline in a time of chaos . . . of
energy in an atmosphere of universal hopelessness, seems to have won
her over also.

I did see quite a number of rough spots in the party doctrines. But I
assumed that they would be polished in time, as has so often happened
in the history of other revolutions. The crucial fact appeared to me that
I had personally to choose between a future Communist Germany or a
future National Socialist Germany since the political centre . . . had
melted away."

E2

GERMAN FARMER YOU BELONG TO HITLER! WHY? The German Farmer stands in
between two great dangers today:

The one danger is the American economic system – BIG CAPITALISM!

The other danger is the Marxist economic system of BOLSHEVISM:

Big Capitalism and Bolshevism work hand in hand; they are born of
Jewish thought and serve the past plan of world Jewry.

Who alone can rescue the farmer from these dangers? NATIONAL
SOCIALISM!

E3

GERMAN WOMEN! GERMAN WOMEN! Our Young People Defiled: Dr Zacarias,
Dresden, reports as follows:

. . . in a German Grammar School for Girls 63 per cent of the girls had
experienced sexual intercourse and 47 per cent had some form of sexual
disease . . . . The number of sexual offences and cases of incest pile up
in the most gruesome manner . . .

This is the result of many years during which our people and in
particular our youth have been exposed to a flood of muck and filth, in
word and print, in the theatre and in the cinema. These are the results
of the systematic Marxist destruction of the family . . . .

German women and mothers. Do you want your honour to sink
further? Do you want your daughters to be playthings and the objects
of sexual lust?

IF NOT then vote for a National Socialist Majority on 31 July.

E4 *'Hitler: Our Last Hope' – a poster of 1933.*

E5 *Cartoon by John Heartfield. The caption reads: 'Millions stand behind me', and the title is: 'The memory of the Hitler salute'.*

E6 *Christopher Isherwood, an English novelist living in Berlin, writes of the weeks immediately after Hitler had become Chancellor in 1933.*

9 *What is the message of the poster (source E4)? How clever a political poster do you think it is? Explain your answer.*

10 *What is the message of the Heartfield cartoon (source E5)? Is it friendly or unfriendly to the Nazis? Explain your answer. Why should Big Business support the Nazis?*

11 *Who are the SA men (source E6)? Why did no one help the Jewish writer?*

12 *Write a short essay explaining how the Nazis were able to win the votes of so many Germans between 1930 and 1933, and why once they were in power they met with little opposition.*

E6

"Almost every evening the SA men come into the café. Sometimes they are only collecting money; everybody is compelled to give something. Sometimes they have come to make an arrest. One evening a Jewish writer ran into a telephone box to ring the police. The Nazis dragged him out and he was taken away. Nobody moved a finger. You could have heard a pin drop, till they were gone .... A young communist was arrested by the SA men, taken to a Nazi barracks and badly knocked about."

Nazism and the churches

Another possible centre of opposition to the Nazis was Christianity, since so many Nazi ideas were clearly anti-Christian. However, both the Protestant and Catholic churches in Germany were strongly anti-communist and favoured strong government. Consequently they began by welcoming the Nazis. For the rest of the 1930s Hitler could count on the support of most Protestants, except for a small group of courageous priests who formed the Confessional Church and whose leaders, Bonhöffer and Niemöller, ended up in concentration camps. The Roman Catholic leadership became increasingly concerned about the barbarism of the Nazis and their treatment both of Catholics and of Jews. In 1937 Pope Pius XI, who had concluded the Concordat with Mussolini (see page 192), openly criticised the government. The Nazi answer was to persecute individual German Catholics, so the new Pope, Pius XII, was less strong in his criticisms, for fear of provoking further persecution.

Controlling people's minds

Influencing German youth

Before long the German public had little information other than what the government was ready to allow (see sources F and G). Newspapers, the radio and the cinema newsreels (an important source of news in those days) were controlled by Goebbel's Ministry of Propaganda. Censorship was strict and books disapproved of by the government were sometimes ceremonially burnt. Hitler was particularly keen to win the hearts and minds of German youth. Teachers whom the Nazis thought unreliable were sacked, syllabuses and textbooks rewritten to fit Nazi principles (see source F1). Young people were encouraged to join the Hitler Youth (see source F2) and League of German Maidens which combined physical training and leisure pursuits with further instruction in Nazi thinking.

Treatment of Jews

Jews began to be ill-treated in 1933 when they were dismissed from the civil service and from university teaching. In 1935 they were forbidden to marry non-Jews and lost their German citizenship. Employment was harder to find and many shops and professions refused them service. Worse followed in 1938 after a Nazi diplomat was assassinated in Paris by a Jewish youth. In revenge Jewish shops and synagogues were looted and destroyed, 20,000 Jews were arrested and 70 killed or seriously wounded. The Jewish community then had to pay for the damage caused. By the time war broke out those German Jews who had been unable to leave the country were somehow surviving in ghettos. As part of the so-called 'Final Solution' of the Jewish problem they were taken away to concentration camps between 1941 and 1945 and killed.

The law-courts and judges became servants of the government so there was no legal defence against Nazi terror. People disappeared and were never heard of again. The concentration camps held a growing number of people arrested without a trial.

Hitler's popularity

None the less, feared though Hitler must have been by many Germans, he was enthusiastically supported by many more. He was a greatly respected, indeed loved, leader both in peace and in war. His personal popularity was always greater than that of his party and came as much from women as from men.

He was popular between 1933 and 1939 because he was successful. He gave a strong lead (see source G1) and apparent unity after years of weak government and social conflict. Through their control of the mass media, youth movements and education, and the use of constant rallies (see source G3) and ceremonial events (particularly the 1936 Olympics) the Nazis maintained an image of confidence and purpose. Moreover there was a rapid economic recovery.

Source F: Nazi youth and education

F1

F1 *The* Nationalist Socialist Educator (*the Nazi guide for teachers*) *recommends a modern history syllabus for senior secondary school pupils.*

1 *During weeks 13–20 what years of German history would be taught?*

2 *What would you expect to be main 'evidence' contained in the Manke and Pierre des Granges books recommended here?*

3 *Horst Wessel was a young member of the SA who died in a street fight with Communists in 1930. Though he seems in reality to have been an unpleasant young thug the Nazis made a legend of him. The 'Horst Wessel' song was the party anthem. Why do you think that the Nazi education chiefs gave so much attention to Horst Wessel? How would you expect him to be portrayed in the recommended book?*

4 *In what ways is this history a) similar to, b) different from the history which you are studying? What conclusions can you draw about the nature of Nazi education and society and your own education and society?*

Weeks	Subject	Relations to the Jews	Reading material
13–16	German Struggle, German Want. Blockade! Starvation!	The Jew becomes prosperous! Profit from German want	Manke: *Espionage at the Front*
17–20	The Stab in the Back	Jews as Leaders of the November Rising	Pierre des Granges: *On Secret Service in Enemy Country*
25–28	Adolf Hitler National Socialism	Judah's Foe	*Mein Kampf*
33–36	National Socialism at grips with crime	Jewish instigators of murder. The Jewish press	Dietrich Eckart: *Horst Wessel*
37–40	Germany's Youth at the Helm! The Victory of Faith	The Last Fight against Judah	*The Reich Party Congress*

F2 *Hitler Youth wait for the Fuhrer at a Nazi rally, Nuremberg, September 1935.*

5 *Why did the Hitler Youth have drums, uniforms and banners? Why were the Nazis so fond of rallies and other party ceremonies?*

6 *If Nazi education was successful, what should the boys in the photograph have been thinking? Is there any evidence that some of them might have been thinking differently?*

7 *What evidence would historians use to work out how effective Nazi education was?*

Economic recovery

Hitler had no interest in economics but he appointed an able financier, Schacht, as his Minister of Economic Affairs. He also ordered a massive programme of rearmament and public works. Big business was encouraged by government contracts and any labour unrest was crushed by the police. Schacht strictly controlled currency exchange rates and made trade deals with Eastern European countries where in return for food and raw materials they received German manufactured goods. Between 1932 and 1937 Germany's gross national product doubled. Unemployment dropped from 6 million in 1933 to 2.5 million in 1934 and to 1.5 million in 1936.

Rearmament

Hitler wanted the economy to be ready for war as soon as possible but he wished to rearm speedily without increasing taxes. Schacht prophesied economic disaster unless rearmament was paid for by higher taxation and he resigned in 1937. Hitler replaced him by Goring, who was already head of the air force and who carried on with Hitler's plans regardless. So swift and far-reaching were Nazi victories in the first part of the war that the immense costs of the German armies were born effectively by the defeated enemy. Not until 1942 were the German people required to make significant economic sacrifices to pay for the war.

Foreign policy successes

Above all Hitler was popular in the 1930s because of the success of his foreign policy (see source G3). He rearmed the army, navy and air force. He reoccupied the Rhineland. He reunited the Germans of Austria and of Czechoslovakia to the Fatherland. As he promised, he had defied the rest of the world, torn up the hated Versailles treaty and made Germany one of the most feared nations in the world.

Source G: Nazism as seen by Germans

G1 *Hitler does the first spadework for the Frankfurt-Heidelberg autobahn, 23 September 1933.*

G2 *A poster outlining the main achievements in Hitler's foreign policy.*

Zug um Zug zerriß Adolf Hitler das Diktat v. Versailles!

1933 Deutschland verläßt den Völkerbund von Versailles!

1934 Der Wiederaufbau der Wehrmacht, der Kriegsmarine und der Luftwaffe wird eingeleitet!

1935 Saargebiet heimgeholt! Wehrhoheit des Reiches wiedergewonnen!

1936 Rheinland vollständig befreit!

1937 Kriegsschuldlüge feierlich ausgelöscht!

1938 Deutsch-Oesterreich dem Reiche angeschlossen! Großdeutschland verwirklicht!

Darum bekennt sich ganz Deutschland am 10. April zu seinem Befreier **Adolf Hitler** Alle sagen: **Ja!**

G3 *A Party rally at Nuremberg, November 1934.*

These are all Nazi propaganda photographs.

1 *What is an autobahn? What is the intention of photograph G1?*

2 *What impression did the Nuremberg rallies (photograph G3) make on Germans and foreigners, do you think? How impressive does it appear to you?*

3 *What are the strengths and weaknesses of such photographs as a reliable record of Nazi Germany?*

4 *You do not need to read German to work out the main message of the list of dates poster. What is it?*

5 *You are a German businessman with English friends. You voted for the Nazis in 1933 since they seemed to you the best hope for Germany. It is now 1938 and you are in no doubt that you made a wise choice five years before. Write a letter to your English friends telling them about Hitler and his government; the information available to you would be similar to sources G1–3.*

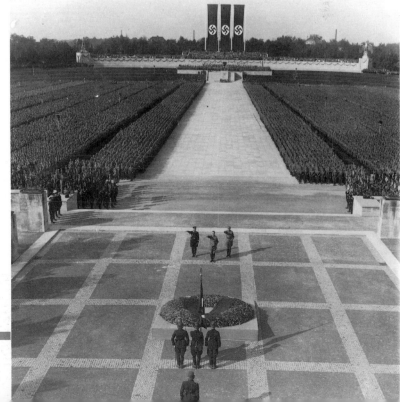

Victories and defeat

Though the outbreak of war was not greeted with popular enthusiasm, the extraordinary victories of 1939–42 were. The Führer seemed possessed of superhuman abilities. As victories changed to defeat, severe losses were experienced on the Russian front, German cities were pounded ceaselessly night and day by British and American planes and strict economic controls were enforced by Speer as he rapidly increased war production. Hitler disappeared from public view (see source H) and was replaced by Goebbels, who kept up national morale by passionate appeals for loyalty to the Führer and for the defence of the Fatherland against the Bolshevik savages. Simultaneously the SS became more powerful still and terrorised possible opponents of the regime.

Opposition to the government

There was therefore little internal opposition to the government. In 1941 the Bishop of Munster, Galen, spoke out from his pulpit against Nazi plans to kill the mentally sick. He was so highly thought of locally that the plans were abandoned. In 1943 young Munich students were less fortunate when they distributed thousands of anti-Nazi leaflets. Several were executed for so doing (see source I). The most important opposition was the group who tried to assassinate Hitler in 1944. They were mainly aristocratic conservatives who realised that Hitler had not only lost the war but was also immensely evil. They came near to success when Count von Stauffenberg was able to place a bomb in Hitler's operations room which blew up when the Führer was there. Unfortunately another officer had moved it quite by chance so that a thick table leg shielded the intended victim who was only slightly injured. The plotters were quickly arrested and killed by slow strangulation.

Attempts to assassinate Hitler

Atrocities of the government

The mass murder of the Jews was kept secret by the government. When they were taken from their homes it was said officially that they were being 'resettled'. While many Germans must have suspected that something dreadful was happening they knew that to speak out would have been extremely dangerous to themselves and their families. Not surprisingly few did. The Nazi regime only ended with complete military defeat and the suicide, flight or arrest of its leaders in 1945.

Source H: Suffering in Germany

H *Speer describes in* Inside the Third Reich *Hitler's reactions to popular suffering in Berlin during the autumn of 1943. By this time the tide of war had turned against Germany. Allied bombers were raiding German cities with increasing frequency and effectiveness.*

1 *What particularly upset Hitler about the bomb damage?*

2 *Why was he so keen to have theatres rebuilt quickly?*

3 *In Speer's view, the German people had more things to worry about than could be ended by attending a good entertainment. What sort of things would they have been worried about by the autumn of 1943?*

4 *Why should Goebbels, in particular, have been keen for Hitler to visit bomb-damaged areas?*

H

"Hitler was shaken by these reports [of bomb damage], although less by the casualties among the populace . . . than by the destruction of valuable buildings, especially theatres . . . . He betrayed a remarkable ignorance of the true situation and the mood of the populace when he answered all objections [to his demand that theatres be immediately rebuilt] with: 'Theatrical performances are needed precisely because the morale of the people must be maintained.' The urban population certainly had other things to worry about.

I tried a few times to persuade Hitler to travel to the bombed cities and let himself be seen there. Goebbels too tried to put over the same idea . . . . But Hitler regularly brushed aside any such suggestion. During his drives . . . he ordered his chauffeur to take the shortest route where formerly he loved long detours. Since I accompanied him several times on such drives, I noticed with what absence of emotion he noted the new areas of rubble through which his car would pass."

5 *What does this extract tell you about Hitler's attitude to the German people?*

6 *How close was Speer to the events he describes in this extract? How fair do you think his comments are?*

Source I: Opposition to Hitler

I1 Opposition to Hitler at Munich University, 1942–3, *a leaflet distributed in the University in 1942.*

I1

"Hitler leads the German people into the abyss. Hitler can no longer win the war, he can only prolong it.

But what do the German people do? It sees nothing and hears nothing . . . Germans, do you and your children want to suffer the same fate as the Jews? . . . Shall we forever be the most hated people in the world? No! Part company therefore with the National Socialist sub-humans . . . . A new war of liberation is beginning . . . . Support the resistance movement and hand out leaflets."

I2

"You know as well as we do that the war is lost," she said. "Why are you so cowardly that you won't admit it?"

I2 *The leaflet writers and distributors were members of the 'White Rose' group led by Hans and Sophie Scholl. They were caught in the university with a suitcase full of leaflets in February 1943, tried, found guilty of treason, and guillotined. Sophie Scholl, who was only twenty-one, had her leg broken by the Gestapo during her interrogation yet had the courage to speak her mind during her mockery of a trial.*

1 *The 'White Rose' leaflet makes three main criticisms of Hitler. What are these?*

2 *What is their main criticism of the German people?*

3 *What did they hope to achieve by their leaflets? How realistic were they?*

4 *If you had been a student in Munich in February 1943 and were beginning to have doubts about the Nazi movement, what effect do you think that the Scholls' example and their dreadful fate would have had upon you?*

5 *What light does this extract throw on the claim of many Germans, once the war was over, that they had no idea what Himmler and the SS were doing to the Jews?*

14 Hitler's war

Hitler's aims

Hitler made his vision of the future clear in 1924 when he wrote *Mein Kampf*. He intended Germany to dominate the world. This domination depended on winning living-space in the East (see source C1 on page 203) where vital raw materials like Ukrainian grain, coal from the Don valley and oil from Romania and the Caucasus would be seized. The Slavs would need to be conquered and made servants of the Aryan master race. A war would also be necessary against France to prevent her coming to the aid of the Eastern Europeans. Once in control of the 'heartland' of Europe and Asia, Germany could live in peace alongside Italy, Japan, a declining British Empire and a USA decaying fast through infection by the Jews.

Unfortunately hardly anyone in the 1930s believed that Hitler still took these astonishing ideas seriously and so, up to 1939, Hitler cleverly played the part of a determined German nationalist who merely wished for the unfair terms of the Treaty of Versailles to be put right. Then he

Source A: Different views in Britain about Hitler

A1

A1 *Lord Lothian writes to a friend in January, 1935. Lothian had been secretary to Lloyd George, the former Prime Minister, and was himself a minister in the National Government of 1931–2. In 1939 he became Ambassador to the USA.*

"I am convinced that Hitler does not want war. I believe that what the Germans are after is a strong but not an excessive army which will enable them to deal with Russia . . . . Hitler is anxious to come to terms with us and I think trusts us . . . of course all the wolves of hatred and fear and suspicion are clamouring to prevent an understanding."

1 *How influential would you have expected Lothian's views to have been?*
2 *Had Germany any reason to fear the Russians? What was the attitude of most Britons towards Russia in the 1930s?*

3 *Explain the phrase 'wolves of hatred and fear and suspicion'. What might these 'wolves' have been saying about Nazi Germany?*

A2

A2 *Sir Horace Rumbold writes to the editor of* The Times *newspaper on 13 June 1936. Rumbold was British Ambassador to Berlin from 1928–33.*

"Hitler has quite consistently applied the principles of *Mein Kampf* in Germany herself. He has now got to apply them in his foreign policy and that's where the trouble is coming. The value of any understanding with Germany is not only that it may bring peace . . . in Western Europe but it may act as a drag on Hitler's adventures in Central and Eastern Europe. Once he embarks on any adventure in those regions war is, to my mind, a dead certainty."

4 *How much would Rumbold have known about Nazism? Would you therefore have regarded his advice as valuable?*
5 *When was* Mein Kampf *written? What principles of* Mein Kampf *would Rumbold have been thinking of when he refers to their being 'consistently applied . . . in Germany herself'?*
6 *Why did he expect Hitler to embark on adventures in Central and Eastern Europe?*
7 *How do Lothian (source A1) and Rumbold*

(source A2) disagree about Hitler? With whom did Chamberlain most agree? Explain your answer.
8 *What kind of understanding with Germany do you think Rumbold had in mind?*

could be trusted to guard the peace of Europe. Not until the war had begun did it become clear that his *Mein Kampf* schemes were as alive as ever.

Britain's policy of appeasement

The most important government to misjudge Hitler was the British. It could not decide what Hitler's plans were. The horrors of the First World War were still vividly remembered and the military experts were convinced that another war would be much worse, since the new bomber planes would get through any defence. Consequently British public opinion was very anti-war. As a 'Peace Ballot' organised by League of Nations supporters showed in 1935, Britons had great confidence in the ability of the League to keep the peace internationally by 'collective security'.

Moreover, where Germany was concerned the view that the Versailles Treaty had treated her unfairly was widely held in Britain, thanks in

Source B: Hitler's thinking (in public)

B

B *Hitler spoke to the Reichstag in November 1936, announcing to delirious applause that German troops were at that moment marching in to the Rhineland.*

"In this historic hour we all unite in two sacred vows. First we swear to yield to no force whatever in restoration of the honour of our people .... Secondly we pledge that now more than ever we shall strive for an understanding between the European peoples, especially for one with our Western neighbours .... We have no territorial demands to make in Europe ... Germany will never break the peace."

Source C: Hitler's thinking (behind closed doors)

C

C *The Hossbach Memorandum is the report of a meeting in November 1937 between Hitler, his Minister of War, and the Commanders in Chief of the armed services. (Colonel Hossbach wrote the report from memory, five days after the meeting.)*

1 *What had the Treaty of Versailles decided about the Rhineland?*

2 *What did Britain and France do about the German troops marching in?*

3 *Why was the reoccupation of the Rhineland such a triumph for Hitler?*

4 *What were Hitler's 'sacred vows' in source B? Why do you think he made them? Did he keep them?*

5 *Is there any evidence in source C that he is planning further expansion? What ideas of* Mein Kampf (*see page 203) does the Hossbach Memorandum repeat?*

6 *What are the chief differences between the aims of Hitler's public speech in the Reichstag and those of his secret military meeting?*

"He [Hitler] wished to explain ... his basic ideas concerning the opportunities for the development of our position in the field of foreign affairs ... he asked that his explanation be regarded, in the event of his death, as his last will and testament. [The Führer continued:]

"The aim of German policy was to make secure and to preserve the racial community and to enlarge it. It was therefore a question of space ... Germany's problem can only be solved by means of force ... After 1943–5 a change for the worse could be expected ... our relative strength would decrease in relation to the rearmament which would then have been carried out by the rest of the world .... It would of course be necessary to maintain a strong defence on our western frontier during ... our attack on the Czechs and Austria .... The incorporation of these two states with Germany meant, from the politico-military point of view, a substantial advantage because it would mean shorter and better frontiers, the freeing of forces for other purposes, and the possibility of creating new [military] units up to a level of 12 divisions, that is, 1 new division per million inhabitants."

7 *What evidence is there that Hitler thought that his statement at the military meeting was particularly important?*

8 *To what extent does the fact that Colonel Hossbach only wrote his report on the meeting five days later from memory lessen the reliability of source C?*

part to Keynes (see page 143). There might be much which did not seem particularly nice about Hitler but if all he really wanted was for Germans to be ruled by a German government, that was hardly worth a major war.

In addition, a war to defend parts of Central and Eastern Europe looked far from easy. The Dominions (Canada, Australia, South Africa and New Zealand) made it clear up to 1939 that they would not assist in another European war. Furthermore the government's military advisers exaggerated the military strength of both Germany and Italy.

For these reasons the National Government, with the wholehearted support of most Britons, followed a policy of 'appeasement'. By this was meant that Britain should give way to Hitler's demands. The Treaty of Versailles should be revised so that Germany would expand to take over all the German-speaking areas on her borders. Once this had happened, the German dictator would be satisfied and war would have been avoided. Linked to the appeasement of Hitler was 'not being beastly' to Mussolini so that the Italian dictator did not team up with the more dangerous German one.

The French attitude

The French never had the same hopes that Hitler could ever be satisfied but they did not feel strong enough to act without Britain. Nor were Anglo-French relations in the 1930s good enough for them to give a strong combined lead either in the League of Nations or in Europe.

Anglo-German Naval Agreement, 1935

The Rhineland reoccupied, 1936

We saw in chapter 13 how Hitler took Germany out of the League of Nations and began rearming and how Britain's response was to sign a joint naval agreement with him. Such a move did not increase France's confidence in Britain's readiness to defend Versailles. Hitler decided that he had little to fear from either the League or France or Britain. In 1936 therefore he ordered his troops to reoccupy the Rhineland (see map opposite) in breach not just of Versailles but of the Locarno Pact too. His was a most risky act taken against the advice of his generals. The German army was not yet strong enough to take on the French and a firm French response backed by Britain would have forced a speedy and humiliating retreat. Instead there was only a feeble protest. France had a temporary government and was waiting for a general election. Her generals overestimated the strength of the German army. For its part the British government considered that Hitler was 'only entering his own backyard' and was not ready to take action.

The reoccupation of the Rhineland was a decisive moment which began the slide of Europe towards the Second World War. Hitler had ignored the advice of his nervous generals. He had trusted his 'sleepwalker's instinct' and had won. Now he was sure that France and Britain did not have the will to resist him. Furthermore Mussolini, who had previously been suspicious of Germany and in particular had opposed the union of Austria and Germany which the Nazis wanted, was ready to work much more closely with Hitler. By the end of 1936 the two dictators boasted of a Rome-Berlin Axis around which the rest of Europe would have to revolve.

The Rome–Berlin Axis, 1936

The Spanish Civil War, 1936–9

They acted jointly and successfully in Spain during the civil war there between 1936 and 1939 (see pages 166–9). They signed the Anti-Comintern Pact with Japan in 1936 to oppose communism in all ways possible, and supported Franco's Nationalists as part of their anti-

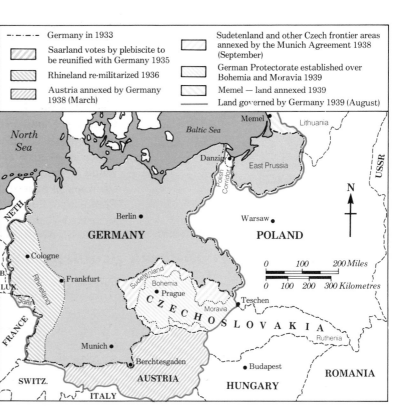

Hitler's aggressive foreign policy, 1933–9.

communist campaign. They sent planes, troops and supplies to help Franco. Mussolini sent the most, but German bombers were the most effective and most atrocious, bombing as they did the undefended town of Guernica on market day. All in all the Spanish Civil War provided useful military practice for the Fascist forces.

The British and French governments, in contrast, tried to follow a policy of non-intervention. Britain, France, Germany, Italy and the USSR all signed a non-intervention agreement in London in 1936 which the last three proceeded to ignore. When Franco was finally victorious in 1939 he joined the Anti-Comintern Pact but stayed neutral throughout the Second World War.

The Anschluss, 1938

Hitler's next move was against Austria. Since 1918 many Austrians had been keen on union (Anschluss) with Germany but it had been forbidden by the Versailles Treaty. Yet simultaneously the treaty had granted self-determination to other peoples; why not us, these Austrians argued.

Hitler, himself an Austrian, was determined to unite Austria and Germany. Already the Nazi Party had been used to try to achieve union in 1934, but though Dollfuss the Austrian Chancellor was murdered, the attempt failed, chiefly because of Mussolini's opposition. The next attempt in 1938, which Mussolini supported, was completely successful. After demonstrations by Austrian Nazis and military threats, German troops occupied the whole country without resistance. To the protests of Britain and France, Hitler argued that his action had the backing of most Austrians.

The Czech crisis

The Anschluss took place in March 1938. The next victims of Hitler, the same year, were the Czechs. The German dictator skilfully played on Britain's guilt feelings about the Versailles settlement. Within Czechoslovakia was a large German minority. It did not like Czech rule and had a Nationalist party which demanded that the Sudetenland (see map D1) where many Germans lived should be transferred from Czechoslovakia to Germany. Hitler took up this claim. All he was after, he said, was genuine self-determination for Germans in Eastern Europe. The Czechs stood firm. Without the Sudetenland their border with Germany would be defenceless and they were sure that Hitler wished to conquer the whole of Eastern Europe. The Czech army was quite strong, and both France and Russia might have fought with the Czechs, had Britain supported them too.

Source D: The Czechoslovak problem, 1938

D1 *The carve-up of Czechoslovakia, 1938–9.*

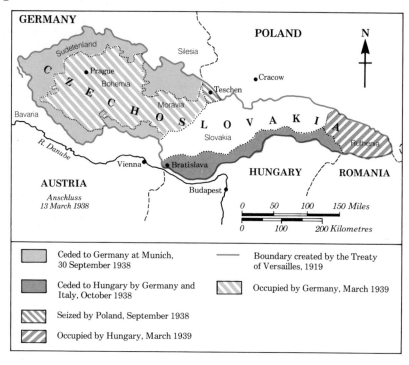

D2 *Neville Chamberlain wrote to a family friend in the USA on 16 January 1938.*

D2

"[The English people] realise that we are in no position to enter light-heartedly upon war with such a formidable power as Germany, much less if Germany were aided by Italian attacks on our Mediterranean possessions and communications. They know that France, though her army is strong, is desperately weak in some vital spots . . .

Therefore . . . until our armaments are strong we must adjust our foreign policy to our circumstances . . . I do not myself take too pessimistic a view of the situation. The dictators are too often regarded as though they were inhuman."

D3 *Lord Zetland, a friend of Chamberlain, had this to say.*

D3

"I remember him saying after he had flown back from Germany that as he saw spread out like a map beneath him the mile upon mile of flimsy housing which constituted the East End of London, he could not bear to think of their inmates lying a prey to bombardment from the air."

The Munich Agreement, 1938

However, the British Prime Minister Neville Chamberlain insisted on appeasement. He negotiated personally with Hitler. Eventually a conference took place at Munich at the end of September 1938 attended by Mussolini for Italy, Daladier for France, Hitler and Chamberlain. The Munich agreement handed the Sudetenland over to Germany. The Czechs, deserted and isolated, had no option but to submit. To add insult to injury, Germany and Italy then insisted (October 1938) that their Hungarian friends should have part of Slovakia (see map D1).

Rearmament

All Czechoslovakia seized, 1939

Memel, 1939

Germany's rearmament programme was accelerating, so Hitler saw little need for restraint. In May 1939 he occupied Bohemia (the Czech half of Czechoslovakia) and made the rest (Slovakia) a protectorate. This aggression finally convinced Chamberlain and British and French public opinion that he could not be trusted and that he would have to be resisted by force. However, the Fascist dictators had by now nothing but contempt for their opponents. The Germans seized the port of Memel from Lithuania, the Italians invaded Albania. They also announced the Pact of Steel, promising to aid each other in the event of a major war.

Poland threatened

In the summer of 1939 it was Poland's turn to be threatened. Hitler demanded that Danzig and the Polish Corridor, with their large German populations, be handed over to Germany. The Polish government refused and prepared for war. This time Britain and France guaranteed their

---

D4 *Entry in Chamberlain's diary, 20 March 1938.*

D5 *Chamberlain wrote to his sister after meeting Hitler at Berchtesgaden in September 1938 at the height of the 'Munich' crisis.*

D6 *This extract is from Peter Calvocoressi and Guy Wint* Total War, *1972.*

1 *Study map D1. What land was Hitler demanding of the Czechs? What were his stated reasons for wanting this land?*

2 *List the reasons which Chamberlain gives in sources D2–5 for not supporting Czechoslovakia. What other reasons did he have (see pages 215–6)?*

3 *What was the Czechs' view? How much did Chamberlain consult them?*

4 *Why do Calvocoressi and Wint (source D6) describe the Munich agreement of 1938 as 'a shameful act'?*

5 *List the reasons which they give for it being a foolish one too. Of the facts which they give, which did Chamberlain know about and of which would he have been ignorant?*

D4

"You have only to look at them to see that nothing that France or we could do could possibly save Czechoslovakia from being overrun by the Germans, if they wanted to do so . . . I have therefore abandoned any idea of giving guarantees to Czechoslovakia."

D5

"I had established a certain confidence which was my aim . . . in spite of the hardness and ruthlessness I thought I saw in his face, I got the impression that here was a man who would be relied upon when he had given his word."

D6

"In 1938 Czechoslovakia was the one country . . . ready for battle. Great Britain and France were not ready, nor was the USSR. More significantly, Germany was not ready. Nor of course was Italy . . . . Czechoslovakia was not only ready but strong, as strong as Germany in all important departments except manpower. The Czechoslovak army of thirty-five divisions faced a German army . . . which was slightly larger . . . . The Czechs were better equipped than the Germans in a number of ways, notably in artillery . . . . Czechoslovakia was the sixth industrial power in Europe . . . .

On a military calculation [Hitler's aggression] was the lunacy which his generals held it to be . . . .

. . . the avoidance of war in 1938 was not only a shameful act but . . . a foolish one."

D7 *Buckingham Palace. The caption to this picture from the* Illustrated London News *of 8 October 1938 read:*
'the crowd beyond the gates was chanting "We want Chamberlain!" . . . They [the King, Queen and Chamberlain] stood there, under the beam of a searchlight while the cheering throng sang "For he's a Jolly Good Fellow". Then the King motioned Mr Chamberlain forward, and he stood alone in front, acknowledging the acclamations [the cheers]'.

D8 *German troops occupy Friedland in the Sudetenland* (Illustrated London News, *8 October 1938).*

6 *From where has Chamberlain just returned? What had he just signed?*

7 *If Calvocoressi and Wint are right (see source D6) and this was such a shameful act, why did Chamberlain get such a hero's welcome?*

8 *Where is Friedland? Who is cheering the German troops and why?*

9 *Comment on the events in Czechoslovakia in early October 1938 from the point of view of Beneš, the Czech President.*

The Nazi-Soviet Pact

War declared, September 1939

War in Europe 1939–41

support. Much closer was Russia, but the Poles feared her, and Britain and France were clumsy in their efforts to achieve an alliance. Instead Stalin, trying it seems to buy time before a war with Germany (see page 180) agreed to a Pact with the Nazis (23 August 1939) and, nine days later, the German invasion of Poland started. Though there was little they could actually do to help the Poles, Britain and France kept their word and declared war on Germany. Only twenty years and ten months after the most terrible war in European history had ended, a second even more terrible one had begun.

The most noticeable feature of the first years of the war was the quality of the German army and its commanders. It used new tactics which it called the 'blitzkrieg' or 'lightning war' in which modern tank divisions attacked in concentrated formations with co-ordinated aircraft action (Stuka dive bombers) and infantry follow-up.

Poland defeated

Poland was defeated in a month. Cavalry, however brave, were no match for tanks and dive bombers, and neither Britain nor France could send effective help. The Russians invaded from the east and the country was divided between the conquerors. The USSR also attacked Finland and succeeded in conquering a large slice of the south of the country. None the less Finnish resistance was tough and it took the Russians until March 1940 to overcome it. Hitler concluded wrongly that the Soviet army was not up to much.

The phoney war

1940: First Denmark then Norway

Meanwhile in the West there was hardly a war at all. Germany had no immediate plans for an attack on France, and though Britain and France had declared war on Germany they contented themselves with a few minor attacks, bombing Germany with propaganda leaflets and declaring an economic blockade. They were particularly keen to prevent Swedish iron ore from reaching Germany and planned to take control of the Norwegian coastline. Hitler, however, read their minds and in April 1940 suddenly occupied Denmark and Norway, from where British troops were forced to make a hurried retreat. The Norway defeat was the end of Chamberlain as Prime Minister. He was replaced by Winston Churchill, who combined a passionate hatred of Nazism with a style of leadership and oratory which inspired the whole country with a will to win, even in the worst moments of defeat.

then the Netherlands, Belgium and France

Dunkirk

Such moments soon occurred. A month later the Germans invaded the Netherlands, Belgium and France. Airborne assaults followed by a surprise tank attack, brilliantly executed through the Ardennes mountains, divided and overwhelmed the Allied forces. The Ardennes attack had by-passed the formidable French defences of the Maginot Line. The Netherlands stopped fighting on 16 May, the Belgians surrendered twelve days later, by which time the British and part of the French army were cornered on the sea-shore at Dunkirk. For reasons which are not entirely clear Hitler delayed the assault on Dunkirk, which allowed the British and some of the French to be evacuated, though they had to leave their arms and equipment behind. France continued fighting for another fortnight but the military position was hopeless. Peace was finally signed on 22 June in the same railway carriage where the German surrender in 1918 had been accepted by Marshal Foch.

Fall of France

A delighted Hitler attended the signing ceremony in person. He had good reason to be pleased. His armies by following what was largely his strategic plan had won one of the more swift and decisive victories in modern warfare. The western and northern coast of France, the Paris region, Belgium and the Netherlands were occupied by his forces. The rest of France was allowed a pretence of independence under the government of Marshal Pétain at Vichy.

The Vichy government

German advantages

The German victory was not won because of any marked advantage in numbers nor in weapons, except in the air. The French and British had as many tanks but spread them thinly across their front line. The Germans' advantage lay in their tactics and their commanders. General Guderian master-minded their 'blitzkrieg' tactics and was ably supported by commanders like Manstein and Rommel.

Britain alone

The British must surely now ask for peace terms, thought Hitler, since their military position was so weak. He had no quarrel with the British Empire, just as long as he was left alone to run Europe as he wished. Yet though Britain was now completely isolated she was determined to fight on, as Churchill made plain in a series of memorable speeches. Reluctantly the German High Command put together a plan for the conquest of the British Isles. Since no invasion would stand a chance of success without control of the air over the Channel, the Royal Air Force and the Luftwaffe fought the 'Battle of Britain' over the southern

Source E: The fall of France

E1 *The German triumph in the West, 1940.*

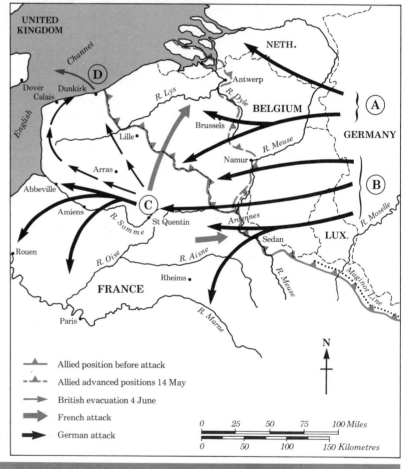

E2 *German tanks advancing through the Ardennes, May 1940.*

E3 *This extract is from* History of the Second World War, *B. H. Liddell Hart, 1970.*

1 *Identify the troop movements at A, B, C and D (source E1). Which was the main German attack? Why did Hitler decide that it should be there rather than further north or further south?*

2 *Which was the movement of the main French army? Why did it go in that direction? Where was the 'hinge of the advance'? What was the Maginot Line? Explain the phrase 'Maginot Line complex'.*

3 *What was so skilful about the German plan and its execution? What were the main mistakes of the French High Command?*

E3

"The German invasion of the West opened . . . on the right flank, against key points in . . . Holland and Belgium. These strokes . . . focused the Allies' attention there in such a way as to distract them from the main thrust – which was being delivered in the centre, through the hilly and wooded country of the Ardennes, towards the heart of France.

. . . the mechanised spearheads of Rundstedt's Army Group had mean-time been driving through Luxembourg and Belgian Luxembourg towards France. After traversing the seventy-mile stretch of the Ardennes . . . they crossed the French frontier and emerged on the banks of the Meuse early on the fourth day of the offensive. It had been a bold venture to send a mass of tanks . . . through such difficult country . . . the thick woods helped to cloak the advance and conceal the strength of the blow.

It was the French High Command however which contributed most to Hitler's success . . . . What proved fatal to the French was not as is commonly imagined their defensive attitude of 'Maginot Line complex' but the more offensive part of their plan. By pushing into Belgium . . . they played into the hands of their enemy . . . . With every step forward that their armies took into Belgium, their rear became more exposed to Rundstedt's flanking drive through the Ardennes. Worse still the hinge of the Allied advance was guarded by a few low-grade French divisions scantily equipped in anti-tank and anti-aircraft guns . . . . To leave the hinge so poorly covered was the crowning blunder of the French High Command."

The Battle of Britain

The Blitz

coastal counties of England during August and September 1940. It was a close-run thing. The Germans had more planes and pilots, the British had better planes and radar which gave them early warning of the size and direction of the German attacks. In August the RAF was reeling from the intense onslaught on its airfields but in September the Luftwaffe switched most of its efforts to the bombing of London (the Blitz). This allowed the RAF to gain the upper hand and in October the planned invasion was indefinitely postponed. The Battle of Britain was the first defeat the Germans had suffered. Hitler was not particularly bothered since Britain was nowhere strong enough to threaten his domination of Europe. However, as long as she remained undefeated she acted as a rallying point for all the enemies of Nazism and, in due course, the launching-pad for the forces which would liberate Western Europe.

1941: Yugoslavia, Greece, Crete

Before the end of 1940 Hitler had decided to proceed with his major aim, the attack on the USSR. He ordered his generals to be ready to move by May 1941. In the meantime he had to sort out south-east Europe where his Italian allies had got into all sorts of difficulties. Having already been defeated by the British in North Africa they were having trouble in the Balkans at the hands of the Greeks, who were being reinforced by Britain. Another superbly executed blitzkrieg conquered Yugoslavia and Greece, including the island of Crete. The British were driven back to Egypt where they were mauled by Rommel's Afrika Korps.

Operation Barbarossa, June 1941

Counterattack, December 1941

The attack on the USSR (Operation Barbarossa) was eventually launched in June 1941. Although it was on a huge scale and a wide front, it took Stalin and the Red Army by surprise. Its immediate success was impressive. Leningrad was besieged, the suburbs of Moscow glimpsed. The Soviet loss of men and equipment was enormous and some of the richest agricultural and industrial areas fell to the invaders. However, Hitler had underestimated both the Red Army and the Soviet people. He thought that within six weeks the army would have no fight left and that within six months the whole country would have surrendered. On the contrary, in December when the winter had set in the Red Army was not only still fighting but was strong enough to counterattack and drive the Germans back from Moscow. New factories were built behind the Urals and the Soviet people settled to the task of clearing the enemy from their soil.

1941 – World War

The USA enters the war

Despite the fact that the Soviet Union was still alive and kicking Hitler did not hesitate to declare war on the USA when his Japanese ally attacked the US naval base of Pearl Harbor in December 1941. By then the USA and Germany were close to war anyway.

In 1939 public opinion in the USA wished that country to stay isolated from the troubles of Europe. It began to change in 1940, especially after the swift collapse of France. F. D. Roosevelt, who was elected President for the third time in 1940, believed Nazi Germany to be a danger to the whole world. He was able to persuade Congress first to give fifty second-hand destroyers to Britain in return for naval bases in the West Indies, and then to sign the Lend-Lease agreement (March 1941) which provided Britain with vital supplies, whether or not they could pay for them. In August 1941 Roosevelt and Churchill met on board ship off the Newfoundland coast and drew up a statement of principles about freedom and democracy, upon which the world should be based once Fascism had

Source F: Britain in 1940

F1 *A cartoon from* Punch: *'At Bay' by Bernard Partridge, published when the British and French armies had retreated to Dunkirk.*

1 *In source F1 explain what is represented by the lion, the arrow, and the meaning of the caption 'At Bay'.*
2 *Of what is the cartoon good evidence?*

F2 *The Battle of Britain – a Spitfire as seen from the gun turret of a Heinkel III as it dives through an attacking bomber formation.*

3 *What precisely would have been the targets of the Heinkel III during the summer of 1940?*
4 *What were its defences against a fighter like the Spitfire?*
5 *Why was there a 'Battle of Britain' in 1940? What was its result and how important was it?*

F3 *Churchill, with his cigar as usual, tours bombed Merseyside in 1941.*

6 *What position did Churchill hold in 1941?*
7 *Why should the Germans have bothered to bomb Merseyside?*
8 *With so much else to do, why should Churchill have taken the time to visit the bomb damage? What does this indicate about his qualities as a leader? What image of him does the photograph give?*

been defeated. This was called the Atlantic Charter. Then in November 1941 armed US merchant ships began carrying military supplies to Britain.

Hitler was not worried. He misjudged the strength and determination of the US as completely as he had exaggerated the feebleness of the Soviet Union. By leading Germany to war against these two mighty nations while Britain and the British Empire were still unbowed, he made Germany's defeat certain if the war lasted any length of time. Consequently the Axis powers had to win a quick victory before their disadvantages in numbers and in economic resources took effect.

1942

Further Axis victories

So 1942 was the crucial year of the war. At first everything went Hitler's way. In the Atlantic German U-boats played havoc with the merchant shipping bringing food and other vital supplies to Britain. In North Africa, Rommel was poised to conquer Egypt and to seize the Suez Canal and Britain's vital oil supplies in the Middle East. In Southern USSR another massive German offensive advanced hundreds of miles across the Don basin, reached Stalingrad on the Volga and threatened the oilfields of the Caucasus. In the Far East the Japanese swept all before them, conquering most of south-east Asia, humiliating the British by the easy capture of their great naval base of Singapore, and advancing on India and Australia.

Nazi power at its greatest extent, November 1942.

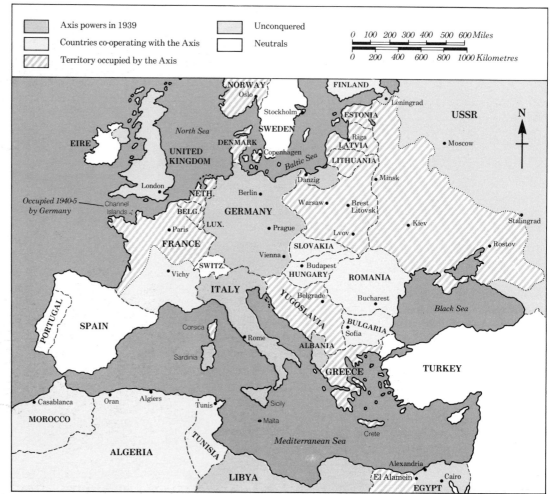

The tide turns

Midway, June 1942

El Alamein, autumn 1942

Stalingrad winter 1942–3

Then suddenly the Axis powers were not winning any more. In June 1942 the US navy inflicted heavy losses on the Japanese navy and forced its retreat from an attack on Midway Island in the Pacific. Midway was the turning-point of the Pacific war. In October and November Rommel's Afrika Korps, heavily outnumbered and outfought by Montgomery's Eighth Army at El Alamein, was driven westwards along the North African coast away from Egypt.

Simultaneously the most important single battle of the war was beginning at Stalingrad. The German Sixth Army of Paulus had been ordered to capture the city so that the advance on the Caucasus oilfields

Source G: Vital battles

G1 *Japanese power at its greatest extent, August, 1942.*

1 *What and where is Midway? What sort of battle was it? If the Americans had lost, which American possession and what important part of the British Empire would have been the next Japanese target?*

2 *Where is El Alamein? Who defeated whom? If the Germans had won, which country, vital sea-routes and crucial supplies might have fallen to them? To which North African city did Montgomery advance to by May 1943? Whom did he meet there? Which part of Europe did they together invade in November 1943?*

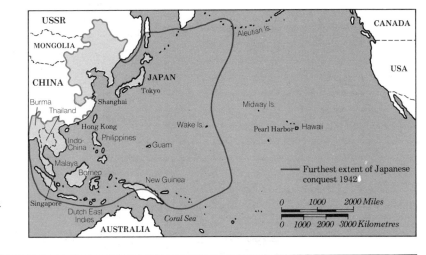

G2 *Allied victories in North Africa and Italy, 1942–4.*

① Eighth Army advance to Tunisia, from the Battle of El Alamein, Oct./Nov. 1942 — Feb. 1943

② Free French forces, supporting the Eighth Army

③ 'Torch' landings of Americans and British towards Tunisia, Nov. — Dec. 1942

④ German reinforcements Nov. 1942

⑤ Allied advance to Tunis, Feb. — May 1943

⑥ Eighth Army advance to Tunis, Feb. — May 1943

⑦ Allied invasion of Sicily and Italy, July-Nov. 1943

⑧ Allied advance in Italy

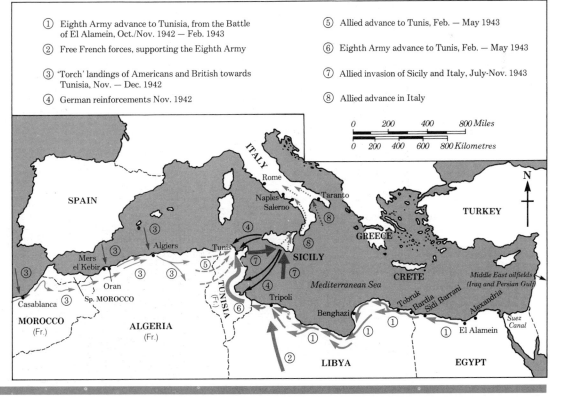

could continue without fear of a Soviet thrust from the north. Throughout the autumn of 1942 the Soviet defenders, though driven into a narrow section backing onto the river, hung on grimly so that Marshal Zhukov could prepare a counterattack, which was planned to catch the Sixth Army in a huge pair of pincers. Paulus's request to retreat was refused by Hitler, the pincers closed and all attempts to relieve him were beaten off. Finally in February Paulus surrendered, ignoring his Führer's instructions to fight to the last man. The Germans lost 250,000 men at Stalingrad and their army in the Caucasus had to beat a hasty retreat to avoid another disaster.

Source H: USSR 1942–3: Stalingrad

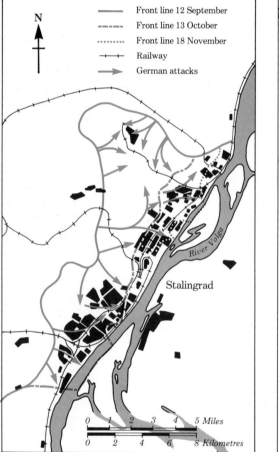

H1 (**Above**) *The struggle for Stalingrad, autumn 1942.*

H2 (**Right**) *The Russian front, 1942–3.*

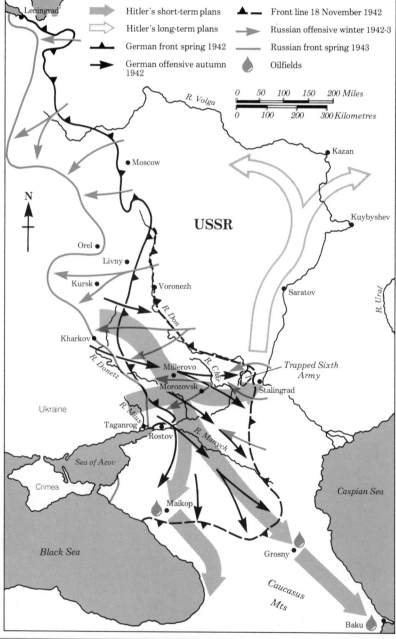

H3

General Franz Halder, Chief of the German General Staff, worked closely with Hitler at the beginning of the Stalingrad battle. He tended to tell Hitler how things really were. He was sacked in September 1942 and replaced by General Zeitzler, from whom the Fuhrer expected a more positive attitude. The description of Hitler in a rage is from his Memoirs. The remnants of the Sixth Army surrendered on 2 February.

"Once when a report was read to him [Hitler] that still, in 1942, Stalin would be able to muster from one to one and a quarter million fresh troops in the region north of Stalingrad ... and which provided proofs that Russian output of tanks amounted to at least 1200 a month, Hitler flew at the man with clenched fists and foam at the corner of his mouth and forbade him to read any more of such idiotic twaddle."

H4

The Russians launched their counter-attack against the German Sixth Army at Stalingrad on 19 November 1942. Zeitzler advised an immediate retreat. Hitler instead ordered the Sixth Army to stand fast. Within four days, the Russians had closed their pincers round the city. These are General Zeitzler's comments.

"On 22 December, I begged Hitler to authorise the breakout .... It was the last chance to save the 200,000 men of Paulus' army. Hitler would not give way. In vain I described to him the conditions inside the so-called fortress; the despair of the starving soldiers, their loss of confidence in the Sumpreme Command, the wounded dying from lack of proper attention while thousands froze to death. He remained impervious to arguments of this sort as to those others which I had advanced."

H5

Radio message from Paulus to Hitler of 24 January 1943.

"Troops without ammunition or food .... Effective command no longer possible ... 18,000 wounded without any supplies or dressing or drugs .... Further defence senseless. Collapse inevitable. Army requests immediate permission to surrender in order to save lives of remaining troops."

H6

Hitler replied by radio.

"Surrender is forbidden. Sixth Army to hold their positions to the last man and the last round and by their heroic endurance will make an unforgettable contribution towards the establishment of a defensive front and the salvation of the Western world."

Study source H2.

1 *If Hitler's plans for 1942 had been successful, what two vital areas would he have captured?*

2 *Why was Stalingrad so important?*

3 *How was the Sixth Army trapped? Which German general tried to save it in December 1942?*

4 *Where had the Russians advanced to by 1943?*

Study source H1.

5 *Did the Germans reach the river? How much of the city did the Russians control by 18 November 1942?*

6 *Why is 18 November the last date given?*

7 *What positions were held by* a) *Halder* b) *Zeitzler,* c) *Paulus?*

8 *Halder and Zeitzler were both writing about Stalingrad after the war was over. How reliable would you expect their memoirs to be?*

9 *Why were 22 November, 22 December and 24 January critical dates for the Sixth Army?*

10 *In what ways were the troops surrounded at Stalingrad suffering?*

11 *How did Hitler justify his 'no surrender' orders? Comment on the arguments which he used. What do they indicate about his state of mind?*

12 *List the weaknesses of Hitler as a military commander, shown by this evidence from the Stalingrad campaign.*

The Battle of the Atlantic, 1942–3

The Battle of the Atlantic took rather longer to win, and 1942 was a black year for the Allies. They lost more than 6 million tons of shipping and the Germans were able to increase the number of U-boats active in the Atlantic from 91 at the beginning of 1942 to 240 in March 1943. Two technical developments swung the struggle in the Allies' favour. The introduction of long-range planes like the Liberator provided much more effective protection for the convoys and short-wave radar enabled the surface vessels to detect U-boats well before the latter detected them. In the summer of 1943 fewer Allied ships were sunk and U-boat losses increased considerably.

Nazi persecutions

Meanwhile occupied Europe was experiencing the dreadful reality of Nazi rule. The Jews were treated the worst. Approximately 5,700,000 were murdered either in the gas chambers of concentration camps like Auschwitz and Belsen or by other methods of mass destruction. The extermination programme carried out by the SS on the orders of Himmler is unique in human history for its scale, efficiency and cold-bloodedness. The Slavs of Eastern Europe also suffered greatly. The Nazis regarded them as sub-human (Untermenschen) and treated them accordingly, stupidly destroying the goodwill of many who at first welcomed the German invasion as a liberation from Stalin's tyranny. The people of Eastern Europe and their land were used simply as resources for the German war effort. By the end of the war 7,500,000 people had been uprooted from their homes and taken as forced labour to the factories of Germany. Any opposition was dealt with mercilessly.

Resistance

Resistance groups soon appeared in every occupied country. Some were directed by governments in exile in London, other communist groups looked instead to Moscow, others had only a local base. They were particularly active in Russia, Poland, Yugoslavia and France, and played a useful part in the war by providing information and by acts of sabotage. For example the Norwegian resistance seriously disrupted the German effort to manufacture an atomic bomb by destroying their 'heavy water' plant. Resistance was very dangerous since the Germans tortured their captives and were ready to order revenge massacres of whole communities like those of Lidice in Czechoslovakia and Oradour-sur-Glane in France.

Source I: The realities of Nazi conquest

I1 *A German housewife, Else Wendel, describes what her husband, Rudolph, told her about the Eastern Front.*

1 *Rudolph Wendel mentions three different kinds of cruelty which his units had carried out. What were these? Why does he consider them foolish as well as wrong?*

2 *Why was the German treatment of the Russians much crueller than their treatment of the populations of Western Europe?*

I1

'"At first it was fine,' he said. 'We swept on adding towns and villages to our score. Then the troops began to get stale .... We behaved like devils out of hell. We left villagers to starve to death behind us, thousands and thousands of them. How can you win a war in this way? Do you think they won't revenge themselves somehow? Of course they will ....

We shoot prisoners at the slightest excuse. Just stick them up against the wall and shoot the lot. We order the whole village to look while we do it .... It's a vicious circle. We hate them and they hate us, and on and on it goes, everyone getting more and more inhuman.

Another of our mistakes was in the Ukraine .... the civilians were all ready to look on us as saviours. They had had years of oppression from the Soviets. They thought that we had come to free them. Does it sound absurd? Perhaps it does. What did we do? Turn them into slaves under Hitler.'"

12 *Hermann Graebe, a German engineer, describes, in the form of a sworn testimony to the War Trials court at Nuremberg in 1945–6, a mass execution of Jews which he saw at Dubno in the USSR on 5 October 1942.*

3 *For what reasons did Hitler order the extermination of the Jews (see page 202)?*

4 *What was the SS (see page 203)?*

5 *What do you think the SS men, described here, thought about their work? How, if brought to trial as war criminals after the war, would you expect them to have explained their actions?*

6 *Comment on the reliability of the source.*

13 *In the specially designed gas chambers of Auschwitz, 6,000 people could be murdered each day. There a million or more Jews died between 1941 and 1945. This is what Albert Speer (see page 206) has to say on his attitude to the concentration camps.*

7 *What posts were held by Hanke and by Speer in 1944?*

8 *Why should Hanke talk 'falteringly' and warn Speer never to visit a concentration camp?*

9 *How fully aware was Speer of what actually was going on at Auschwitz?*

10 *What did he do after his talk with Hanke? What could he have done? Would it have had any effect? What should he have done?*

11 *Hitler and Himmler both committed suicide. How would you expect the SS men in charge of the concentration camps to have defended their actions? How responsible do you consider such a defence?*

12 *From Speer's account, how much would you expect ordinary Germans to have known about Auschwitz?*

12

"The people who had got off the trucks – men, women and children of all ages – had to undress upon the order of an SS man who carried a riding or dog whip .... Without screaming or weeping these people undressed, stood around in family groups, kissed each other, said farewells and waited for a sign from another SS man, also with a whip in his hand .... An old woman with snow-white hair was holding a one-year-old child in her arms and singing to it and tickling it. The child was cooing with delight. The parents were looking on with tears in their eyes. The father was holding the hand of a boy about ten years old and speaking to him softly; the boy was fighting his tears. The father pointed to the sky, stroked his head and seemed to explain something to him ....

I walked round and round and found myself confronted by a tremendous grave. People were closely wedged together and lying on top of each other so that only their heads were visible. Nearly all had blood running over their shoulders.

The pit was already two-thirds full. I estimated that it contained about a thousand people. I looked for the man who did the shooting. He was an SS man who sat, his feet dangling into the pit. He had a tommy gun on his knees and was smoking a cigarette."

13

"One day, some time in the summer of 1944, my friend Karl Hanke, the Gauleiter [local Nazi Chief] of Lower Silesia, came to see me. In earlier years he had told me a great deal about the Polish and French campaigns ... and in talking about these things had shown himself a man of sympathy and directness. This time, sitting in the green leather easy chair in my office, he seemed confused and spoke falteringly, with many breaks. He advised me never to accept an invitation to inspect a concentration camp in Upper Silesia. Never, under any circumstances. He had seen something there which he was not permitted to describe and moreover could not describe.

I did not query him. I did not query Himmler [Head of the SS and responsible for the concentration camps], I did not query Hitler, I did not speak with personal friends, I did not investigate because I did not want to know what was happening there. Hanke must have been speaking of Auschwitz .... This deliberate blindness outweighs whatever good I may have done or tried to do in the last period of the war. Because I failed at that time, I still feel to this day responsible for Auschwitz in a wholly personal sense."

Source J: The French experience

J1 *German troops in Paris, 12 June 1940.*

J2 *De Gaulle broadcast from London to the French on 18 June 1940. De Gaulle, who was in command of a brigade of tanks in May 1940, was one of the few French commanders to distinguish himself during the German invasion. On 6 June Reynaud, the French Prime Minister, appointed de Gaulle Under-Secretary for War. Since the Germans were clearly victorious, he fled to London determined to continue the fight.*

J3 *Paris had just been liberated. That afternoon de Gaulle met the generals of his Free French army and Resistance leaders at the Arc de Triomphe. There, on the grave of the Unknown Warrior, the memorial to the fallen of the First World War, he laid a wreath. Then he walked down the greatest avenue of Paris, the Champs Elysées, through a delighted crowd of more than a million Parisians. This is what he wrote in his Memoirs for 26 August 1944.*

J2

"Nothing is lost to France. The same means that have defeated us can one day bring victory. For France is not alone! She is not alone! .... she can ally with the British Empire which holds the seas and continues the struggle. She can, like England, use without limit the tremendous industry of the United States.

I, General de Gaulle, at present in London, invite the French officers and men ... engineers and skilled workers in the arms industries who are in the British territory to get in touch with me.

Whatever happens the flame of French resistance must not be extinguished and shall not be extinguished."

J3

"I went on ... trying as I advanced to look at every person in that multitude in order that every eye might register my presence, raising and lowering my arms to reply to the cheers. This was one of those miracles of national consciousness ... which sometimes in the course of centuries light up the history of France."

J4 *A shaven-headed female collaborator carries her baby out of the town of Chartres after its capture by Allied troops, October 1944.*

J5 **(Below right)** *Paris, 26 August 1944.*

1 *What happened to France in the summer of 1940?*

2 *How and by whom was France ruled from 1940 to 1944?*

3 *What was meant by a) Resistance, b) collaboration?*

4 *What was de Gaulle's aim in his 1940 broadcast (source J2)? To what extent had he succeeded by August 1944? He made sure that he, alone, led the parade down the Champs Elysées. What does this tell you about him a) as a person, b) as a political leader?*

5 *You are a Parisian, fourteen years old in 1940, and you have heard the 18 June broadcast. It is September 1944 and you have a cousin in Switzerland. Write to him/her about the events in France in the summer of 1944 and your feelings about them. Build your letter round sources J1–5.*

Study source J4.

6 *Why does the woman with the baby have her head shaved?*

7 *What do you think is the attitude of the people around her?*

8 *Why was there such bitterness in France after liberation?*

Study source J5.

9 *Who is receiving the cheers of the crowd?*

10 *What had happened in the summer of 1944 which made possible the liberation of Paris?*

The defeat of Fascism: North Africa and Italy

After Stalingrad the Axis forces were everywhere in retreat. The Americans landed in Morocco, joined up with Montgomery's Eighth Army and cleared the Axis out of North Africa. In 1943 they invaded Italy and toppled Mussolini. However, there was no swift advance northwards up the peninsula. The Germans made good use of the mountainous countryside to mount an effective defence. The bulk of the German forces were concentrated against the Red Army, which they were unable to hold back since it was growing daily in numbers, in the strength of its armour and in confidence. The Russians were victorious in a major tank battle in the Kursk area and, at the beginning of 1944, crossed into Poland.

1944 The battle of Kursk

D-Day landings in Normandy

Stalin had frequently requested that Britain and the USA should open a second front in France and relieve some of the pressure on the USSR. At last, in the summer of 1944, a carefully organised Anglo-American seaborne invasion led by General Eisenhower attacked the coast of Normandy. These D-Day landings were successful and Eisenhower's forces, having broken out from the beaches after heavy fighting, swept across Northern France and liberated Paris in August (see sources J1–5). Hitler's orders forbidding any retreat made it much harder for his commanders to organise an effective defence.

Terror bombing

In Europe the Allies had won complete command of the air. This they used to bomb Germany very heavily. They aimed not only to destroy her economically but to terrorise her inhabitants into submission. They failed on both counts (see source K).

Hitler's hopes in secret weapons

By the end of 1944 Hitler was living in a fantasy world. His health had broken down and he relied heavily on drugs to keep going. He convinced himself that the war could still be won by secret weapons, by V-bombs, the Tiger tank, the super U-boat and the jet plane. However, none of these weapons could be manufactured in enough quantities to affect the course of war. There was only one weapon, the atomic bomb, which could have changed the outcome, but German scientists were still far from success in making one. Hitler also believed that he would be saved at the last moment by his enemies quarrelling amongst themselves, just as Frederick the Great of Prussia had been saved in 1762 at the end of the Seven Years War. What he failed to realise was that serious though the differences between the Allies were the dreadful things that Nazism had done would unite them until they had brought about its destruction.

Battle of the Bulge

In December 1944 Hitler managed to put together a force strong enough to counterattack in the West through the Ardennes. The Anglo-American armies were caught by surprise and in this Battle of the Bulge were driven back many miles before fuel shortages halted the German advance and allowed them to reorganise their defences. This was the last gasp of the German army. At the end of January 1945 the Russians had crossed the eastern frontier of Germany and, as Hitler sent a ever-larger proportion of his troops to slow them down, the Anglo-American forces got across the Rhine. There was hardly any resistance to them so they sped eastwards to the Elbe River which they reached on 11 April. There they halted to await the Russians.

Source K: The bombing of Germany 1943–5

K1 *Philip Knightley:* The First Casualty, *1975.*

1 *What was the true reason for the Dresden raid? Do you think that it was justified in the circumstances of February 1945?*

2 *Why was the truth kept from the British newspapers?*

3 *Was the killing by bombing of refugees in Dresden by the RAF morally any better than the killing of Jews by the SS? Explain your answer.*

4 *Knightley is a journalist. His book is less about war than about how journalists report wars and the effects of censorship. How reliable would you expect his account of the Dresden raid to be? What other sources would you use to check the account?*

5 *How useful would you expect newspapers to be to historians trying to work out what actually happened during a campaign? Explain your answer. If, like Liddell Hart, you planned to write a* History of the Second World War, *what do you think would be your most valuable source?*

K2 *Hamburg, autumn 1943. During the summer of 1943 Hamburg was bombed in much the same way as Dresden. Half the city's buildings were destroyed and 50,000 people were killed.*

6 *The bombing of Hamburg was also part of the attempt to break the spirit of the German population. How might the RAF Bomber Command have used photographs like source K2 to support its bombing? Is there anything in the photograph which could have been used by critics of the bombing?*

7 *On the whole 'terror' bombing seems to have strengthened the determination of the German population. What evidence would historians have used to reach conclusions about the effect on German morale of Allied bombing?*

K1

"[The British government decided] on a raid so great and terrible that it would precipitate the end of the war before Hitler could deploy his new V-weapons [rocket bombs].

Dresden was chosen and on the night of 13 February 1945 . . . the RAF struck at the city, crowded with refugees from the Russian advance, and dropped three-quarters of a million incendiary bombs which created a fire-storm, an artificial tornado in which air is sucked into the fire centre at an ever-increasing speed. At Dresden, winds approaching 100 miles [160 kilometres] per hour swept debris and people into the fire centre where temperatures exceeded 1000 °C. The flames ate . . . everything that would burn. People died by the thousands, cooked, incinerated, suffocated. Then American planes came the next day to machine gun survivors as they struggled to the banks of the Elbe. Precise casualty figures will never be known. The German authorities stopped counting when the known dead reached 25,000 and the missing 35,000. Some post-war sources put the number of dead at more than 100,000 which would greatly exceed the number killed in the atom-bomb of Hiroshima . . . and would make the Blitz total of 51,500 look small indeed.

The British newspapers at first accepted and published without query the official line, that Dresden was an important military target . . . but the railway marshalling yards were not even attacked . . . The truth first came out of Sweden . . . then in the United States the Associated Press reported 'Allied Air Chiefs have made the long awaited decision to adopt deliberate terror bombing of German population centres as a ruthless expedient of hastening Hitler's doom' . . . (this news did not appear in British newspapers until 5 March, nearly three weeks after the event)."

The end of the war – and its cost

Hitler's death

Hitler's failure

The defeat of Japan, 1942–5

From his bunker in Berlin Hitler ordered that Germany should be laid waste as the invaders advanced (see sources L1 and 2). Speer, Minister of Economic Affairs, refused to carry out this order and persuaded most industrial leaders and generals to ignore it. Berlin was surrounded by the Russians on 25 April. Five days later Hitler committed suicide: so too did Goebbels. All fighting formally ceased on 7 May 1945.

Just as Hitler had made an important personal contribution to the victories of 1939–42 so he had a major responsibility for the defeats of 1942–5. We have seen how he badly underestimated his opponents, especially the Russians and the Americans. He was also by nature quite unsuited to waging a defensive war. Moody, impatient and frequently unrealistic, he would order his armies not to give an inch of ground when a well-timed withdrawal and regrouping was called for. His generals found him increasingly difficult to work for but faced the sack and worse if they criticised him.

After their defeat at Midway Island in 1942 the Japanese were slowly driven back. But they refused to give up. Their military code made it impossible for many of them, particularly their officers, to think of surrender, however hopeless their situation. They defended every island and inflicted heavy casualties on the Americans. Their 'kamikaze' suicide pilots menaced the American navy. By the end of 1944 parts of the Philippine and Mariana Islands had been recaptured and the new giant B29 bombers were able to bomb the Japanese mainland. One raid on Tokyo killed 80,000 inhabitants. Yet still Japanese resistance continued.

Eventually in July 1945 President Truman of the USA decided to use the atomic bomb which Allied scientists had succeeded in inventing after

The defeat of Japan, 1943–5.

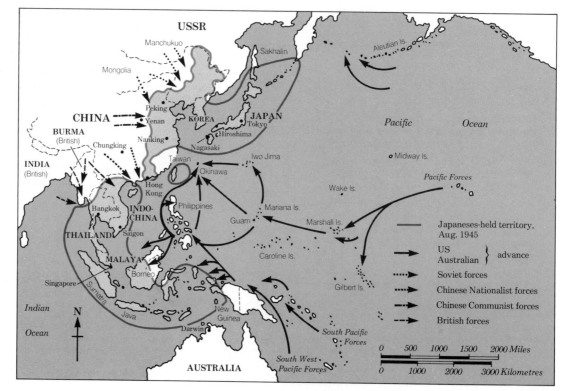

The first nuclear weapons

an intense research programme (the Manhattan Project, 1942–5). One atomic bomb was dropped on Hiroshima on 6 August 1945 and a second on Nagasaki on 9 August. Between them these two bombs killed 100,000 people. As a new frightening nuclear age began, the terrible war at last ended. The day after the Nagasaki bomb the Japanese agreed to surrender.

The costs of the Second World War

Like the First World War, only more so, the costs of the Second World War were so large as to be impossible to calculate accurately. The total number of dead was somewhere between 40 and 50 million. The USSR lost 18 million, Poland 6 million, Germany 4 million, Japan 2 million, Yugoslavia 1.5 million, France 530,000, Britain 350,000 and the USA 300,000. Cities were damaged and countryside laid waste on a similar scale. For example, France lost 70 per cent of her merchant ships, 40 per cent of Germany's buildings were damaged, 30 per cent of Poland's destroyed, as were 40 per cent of Yugoslavia's vineyards. Twenty-one million Europeans were homeless refugees and the economic life of the continent was as ruined as its major cities.

Source L: The last months of the war

L1 *The bridge across the Rhine at Remagen was not blown up in time to prevent the Allies crossing the river. On 15 March 1945 the German army newspaper reported that on the Führer's orders four officers had been executed for this failure. This is Speer's comment.*

L2 *Hitler's directive of 18 March 1945.*

Read sources L1 and L2.

1 *What was the military situation when this order was issued?*

2 *How does Hitler indicate that he still did not believe that the war was lost?*

3 *If you were the military commander of a small German town from which you were about to retreat what would you have to do to carry out this order to the letter?*

4 *Some commanders did obey the order. How would they have justified their action? Others disobeyed it. How would they have explained their disobedience?*

5 *What does this order indicate about Hitler's personality and state of mind?*

L1

"they were completely innocent but this 'shock of Remagen' kept ... [officers] in a state of terror until the end of the war".

L2

"The struggle for the very existence of our people forces us to seize any means which can weaken the combat readiness of our enemies and prevent them from advancing .... It is a mistake to believe that when we win back the lost territories we will be able to retrieve and use these transportations, communications, production, and supply facilities that have not been destroyed ... when the enemy withdraws he will leave us only scorched earth ....

Therefore I order: All military transportations, communications, industrial and food-supply facilities, as well as all resources within the Reich which the enemy might use either immediately or in the foreseeable future for continuing the war are to be destroyed."

15 Europe between the superpowers since 1945

In April 1945 cheerful and triumphant Russian and American troops met on the banks of the River Elbe. As allies they celebrated together as the remnants of the German armies laid down their arms. Their meeting marked the end of an era of world history. During the four previous centuries the continent of Europe had dominated the world. First the Portuguese and Spanish, then the Dutch, French and British had headed the list of Great Powers. Recently Germany had elbowed her way to the front. Now the German armies were destroyed, on the Eastern Front by the Russians – as many of whom were from Asia as from Europe, – and on the Western Front by an Allied army which was mainly American. Simultaneously in the Pacific the USA had defeated Japan virtually single-handed. In 1945 the USSR and the USA were by far the most powerful nations in the world; the USSR because of the size and proven fighting record of her armed forces, her large population and her potential rather than actual economic strength; America because of her military and industrial might and her scientific and technological know-how. Of the once great European powers, Germany was defeated and occupied, France humbled by the Nazi victories and occupation of 1941, and Britain, though undefeated, physically and economically exhausted.

Steps towards the 'Cold War'

Post-war Europe therefore had to recover and develop whilst caught between two superpowers who, within three years of their victory over Germany, were the bitterest of enemies. This enmity, which in the next forty years sometimes threatened but never actually caused a third world war, became known as the 'Cold War'. Every continent was affected by the Cold War, but Europe particularly so.

Its causes

Communism v. Capitalism

Tragic though the Cold War was, following so soon after the anti-Nazi alliance, its coming was not surprising. It stemmed from the deep and important differences between Soviet Communism and American Capitalist democracy, about the nature of society and political values. The USSR had had a Communist government since 1917. Communists believe that private property is wrong. In a good society all the means of production such as factories, mines, banks, farms and so on should be owned by the state representing the people and run in the interests of all citizens. Private ownership allows the rich to bully the poor and makes genuine equality impossible. Individual freedom is less important than the common good. Consequently Communism looks forward to a world-wide revolution which would bring Communist governments to power everywhere. In contrast the Americans believe in private enterprise. They are suspicious of public ownership, which is likely in their opinion to be inefficient. They also highly value individual freedom and consider that the greater the strength of the state and of state officials the less freedom will exist.

The governments of the USA and Western Europe had not welcomed

Distrust between
East and West

Lenin's successful revolution in 1917. On the contrary, as the Soviet government never forgot, the USA, Britain and France sent supplies and reinforcements to the White armies which unsuccessfully tried to overthrow the Bolsheviks. So much did Britain and France distrust Stalin's Russia that they were unable to form an alliance against Germany in 1939. Only Hitler's ceaseless aggression created the Grand Alliance of 1941–5. With Nazism destroyed, the profound differences between Soviet Communism and Western Capitalism resurfaced. Differences caused lack of trust, suspicion and fear. In 1945 the USA was the sole owner of the atomic bomb but by 1953 both powers had developed the hydrogen bomb.

Nuclear
weapons and
the arms race

Over the next four decades they committed themselves to an arms race of nuclear bombs and missiles that virtually guaranteed that in the event of war each could obliterate the other (and most of the rest of the world too). This Mutually Assured Destruction (MAD) may have helped to preserve peace but did nothing to encourage friendship and understanding.

The peace
settlement
Tehran, 1943
Yalta, 1945

Potsdam, 1945

Three major conferences were held between the USA, the USSR and Britain to decide the shape of Europe once Germany was defeated. The first two, Tehran in Persia (1943) and Yalta in the Crimea (1945) were held while the war was still in progress and were attended by Stalin for the USSR, Roosevelt for the USA and Churchill for Britain. The third was held at Potsdam, near Berlin in 1945 after the war in Europe had ended. Stalin again represented the USSR but for the USA Truman came in place of Roosevelt, who had recently died, while for Britain Churchill led the British delegation for the first week but then, having lost the general election back home, was replaced by Attlee, the new Prime Minister.

Agreements

There was agreement on some matters. The United Nations was set up. The surviving Nazi leaders were tried at Nuremberg. Peace treaties were signed with Italy, Finland, Bulgaria and Romania. Eastern Europe was to be a Soviet 'sphere of influence', Greece a British one. However, no agreement could be reached on three important issues; the future of Germany, the frontiers of Poland, and the character of the new governments of Eastern Europe. Disagreements on these vital matters brought the Cold War into existence. In 1946, while visiting the USA, Churchill warned that an 'iron curtain' was descending across Europe, dividing the Eastern Communist half from the anti-Communist West. By 1950 a barrier of minefields, walls and fences, patrolled by heavily armed guards and stretching more than 1,500 kilometres from the Baltic to the Black Sea, had become a reality.

Disagreements

Germany

The original plan for Germany was to keep her as a single country divided into four occupation zones, Soviet, American, British and French. Berlin the capital, which lay inside the Soviet zone, was also divided into four zones. A joint Allied Control Commission was set up to ensure co-operation between the four occupying powers. Though the USA, Britain and France had agreed that Germany should pay reparations, they decided before long to encourage the economic recovery of Germany, to treat their zones as a single economic unit and to reduce their reparations demands. In contrast the USSR continued to insist on reparations which included heavy machinery and other items from the zones of the other Allies. Meanwhile in local elections in the Soviet zone Communists did well. In the rest of Germany anti-Communist parties prevailed.

The Berlin airlift, 1948–9

An acute crisis erupted in 1948. A plan to reform the German currency angered the Russians. They walked out of the Allied Control Commission and cut all the land links between Berlin and West Germany: roads, railways, gas and electricity. The Western Allies believed that the Russians were putting their determination to the test. If they failed to act, first West Berlin and then perhaps other parts of Europe would fall to Communist aggression. Consequently they flew in vital supplies to West Berlin by air through the winter of 1948–9. The Berlin airlift was an expensive and difficult operation but it worked. The citizens of West Berlin refused to be intimidated into co-operation with Communist East Berlin and the Russians realised that to interfere with the airlift was likely to cause another war. In May 1949 they reopened the land links. One result of this crisis was the division of Germany into two parts. The Soviet zone became the German Democratic Republic (DDR) and the

Europe after the Second World War.

Western zones formed the German Federal Republic (FDR). The DDR was tied firmly into the Communist bloc of Eastern Europe while the FDR remained clearly in the American sphere. West Berlin was a capitalist island in a communist lake.

Poland

Poland also caused many difficulties. Britain and France had gone to war in 1939 to defend the Poles from Nazi aggression. After the Nazi conquest they had recognised the Polish government in exile as the rightful government. However, the exiled Poles, led by Mikolajczyk, were fiercely anti-Russian. For his part, Stalin regarded Poland as 'the corridor through which the enemy advances to attack Russia' and intended that the new Poland should be reshaped in the USSR's interest. This he was able to do since the country was liberated and occupied by the Red Army. A wide band of inter-war Poland now became part of the USSR, the Poles being compensated by a big slice of East Germany. The rivers Oder and W. Neisse became Poland's western border. At first Stalin agreed that members of the Polish government in exile could join a communist-dominated Provisional Government but, in the election of 1947, the anti-communist parties were so harassed by the secret police that they were swept away in a communist landslide. The Western Allies protested but there was nothing which they could effectively do.

The communist advance in Eastern Europe, 1945–9

Much the same happened in the other Eastern European countries, liberated from the Nazis by the Red Army. Broadly-based coalition governments were set up in which the Communist Party was strong. Key posts like the Ministry of the Interior (which controlled the police and security forces) would be held by communists. When elections were held, anti-communist political leaders were terrorised. Some were threatened personally, others feared for their families. Other were imprisoned and Jan Masaryk, a Czech leader, fell to his death from an upper floor window in mysterious circumstances. Moreover, ballot papers were lost or forged. By such methods the communists won overwhelming victories and in East Germany, Hungary, Czechoslovakia, Bulgaria and Romania were able to set up one-party communist governments closely linked to Moscow.

Stalin's aims

Of all of the Allied leaders Stalin had the clearest war aims. Having defeated Germany he wished to make sure that the USSR, who had lost 20 million people as a result of Hitler's aggression, could never again suffer the same way. Germany must be permanently weakened and a buffer be made by turning the nations of Eastern Europe into reliable allies. Only by installing communist governments could he be sure of their reliability. Thanks to the Red Army and his own brand of ruthless determination, he met with considerable success in achieving these aims.

Yugoslavia resists Stalin

Only Yugoslavia managed to defy Stalin. Tito, leader of the communist resistance, had liberated the country without the help of the Red Army. Popular and resourceful, Tito crushed the internal opposition and set up his own one-party state. At first Stalin had nothing but praise for his Yugoslav brother. However he soon began to find him too independent. Tito was recklessly anti-American. More seriously he had plans for alliances between the nations of south-east Europe which did not include the USSR. In 1948 Stalin ordered the Soviet newspapers and radio to brand Tito as an American spy! He attempted to have Tito overthrown by an internal plot, imposed a trade blockade and even considered an armed invasion. Tito survived however and enjoyed the staunch support of most Yugoslavs. His success made Stalin uneasy about the other communist leaders of Eastern Europe. Might they follow the Yugoslav example and develop their own kind of communism? To make sure that they did not he let loose a purge similar to those within the USSR in the 1930s. Leading politicians were placed on trial and amazed the capitals of Eastern Europe with their confessions of unbelievable crimes. Many were executed. In Poland 500,000 and in Czechoslovakia 300,000 members were expelled from the Communist Party. The new leaders were absolutely loyal to Moscow.

Source A: Tito's Yugoslavia

A1 (**Right**) *A Soviet cartoon of Tito published in 1949.*

1 *Who was Tito? What part had the Red Army played in driving the Germans out of Yugoslavia?*

2 *What did Stalin dislike about Tito?*

3 *In source A1 explain the top hat and swastikas. What is the message of the cartoon?*

A2 (**Below**) *Cartoon by David Low for the* Evening Standard, *March 1949.*

4 *Explain the Low cartoon.*

5 *What major geographical advantage did Yugoslavia have, compared with Poland or Hungary or Czechoslovakia, when it came to resisting the Soviet Union?*

Source B: Poland

B1 *Poland after the Second World War.*

Study map B1 and the map on page 240.

1 a) *Which two main powers had been neighbours of Poland between 1919 and 1938?*
b) *Why was Stalin determined to have a say in Poland's future?*
c) *How did Poland's post-war borders compare with those of 1939? Who gained? Who lost?*
d) *Why did Britain feel a particular responsibility towards Poland?*

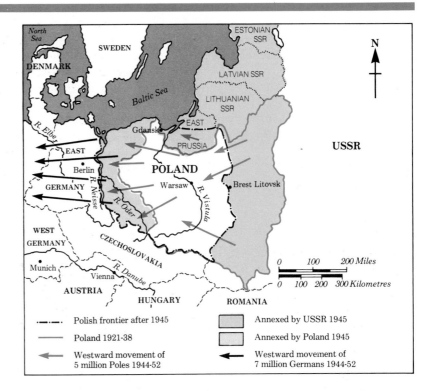

B2 *Communist rule comes to Poland. The Nazis were driven out of Poland by the Red Army during 1944–5. The boundaries fixed by the Big Three at Yalta and Potsdam shifted the country markedly to the west (see page 241). The Soviet Union gained much Polish land, while Poland gained at the expense of Germany. Most Poles moved out of the Soviet areas to be in Poland and 5 million Germans were expelled from the western areas.*

The following extracts are taken from a history of Poland by Norman Davies called God's Playground. *It was published in 1982.*

Read source B2.

2 a) *Why was Stalin in a strong position in 1945 to get Poland the way he wanted?*
b) *What evidence does Norman Davies give of the Soviet government bullying the Poles?*
c) *Where does he get his evidence from? Comment on its reliability.*

3 *List the ways in which the Polish elections of 1947 were neither 'free' nor 'unfettered' (source B2). How would a properly free and unfettered election have been organised?*

4 *Who was Mikolajczyk? What happened to him?*

5 *Why was there so little opposition to the Communist takeover of Poland?*

B2

"The Provisional Government [set up in 1944] ruled by permission of the Red Army. Bierut, the Polish Communist leader, was ordered by Stalin 'to change his methods or clear out' . . . .

Mikolajczyk [the leading anti-communist in the government] believed that every Thursday morning the Communist leaders met a Soviet Colonel [of the secret police] . . . to receive their orders . . . .

The January election of 1947 gave the Communist-led Democratic Bloc 80 per cent of the vote . . . . The election was neither 'free' nor 'unfettered' [as had been agreed by the Big Three at Yalta]. The list of candidates had been vetted in advance by the government. Two million voters had been struck from the registers by government-controlled electoral committees. Factory workers were marched to the polls by their foremen and told to vote for the government on pain of losing their jobs. The rules of secret balloting were ignored. The count was organised . . . by government officials.

In the Sejm [Assembly] the government had 394 seats against Mikolajczyk's 28. He was publicly denounced as 'a foreign spy' . . . and fled for his life [to an English exile].

The success of the Communists had proved far easier than anyone in 1945 had supposed . . . . Power passed directly and smoothly from the German Occupation forces to the Soviet Army, from the Soviet Army to the Soviet-controlled Provisional Government and then to the 'elected' Communist government. The Communists were handed Poland on a platter and successfully obstructed all attempts to share power thereafter."

*Civil War in
Greece*

The USA had hoped for friendlier relations with the USSR at the end of the war but Stalin's actions over Germany and Poland made her think again. Then in 1947 there was a crisis in Greece. A cruel civil war was being fought between communists and anti-communists. The former were winning and the British, whose sphere of influence Greece was, decided that they no longer had the resources to continue the fight against them. President Truman, arguing that if Greece fell to the communists many other European nations could do so too, persuaded the American Congress not only to agree to support the anti-communists in Greece but more generally 'to support free peoples who are resisting attempted subjugation by armed minorities or by outside pressures'. This policy, the Truman Doctrine, meant that the USA was ready to take action internationally to prevent the spread of communism. With American help, the anti-communist forces gained victory in Greece.

*The Truman
Doctrine, 1947*

*The Marshall
Plan, 1947*

Also in 1947 the USA offered a massive package of economic aid to Europe. Called the Marshall Plan (see sources C2 and C4) after the Secretary of State who announced it, the Plan was intended to bring about the economic recovery of Europe. It was offered to Eastern as well as Western Europe. While both generous and imaginative, it was also in the USA's long-term interest. A prosperous Europe with strong commercial links with the USA was less likely to fall under communist influence. For their part, the Russians treated the Marshall Plan simply as a capitalist plot 'to enslave Europe' and prevented their Eastern European neighbours from accepting aid. Czechoslovakia, who had attended the first 'aid' conference, withdrew with great reluctance.

The divisions harden

The Marshall Plan was a success and helped the nations of Western Europe into a spectacular economic recovery which was to continue through the 1950s and 1960s. The USSR's counter-move was to set up the Council for Mutual Economic Aid (Comecon) in 1949 to co-ordinate the economic development of Eastern Europe.

Comecon

Comecon aimed to guide the economies of the USSR and her satellites so they developed to each other's best advantage. Critics in the West argued that the Russians intended Comecon to work chiefly to benefit them. However from 1949 to 1956 most Eastern European nations aimed to make themselves self-sufficient rather than economically dependent on each other and when, after 1956, reacting to the success of the Common Market (see pages 258–9) Khrushchev attempted to get agreement on more co-operative policies, he met strong and successful opposition led by Romania. None the less there were some major co-operative achievements, particularly concerning energy supplies. The world's longest oil-pipeline – 'Friendship' – was built from the USSR to Poland, East Germany and Hungary, with links to Bulgaria and Romania.

NATO, 1949

The economic division of the continent was accompanied by its division into military alliances. The scare of the Berlin airlift crisis caused the USA, Canada and most of the nations of Western Europe to form the North Atlantic Treaty Organisation (NATO) in 1949. Its aim was to defend Western Europe from communist attack. Its members agreed to maintain powerful military forces to contain the USSR, in particular a large army in West Germany. Greece and Turkey joined NATO in 1952 and West Germany in 1954. The USSR said that NATO was 'a weapon intended to establish Anglo-American world domination' and in 1955 reorganised the armed forces of the communist bloc into a new alliance, the Warsaw Pact. So Europe was divided between the two superpowers.

*The Warsaw
pact, 1955*

Source C:
East–West divisions

C1 *An American cartoon from the* Cleveland Press, *late 1940s.*

1 *Study source C1. Who was Truman? What was his programme? Who is smoking the pipe? Explain the symbol on the pipe and the message of the cartoon.*

C2 *'Free pass for the Marshall Plan': a German poster of 1950.*

2 *Study source C2. Who was Marshall? What was his plan? Explain the flags on the lorry and the message of the poster.*

3 *Re-design the poster as if you were a cartoonist working for Cominform (see source C5).*

C3 *The Truman Doctrine. Speech by President Truman to Congress on 12 March 1947, requesting $400 million to intervene in Greece and Turkey (quoted by F. L. Schuman, in* Russia since 1917 *published in 1957).*

4 a) *What had been happening in Greece between 1945 and 1947 which so worried the USA?*
b) *What precisely did Truman mean by 'armed minorities' and 'outside pressures'.*

C3

"The very existence of the Greek State is now threatened by the terrorist activity of several thousand armed men, led by Communists, who defy the Government's authority .... Greece must have assistance if it is to become a self-supporting and self-respecting democracy ....

The US has made frequent protests against coercion and intimidation in violation of the Yalta agreement in Poland, Romania and Bulgaria .... I believe that it must be the policy of the US to support free peoples who are resisting attempted subjugation of armed minorities or outside pressures ..."

C4 *The Marshall Plan. An extract from a speech by George C. Marshall, US Secretary of State (Foreign Minister), on 5 June 1947.*

5 *What did Marshall fear would be the result of the economic, social and political deterioration to which he referred?*

C5 *The Manifesto of Cominform, October 1947. Cominform was the Communist Information Bureau set up in 1947 to spread communist ideas world-wide.*

6 a) *What was Cominform?*
   b) *Why was it so hostile to the ideas of Truman and Marshall?*
   c) *Truman and Cominform both claimed to be champions of democracy. How did their versions of democracy differ?*
   d) *What do you understand by democracy?*

C6 *Soviet protest on the formation of NATO, 1 April 1949.*

C7 Newsweek *magazine, 17 May 1948, quoted General Kenney, Commander of the US Strategic Air Command.*

C8 *Admiral Standley, US Ambassador to Moscow 1943–5 said this.*

7 *How did the USSR explain its close alliances with the countries of Eastern Europe? How likely does it seem to you that the USSR would have conquered Europe if she possibly could have between 1945 and 1950? Give your reasons.*

C4

"Europe's requirements for the next three to four years of foreign food and essential products – principally from America – are so much greater than her present ability to pay that she must have substantial additional help or face economic, social and political deterioration of a very grave nature . . . .

Our policy is directed not against any country or doctrine but against hunger, poverty, desperation and chaos. Its purpose should be the revival of a working economy so as to permit the emergence of political and social conditions in which free institutions can exist . . ."

C5

"Two opposite political lines have formed.

On the one side the policy of the USSR and democratic countries directed towards undermining imperialism and strengthening democracy; on the other hand is the policy of the USA and England directed towards the strengthening of imperialism and the weakening of democracy . . . .

The Truman-Marshall Plan is only a constituent part, the European, of the general plan of the world expansionist policy carried out by the United States in all parts of the world. The plan of economic and political enslavement of Europe by American imperialism is supplemented by plans for the economic and political enslavement of China, Indonesia and South America."

C6

"To justify the conclusion of the North Atlantic Treaty Organisation, references are being made to the fact that the Soviet Union has definite treaties with the countries of the Peoples' Democracies [the Communist nations of Eastern Europe] . . . . All these treaties of the Soviet Union . . . are dedicated solely against the possible repetition of German aggression. The possibility of interpreting these treaties as in any way aimed against the Allies of the USSR in the late war is absolutely out of the question . . ."

C7

"American strategists are thinking . . . of closing the circle of air bases around Russia, making it smaller and smaller, tighter and tighter until the Russians are throttled. This means getting closer to Russia's heartland through combined air, sea and ground operations then using the bases for sustained bombing and guided missile attack."

C8

"I have been wrong about the Soviet Government and its leaders but I have never been wrong about Communism. It is the religion of the devil, it is the distillation of evil; it is the very anti-Christ. We shall never be safe from this evil faith until it is driven back to the hell from whence it came."

8 *If you were a Russian and could read and understand General Kenney and Admiral Standley, what conclusions would you have drawn?*

The USSR and Eastern Europe since Stalin

Khrushchev

A year of two of 'collective leadership' followed Stalin's death. Then Khrushchev, First Party Secretary with many supporters among senior party members, emerged as the Soviet leader. He was a lively down-to-earth character with strong views, a sense of humour and a quick temper (see source D). One of his priorities was to give to ordinary Russians a better standard of living. He shocked the Twentieth Congress of the Communist Party in 1956 by severely criticising Stalin. In a speech which was never published within the USSR he portrayed the former revered statesman-who-never-erred as a blundering madman with criminal tendencies.

De-Stalinisation

His anti-Stalin line had a number of effects. It caused many Russians, particularly government officials and party members, to look critically at the past and to consider new approaches. For a time it meant less censorship of writers and artists. Solzhenitsyn's novel, *One Day in the Life of Ivan Denisovich*, the publication of which would have been unthinkable in Stalin's day, was a best-seller in 1962. Stalin's body was removed from its place of honour beside Lenin's in Red Square. These changes were, however, limited and did not alter the basic nature of Soviet rule, as Hungarians discovered to their cost.

Hungary, 1956

De-Stalinisation was infectious. In Hungary the Stalinist rulers were hated. Students and workers organised demonstrations against them and rose in revolt when the security police opened fire on them. The revolt brought to power a coalition government led by Imre Nagy (a communist disgraced by Stalin) which included non-communist parties. It demanded that Hungary should leave the Warsaw Pact and take a position of

Source D: Khrushchev and abstract art

D *The 'thaw' in censorship which followed Khrushchev's de-Stalinisation speech saw not only much more lively novels and poems but experimental painting and sculpture. This account of the Soviet leader's visit to such an art exhibition is taken from a biography of Khrushchev by R. Medvedev published in 1982, which quotes one of the sculptors who was exhibiting.*

D

"Khrushchev began his inspection in the room in which paintings by Bilyutin and some other friends of mine had been hung. He swore horribly and became extremely angry about them. It was there that he said that a donkey could do better with its tail . . . .

He said that I devoured people's money and produced shit. I told him that he knew nothing about art . . . . In spite of the fear in the air, I found him easy to talk to . . . . He spoke frankly – ignorantly but frankly – which meant that I could answer him back frankly.

My talk ended like this. He said, 'You're an interesting man. I enjoy meeting people like you. But inside you're an angel and a devil. If the devil wins, we'll crush you. If the angel wins, we'll do all we can to help you.' And he gave me his hand . . ."

[*The next day* Pravda, *the official government newspaper, printed this report.*]

"These people must recognise their mistakes and begin to work for the people."

1 *What does source D tell you about Khrushchev as a person?*

2 *If you were an artist at that exhibition, what would you have understood to be the Soviet government's policy towards the arts as a result of Khrushchev's visit?*

neutrality between East and West. Such a demand put at risk all the Soviet gains in Eastern Europe since 1945 and was completely unacceptable to Khrushchev. In November Soviet tanks rolled into Budapest and crushed the revolution. The leaders of the revolt were imprisoned, tried and executed in secret. More than 150,000 Hungarians went into exile. A government loyal to Moscow, headed by Josef Kadar, was installed.

Source E: Hungary 1956

E1 *A facsimile reproduction of the front page of the* Daily Express, *27 October 1956.*

1 *Read source E1. Note the date. Who is massacring whom? Who is reporting? Where is he? From where is he getting his information? How old is the news which he is reporting?*

DAILY EXPRESS

No. 17,553   SATURDAY OCTOBER 27 1956   3 a.m. forecast: Fine but cold   Price 2d.

Singing Hungarians fraternise — and then a Soviet tank opens fire
Red troops and secret police swoop on a border village

THE MASSACRES

600 'victory' marchers shot in Budapest Parliament-sq.

BUT REVOLT IS SPREADING

From SYDNEY SMITH: Austrian-Hungarian Border, Friday night

REPORTS of two massacres in which unarmed demonstrators were mown down by Russian tanks or motorised infantry reached me tonight on the Austrian border, the only escape point from embattled Hungary.

Tanks move in from Russia

SURRENDER OR DIE, NAGY WARNS THE INSURGENTS

From LAWRENCE DAVIS
AUSTRIAN-HUNGARIAN BORDER, Friday.

SOVIET tanks and troops are moving into Hungary tonight from Rumania and over the Carpathians from Russia itself.

The aim: To reinforce the Red Army trying to quell the uprising which is spreading from Budapest throughout the land.

Railways on the eastern borders are choked with Soviet infantry coming in and wounded moving out.

All the indications tonight are that fighting continues in Budapest — and insurgents are in control of many areas in the south of the country.

The situation that faces new Premier Imre Nagy and Party chief Janos Kadar tonight is completely out of control.

THE Government, in repeated, often

❶ A group of Russian tanks were stationed in Budapest's Parliament square and the soldiers were fraternising with the happy, cheering crowd, singing the old Hungarian anthems.

Then, without warning — a returning German business man told me — one of the tanks opened fire. There were 600 casualties from this one incident alone.

This incident was confirmed by Mr. Leslie Fry, British Minister in Budapest, reporting to the Foreign Office in London: As elsewhere in the town, the demonstrators were waving Hungarian flags with the Communist star cut out or obliterated. Almost without exception they were unarmed because they were confident they had overthrown the existing regime.

Suddenly a tank opened fire with "main armament" (cannon) and machine guns. Diplomatic observers estimate that there were at least 600 casualties within minutes.

❷ Three doctors crossing here tonight said that 70 people were killed and 290 wounded in a battle with Russian motorised infantry and secret police near Magyarovar, 16 miles from the border.

The doctors appealed for blood plasma, serums, and bandages for wounded they brought in an ambulance. Blood plasma and medical equipment is being rushed to the border from Vienna.

A Hungarian Army doctor — his Red Star emblem torn from his coat and replaced by a small green, red, and white national flag — told me as he went on to Vienna: —

"We are going to get food, medicines, and blood plasma, above all plasma. We need it for a hospital and first-aid station where there has been a lot of

2.35 p.m. — and the tanks roll in

Time: 2.35 p.m.   Place: A bridge over the Danube

Puskas dies in battle says report

FLOUR TO BE DEARER FROM MONDAY

By KENNETH PIPE

BAKERS will have to pay 2s. a sack more for their flour from Monday. Millers decided this yesterday

4.30 a.m. LATEST LIFEBOAT DRAMA

[See Page 5.]

Kelch Orenda put out dramatic call early today for assistance. Message said: "We have two sick men on board, one suffering from exposure, the other fallen from helicopter." Salcombe lifeboat went to their aid.

Economic developments

In economic matters Khrushchev achieved some success. The economy continued to grow at a healthy rate as did those of the East European 'satellites' (see sources F1–6). Khrushchev encouraged the construction and light engineering industries so that the population did enjoy better living standards. However, he foolishly boasted that by 1970 Soviet living standards would have caught up with American ones, a completely unrealistic claim. He was also unable to fulfil another boastful promise – that he would transform Soviet agriculture. Though he pushed through the sensible reform of abolishing the machine tractor stations, his ambitious 'virgin lands' scheme, which was intended to turn into good wheat-growing farmland previously unploughed regions of south-west Siberia, was an expensive failure. By 1964 his colleagues had had enough of him. They got together while he was on holiday and forced him from office, accusing him of 'hare-brained schemes' and of 'inability to take advice'. They were particularly critical of his reckless foreign policy and overambitious economic programme. The new leadership, dominated by Brezhnev, gave calmer, firmer and safer government, with sterner censorship and a renewed emphasis on military strength.

Khrushchev's fall, 1964

E2 *Some important dates taken from recent secondary accounts of the Hungarian Rising.*

E2

Early October 1956: Growing popular unrest in Hungary.

23 October: Huge anti-Soviet marches. Demands that Imre Nagy become premier instead of Gero. Soviet police and Soviet troops fire on crowd.

24 October: Nagy becomes Prime Minister.

27 October: Soviet army leaves Budapest. Nagy allows non-communist parties to revive.

30 October: Soviet reinforcements enter Hungary. Nagy forms new government including non-communists. Nagy takes Hungary out of Warsaw Pact.

4 November: Soviet troops re-enter Budapest. Declare Kadar to be the new head of the government.

14 November: All resistance finally crushed.

June 1958: Nagy tried and executed in secret.

E3 *Soviet tanks in Budapest: a telephoto released by the United Press photographic agency, dated 29 October. Its caption read 'Russian tanks stand guard . . . to stop rioting after a night of wild fighting. It is estimated that over 7,000 people have been killed . . . Premier Nagy announced over Budapest radio that all Russian troops are to withdraw from Budapest and appealed for a cease fire.'*

2 *Study sources E2 and E3. In what form did source E3 appear? Explain the apparent contradictions in the dates of E2 and E3. What did the Russian tanks do in the next few days?*

3 *What bias would you expect in these sources? Can you find any examples of bias?*

4 *What do the events in Hungary in 1956 suggest to you about the Soviet Union and Nikita Khrushchev?*

5 *Comment on the value of E1 and E3 as sources for the Hungarian Rising, 1956.*

Source F: Economic growth in the USSR and Eastern Europe

F1 *Annual percentage increases in net material product.*

	Bulgaria	Czechoslovakia	East Germany	Hungary	Poland	Romania	Yugoslavia
1949-54	10.4	8		8	9	13.9	
1956-63							9.6
1950-67	8	5.2	6.1	5.8	6.7	8.3	
1963-73							5.9
1966-70	8.7	6.9	5.2	6.8	6	7.7	
1974							8.5
1974-5	7.9	5.7	5.4	6.3	9.8	11.3	
1976							3.9
1978							6.9
1979							7
1976-80	6.2	3.7	4.1	3.2	1.6	7.1	

F2 *Ownership of wireless receivers and television sets (in thousands).*

	Bulgaria	Czechoslovakia	East Germany	Hungary	Poland	Romania	Yugoslavia	UK
Wireless receivers								
1949	205	2229			1055	226	220	
1959		3050	5061	1775	5000			
1968	2245	3200	5940			3030	3171	
1973	2266	3110		2533	5800	3100		
1979		3778	6290	2590	8560	3200	4600	
Television sets								
1958		328	318		▲1883			8900
1961	31			○605		■245		■12789
1968	620	2600	4170			1200		15506
1973	1381	3400		2199	5670	2100	2245	17293
1978	*2047	□4048	□5630	2630	7710	3600	4200	□18268

*Figure for 1980   □ Figure for 1979   ○ Figure for 1964
■ Figure for 1963   ▲ Figure for 1959

F3 *Number of physicians and hospital beds per 10,000 population.*

1 *Refer to F1, 2 and 3:*
a) *Which Eastern European country had the fastest rate of growth between 1949 and 1980; which the slowest?*
b) *What conclusions can you draw about the comparative standard of living of the DDR, Czechoslovakia and Bulgaria?*

2 *What conclusions can you reach about the comparative standard of living between Czechoslovakia and the United Kingdom?*

3 *Governments love statistics and are clever at presenting them in such a way as to suggest that things are always getting better as long as they are in power. In what other ways can standards of living in different countries be compared?*

	Bulgaria	Czechoslovakia	East Germany	Hungary	Poland	Romania	Yugoslavia	UK
Physicians								
1948		9		10	3.5			
1960	17	17.5	12.2	15.3	12.7	13.5	*7.1	12
1970	18.6	20	16.8	19.2	15.2	12.1	10	12.7
1977	22.6	25.3	18.9	23	16.5	13.6	13	15.8
Hospital beds								
1948		58		52	28	28		
1960	82.5	78.1	119	87.2	70.3	72.5		
1970	77.5	103	117.6	81.3	76.3	83.3	56.5	94.3
1977	87	123.5	106.4	87.7	76.3	91.7	60.2	112.4

*Figure for 1962
UK figures based on different calculations: not directly comparable

F4 *The Seven-Year Plan 1959–65.*
This was begun when Khrushchev was in
power. It caused him to boast that the USSR
would soon have a standard of living equal to
that of the USA. The following was the
opinion of Western economic experts, quoted by
Riasanovsky in his History of Russia (*1969*).

F4

"The industrial goals of the Plan were . . . realistic. If it is assumed that industry in the USA will continue to expand at about 4% and that the rate of growth planned by the Russians for their industry is actually achieved, their industrial output will rise from about 45% of ours at the beginning of the seven-year period to about 61% at the end. In other words they will still be far behind us (and even further behind in terms of per capita output . . .) though they will certainly have made a remarkable gain on us."

F5 *East-West cooperation, 9 July 1974.*
Leonov (right, USSR) and Stafford (left, USA)
train together for their joint successful space
mission.

F6 *'To train future specialists' reads the*
caption of this photograph of the Novosibirsk
Polytechnic published by the Novosti Press
Agency in August 1984.

4 *Read source F4. Why did Western economic*
experts disagree with Khrushchev's boast
that the USSR would soon equal the USA's
standard of living?

5 *Sources F5 and F6 are provided by Soviet*
information agencies. Such photographs
appear frequently in Soviet books.
a) Why do you think Soviet authors would
choose these photographs?
b) What are the strengths and weaknesses
of photographs as historical evidence?

Tanks in Czechoslovakia, 1968

Towards Eastern Europe Soviet policy remained the same, as events in Czechoslovakia in 1968 proved. Novotny, the Czech leader, was an old-style Stalinist. His government was rigid, cruel and increasingly clumsy. He upset students by strict censorship and the Slovak part of the population by his refusal to show much interest in their group identity. He also failed to carry out much-needed economic reform. Popular demonstrations caused him to be replaced by a more reforming communist, Dubček.

The new government relaxed the censorship laws and the country was agog with excited discussions about reforms, greater individual freedom and 'socialism with a human face'. Though Dubček assured Moscow that his country would remain loyal to the communist bloc, Ulbricht in East Germany and Gomulka in Poland took fright. They were sure that if the Czechoslovak reforming mood spread to their peoples they would be overthrown and the communist hold on Eastern Europe be at risk. Brezhnev agreed. Warsaw Pact tanks rumbled into Prague in August 1968. Dubček and his ministers were summoned to Moscow and bullied into agreeing to an army of occupation until the popular unrest, said by Moscow to be inspired by capitalist, mainly West German plotters(!), was ended. Dubček and other reforming ministers were eased out of power in 1969 and replaced by Moscow loyalists. Economic reforms were ended, censorship resumed and the security police reappeared.

The Brezhnev Doctrine 1968

The Czech crisis caused Brezhnev, the Soviet leader, to state that if a communist government of any nation seemed likely to be replaced by a more capitalist one, then other communist states would actively seek to prevent such a change. This became known as the 'Brezhnev Doctrine' and was to a large extent the Truman Doctrine in reverse.

Restless Poland

During the 1970s the USSR and Eastern Europe were ruled by men who were generally old and cautious. Most of the countries grew more prosperous and stayed quiet. The exception was Poland which was economically depressed and restless. It had a strong Roman Catholic Church which had at best an uneasy relationship with the communist government. Strikes and riots overthrew one government in 1970 (Gomulka's)

'Solidarity'

and another (Gierek's) in 1980. A free trade union, 'Solidarity', built up huge popular support until it was repressed in 1981 by the Polish army backed by Moscow.

Soviet foreign policy 1953–73

The West never knew quite where it was with the Soviet Union during these twenty years. Periods of 'thaw' in the Cold War when the Russians seemed genuinely seeking peace and disarmament were interrupted by major crises. No doubt the Russians felt the same about the West, so deep ran Cold War suspicions.

Hungary and Suez, 1956

The period 1953–5 was a hopeful one of summit talks. A thaw, it seemed, was taking place in the Cold War. However, 1956 was dreadful, with the Soviet invasion of Hungary (see sources E1–3) and threats of nuclear attacks on Britain and France because of their Suez invasion (see page 272). The years 1957–60 were better. Khrushchev visited both Britain and the USA. Disarmament talks began in Geneva which achieved some limited success with the Test Ban Treaty of 1963. In contrast 1960–62 were years when nuclear war seemed close. When an American U-2 spy plane was shot down over the USSR in 1960, Khrushchev refused to attend an important summit conference. Also in 1960 the

The Berlin Wall, 1961

East German government was becoming most concerned about the situation of West Berlin, through which some of its most able citizens were escaping to the West with its higher living standards and greater freedom. By July 1961 10,000 were fleeing each week and the DDR faced economic disaster. With Soviet backing the DDR government threatened to take over West Berlin. President Kennedy flew into the city and made clear that the West would stand as firm as in 1948. The communist response was not a blockade but the closing of all border crossings in the city and the building of a high fortified wall which made any further escapes virtually impossible.

The Cuba Crisis, 1962

In 1962 the area of crisis was the island of Cuba in the Caribbean. It had a communist government, led by Castro, which Khrushchev agreed to supply with nuclear missiles. President Kennedy insisted that they be removed and sent the American navy to intercept Soviet supply ships on their way to Cuba. Only at the last minute did Khrushchev back down and order that the missiles be taken away.

This acute crisis had some beneficial results. A 'hot-line' telephone link was made between Moscow and Washington and Strategic Arms Limitation Talks (SALT) took place which ended in agreement in 1972 on the number of long-range missiles to be held by each of the superpowers.

The USSR and China

Meanwhile the focus of the USSR's interests was shifting. She shared a common border thousands of miles in length with China. The population of China was the largest in the world and growing, as were her industries and her military strength. She had nuclear weapons, and border claims against the Soviet Union. Though the two communist governments seemed close allies in the early fifties, they fell out badly after 1958. Consequently the USSR was less inclined to look for trouble in Europe.

Less tension in divided Germany

Within divided Germany, the most dangerous area of the Cold War in Europe, tensions lessened considerably in the 1960s and 1970s. The Berlin Wall, brutal though it was, had the effect which the DDR government intended. East Germany prospered and responded favourably to Brandt's Ostpolitik (see page 256). In 1973 the FDR and DDR recognised each other as independent nations and were admitted to the UN.

A major conference was held at Helsinki in 1975 attended by the USA, USSR and thirty-three other states. They all agreed to recognise the existing frontiers of Europe, including East and West Germany and East and West Berlin.

France 1945–62

De Gaulle, 1944–5

The Third Republic collapsed with the military defeat of 1940. General de Gaulle, who had led the liberation forces, headed a provisional government during 1944–5. However when he failed to persuade the country to have a constitution which gave less power to parliament and more to a president, he retired, though he let his countrymen know that he was ready to come to his country's aid should destiny so decide.

The Fourth Republic, 1946–58

The Fourth Republic began in 1946. Though its constitution was supposed to encourage governments which lasted longer than those of the Third Republic, its coalitions came and went at a high rate (nineteen in twelve years). The strongest parties were the Catholic MRP, the socialists and the communists. The coalition governments of the Fourth Republic were more effective than their frequent comings and goings suggested. From 1946 to 1954 France had only two Foreign Ministers, Bidault and Schuman, both of high competence. The economy was directed with great effectiveness by a non-party commission headed by Monnet. With the help of Marshall Aid and four well-considered national plans between 1947 and 1961, French industry was transformed. The average growth rate between 1954 and 1959 was 5½ per cent. The driving force of this remarkable change was not so much businessmen or trade unions but intelligent civil servants, well educated in science and technology and aware of the needs of modern industry.

Economic progress

Decolonisation problems in Indo-China

What the Fourth Republic could not cope with was decolonisation (see pages 266–74). Neither the French colonial officials nor the French army were ready to give up the colonies. Both in Indo-China and in Algeria the generals intended to recover some of the glory lost in the Second World War. Not until the complete defeat of the French army by the Vietnamese at Dien Bien Phu in 1954 was Indo-China given up.

Algeria

The struggle for Algeria was even more bitter since the colony was much closer to France. Algerian deputies sat in the National Assembly and there were a million French settlers in no mood to abandon their homes. The independence struggle began in 1954. By 1956 it had become a full-scale war with frightful atrocities. No only did the leaders of European settlers defy the French government's orders in Algeria but they plotted its overthrow. The Paris government began to doubt that it could trust the police to obey it. In 1958, with the country in a state of political paralysis, de Gaulle was voted in as Prime Minister. He drew up a constitution which had a strong president and a weaker parliament. When this constitution was accepted by the electorate he became the first President of the Fifth Republic. Perhaps his greatest achievement in his eleven years as President was to grant independence to Algeria despite the violent opposition of sections of the army. He survived a number of attempts to assassinate him.

De Gaulle returns

The Fifth Republic, 1958

De Gaulle as President, 1958–69

De Gaulle's nationalism

During his time as President, de Gaulle proved to be a prickly nationalist. He disliked France being overshadowed by anyone, particularly the USA, and insisted on developing nuclear weapons independently. Though he remained within NATO he would not have NATO troops on French soil nor would he sign the Nuclear Test Ban treaty of 1963 with the USA, USSR and Britain. He also successfully opposed Britain's entry to the Common Market (see pages 288–9). More positively he created an effective working partnership with West Germany.

For much of his presidency, he was extremely popular but, after ten years, France experienced a change of mood. There were some economic setbacks and then in 1968 an extraordinary student revolt (see sources G1–2).

The 1968 student risings

Discontent had been bubbling in the universities of Western Europe for a number of years. Partly the universities themselves were criticised for overcrowding and poor teaching, partly the modern world, particularly the world of capitalism with its big businesses and big governments was seen as sick and limiting genuine freedom. The American military action in Vietnam was especially hated. In 1968 trouble erupted in French universities, particularly in the new university of Nanterre in Paris. Students raised barricades in the streets of the capital. Clumsy and rough attempts by the police to end the demonstrations increased the violence. In contrast to Germany and Italy, French workers joined the students. A wave of strikes in May plus further disorder seemed for a moment to be about to topple de Gaulle. However, having made sure that the army would support him if the situation got worse, he stood firm and appealed for support against communism and the breakdown of law and order. Huge demonstrations against the students followed and in the June elections (the referendum of source G2 was never held) he won a convincing majority. Calm returned to France. De Gaulle resigned the following year, aged seventy-seven.

Source G: France 1968

G1 Illustrated London News, *25 May 1968.*

G2 Daily Mail, *25 May 1968.*

1 *The* Illustrated London News *is a weekly magazine. Is its news less or more up-to-date than that of the* Daily Mail?

2 *Study source G1. Who is in the clown's audience? Where would they normally be on a May weekday? What is happening in France?*

3 *Explain the words 'referendum' and 'ultimatum'. De Gaulle actually called a general election rather than a referendum. What sort of people would you expect to have voted for him and who against? Explain your answers.*

ALL OF FRANCE IS A STAGE FOR STRIKERS, MARCHERS AND THE CLOWN

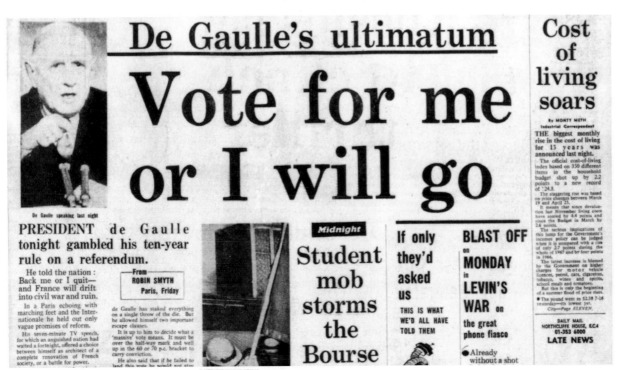

West Germany 1945—63

Adenauer

From 1945 to 1948 Germany was run by the armies of occupation. The Cold War and the Berlin Airlift effectively divided the country into two and in 1949 the first general election of the Federal Republic of Germany (the FDR or West Germany) was held. The Christian Democrats won so their leader, Adenauer, became Chancellor. Adenauer was a convinced Catholic. He had been Mayor of Cologne but had left politics when the Nazis came to power. Aged seventy-three when he became Chancellor for the first time, he won election after election until his retirement in 1963 at the age of eighty-seven. He feared communism and experiments. His chief aim was to provide stability and peace.

The economic miracle

The main feature of the Adenauer years was economic growth so rapid and continuous that it was referred to as an 'economic miracle'. In 1945 Germany was in ruins. Most people therefore concentrated their energies on making good the damage and then creating greater prosperity. The Marshall Plan helped. So did the skill of Ludwig Erhard, the Economics Minister, who allowed market forces more scope and planned less than the French. Industrial production rose 600 per cent and unemployment fell from 8 to 1 per cent. In the same period the number of Germans working in farming fell from 5 to 3 million yet agricultural production rose 250 per cent.

Erhard followed Adenauer as Chancellor. Then in 1966 the long years of Christian Democratic majorities ended. The other major party, the Social Democrats, first shared power and then became the senior party of the coalition with the much smaller Liberals. Willi Brandt, Foreign Minister from 1966, became Chancellor in 1969 and stayed in office until 1974 when a spy scandal forced his resignation. Brandt's major achievement was his 'Ostpolitik' or policies towards Eastern Europe. Hitherto West Germany had refused to accept that Germany was partitioned and had lost land to Poland. Moreover it had been hostile to the Soviet Union and the whole communist bloc. In 1969 West Germany agreed not to make nuclear weapons. She also signed treaties of non-aggression with the USSR, Poland and East Germany. Poland's frontiers were accepted, as was the division in two of both Germany and Berlin.

Italy 1945—60

The fall of the monarchy

The dominance of the Christian Democrats

Immediately after the war the Communists who had played an important part in the struggle against the Germans and the overthrow of Mussolini were a strong force politically, so were the Socialists and the Christian Democrats. By a plebiscite in 1946 the monarchy was replaced by a republic and in the general election of the same year the Communists and Socialists polled about 40 per cent, the Christian Democrats 35 per cent. Since the Communists and Socialists found themselves unable to work together, it became normal for Italy to be governed by coalitions dominated by the Christian Democrats. The first post-war Christian Democratic Prime Minister, Alcide de Gasperi, was very able. He stayed in power until 1953.

Economic advance

Like West Germany the main feature of Italy's post-war history was spectacular economic growth. It was especially marked in motor vehicles, office machinery and electrical goods. During the early 1960s Italy's growth rate was the fastest in the industrial world. While the north became as rich as anywhere in Europe, the south remained backward and millions migrated northwards and overseas. Agriculture did not advance at the same pace as industry. Nor did investment in education and the social services compare with that of France or West Germany.

Source H: Conditions in Germany 1945-7

H *These extracts are taken from* The Rise of West Germany *by Aidan Crawley, published in 1973.*

H

"William Shirer writes for the New York *Herald Tribune* about Berlin in 1945. 'This is more like the face of the moon than any city I have ever imagined. The destruction makes the senses reel, for it is difficult to imagine how anyone has survived the thousands of tons of bombs and shells which have almost erased the city from the map . . . . The spacious avenues, once the pride of the city . . . are so covered with debris that bulldozers are set to work to clear a passage even for tanks and armoured vehicles . . . . And everywhere comes the putrid smell to remind the living that thousands of bodies still remain beneath the funeral pyres of rubble.' . . .

In February 1946 the meagre ration of the British zone had been reduced to a level which, according to the correspondent of the *Manchester Guardian*, meant that the daily diet of a German in the Ruhr consisted of 'two slices of bread, with perhaps a smear of margarine, a spoonful of porridge and two not very large potatoes'. Even this ration could not be met. Men and women would stand in queues all day only to find that at the end there was no food left. Wuppertal was without bread for ten days; almost the whole population of Hamburg had eaten their bread ration in the first half of March and had nothing left for the second . . . .

The winter of 1946-7 was one of the coldest on record in Europe and Germany was still desperately short of coal; a household was lucky if it could scrounge a few lumps a week . . . . In Berlin 200 people were recorded as 'frozen to death' . . . . Journalists reported widespread signs of starvation: 'earth-coloured faces and hollow cheeks', children begging in the streets and emaciated women harnessed to carts pulling piles of wood or felling trees; and always endless queues of people so listless that motorists had to take special care not to run them down as they crossed the streets. . . .

'You had to be clever,' said Georg Schroder who lived through the occupation with a wife and three children. 'I spent two years doing nothing except scrounge food for my family. I travelled endlessly, sometimes acting on my own behalf and sometimes acting as agent for others. I exchanged everything I possessed and a lot more that I acquired for food . . . . A lot of my friends thought that you were out to exterminate us but perhaps I understood more of what was going on. The truth was that the State had collapsed.'"

1 *Imagine that you were a twelve-year-old in Hamburg in 1943. Describe your experiences from 1943 to 1953 basing your account on the evidence in this chapter and especially source H and pages 234-5 in chapter 14.*

2 *What were the main concerns of the Allies in Germany between 1945 and 1947?*

3 *Did the Germans suffer much more than the British (see page 280) immediately after the war?*

4 *For what reasons were the British not specially bothered by the suffering in Germany?*

Terrorism

Christian Democrats challenged from the left

During the 1960s and 1970s Italy's coalition governments came and went more and more frequently. Her economic growth slowed and extreme left-wing terrorists kidnapped and murdered politicians including a prime minister, Aldo Moro, in 1978 and businessmen. Though the Christian Democrats remained strong the Socialists gained support. In 1981 a socialist, Giuseppe Spadolino, became the first Prime Minister since 1945 who was not a Christian Democrat.

Unifying Western Europe

The experience of two catastrophic wars in less than fifty years convinced many thoughtful Europeans that the best hope for the future of Europe lay in unity. Various unifying organisations came into existence after

Moves to greater unity

1945. The Organisation of European Economic Co-operation was set up in 1947 to administer Marshall Aid. The Council of Europe was established the following year to discuss mainly cultural matters. However, the acorn from which the most flourishing oak of European co-operation grew was the European Coal and Steel Community (ECSC) which was

ECSC

formed in 1951. The ECSC was the brainchild of Monnet, a French diplomat and civil servant who believed that genuine European political union would follow from effective economic co-operation. He suggested that France and Germany should have a common plan for their coal and steel industries. There were powerful geographic and economic reasons

Monnet and Schuman

for so doing. Schuman, the French Foreign Minister, took up Monnet's scheme with enthusiasm (it became known as the Schuman Plan). So did Adenauer of West Germany and de Gasperi of Italy. Six countries – France, West Germany, Italy, Belgium, the Netherlands and Luxembourg – joined the ECSC and allowed the coal and steel industries of their countries to be managed as a single unit. The ECSC was a great success under Monnet's personal direction. Between 1953 and 1958 it improved production by 42 per cent.

The Messina Conference, 1955

The success of the ECSC convinced its six members that they could attempt a more ambitious scheme of economic co-operation. At a conference in Messina in Sicily in 1955 they decided in principle to create a common market. The details of the organisation of this market were worked out by a committee headed by Spaak, a Belgian. In March 1957

The Treaty of Rome, 1957

the Treaty of Rome, the foundation document of this Common Market or European Economic Community (EEC), was signed. Though the long-term aim of the EEC was the greater political unity of Europe, its immediate concern was the lowering and eventual elimination of trading barriers between the member states. The new Market was to be run by a nine-man Commission with a rotating president. Major policy decisions would be made by the Council of Ministers which had a representative from each of the member states. Like the ECSC, the Common Market was an immediate success. Between 1957 and 1967 the volume of trade between the Six rose by 400 per cent. By 1964 it had become the world's largest trading unit.

Britain and the EEC

The Six had been keen to have Britain as a member both of ECSC and the EEC but neither the Conservative nor Labour parties were keen to join. They did not think that either organisation would succeed and were confident that Britain would do better from her well-established Commonwealth trading links. Both parties disliked the idea of any part of British industry being run by foreigners and Labour in particular saw the EEC as an organisation for businessmen rather than for workers. Macmillan's Conservative government combined with other non-EEC countries to form a rival trading unit, the European Free Trade Associ-

EFTA

ation (EFTA), but sensing that it had misjudged the EEC's prospects, applied to join in 1961.

De Gaulle's veto

Unfortunately for Britain, de Gaulle was now President of France. He was not keen on the political union of Europe but he saw that France was doing nicely out of the EEC and, with West Germany, was the strongest nation within it. He considered that Britain was too closely linked with the USA, whose dynamic industry might use the British connection to move into and dominate the Common Market. He therefore vetoed Britain's application in 1963, arguing that Britain was still too

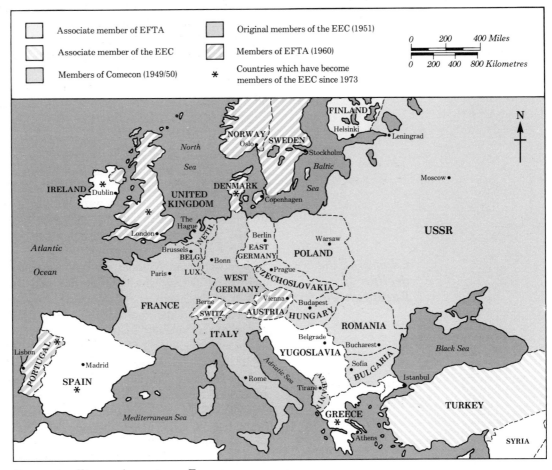

Economic alliances in post-war Europe.

much bound up in her island ways and too concerned with her Commonwealth to be a good member of the EEC (see pages 288–9).

De Gaulle came near to wrecking the Common Market. The other members were angry about the veto. In 1965 de Gaulle provoked a huge row over agricultural policy; then in 1967 he vetoed a second application for membership from Britain, this one submitted by Wilson's Labour government. To his former arguments he added Britain's continuing economic weakness. Only after his retirement in 1969 was the expansion of the EEC possible. Britain finally gained entry in 1973, along with Denmark and Ireland. Greece joined in 1981 and Spain and Portugal in 1986. However by the 1970s much of the high hopes for a united Europe had been forgotten. The EEC worked reasonably well as an economic organisation but there was no popular enthusiasm for it. On the contrary it tended to provoke grumbles about its over-large bureaucracy and extravagant agricultural policies.

Six to Nine 1973

Nine to Ten 1981

Ten to Twelve 1986

16 The end of European empires

Nothing showed more clearly the reduction in Europe's power in the world than the swift disappearance of European empires after 1945. At the beginning of the Second World War virtually all Africa and much of the Middle East and Asia were directly or indirectly controlled by Europeans. Forty years later the only remnant of these empires of any size still under European control was South Africa.

Causes of the decline of European power

There were many reasons for this remarkable change. One was the humiliating defeats which the British and Dutch suffered in Asia in 1941–2 at the hands of the Japanese. Previously the white man had appeared unbeatable. Now that opponents of European rule could see the possibility of success their confidence and determination greatly increased. Secondly, Europeans were less enthusiastic about their empires which no longer seemed likely to be the source of great and easily-won wealth. Nor did the conquest and control of far-flung corners of the world have the glamour of the pre-1914 era. On the contrary many Europeans felt uncomfortable about colonial rule which meant the domination of large non-white majorities by small white minorities. After all the Second World War had been fought to save freedom and democracy from tyranny. Moreover the destructive lunacy of Nazi racial ideas made the post-war world very suspicious of any system based on racial inequalities.

Nationalism

Within the non-European populations the European ideals of nationalism, democracy and racial inequality were inspiring, especially to the small but growing educated class (see sources A1–5). Before the war nationalist groups had begun to be organised which demanded independence. They grew more vigorous during the war. After 1945 they could count on the sympathy of the superpowers. The USA, which had come into existence at the end of the eighteenth century by revolting and breaking free from the British Empire, basically disapproved of the European empires, while the USSR was openly hostile to them. It was a central communist belief that the capitalist powers of Western Europe had conquered much of the world to take the wealth of the colonies and make their own workers more prosperous and content, so avoiding the revolution of the proletariat against the ruling bourgeoisie which Marx had predicted.

Asia

The British in India

Since India was the 'jewel in the crown' of the British Empire, which was much the grandest of the European Empires, what happened there was of world-wide significance. An Indian nationalist movement had existed even before the First World War, centred on the Congress Party which had been founded in 1885. At this stage it was limited to a tiny minority of the educated middle class. It grew stronger as a result of the First World War when more than a million Indians, who had fought for the British cause against Germany and Turkey, returned to their homeland

Source A: *The force of nationalism*

A1 *This is by the Rev. Attoh Ahuma (principal of a Gold Coast secondary school), from* The Gold Coast Nation and National Consciousness, *1911.*

A1

"Let us help one another to find a way out of Darker Africa. We must emerge from the savage backwoods and come into the open where nations are made."

A2 *8 January 1912, Bloemfontein, South Africa. Delegates from all over South Africa met to form the South African Native National Congress. It was addressed by P. I. Seme, a lawyer and founder of the ANC. (From* The Struggle for a Birthright *by Mary Benson, 1963.)*

A2

"We have gathered here to consider and discuss a scheme which my colleagues and I have decided to place before you. We have discovered that in the land of their birth, Africans are treated as hewers of wood and drawers of water. The white people of this country have formed what is known as the Union of South Africa – a union in which we have no voice in the making of laws and no part in the administration. We have called you therefore in conference so that we can find ways and means of forming our national union for the purpose of creating national unity and defending our rights and privileges."

A3 *Editorial in a Madagascar newspaper,* La Nation Malgache, *April 1946. (Quoted by Basil Davidson in* Africa in Modern History, *1978.)*

A3

"We know very well that the colonialism and racism which some persons claim to reject is still alive within them. But such people must understand that the era of colonial conquest and domination is now ended. We are now in a new era to whose existence . . . the Atlantic Charter and the United Nations are the historic witness."

A4 *The Atlantic Charter was a list of agreed war aims for Britain and America drawn up by Churchill and Roosevelt at the end of a ship-based conference off the coast of Newfoundland in August 1941. This was their third principle.*

A4

". . . they respect the right of all peoples to choose the form of government under which they will live; and wish to see sovereign rights and self-government restored to those who have been forcibly deprived of them".

A5 *Harold Macmillan, Prime Minister of Britain, to the white South African Parliament in Cape Town, February 1960. (Quoted in Colin Cross,* The Fall of the British Empire, *1968.)*

A5

"Ever since the break-up of the Roman Empire one of the constant facts of political life in Europe has been the emergence of independent nations . . . . In the twentieth century, and especially since the end of the war, the processes which gave birth to the nation-states of Europe have been repeated all over the world. We have seen the awakening of national consciousness in peoples who have lived for centuries in dependence on some other power.

Fifteen years ago this movement spread through Asia. Many countries there of different races and civilisations pressed their claim to an independent national life. Today the same thing is happening in Africa. The most striking of the impressions I have formed since I left London a month ago is the strength of this African national consciousness. In different places it may take different forms, but it is happening everywhere.

The wind of change is blowing through the continent."

1 *Both Ahuma (source A1) in the Gold Coast in 1911 and Seme (source A2) in South Africa in 1912 believed that their peoples had some way to go before they were a nation. How could they achieve nationhood?*

2 *What does the newspaper editor (source A3) mean by a) 'colonialism', and b) 'racism'?*

3 *What changes in the way the British Empire was ruled would educated Asians and Africans have expected as a result of the Atlantic Charter (source A4)? Churchill argued that it was not meant to apply to the British Empire. How could he justify such an attitude?*

4 *What did Macmillan mean by 'the wind of change' in source A5? Did he approve of it? What would the attitude of most of his audience have been? Explain your answer.*

Gandhi

to find that the British would still allow them virtually no say in its running (see source B3). Indian nationalism was made into a mass movement by Mohandas Gandhi who in 1915 returned to India from South Africa, where he had already made himself famous by organising non-violent resistance among the Indians of that country to the government's policies of racial discrimination. Gandhi was quite exceptional. He was deeply religious and recommended a most simple life in food, dress and work. He practised what he preached and gave up a comfortable lawyer's life for a semi-peasant life of contemplation, weaving and politics. The Hindu peasantry in their millions regarded him as a saint and referred to him as Mahatma, the great-souled.

The Montagu-Chelmsford reforms 1919

The year 1919 was eventful. While the British put into effect the so-called Montagu-Chelmsford reforms which gave Indians more influence in both central and provincial government (and also promised Indian self-government at some indefinite time in the future), they also took

Source B: The British in India

B1 *These extracts describing the Amritsar massacre of 1919 are taken from Michael Edwardes' biography of Nehru, 1973.*

B1

"Protests against the new security measures took place . . . on 9 April Gandhi was arrested . . . . In the Punjab the administration, determined on a show of force, arrested two popular Congress leaders on 10 April and when a crowd began a protest march on the European section of the city of Amritsar, the police opened fire. Turned back, the crowd looted two banks and burnt the railway station. Four Europeans were murdered by the mob and others beaten up, including a woman missionary who was left for dead . . . . All public meetings and assemblies were banned.

Despite the ban, on 13 April a large crowd estimated at some 20,000 men, women and children gathered in an enclosed space known as the Jallianwalla Bagh. When he heard of this General Dyer went personally to the spot with ninety Gurkha and Baluchi soldiers and two armoured cars. As the entrance was too narrow for the armoured vehicles to pass through he used them to block the only exit. He then ordered the crowd to disperse. It does seem likely that Dyer, who was a stranger to Amritsar, did not know that there were no other convenient exits and that, when the crowd did not disperse because it could not, he panicked. Without warning Dyer ordered his soldiers to shoot into the crowd. He admitted later that he fired all the ammunition he had with him and then withdrew, leaving, according to official estimates, 379 dead and 1,200 wounded. The armoured cars were left blocking the entrance so that no one could leave and no medical aid could get in . . . .

[In the weeks that followed] Indians were forced to walk on their hands and knees past the spot where the woman missionary had been attacked . . . and public floggings were inflicted for such minor offences as . . . failure to salaam to a commissioned officer, disrespect to a European . . . .

Dyer commented, 'I realised that my force was small and to hestitate might induce attack. I immediately opened fire . . . . It was no longer a question of merely dispersing the crowd, but one of producing a sufficient moral effect from the military point of view, not only on those who were present, but more especially throughout the Punjab.'

The Lieutenant-Governor of the Punjab: 'If Dyer had not opened first, his small force would probably have been swept away like chaff before the wind.'"

The Amritsar massacre, 1919

Gandhi's march to the sea

emergency powers to deal with nationalist disturbances which were then widespread. Gandhi led a non-violent campaign against the emergency laws but he was unable to prevent violence by some nationalist extremists. Angered by violence against Europeans in Amritsar a British general, Dyer, responded with violence of his own. His soldiers fired on a peaceful demonstration killing nearly four hundred (see source B1).

The Amritsar massacre solidified Indian resistance to British rule (see source B3). Gandhi worked closely with the Congress leader, Motilal Nehru, and Nehru's son, Jawaharlal. 'Father, Son and Holy Ghost', as they were nicknamed by the British, organised campaigns of mass disobedience which had them in and out of prison. In 1929 the British government appointed the Simon Commission to investigate what changes should be made to the ways in which India was governed. However, from the start, it enraged Indian opinion by failing to include a single Indian on the commission and not surprisingly the Congress leaders refused to help. Instead they began a new campaign in 1930, this time aiming for complete independence. Gandhi's contribution was a spectacular mass walk to the sea at the end of which he publicly defied the government by making salt, in breach of a hated government monopoly. By 1935 the British were ready to grant further powers to the

B2 Winston Churchill, then Secretary of War, dismissed Dyer and explained his action to the House of Commons.

B2

"Governments who have seized power by violence . . . have often resorted to terrorism in their desperate efforts to keep what they have stolen . . . but the august and venerable structure of the British Empire, where lawful authority descends from hand to hand and generation after generation, does not need such aid . . . . Our reign in India or anywhere else has never stood on the basis of physical force alone, and it would be fatal to the British Empire if we were to try to base ourselves solely on that."

B3 Gandhi's advice to the Congress Party in 1920 was as follows. (Quoted by Colin Cross in The Fall of the British Empire, *1968.)*

1 *What caused the unrest in the Punjab in 1919?*

2 *What was the crowd doing on 13 April? Why did Dyer order it to disperse?*

3 *How did the Lieutenant-Governor justify Dyer's action (see source B1)? To what extent does the evidence support the view that Dyer did the minimum necessary to keep order?*

4 *Many Britons in India and in Britain believed that Dyer had acted sensibly and with courage. What arguments might they have used to support that view?*

5 *From the viewpoint of a moderate Indian Nationalist who was in his or her early twenties in 1919, explain what happened in Amritsar in April and May 1919 to your grandchildren in the 1960s, and its importance in the history of India.*

6 *What else would Churchill have believed to be the basis of the British Empire other*

B3

"If the British connection is for the advancement of India, we do not want to destroy it. But if it is against our national self-interest, then our duty is to destroy it . . . . There is room in this resolution [in favour of 'swaraj' – self-rule] for both those who believe that by retaining the British connection we can purify ourselves and purify the British people, and those who have no such belief.

I want you to accompany the carrying of this resolution with a faith . . . that nothing on earth can move that you are intent upon getting 'swaraj' by means that are legitimate, that are honourable, and by means that are non-violent, that are peaceful. You have resolved upon this thing that so far as we can see today we cannot give battle to this government by means of steel, but we can give battle by exercising what is often called soul-force."

than 'physical force alone' (source B2)? What evidence is there in source B3 that some Indians might have agreed with him?

7 *What did Gandhi mean by 'swaraj' (source B3)? How did he want it to be gained? What success had been achieved by the time of his assassination in 1948? How important a part had he played in this achievement?*

The Government of India Act, 1935

Religious rivalry in India

Jinnah and the Muslim League

The Second World War and the 'Quit India' campaign

Mountbatten and Partition, 1947

Massacres

The Dutch and Indonesia

Sukarno and Hatta

provincial assemblies by the Government of India Act, but it was too little too late. The nationalists were set on full independence.

However there was another obstacle to independence quite as large as the British: the bitter religious rivalry between the Hindus and the Muslims. The main Muslim areas were in the north-west and north-east but they were scattered widely across the sub-continent (see map C3). Mohammad Ali Jinnah, leader of the Muslim League, had hoped like Gandhi that Muslims and Hindus would be able to live in peace in a single independent nation but in 1937 he changed his mind. Such a nation would have an overwhelming Hindu majority and extremists of both religions were numerous and increasingly intolerant of each other. Jinnah therefore began campaigning for an independent Muslim state, Pakistan.

At the beginning of the Second World War Gandhi and the Congress leaders called on Britain to grant independence or 'quit India'. Britain did neither and locked up many of them. However, when peace came in 1945, Britain's new Labour government decided that the time had come to leave. Its intention was to grant independence in 1948. It expected independent India to include Hindus and Muslims alike and appointed Viscount Mountbatten as the last Viceroy to supervise the change-over. When Mountbatten arrived, however, he found communities split apart by religious rivalries and thousands of deaths from intercommunal violence. He persuaded the British government to accept that the country should be partitioned and both Hindu India and Muslim Pakistan be granted independence as quickly as possible. Independence Day for India was 14 August 1947, Pakistan's the following day. Jawaharlal Nehru was India's first Prime Minister, Pakistan's was Jinnah. The new states were born in appalling bloodshed. As millions of Muslim refugees headed for Pakistan and Hindu refugees in the opposite direction they were savagely attacked. About 500,000 lost their lives.

Having given up India Britain did not linger long in her other main Asian colonies. Sri Lanka (formerly Ceylon) and Burma were granted independence in 1948, Malaysia (formerly Malaya) in 1957 after a jungle war against communist revolutionaries.

The second largest European empire in Asia was the Dutch, based on the East Indian (Indonesian) islands of Sumatra, Borneo, Java and New Guinea. An Indonesian nationalist movement was founded before the First World War. Like the British in India, the Dutch did not take it seriously enough and gave too little too late. Though they allowed an advisory council in 1918 they gave little genuine power to the Indonesians and dealt sternly with disturbances, especially the communist-led rebellion of 1926–7. Their authority was fatally wounded by the events of the Second World War when the Netherlands were occupied by the Germans and Indonesia by the Japanese, but they still tried hard to win back control after 1945. They failed partly because of the strength of the nationalist movement and partly because of the opposition of the USA. The nationalist leaders Sukarno and Hatta had co-operated with the Japanese during their occupation and declared Indonesia independent when they retreated. The USA considered that an independent Indonesia was likely to be anti-communist. After four years of fighting the Dutch gave up and in 1949 recognised the effective independence of Indonesia with Sukarno as President and Hatta as Prime Minister. The last formal ties with the Netherlands were broken in 1954.

Source C: The partition of India

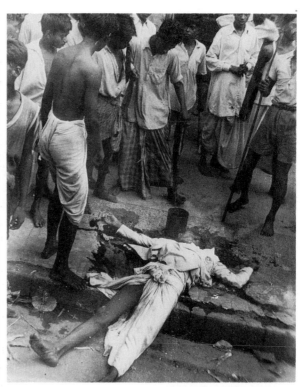

C1 (**Above**) *Mountbatten (centre), Jinnah (right) and Nehru (far left) in New Delhi, 7 June 1947, announcing the partition plan for India.*

C2 (**Above right**) *A dead Hindu is surrounded by a crowd of Muslims armed with wooden sticks, Calcutta, 24 August 1946.*

C3 (**Right**) *The partition of India, 1947.*

1 *Who were Mountbatten, Nehru and Jinnah?*

2 *At this meeting (source C1) they were discussing the partition of India. Who was for partition? Who against? Why did it become necessary?*

3 *Find Calcutta on source C3. Why was there such serious rioting there? In which country was Calcutta placed by the partition?*

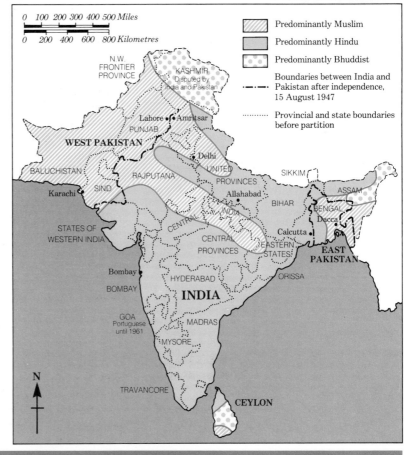

The French and Indo-China

The war in Vietnam.

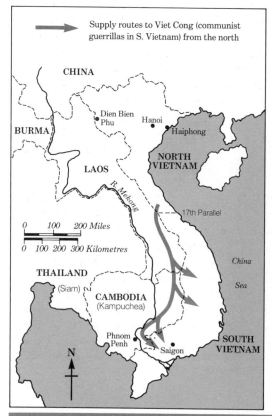

The third largest European empire in Asia, French Indo-China (Vietnam, Cambodia and Laos – see map left), ended in the greatest turmoil. Between the wars the most effective opposition was the Vietnamese Communist Party led by Ho Chi Minh. It joined other nationalist groups in revolts in Tongking and Annam in 1930–31. These the French crushed without much difficulty and Ho Chi Minh fled to Moscow. During the Second World War the Japanese allowed French officials of the Vichy government which was collaborating with the Germans to continue running Indo-China but the various nationalist groups formed themselves into an independence movement called the Vietminh. During the summer of 1945 as the Japanese retreated and the Vichy government collapsed, Ho Chi Minh – on behalf of the Vietminh – declared Vietnam independent. But neither America nor Britain nor France nor Chiang Kai-shek, the Chinese Nationalist leader whose troops occupied the northern part of Vietnam, were ready to accept this.

The French took over the south and Ho Chi Minh feared the Chinese Nationalists were ready to do a deal with the French. It was agreed by the new French government in Paris that Vietnam would become independent within a new French federation of Indo-China. However this deal was sabotaged by the French in Vietnam. In the south they set up a separate state, Cochin-China, and as tension increased in the north sent the French navy to bombard and occupy Hanoi, the northern capital. Six thousand were killed in the bombardment and the Vietminh had to retreat to the mountains.

The French were now determined to regain complete control of Indo-China and to destroy the Vietminh. They could count on the backing of the USA which was suspicious of Ho Chi Minh's communism, all the more so after 1947 when his guerrilla armies were supplied from China

Source D: The French in Indo-China

D1 *With the collapse of Japanese rule in Indo-China, Ho Chi Minh's Vietminh forces took control of the Hanoi area. On 2 September 1945 Ho declared Indo-China to be independent and had this to say about the French:*

D1

"For over eighty years the gang of French colonialists, operating under the three colours which are supposed to stand for liberty, equality and fraternity, have stolen our land and oppressed our people .... The French have not given us political freedom, they have instituted a barbarous legal code, they have opened more prisons than schools, they have drowned all our attempts at revolt in rivers of blood, they have sought to besot our race with opium and alcohol .... In the economic sphere they have stripped us to the bone, they have stolen our paddy fields, our estates, our forests, our mines.

So we, the Provisional Government of the new Vietnam, the representatives of the people, declare that we repudiate the French colonialist regime ... the treaties signed between France and our own country and all the privileges which the French claim over our country .... The people are of one heart in affirming their determination to fight the French colonialists ..."

D2

D2 *As the French generals set about winning back Indo-China and drove the Vietminh into the hills, Ho said this to an American journalist. [Sources D2 and D3 are taken from Jean Lacouture's biography of Ho Chi Minh, 1969.]*

"If the tiger ever stands still the elephant will crush him with his mighty tusks. But the tiger does not stand still. He lurks in the jungle by day and emerges by night. He will leap on the back of the elephant, tearing huge chunks from his hide, and then he will leap back into the dark jungle. And slowly the elephant will bleed to death."

War, 1946

Dien Bien Phu, 1954

The French withdraw

The USA intervenes in South Vietnam

The Vietnamese War

The USA defeated, 1973

Vietnam united, 1975

where the communist Mao Tse-tung had overthrown Chiang Kai-shek, America's ally. The Vietminh armies could count on popular support and were brilliantly led by General Giap. Despite increasing American aid the French were outfought. Eventually in 1954 a French army was cut off in the mountains at Dien Bien Phu (see sources D4–7) and forced to surrender. By now there was little popular support within France for the war. At a peace conference in Geneva the French agreed to hand over all of Vietnam north of the Seventeenth Parallel to the Vietminh, while the Vietminh agreed to withdraw from the south. Elections were to be held in South Vietnam in order that the population could state what sort of government it wanted. The USA refused to accept the Geneva agreement. Fearing that communism might spread all over South-East Asia she replaced France in South Vietnam and did her utmost to prop up anti-communist governments.

Another guerrilla war followed. Vietcong (communist) guerrillas, directed by General Giap and supplied from North Vietnam, fought to overthrow the American-backed governments of the south. The Vietcong could count on the assistance of the rural population and had the South Vietnamese governments almost continuously on the defensive. The American government increased its support adding first military advisers to its supplies and then units of the US Army, Navy and Air Force. Yet the ruthless use of some of the most advanced weapons in the world could not turn the tide. The American public who saw some of the hideous realities of the war on their television* screens was increasingly convinced that it was unjust and unnecessary. American forces were withdrawn in 1973 and South Vietnam was conquered and united with the north into the single communist state of Vietnam in 1975.

* The first practical television transmission was made by J. L. Baird in 1926. Ten years later the BBC began some television broadcasting but only to a small audience. The USA began regular television broadcasting in 1941 and by 1950 there were ten million American receivers. European television expanded rapidly in the 1950s and 1960s. By the 1960s television was by far the most popular source of news, much more so than the newspapers.

D3 Sainteny was head of the French Military Mission who met Ho frequently during the difficult months of 1945–6. This is how he described him.

1 *What was the Vietminh? Who was Ho Chi Minh? How did the French get back into power in Indo-China after the Second World War?*

2 *In his bitter speech of 2 September 1945 (source D1) explain Ho Chi Minh's reference to the French belief in 'liberty, equality and fraternity'.*

3 *What does he mean by 'to besot our race with opium and alcohol'?*

4 *Which of his criticisms of the French sounds to you the most exaggerated? How would a historian set about testing its accuracy? If a French colonial official had spoken after Ho Chi Minh, which points*

D3

"From my first dealings with Ho Chi Minh I derived the impression that this ascetic man whose face reflected a mixture of intelligence, guile and subtely was a person of the highest calibre .... His vast culture, unbelievable energy and total unselfishness had earned him unparalleled prestige and popularity in the eyes of the whole people. His talk, his deeds, his bearing, everything about him served to convince one that a solution by force of arms was repugnant to him. There can be no doubt that he had hopes throughout this period of becoming the Gandhi of Indo-China."

might he have made in defence of the French colonial record?

5 *In source D2 who is the tiger and who the elephant? To what extent did this prophecy of Ho's prove an accurate one between 1946 and 1975?*

6 *Which source indicates that Ho Chi Minh was not a particularly warlike character? Comment on the reliability of this source.*

D4 *The setting of Dien Bien Phu.*

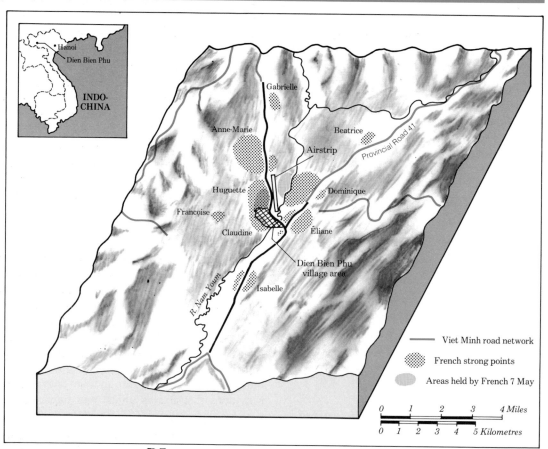

INDO-CHINA

Hanoi
Dien Bien Phu

Gabrielle

Anne-Marie

Beatrice

Provincial Road 41

Airstrip

Huguette

Dominique

Françoise

Claudine

Éliane

Dien Bien Phu village area

R. Nam Youm

Isabelle

Viet Minh road network

French strong points

Areas held by French 7 May

0   1   2   3   4 *Miles*
0   1   2   3   4   5 *Kilometres*

D5 *The last telegram from the French Command:*

D6 *Helicopters hover over the trenches during the battle of Dien Bien Phu, 26 March 1954.*

D5

"1600 hrs 7 May
Situation at 16 hours Stop Eliane 3 Fallen Stop Attacks continue Stop Massive Infiltrations on the West Front Stop and End."

D7 Dien Bien Phu 1953–4: The Decisive Battle of the Struggle for French Indo-China. *Extracts from Alistair Horne's 1968 account of the battle.*

7 *Study map D4 and the map on page 266. What was Navarre's strategy at the end of 1953? Why did he choose Dien Bien Phu as his base?*

8 *Study the photograph source D6. Whereabouts in the picture are Giap's forces? Who had command of the air? Why is the helicopter probably not in great danger?*

9 *Imagine that the wireless operator who sent the last telegram from Dien Bien Phu became a prisoner of war. Write the story of the afternoon of 7 May 1954 as he might have done. (Make as much use as you can of sources D4 and D6.)*

10 *Navarre made two miscalculations about Giap's forces (see source D7). What were these and why did they prove so serious?*

11 *Where precisely did Giap get his anti-aircraft guns from?*

D7

"Navarre [the French commander] aimed at both relieving the threat to Laos and at inflicting a major defeat upon the Vietminh before Chinese aid could become effective .... On 21st November 1953 a strong French paratroop force ... dropped onto the isolated village of Dien Bien Phu ... Navarre's plan was to bait the trap for Giap [the Vietminh commander] by establishing a powerful and aggressive garrison there.

The attraction of Dien Bien Phu lay in the fact that it possessed an airstrip ... but it was under 100 miles [160 km] from the Chinese border and almost 200 (320 km) from the French bases round Hanoi ....

Navarre was confident .... He knew Giap had artillery but hitherto he had used nothing bigger than Japanese and Chinese 75 mm field guns ... and only a few anti-aircraft weapons .... His system over the tortuous jungle trails would be incapable of [supplying the Vietminh adequately].

Giap willingly accepted Navarre's challenge. With superhuman effort some 50,000 coolies ... wheeling specially strengthened bicycles that could carry 450 lb [200 kg] cargoes were methodically moving up a siege train of over 200 guns. Many of them were American medium 105 mm pieces, captured by the Chinese .... Giap's gunners burrowed through the crests of the hills wrested from the French so that the muzzles of the guns poked out of small tunnels directly down on to the French garrison, presenting targets almost impossible to hit ....

From China Giap had massed a formidable array of anti-aircraft weapons .... Losses hard to replace from the French airforce's slender resources mounted steadily ....

Although Dien Bien Phu still held out with incredible heroism and continued to receive small paratroop reinforcements there was now no hope of escape for the beleaguered garrison .... Moreover much of the arms and ammunition parachuted in fell into Giap's hands. On May 7th 1954, Dien Bien Phu was overwhelmed. It never surrendered."

Laos and Cambodia

As far as the rest of Indo-China was concerned, Laos and Cambodia gained self-government from France in 1949 and complete independence by 1954. For the next twenty years both countries were seriously affected by the Vietnam war. Cambodia, having had a king previously, became a republic in 1970. Five years later the communist Khmer Rouge government seized power. It followed some grotesque policies including the enforced evacuation of the population of the capital, Phnom Penh, into the countryside. In four years perhaps as many as a million of a total population of eight million died. In 1979 Vietnam invaded the country and replaced the Khmer Rouge with another communist government.

The Middle East and North Africa

The European powers with the most influence in this mainly Arab-inhabited area were Britain and France (see map on page 270). The Suez Canal (a vital link in the sea route to India) and the oil of the Persian Gulf were Britain's main interests. France's most important colony was Algeria and she also had important financial and trading interests in Syria and Lebanon. The Ottoman (Turkish) Empire had collapsed at the end of the First World War and the League of Nations had given the former Ottoman provinces of Syria and Lebanon as mandates to France, and Palestine, Transjordan and Iraq to Britain.

The British in Egypt

Though Britain claimed to regard Egypt, through whose territory the Suez Canal ran, as an independent kingdom as early as 1922, she kept an army there to defend the Canal area and also ruled the Sudan jointly with Egypt. The Wafd, Egypt's main nationalist party, wanted the British army out and the Sudan united with Egypt. Continual agitation by the Wafd and some serious violence which included the assassination of British officials led to an agreement in 1936 that in due course British forces should be reduced in size and limited to the Canal Zone. The Second World War intervened, during which Egypt was absolutely vital to the British war effort, and British influence over the country became once again very strong. Not until after the Suez Crisis of 1956 (see page 272) could Egyptian nationalists claim that their country was genuinely free of British influence. That same year the Sudan became independent of both Britain and Egypt.

The French and Syria

Syria's nationalists had expected independence at the end of the First World War when their Ottoman rulers had been defeated. They were angered by the decision of the League of Nations to place them under a French mandate. Revolts took place in 1925 and 1927 and elections to the national assembly proved that the nationalists were genuinely popular. Though French and Syrian representatives agreed in 1936 that Syria should be given complete independence the Paris government delayed confirming the agreement. It needed the Second World War and pressure from America and Britain before France finally agreed. Lebanon became independent the same year (1946).

Britain and Palestine

The problems posed by the Syrian mandate for France were as nothing compared to those of the Palestine mandate for Britain. Palestine had also been part of the Ottoman Empire and had been inhabited mainly by Muslim Arabs. Towards the end of the nineteenth century a movement of European Jews, Zionism, set itself the task of creating a Jewish nation in Palestine. During the First World War the British government promised the Zionists, by the Balfour Declaration of 1917, to support the

The Middle East in the 1950s.

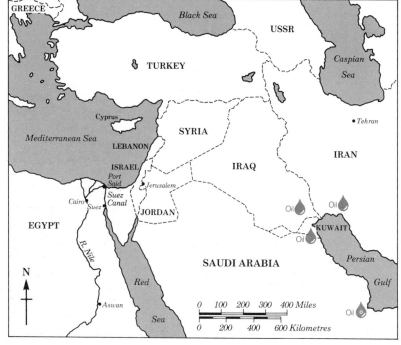

establishment of a national home for the Jews in Palestine. It also gave the Arabs reason to believe in letters from McMahon, High Commissioner for Egypt to the leaders of the Arab rebellion, that it would help them to complete independence. In fact, to support both Jews and Arabs in Palestine was impossible. The Zionists were determined to create a homeland for themselves yet the area was the home of multitudes of Arabs. If the Zionists were successful in establishing a Jewish national home, the Palestinian Arabs must be the losers, whatever pious hopes the British government might express in its official documents.

In 1929 there was serious fighting between Jews and Arabs in Jerusalem and after 1933 tension further increased as the number of Jewish refugees entering Palestine grew rapidly as a consequence of Nazi persecution in Germany. Between 1936 and 1939 an Arab revolt, sparked off by fear of Britain handing Palestine over to the Jews, cost 3,500 lives. In 1939 Britain did try to limit Jewish immigration but the appalling sufferings of the Jews of Europe during the Second World War and America's powerful support of the Zionist cause led to another flood of Jewish refugees into Palestine in 1945 and 1946. Both Arabs and Jews prepared for war and Jewish terrorists murdered Britons as well as Arabs. As with India, Attlee's government considered that the situation was out of control and this time passed the problem on to the United Nations, which decided that partition was the only answer. Such an answer was acceptable neither to the Jews nor to the Arabs. As British troops finally withdrew in May 1948, the Jews proclaimed the new state of Israel and were immediately attacked by their Arab neighbours. The Israelis won and a million Palestinian Arabs fled from their homes. In the following years they were sheltered in refugee camps in nearby Arab states and swore that some day they would win back their lost lands.

The creation of the state of Israel transformed the Middle East. The Arabs united against it and against the nations which had helped to bring it into being, especially the USA, but also to some extent Britain and France. Since Israel was closely linked to the USA, the USSR lined up with the Arabs.

The new state of Israel

Source E: Refugees in Palestine

E *The* Theodor Herzl *arrives in Palestine with 27,000 refugees on board, 24 April 1947. The refugees put up a strong resistance when a naval boarding party went on board and two of the refugees were killed.*

1 *Where are these refugees from?*
2 *Who ruled Palestine at the time of this photograph?*
3 *What was 'illegal' about this ship and why the boarding party?*
4 *Explain the banner on the ship's side.*
5 *How had Britain got herself into such a fix in Palestine? What eventually did she do? What then happened?*

The Suez Canal Crisis, 1956

The hostility between the Jews and Arabs and superpower suspicions in the Middle East played their part in a crisis which showed most vividly how comparatively weak the once proud and aggressive European nations had become: Suez. Egypt had a new ambitious nationalist leader, Nasser. In 1956 he had got Britain to withdraw her troops from the Canal Zone and persuaded America, with France and Britain, to help finance a vast dam on the Nile at Aswan (see map on page 270). Simultaneously he was buying arms from the communist bloc. In 1956 the Western powers pulled out of the dam scheme. Nasser retaliated by nationalising the Suez Canal which was chiefly owned by British and French shareholders. While the British government regarded Nasser as a little Hitler who needed to be taught a lesson, the French were sure that he was sending aid to the Algerians rebelling against their rule. A secret meeting of British, French and Israeli representatives put together a plan: Israel would attack Egypt, acting as if on her own; Britain and France would then send troops themselves to repossess the Canal, saying that they were acting as peacemakers since they would keep apart the Egyptian and the Israeli armies by their occupation of the Canal Zone.

The Israelis advanced and British and French troops entered the Canal Zone as planned. Then the storm broke. The rest of the world was outraged. The Americans were angry since they had not been consulted and, realising that this rash Anglo-French action could only improve the USSR's standing in the Middle East, voted against Britain at the United Nations. Britain ran into a major financial crisis and public opinion was fiercely divided (see sources F1–2). The troops were withdrawn and the Egyptians, though militarily savaged by the Israelis, were left in possession of the Canal (see source F3). Nasser was more popular than ever. The British and French governments had made a colossal miscalculation. Times had changed. Military action of the Suez type had no chance of success without American backing.

Source F: The Suez Crisis

F1 *A Soviet cartoon of the Suez crisis.*

1 *Identify the sphinx, the cockerel and the lion in the Soviet cartoon. What is its message?*

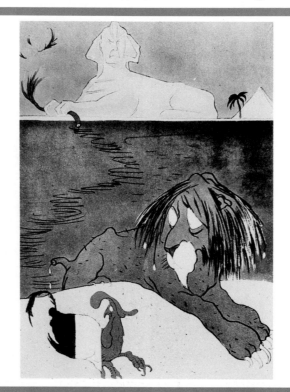

F2 Daily Express, *1 November 1956.*   F3 Daily Mirror, *1 November 1956.*

F2   **F3**

The Suez Crisis, 1956: conflicting opinions.

Look at sources F2 and F3.

2 *From the* Daily Mirror *(F3) write down three sentences which are statements of fact and three which are opinions.*

3 a) *Summarise in your own words the* Daily Express *article.*
b) *In what main ways does it disagree with the* Daily Mirror*? Which paper supported the Labour Party and which the Conservatives?*

4 *Why did Britain invade the Suez Canal area in 1956? What fighting actually took place? When and why did British forces withdraw? What were the consequences of this 'Suez Crisis'?*

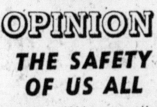

DAILY EXPRESS
THE GUARDIAN OF PUBLIC LIBERTIES

OPINION
THE SAFETY OF US ALL

THE military action undertaken by Britain in Egypt has a clear motive which should commend itself to all the people :—

To safeguard the life of the British Empire.

For that reason the country should rally to the Prime Minister. The nation should acknowledge the resolution that inspires his decision and the deep necessity that imposes it upon him.

This is not a concern remote from the national life as was the integrity of Poland in 1939. This is an issue on which the livelihood and very existence of our people depend.

Guard the lifeline

THE peace of the lands which surround the Suez Canal has been broken. The future of that area is dark and dismal.

Yet the Canal is the lifeline of the Empire. If it passes into hostile hands or passes out of use on account of a violent outbreak, the Empire is destroyed and Britain, as we know it, is at an end.

Without a manifestation of strength and courage such as Sir Anthony Eden has launched, living conditions here must sink to so low a level that there will be nothing but misery in the country, with oblivion as the next chapter in the story.

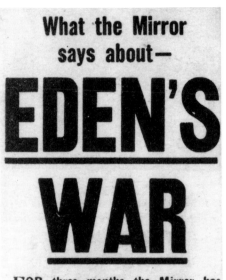

What the Mirror says about—
EDEN'S WAR

FOR three months the Mirror has warned the nation that Sir Anthony Eden's handling of the Middle East crisis might lead us into war.

Time and again the Mirror has attacked gunboat diplomacy.

Today those warnings stand fully justified.

British bombs fall on Egypt.

British and French troops are poised to seize Egyptian territory.

Tory spokesmen in the Commons and some Tory newspapers claim that Eden's action against Egypt is a triumph for the rule of law. That is claptrap.

The truth is this:

There is NO treaty, NO international authority, NO moral sanction for this desperate action.

This is Eden's War.

Unlike some newspapers which are whooping with joy at this grave news, the Mirror has no shameful record of appeasement to live down.

Orders

Clearly everyone's thoughts at this moment must first be with the British soldiers whose job it is to carry out the Government's orders.

This newspaper has taken no part and will take no part in inciting discontent among the troops.

But in a democracy that must not mean that all criticism of the Government has to be stifled once shooting starts.

The Mirror declares that the attack on Egypt is the culminating blunder in Eden's disastrous Middle East record.

France and Algeria

The French had one more bitter pill to swallow, this one fed them by Algerian nationalists. Algeria was one of the oldest French colonies and had a large French settler population nearly a million in number. However sympathetic Paris governments might be to greater self-government for the Algerian Arabs, the settler population was resolutely against it.

A major uprising organised by the nationalist movement, the FLN, began in 1954. A cruel guerrilla war followed. Massacres of French settlers were countered by large-scale executions of captured guerrillas. Villages were resettled and suspects tortured. The Algerian war caused a major political crisis within France and brought the French Resistance leader, General de Gaulle, to power in 1958. He decided that there was no alternative but Algerian independence and brought this about in 1962, despite a European rising in Algiers and attempts to assassinate him. Most French settlers left Algeria.

Iran (Persia) and its oilfields

In contrast the Western powers did rather better in Iran with its important oilfields. They faced a serious crisis there in 1951 when Mossadegh, the Prime Minister, nationalised the oilfields. Two years later a military revolt assisted by American secret agents caused Mossadegh's downfall. For the next twenty years under the influence of the Shah of Iran the Iranian government was thoroughly pro-Western.

West, Central and Southern Africa

Nationalism in Africa

In October 1945, in a suburb of Manchester, a group of young and at that time obscure African politicians calling themselves the Pan-African Congress passed this resolution: 'We demand for Black Africa autonomy and independence'. Most European colonial officials in Africa would not have heard of the meeting and would have considered the resolution idiotic. The vast majority of black Africans were illiterate and their educational opportunities very limited. In addition few of them had experience of government and administration. None the less African nationalism was to prove as irresistible as the Arab and Asian form.

Ghana

The first of the British colonies to go was the Gold Coast (Ghana). Nkrumah, a keen and ambitious nationalist politician, had been at the Pan-African Congress meeting. He returned home in 1947 and built up a mass nationalist movement. The following year, in Accra the capital, police opened fire on a peaceful demonstration, killing twenty-nine people. Nkrumah was locked up in the state of emergency which followed. Britain's Labour government then carried out inquiries which made clear how strong Ghanaian nationalism has become. Nkrumah was released. He became Prime Minister in 1952 and led Ghana to full independence in 1957.

Nigeria, Sierra Leone and Gambia

Ghana's example was infectious. Within Britain there was no longer the will to oppose the principle of independence. The main issue with which Colonial Ministers grappled was the speed with which it should be granted. Where there was no sizeable group of white settlers as in West Africa the change-over was reasonably straightforward. Nigeria gained independence in 1961, Sierra Leone in 1962 and the Gambia in 1965. Where white settlement had taken place, as in Kenya and Southern Rhodesia, things were much more difficult.

Kenya

Kenya had a rich and influential white community which owned some of the best land, the White Highlands. Its Kikuyu people had an able nationalist leader, Kenyatta, who had also been at the 1945 Pan-African Congress. The 1950s in Kenya were dominated by the strange and cruel Mau Mau rebellion which though directed against European landowners also killed many Africans. At the height of the rebellion the colonial government held 80,000 Africans in concentration camps, at one of which some inmates were beaten to death by the warders. In Britain Macmillan's Conservative government decided that it could no longer afford the cost nor the international unpopularity of holding down African nationalism by force. Kenya became independent in 1963 with Kenyatta as President.

Rhodesia

The white settlers of Southern Rhodesia resisted black nationalism with great determination. They had been granted self-government in 1923 and had watched Britain's retreat from Empire with growing dismay. A complicated scheme to merge Northern Rhodesia (Zambia), Nyasaland (Malawi) and Southern Rhodesia into a Central African Federation failed in 1962 because of the opposition of African nationalist leaders. While Zambia and Malawi both gained independence in 1964 under black nationalist governments, white Rhodesians united together in the Rhodesian Front party and refused to allow any major improvements in the political situation of their African population. When Harold Wilson, Britain's Prime Minister, pressed for further reforms, Ian Smith, the Rhodesian Front leader, declared Rhodesia to be independent. Britain huffed and puffed but refused to use force against what was in fact a white rebellion. There was an outcry internationally and an economic blockade. This the white settlers survived quite easily, thanks to aid from South Africa. What eventually defeated them was a guerrilla war with nationalist armies supplied and trained by the communist bloc. These guerrillas were able to invade with great effectiveness after the collapse of Portuguese power in neighbouring Angola and Mozambique during the 1970s.

Unilateral Declaration of Independence

Zimbabwe

The USA became convinced that the existence of a white minority government in Rhodesia encouraged the spread of communism in Africa. It persuaded the South African government to withdraw its support from Smith and the Rhodesian Front. In 1980 Rhodesia briefly returned to British rule before being handed over as independent Zimbabwe to Mugabe, former guerrilla leader and winner by a wide margin of the first 'one man one vote' general election.

South Africa

Only South Africa stayed under European control. There were three main reasons for this. The settler population was comparatively large (3,100,000 in 1960 against Rhodesia's 240,000). Secondly the dominant European group, the Afrikaners of Dutch descent, did not regard Europe as home. South Africa, they believed, was their God-given homeland which they had developed and would continue to develop as a Christian and civilised land. Thirdly, the country was immensely rich with gold and other minerals of great importance to the Western world. However much the West disliked aspects of white rule in South Africa it did not take action against it for fear of its riches falling into unfriendly hands, particularly communist ones.

Apartheid

Though the British had won the Boer War in 1899–1902 they were slightly outnumbered by the Boer (Afrikaner) population and in the Union of South Africa, created in 1910, a united Afrikaner population could win a general election. Such a victory was achieved in 1948 by Malan's Nationalist party. Malan and his colleagues were completely out of step with the rest of the world and gloried in the fact. They believed that whites were superior to blacks and that South Africa had no future unless it was dominated by the whites. They kept the country's 'colour bar' and made it more systematic by introducing 'apartheid' or 'separate development'. The various races were to be separated; their traditional tribal lands were named their 'homelands'; and they could only enjoy political rights in these homelands even if they lived and worked hundreds of miles away. Much the best agricultural, industrial and residential areas were reserved for the whites. So were the best jobs. Whole non-white communities were uprooted from their homes of long standing and forcibly resettled to fit the schemes of the 'apartheid' planners (see sources H1–5).

Sharpeville shootings

Apartheid made South Africa the most hated country in the world and it became impossible for her to remain part of the British Commonwealth which was committed to racial equality. Internal opposition was considerable and dealt with ruthlessly by the government. In 1960, at Sharpeville not far from Johannesburg, police opened fire on a demonstration and killed sixty-seven people. The African opposition turned to violence and terrorism but some of its best leaders, including Nelson Mandela (see source H4), were hunted down and imprisoned with long sentences. Others, like the young Biko, died in police custody. Through the 1960s and 1970s South Africa flourished economically and could afford a modern well-equipped army and a large security police force.

Opposition leaders hunted

Southern Africa since 1964.

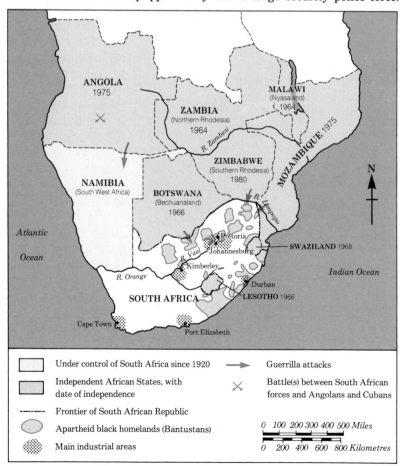

Source G: Rhodesia

G1 *A Rhodesian cartoon of 5 January 1966.*

1 *Identify the man in the cooking pot and his white cook. Explain the words on his hat.*

2 *Explain the caption and the Chinaman in the long grass.*

3 *What do you think were the political views of the cartoonist? Explain your answer.*

"HIM GOOD COOK, LIKE US!"

G2 *The Problem of Southern Rhodesia.
In October 1965 Prime Minister Wilson flew out from London to Salisbury in an attempt to prevent Smith, the leader of the Rhodesian Front government which had overwhelming support from the white settlers, from declaring independence illegally. Having talked to Smith he then consulted other Rhodesians, including Africans. This is how the consultations went, according to his 'Personal Record'. (No agreement proved possible between the British government and the Rhodesian Front government which made its Unilateral Declaration of Independence (UDI) on 11 November.)*

4 *Explain the phrases 'no independence before majority rule': 'one man, one vote'.*

5 *What was UDI? Who led the Rhodesian Front Party? Who were his supporters? At the time of UDI who of Rhodesia/Zimbabwe's adults had the vote?*

6 *What was the general opinion of the Rhodesians whom Wilson consulted on 26 and 27 October? What sections of the Rhodesian population did these people represent?*

7 *Why was Smith so keen for Wilson to meet the Council of Chiefs? For what reasons did Wilson form a low opinion of their views? Was this sensible of him?*

8 *How and when did Rhodesia become Zimbabwe?*

G2

"At 2.30 p.m. [on Tuesday 26 October 1965] I saw the leader of the parliamentary Opposition; at 3.45 p.m. Mr Palley the white liberal elected by . . . Africans; at 5 p.m. a delegation from the Asian community; and a 6 p.m. the representative of a . . . separate coloured community. All of these were flatly opposed to the Rhodesian Front proposals, almost all to any independence before majority rule . . . .

[The next day] at 11.15 a.m. Mr Nkomo was brought in with his colleagues of the Zimbabwe African People's Union (ZAPU) from [various] detention centres . . . . Our talks rapidly made it clear that Mr Nkomo and his supporters had no intention whatsoever of accepting any settlement without prior majority rule . . . . At 5 p.m. the Reverend Sithole came in with his supporters [of the Zimbabwe African National Union]. They immediately dismissed any suggestion of working with ZAPU but . . . whatever the personal antipathies [dislikes] they took exactly the same line as Nkomo . . .: one man, one vote.

Thursday 28 October was certainly the most colourful day of my visit. The Council of Chiefs paraded on the lawn . . . . I took them to the conference room . . . and made clear my concern to test Mr Smith's claim that the chiefs clearly represented the opinion of four million Africans. In response to question after question, they assured me that they did.

I asked them how they came to know what the Africans were thinking; what were their methods of consultation and discussion? Two or three of them insisted that they simply knew, because they owed their position to the divine law of chiefly blood and this made them the best judge of what the Africans wanted."

[*Wilson then explained to the Chiefs the constitutional proposals which he had been discussing with Smith and with the other political groups.*]

"I stopped and asked whether there was a single one of the thirty chiefs present who had the remotest idea of what I was talking about . . . . There was a prolonged silence until one of the chiefs . . . essayed an attempt at it but did not even get near to a correct rendering of what the problem was about. This test satisfied me that their claims to be a respresentative group capable of expressing the opinion of the Africans were totally false."

Soweto riots

Though all races benefited from economic expansion, opposition continued. The young people of Soweto, a huge black township near Johannesburg, rioted in 1976 in protest against the poor quality of their education. Troops were used to crush the riots. Hundreds died. There was renewed terrorist activity and some skirmishes along the borders with Black Africa. The Nationalist government was able to hold the support of most of the white population. Though it took some steps to limit the more cruel and humiliating details of apartheid, it remained absolutely committed to white supremacy in defiance of world opinion.

Independence of French colonies

For ten years after the Second World War the French tried to forge closer links with their African colonies and discouraged independence movements. However in 1956 they changed this policy. Morocco and Tunisia in the north gained full independence, and the other colonies self-government. From then on the French had no intention of trying to stem the nationalist tide. All their African colonies were independent by 1960.

Belgian Congo

Probably the most tragic case of decolonisation was that of the Belgian Congo. Quite suddenly in 1959 the Belgian government decided to grant independence to a population which was completely unprepared for such a step. In 1960 Lumumba, a former postal clerk, became the first Prime Minister of an independent Congo. The army mutinied, a civil war began and by 1961 Lumumba had been murdered. Despite the arrival of a United Nations force to restore peace, war continued for another nine years causing much destruction and suffering.

The end of European empires

It would be wrong however to conclude that European empires ended only in bloodshed and bitterness with the nationalists wishing to rid their countries of all European connections. During the years of Empire many ties of education, culture, trade and friendship had been made which were valued by both sides. Almost all the former British colonies remained members of the Commonwealth, whose head was the British monarch and whose chief aim was to maintain the friendly links. The former French colonies had similar ties with France.

Source H: South Africa 1964–80

H1–3 *Verwoerd was appointed Minister of Native Affairs in South Africa in 1950. He held this post for eight years until he became Prime Minister. Here are some of his views. They are taken from Alexander Hepple's biography of Verwoerd published in 1967.*

1 *What is meant by the term 'Native Reserves' (source H1)? What kind of future did Verwoerd foresee for Africans on the Reserves (or Bantustans) compared with the Africans living in European areas?*

2 *What did he mean by the sentence in italic in source H3?*

H1

"I want to state unequivocally [absolutely clearly] now . . . that South Africa is a white man's country and he must remain the master here. In the Reserves we are prepared to allow the Natives to be the masters, . . .but within the European areas, we, the white people of South Africa are and shall remain the masters . . ."

H2

"The Bantu in the cities are not distinct from the Bantu in the Native Reserves. They belong to one another and . . . the urban Bantu are visitors in the white areas . . . for their own economic benefit. Their roots are in the Native Reserves. The opportunities for them to enjoy rights, whether they be social or political rights, are available to them in their home areas . . ."

H3

"I will reform it [African education] so that the Natives will be taught from childhood to realise that equality with Europeans is not for them ... racial relations cannot improve if the wrong type of education is given to the Natives. *They cannot improve if the result of Native education is the creation of a frustrated people who ... have expectations in life which circumstances in South Africa do not allow to be fulfilled...*"

H4

H4 *In the early sixties some leaders of the African National Congress, including Mandela, decided to turn to violence, particularly acts of sabotage. They were arrested in the Rivonia surburb of Johannesburg in 1963 and brought to trial in 1964. This is the final section of Mandela's speech in the court. This extract is taken from Mary Benson's* The Struggle for a Birthright, *1963. Mandela and the other accused were found guilty and sentenced to life imprisonment.*

"Africans want to be paid a living wage. Africans want to perform work which they are capable of doing.... We want to be allowed to live where we obtain work and not to be endorsed out of an area because we were not born there. We want to be allowed to own places where we work ... African men want to have their wives and children to live with them where they work ... our women want to be with their menfolk and not to be left permanently widowed in the reserves. We want to be allowed out after 11 o'clock at night and not to be confined to our rooms like little children. We want a just share in the whole of South Africa.

Above all we want political rights.

Our struggle is a truly national one. It is a struggle of the African people inspired by our own suffering and our own experience. It is a struggle for the right to live.

During my lifetime I have dedicated myself to this struggle of the African people. I have fought against white domination and I have fought against black domination. I have cherished the ideal of a democratic and free society in which all persons live together in harmony with equal opportunities. It is an ideal which I hope to live for and achieve. But if needs be, it is an ideal for which I am prepared to die."

H5 *Victims of riots in Soweto, June 1976.*

3 *What effects, according to Mandela (source H4) did apartheid have on the life of most Africans?*

4 *Why did Mandela and other nationalist leaders turn to violence?*

5 *Europeans managed to stay in control of South Africa after 1945 while everywhere else they retreated before the advance of Asian and African nationalism. How were they able to stay in power? At what cost? (See sources H4 and H5.)*

17 Britain since 1945

Britain had played a heroic part in the Second World War. She had emerged victorious, her huge empires still intact. Not surprisingly most Britons believed their country to be one of the Big Three world powers, nearly, if not quite, the equal of the USA and the USSR.

Such a belief was based however on appearances, not realities. Britain was exhausted economically. As part of the struggle to save Europe from Nazism, she had had to sell more than £1,000 million of overseas investments. £1,500 million worth of damage had been done to factories and homes, 15.9 million tonnes of shipping had been sunk. Her economic position was made worse in August 1945 when President Truman of the USA suddenly cancelled the wartime Lend-Lease agreement. Although Canada and the USA lent Britain some money to help her through the first years of peace, her financial position remained weak. Marshall Aid (see page 244) was needed to end one financial crisis in 1947, but another, two years later, caused the pound to be devalued against the dollar from £1 to $4.03 to £1 to $2.80. Moreover, the strength of the British Empire was an illusion, as the events of the next twenty years were to show. A major question of Britain's post-war history was how successfully her government and people would adjust to the realities of a greatly changed world.

The 1945 general election

The result of the 1945 general election surprised the world. Churchill, the great war leader, and his Conservative Party lost to Labour by a wide margin (Labour 393 seats, 48 per cent of the votes, Conservative 213, 40 per cent). Churchill was voted out, not because of his wartime record, but for his pre-war peacetime one. The voters wanted a new society, better than that of the 1930s, with less unemployment and better living conditions for everyone. For this Labour seemed the best bet.

Attlee

The new Prime Minister was Attlee who, during his life, was underestimated by almost everyone. He was a small, modest and quiet man, but very determined and exceptionally good at choosing ministers and at running them as a team. During his six years as Prime Minister he led one of the most effective reforming governments in British history (see sources B1–4).

Labour reforms, 1945–50

The Beveridge Report

Its major achievement was the creation of what became known as 'the welfare state'. In 1942 Sir William Beveridge had been asked to write a report on how social insurance might be organised once the war was over. His report did rather more than discuss new methods of organising insurance. It explained how Want, Disease, Ignorance, Squalor and Idleness, which made the lives of too many of the population more miserable than they need be, could be lessened by government action. Labour welcomed the Beveridge Report and was deeply influenced by it. In 1946 Attlee's government passed the National Insurance Act. This built on the Liberal 'welfare' reforms of 1906–14. Unemployment benefit, old age and widows' pensions and death grants were made available to all citizens who paid their national insurance stamps. Since many of the welfare services were paid for by a tax system which required more taxes from the higher paid, the needs of the poor and weak would be met by the rich and strong.

***The National
Health Service***

The National Health Service (NHS) Act was passed the same year. Its aim was to provide good free medical care to everyone who needed it; an enormous advance over previous practice. The NHS Act was much more controversial than the National Insurance Act partly because of its expected cost, partly because doctors believed that it would reduce their fees and their freedom and partly because Bevan, the Minister of Health, was himself a controversial character. Born the son of a Welsh miner,

Source A: Britain after the Second World War

FIRST IN THE QUEUE

A1 *A cartoon on Beveridge, which appeared in the* Daily Express, *17 February 1943.*

A2 *Living conditions 1945–9, as described by A. Marwick in* Britain in our Century, *1984.*

Refer to source A1.

1 a) *Who is holding the board?*
   b) *Explain 'social security' and 'tenders invited'.*

2 *Explain the point of view of the cartoonist.*

3 *What got built on the building site after the war?*

4 *Look at the rations allowance in source A2. How does this compare with your present weekly food consumption? You will find people who say that they were never healthier than during the years of rationing. How could this be?*

5 *Explain the Tory slogan 'shiver with Shinwell and starve with Strachey'. What might have been a Labour slogan for the 1950 election?*

A2

"the years [1945–9] undoubtedly brought harassment for the ordinary housewife coping with shortages and juggling with the various forms of rationing. Basic foodstuffs were on 'coupons', clothing on 'clothing coupons', tinned fruits and dried fruits on one kind of 'points' and chocolate and sweets on another, popularly known as 'sweetie coupons'. Rations fluctuated, but in 1948 they worked out at a weekly allowance per person of 13 oz [370 g] of meat, 1½ oz [40 g] of cheese, 6 oz [170 g] of butter and margarine, 1 oz [30 g] of cooking fat, 8 oz [240 g] of sugar, 2 pints of milk and one egg. In neither world war ... had it proved necessary to institute bread rationing but in 1946 the Minister of Food, John Strachey, introduced this ultimate symbol of belt-tightening, which lasted from July 1946 to July 1948. The big freeze-up associated with the fuel policies of Emanuel Shinwell brought forth the anti-Labour slogan in the Tory press: 'shiver with Shinwell and Starve with Strachey'. Already modest rations were further reduced in the aftermath of the financial crisis of 1947, when there was at no time greater popular enthusiasm for the various delicacies offered by the Ministry of Food such as whale meat and the mysterious but aptly named canned fish snoek."

he was a fiery speaker and firmly on the left wing of the party. However he proved to be a skilful negotiator. He had to be, since the doctors, acting through the British Medical Association (BMA), strongly opposed the scheme. At one stage 90 per cent threatened to resign rather than join the new service. Bevan did not give way on any major point of principle but made some well-timed compromises which caused the medical opposition to crumble away. The NHS came into existence in 1948 and quickly won support from most patients and doctors.

Nationalisation

Another priority for Labour was nationalisation. Socialists believed that the best interests of the people would be served if major industrial and financial institutions were run for the benefit of the public, not for private profit. Between 1946 and 1951 the Bank of England, civil aviation, the coal mines, railways and road haulage, gas, electricity, cable and wireless, iron and steel were all nationalised. With the exception of iron and steel, the Conservatives were not too angry about this change of ownership, massive though it was. You did not have to be a socialist to support state control of key industries like cable and wireless, gas and electricity. Moreover old industries, like coal and the railways, were running at a loss, and the compensation offered to their former owners by the Labour government was quite generous. The main weakness of the nationalisation scheme was that it had not been considered carefully enough before being put into effect. It did little to change the management methods within the industries and less to encourage within them a new approach to public service. As time passed, the Labour leadership became less keen on nationalisation, partly because it was not popular with the electorate.

Foreign policy

The Foreign Minister was Ernest Bevin, a former trade union boss, tough, intelligent and effective. He kept Britain a close ally of the USA through the difficult years of the Cold War. In immediate crises he had a realistic idea of Britain's limited capabilities and pulled troops out of both Greece and Palestine when the situation became impossible. He also realised that Britain could not stay in India. None the less he still believed that he was Foreign Secretary of a major world power which should keep armed forces large enough to operate anywhere in the world. Attlee, with Bevin and a few senior ministers, decided in 1946 that Britain should make her own atomic bomb, lest she became too dependent on the USA. The decision was a secret one. Parliament was not informed, let alone consulted.

The 1950 general election

There was real hardship between 1945 and 1950. Food and other goods were rationed. Housing was in short supply, as was fuel, particularly during the cold winter of 1947 (see source A2). People grumbled against the government and Churchill spoke out loudly about errors of socialism with its bad planning and too many controls. None the less Labour won the 1950 general election, though its majority was greatly reduced (Labour 315, 46 per cent, Conservative 298, 43.5 per cent).

Labour defeat, 1951

Labour's majority over all the parties combined was only six. Its leaders were worn out. Yet they had immediately to face the crisis of the Korean War. As allies of the USA and members of the UN they agreed to send troops as part of the UN force defending South Korea against Communist North Korea. Gaitskell, Chancellor of the Exchequer, raised income tax and charged fees for prescriptions, spectacles and false teeth

Source B: The Labour Government 1945–51

B1 *Attlee on Cabinet government. (This and the following extracts are taken from the biography of Attlee by Kenneth Harris, 1982.)*

B1

"A Prime Minister has to know when to ask for an opinion. He can't always stop some Ministers offering theirs – you'll always have some people who'll talk on everything. But he can make sure to extract the opinion of those he wants when he needs them. The job of the Prime Minister is to get the general feeling – collect the voices. And then when everything reasonable has been said, to get on with the job and say, 'Well, I think the decision of the Cabinet is this, that or the other. Any objections?' Usually there aren't. I didn't often find my Cabinet disagreeing with me. To go through the agenda you must stop people talking – unnecessary talk, unnecessary approval of things already agreed, pleasant byways that may be interesting but not strictly relevant. And you should not talk too much yourself however good you are at it."

B2 *For some weeks after the decision had been taken to nationalise the railways, one minister continued to send papers to Attlee asking that the Cabinet reconsider its 'proposals'. Attlee terminated the correspondence with one minute (note): 'The Cabinet does not propose; it decides'.*

This is the opinion of a distinguished civil servant who served under five Prime Ministers.

B2

"[Attlee was] orderly, regular, efficient and methodical to a degree which put him in a different class from any of the prime ministers who followed him . . . the country was never so well-governed, in this technical sense, in living memory . . .".

B3 *Attlee thought that choosing ministers was one of a Prime Minister's most exacting tasks . . . . The fatal mistake was to select 'docile yes-men'. To guard against this Attlee sometimes chose to 'put in people who are likely to be awkward'. These were always warned in advance: 'If you don't turn out all right I shall sack you .' . . . He thought it essential for a Prime Minister to pick his ministers himself.*

B3

"My general experience was that when I accepted advice it wasn't very good. I did once or twice have people foisted on me. People don't always understand why a man who seems very clever may not turn out to be particularly good as a Cabinet Minister."

B4

One junior minister . . . was summoned precipitately to Number 10, to be congratulated on the work of his department, so he thought. 'What can I do for you, Prime Minister?' he said, as he sat down. 'I want your job', said Attlee. The minister was staggered. 'But why, Prime Minister?' 'Afraid you're not up to it', said Attlee. The interview was over.

1 What is 'the Cabinet'? What did Attlee believe to be the main job of a Prime Minister in Cabinet meetings?

2 What qualities had Attlee which made him a good Prime Minister?

3 What were the main achievements of his government between 1945 and 1951?

4 How good a source does Harris's biography seem to be? What other sources would you turn to for a balanced view of Attlee's strengths and weaknesses?

in order to pay for the war. These health service charges caused Bevan and Wilson to resign from the Cabinet. These resignations reflected an important and lasting argument within the Labour Party about the nature of British socialism. Bevan and Wilson represented the left wing of the party who wanted greater social change and no compromise of the principle of free medical service for all citizens. Attlee and Gaitskell represented the more moderate section of the party. They were suspicious of too much talk of principles and believed that governments sometimes had to make compromises if they were to be effective.

The summer of 1951 brought another financial crisis. Finding it difficult to control the House of Commons with only a small majority, Attlee called another general election. This time, though they still won fewer votes, the Conservatives won a majority in Parliament (Conservatives 321, 48 per cent, Labour 295 49 per cent).

Conservative government, 1951–64

Churchill Prime Minister

Churchill was now seventy-seven, an old man, who tended to surround himself with old friends. None the less he did not try to turn back the clock. The Conservatives accepted that the welfare state had come to stay and nationalisation too, except for iron, steel and road haulage which they denationalised. Their main achievements while Churchill was Prime Minister were to end rationing, lower income tax and, in 1953, build 300,000 new homes. Butler, Chancellor of the Exchequer, won credit for the sense of growing prosperity, Macmillan for the success with house-building, but, after Churchill, the leading Conservative was Eden, the Foreign Secretary. He added to his already considerable reputation by successes in 1954. He helped to end the Indo-China war between the French and the communists. He also persuaded the French, West Germans and British to agree on the tricky subject of German rearmament. That same year Churchill announced that Britain would make its own hydrogen bomb. It was his last major political decision. He retired in 1955.

Eden Prime Minister

The 1955 election

Eden, his successor, called a general election almost immediately. Labour was divided. Its left wing, led by Bevan, criticised the party leadership for its loyalty to the USA and it acceptance of a high level of military spending. In his budget just before the election, Butler again cut income tax and the Conservatives told the electorate that they were the party of prosperity. They won a large majority (Conservative 344, 50 per cent, Labour 277, 46 per cent).

The Suez crisis, 1956

Eden had been a good Foreign Secretary but proved a poor Prime Minister. He was not fully fit. His choice of ministers and his handling of them was clumsy. They found him a fussy and muddled leader. The Suez crisis of 1956 broke him. It was his excited and inaccurate comparison of Nasser with Hitler which was the chief cause of the fiasco (see page 000). At the height of the crisis his health broke down and he went to Jamaica to convalesce leaving Butler the unhappy task of pulling British troops out of the Canal Zone. He eventually resigned in 1957.

Macmillan Prime Minister

Macmillan and Butler were the rivals to succeed him. The Conservative method of choosing a leader was for influential members to take 'soundings' across the party membership. Their choice was Macmillan. He was witty, unflappable and apparently easygoing yet hard-working, decisive, ambitious and well-connected. In comparison Butler seemed lacking in strength and fire, though he was experienced, intelligent and extremely conscientious.

Macmillan was an immediate success as Prime Minister. Having an American wife and being a personal friend of President Eisenhower, he soon regained the confidence of the US government which Eden had lost. He announced a revised defence policy based on the H-bomb and a small professional army. This allowed him to end national service (conscription) and to reduce defence spending. In 1958 he sacked his Chancellor of the Exchequer, Thorneycroft, because his policies of financial restraint were increasing unemployment. Next year, 1959, was election year.

Source C: Divisions within the Labour Party

"SOCIALISTS!"

C1 *Vicky cartoon from the* News Chronicle, *July 1951.*

C2 *Aneurin Bevan's resignation speech in January 1951 to the House of Commons. The cause of Bevan's resignation was the plan of Gaitskell, the Chancellor of the Exchequer, whom he loathed, to pay for an increased spending on armaments by various means including the introduction of fees in the National Health Service. Gaitskell's plan had been approved by the Cabinet.*

1 *In source C1 identify the largest hooligan (a former Minister of Health), the man leading the file of top-hatted children (the Prime Minister), and the child immediately behind him (the Chancellor of the Exchequer).*

2 *Explain the 'Keep Left' and 'One Way Only' signs.*

3 *'Socialist' is being used as a term of abuse in the cartoon. Why is this?*

4 *What was the event which caused this cartoon to be drawn?*

5 *What were the main points Bevan made in his speech (source C2)? To what extent do you think that he was correct?*

C2

"I therefore say with the full solemnity of the seriousness of what I am saying that the £4,700 million arms programme is already dead. It cannot be achieved without irreparable damage to the economy of Great Britain and the world.

Over and over again I have said that these figures of arms production are fantastically wrong . . . . May I be permitted in passing to give a word of advice to my colleagues in the Government . . . . Take economic planning away from the Treasury, they know nothing about it . . . . It has been perfectly obvious that there are too many economists advising the Treasury and now we have the added misfortune of having an economist in the Chancellor of the Exchequer himself.

I now come to the National Health side of the matter. Let me say to my Hon. Friends on these benches: you have been saying in the last fortnight . . . that I have been quarrelling about a triviality, spectacles and dentures.

The Chancellor of the Exchequer has taken £23 million out of the Budget total of £4,000 million. If he finds it necessary to mutilate or begin to mutilate the Health Service for £13 million, what will he do next? . . . Prescriptions? Hospital charges? Where do you stop? . . .

I say this in conclusion. There is only one hope for mankind – and that is democratic Socialism. There is only one Party in Britain which can do it – and that is the Labour Party. But I ask them carefully to consider how far they are polluting the stream. We have gone a long way – a very long way – against great difficulties. Let us not change direction now."

There were cuts in both income and purchase tax. Newspapers referred to Macmillan as 'Super-Mac' and the Tory election slogan was 'Life is better under the Conservatives. Don't let Labour ruin it.' Labour, now led by Gaitskell, was still badly split – mainly over defence and nationalisation. In the by-elections of 1957 and 1958 the Liberals rather than Labour picked up the anti-government vote. The 1959 general election was a Conservative triumph (Conservative 365, 49 per cent, Labour 258, 44 per cent, Liberal 6, 6 per cent.) Though the Liberals doubled their vote, they did not gain any more seats.

The 1959 general election

Macmillan faces some major problems 1959–63

Economic difficulties

Macmillan had another four years as Prime Minister but the period 1959–63 was an anti-climax. The pre-election budget had been good for votes but was bad economics. The boom petered out. Because more foreign goods were imported than British goods exported there was a balance of payments crisis. Attempts to hold down wages led to serious strikes in 1962, including railwaymen, postmen and nurses. During the winter of 1962–3 unemployment rose to 800,000 after a decade when the country had come to take full employment for granted.

Defence

Furthermore Conservative defence policy got into knots. In 1957 Britain had a nuclear deterrent which was genuinely independent. British-built V-bombers (see source D1) carried British built H-bombs. By 1960 the missile systems developed by the Americans and Russians made Britain's deterrent obsolete. An attempt to build a British missile, the Blue Streak, failed. Consequently Macmillan had to persuade the Americans, through the 'Nassau agreement' (1962), to sell Britain their Polaris submarine missile system (see sources D2 and D3).

The Common Market

Another important Conservative plan came to nothing the following year, Britain's attempt to join the Common Market (see page 258). In 1962 an American expert on foreign affairs, Dean Acheson, commented that 'Britain has lost an Empire and not yet found a role'. Since the truth often hurts, many Britons were upset by this remark and retorted that it was wrong as well as unfriendly. Others, realising its essential accuracy, began to ask more often what kind of society they wanted in Britain and what part their country should play in the world.

Meanwhile the Labour Party was recovering. Gaitskell had managed to persuade most of the party to support NATO and nuclear weapons. There was almost complete unity against the Common Market. Unity was further strengthened by brilliant attacks on the Conservative record by the new leader Wilson who had succeeded Gaitskell when the latter died in 1963.

Macmillan resigns, 1963

Wilson had plenty of ammunition. Macmillan's government was rocked by one spy scandal in 1962 and another more scandalous still in 1963, involving spies, sex and a minister lying to the House of Commons (the Profumo affair).

Simultaneously some London landlords were discovered to be badly treating their tenants thanks to the Conservative Rent Act of 1957. Macmillan resigned in 1963 for health reasons. The usual Conservative 'soundings' produced not Butler, much the most experienced minister, nor another capable minister with a seat in the House of Commons, but the Earl of Home, a pleasant modest aristocrat who had been a Foreign Secretary of no special distinction since 1960. Two of the most able of Macmillan's cabinet, Macleod and Powell, refused to serve under him.

Home Prime Minister

Source D: Deterrence – independent, or dependent on the USA

D1 *Three V-bombers during training at RAF Waddington, September 1957. V-bombers flew at 500 mph (800 km per hour).*

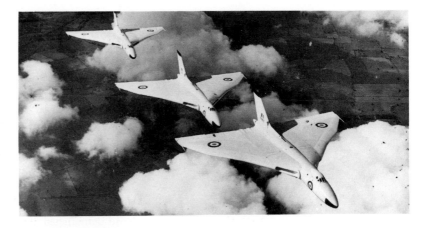

D2 *Polaris fired from a nuclear submarine which could stay under water for sixty days. Its speed was about 6,000 mph (9,600 km per hour) and its range was 2,500–3,000 miles (4,000–4,800 km). This demonstration took place in November 1960.*

D3 *An American pilot by Skybolt in December 1962. The Skybolt missile was made in the USA and bought by the British because their Blue Streak never worked satisfactorily.*

1 *If there had been a nuclear war in the 1950s how would Britain have launched a nuclear attack?*
2 *Using sources D1–3 explain how Britain's independent deterrent had become obsolete by 1960.*

Source E: Britain and the Common Market

E1 *Macmillan proposed to the House of Commons in 1961 that Britain should apply to join the Common Market. This description is taken from the biography of Macmillan by Nigel Fisher, published in 1982.*

E1

"He argued for an outward-looking Europe, ready to help under-developed countries, to which Britain with its world-wide ties could make a valuable contribution. 'I believe that our right place is in the vanguard of the movement towards the greater unity of the free world and that we can lead better from within than outside'.

He went on to claim that membership of the Community would strengthen Britain's economy and so enable her to help the Common-wealth more effectively. It would be a mistake, he thought, to regard her European and Commonwealth interests as conflicting. He believed the weight of opinion in British industry was in favour of joining the EEC since it would provide a market comparable in size . . . to Russia or the United States.

He demolished the argument of diminished national sovereignty by pointing out that every treaty was a limitation of a nation's freedom of action, but in this case he had noticed no loss of French or German national liberty."

E2 *Gaitskell, leader of the Labour Party, stated his position on the Common Market at the 1961 Labour Party Conference. This extract is taken from the biography of Gaitskell by P. Williams, published in 1982. (Privately Gaitskell thought the Common Market arguments 'always a bore and a nuisance'.)*

E2

"We would gain in markets where we sell less than one-fifth of our exports and lose in markets where we sell about half our exports . . . . We are to be obliged to import expensive food from the continent of Europe in place of cheap food from the Commonwealth . . . . You cannot have it both ways. It is either better for industry to have tougher competition – which it will certainly get at home – or better for it to have easier conditions which it will get in the markets of the Six. Both arguments cannot be true . . . . It is not mainly because of the Common Market that Europe has had this remarkable growth recently . . . . The truth is that the faults lie not in our markets nor in the tariffs but in ourselves.

[It could mean] the end of Britain as an independent state . . . the end of a thousand years of history . . . . Becoming a province of Europe must mean the end of the Commonwealth . . . . We are told that the British people are not capable of judging the issue – that the Government knows best . . . . What an odious piece of arrogant rubbish this is!"

E3 *A German cartoonist's view of Macmillan's application, October 1961.*

E4 *Macmillan and de Gaulle. This extract is taken from a biography of de Gaulle by Don Cook, published in 1984. De Gaulle announced his veto on Britain's entry at a news conference on 14 January 1963.*

E5 *The French Minister of Agriculture said this in conversation with the British Ambassador, not long afterwards.*

E6 *Macmillan's diary entry after de Gaulle's veto:*

E7 *A cartoon of de Gaulle, from the* Daily Express *1967.*

1 *What positions were held in 1962 by*
  a) *Macmillan* b) *Gaitskell,* c) *de Gaulle?*

2 *List:*
  a) *the reasons given by Macmillan for going into the Common Market.*
  b) *the reasons given by Gaitskell for staying out.*
  c) *Whom do you think events have proved to be the more accurate in his predictions? Explain your answer.*

3 *Gaitskell thought the Common Market a nuisance because it distracted attention from what he believed to be more important questions for British society. What do you think these more important questions were?*

4 *The rower in the boat (source E3) is Erhard the German Economics Minister, on board ship is de Gaulle. Explain the cartoon and indicate the cartoonist's attitude. How fair a comment is it?*

5 *What were de Gaulle's main reasons for opposing Britain's entry?*

6 *Why should Macmillan (source E6) in 1963 have been really depressed by de Gaulle's veto while Wilson in 1967 was not especially bothered?*

7 *Explain the cartoon in source E7.*

E4

"Macmillan was certainly sincere in his conviction that Britain had to join Europe ... and taking Britain into Europe would have been the crowning act of a very successful career .... But joining Europe was deeply divisive within his own party as well as with the Labour opposition ... so he chose to tiptoe cautiously round the problem .... He enjoyed a good conversational and personal relationship with de Gaulle and he believed that ultimately the General would support Britain out of logic and persuasion ... he did not realise or did not accept the real depth of de Gaulle's anti-British feelings."

E5

"My friend. It is very simple. Now with the Six there are five hens and one cock. If you join (with other countries) there will be perhaps seven or eight hens, but there will be two cocks. That would not be a happy arrangement."

E6

"All our policies at home and abroad are in ruins ... European unity is no more; French domination of Europe is the new and alarming feature; our popularity as a government is rapidly declining. We have lost everything except our courage and determination."

The 1964 general election

In their opinion Home was not an appropriate leader for Britain in the 1960s. They were probably right. During the 1964 election campaign Wilson, who was an excellent television performer and cleverer than Home, projected himself as the man of the future with a clear understanding of how science and technology could be harnessed to create a better Britain both economically and socially. In comparison Home appeared ill at ease and out of touch. The result was very close but Labour scraped home (Labour 317, 44 per cent, Conservative 304, 43 per cent, Liberal 9, 11 per cent).

The Thirteen Years

Conservative rule

In some ways the thirteen years of Conservative rule since 1951 were quite successful. Most Britons were better off. They had more cars, washing machines and televisions. The difficult task of decolonisation had been carried out reasonably smoothly – particularly in comparison with France and Belgium. Despite Suez and defence cuts Britain still seemed a major world power. None the less the Labour election slogan of 'thirteen wasted years' had substance to it. The Conservatives had not faced up to the critical weakness of the economy, its increasing uncompetitiveness internationally against rivals like the Japanese, the West Germans and French. They seriously misjudged the effectiveness of the Common Market and failed to apply for entry until too late. They left to fester the running sore of bad relations between employers and trade unions. By spending heavily on an out-of-date defence policy, they had little to spare for modernising hospitals, schools, prisons and suchlike.

Economic problems

Indeed, how to reverse Britain's comparative economic decline was the central political issue of the 1964–83 period. This table shows how the British economy grew in comparison with her neighbours:

Percentage growth per annum in Gross National Products

	1950–60	1961–70
France	4.5	5.5
West Germany	7.8	4.6
Italy	5.4	5.9
Netherlands	4.8	4.8
Britain	2.7	2.9

Stop-go

Not only were Britain's growth rates among the lowest in the industrial world, but her share of international trade and the competitiveness of her manufacturing industry were declining too. Moreover, the economy grew in fits and starts: stop-go was how the newspapers described it. 'Go' was when governments lowered taxes and interest rates to encourage economic growth. More foreign goods were then imported into Britain than British good were exported overseas, so 'balance of payments' crises occurred. These then led to 'stop' policies when governments raised taxes and interest rates. These dealt with the balance of payments problem but slowed down economic growth.

Labour in power, 1964–70

Wilson Prime Minister

Immediately he became Prime Minister Wilson displayed energy and imagination. During his first year of office there were three budgets to deal with a financial crisis which, he persuasively argued, was the fault of the Conservatives. The unions were persuaded to co-operate with the government and to raise production without demanding large wage increases. Defence cuts were announced. Moreover two important social reforms were made in 1965. The Race Relations Act forbade racial discrimination and activities likely to stir up racial hatred; the Rent Act gave tenants greater protection against private landlords. In foreign affairs Wilson broadly supported the Americans in Vietnam and, though he was unable to bring to an end the white settler rebellion in Rhodesia, his policy of economic sanctions kept Labour united. Meanwhile Home had resigned the Conservative leadership to Heath. Wilson called a general election for March 1966. His timing was skilful, taking advantage of the fact that he was much better known to the electorate than Heath. His slogan was 'You *know* Labour government works'. The result was a convincing Labour win (Labour 363, 48 per cent, Conservative 253, 42 per cent, Liberal 12, 8.5 per cent).

The 1966 general election

Economic crisis of 1967–8

An acute economic crisis hit Labour soon after this triumph. International confidence in the government's handling of the economy was weakened by a damaging seamen's strike. Sterling was in trouble on the foreign exchanges. The government faced the choice either of devaluing the pound or imposing tax increases and strict wage controls. To the fury of its left wing it chose the latter course, without success. There was a dock strike in 1967 and another balance of payments crisis. The pound had to be devalued from $2.80 to $2.40 and financial support requested from the International Monetary Fund. Economic weakness continued into 1968 and led to a tough budget of higher taxes mainly on cigarettes, alcohol and petrol.

'In Place of Strife', 1969

In 1969 the government tried to reform the trade unions. Wilson and most of his cabinet believed the country was being damaged by too many strikes which were too often organised by small unrepresentative groups of workers. They had the report of the Donovan Commission but planned to go further than Donovan recommended and make unofficial strikes illegal. They made their intention clear in the document, 'In Place of Strife', published in 1969. Though public opinion was strongly in favour of trade union reform, the trade union leadership and the left wing of the Labour party were obstinately opposed to it (see sources F1–4). When Wilson realised that the only way that he could have got it through Parliament would have been by deeply splitting his party, he gave up the attempt.

The Common Market

The previous Labour policy of opposition to the Common Market was reversed and application for entry made in 1967. De Gaulle vetoed this application (see source E7). Two attempts to negotiate a Rhodesian settlement with Smith, the first on HMS *Tiger* in 1966, the second on HMS *Fearless* in 1968, also failed.

1968 student troubles

Between 1966 and 1969 Labour was very unpopular with the electorate. It lost by-election after by-election. In Scotland and Wales nationalist parties attracted new levels of support. Throughout the country there was dissatisfaction with traditional party politics and with many aspects of society. The international student disturbances of 1968 affected British universities, notably the London School of Economics, though nowhere near so severely as in France or the USA. For those who believed that Britain needed radical change, Wilson's government was a great disappointment. Within the Labour movement the tensions between the moderates and the more radical left grew.

The 1970 general election

However, Labour's standing in the opinion polls improved with better economic news. When Wilson called a general election in 1970 he, and many political experts, were confident of a Labour victory. They were wrong. Heath led the Conservatives home (Conservative 330, 45 per cent, Labour 287, 43 per cent, Liberals 6, 7.5 per cent, Scottish Nationalists 1, 1 per cent).

The 1970s: a decade of crisis

Heath Prime Minister

Heath was determined to set the country on a new course. Economic growth would be achieved by the firm control of public spending; badly managed out-of-date 'lame duck' companies should go out of business. They should not be bailed out with taxpayers' money. Industrial relations would be improved by making strikes more difficult.

Economic crisis, 1971–2

The Conservatives suffered a severe setback soon after the election when Macleod, Chancellor of the Exchequer and one of their most able and experienced ministers, died. Barber, his successor, tried to encourage growth by cutting taxes and public spending. However he did not reach his growth targets and unemployment and prices both rose. During a serious international inflationary crisis Britain's balance of payments worsened and the pound fell sharply in value. These pressures persuaded Heath to do a U-turn during 1972–3 and use many of the policies for which he had previously so criticised Wilson – controlling both wages and prices in order to limit inflation and increasing government spending to boost industry. Bankrupt companies like Rolls-Royce and Upper Clyde Shipbuilders were saved with taxpayers' money. Simultaneously the government was fighting a bitter battle with the trade unions. Its Industrial Relations Act of 1970 made agreement between employers and unions legally binding and set up the National Industrial Relations Court to enforce them. The unions refused to accept the Act or to co-operate with the government's schemes of prices and wages control, and 1971 was a bad year for strikes. In 1972 the miners won for themselves a pay increase three times the size of that originally offered by the Coal Board by striking and by preventing the movement of coal to power stations by mass picketing. A dock strike followed which was a direct challenge to the Industrial Relations Act. The government backed off, its plans for controlling the unions in tatters.

Industrial conflict

Source F: Trade union reform 1969

F1 *Wilson and Barbara Castle were on the point of putting their 'In Place of Strife' proposals into a bill to place before Parliament. Many members of the Labour Party were unhappy about them since they believed them to be too hard on the unions. In April Wilson spoke to a meeting of Labour MPs. (Quoted from Harold Wilson: The Labour Government 1964–70: A Personal Record, 1971.)*

F1

"We have told the TUC on many occasions . . . that if they would come forward with their own measures, equally effective, equally urgent in time, to our proposals to deal with unofficial strikes, we would be prepared to consider their alternative suggestions. So far they have not indicated that this would be possible but they have been again invited to come forward with alternatives if they wish to do so . . . . The Bill we are discussing tonight is an essential Bill. Essential to our economic recovery. Essential to the balance of payments. Essential to full employment. It is an essential component of ensuring the economic success of the Government. It is on that economic success that the recovery of the nation led by the Labour Party depends. That is why I have to tell you that the passage of this Bill is essential to its continuance in office. There can be no going back on that . . ."

F2 In June it became clear that opposition to the proposals was strong in the trade unions, the Labour Party and in the Cabinet itself. Wilson and Castle met the TUC leaders.

F2

"I opened the discussion [Wilson records] and stressed strongly what we required ... I said that we were prepared to consider a binding undertaking and to recommend it to the Cabinet, provided that it was clear, specific and met all the points on which we insisted .... We presented them with a draft and left them to consider it .... When we met again Vic Feather [Secretary to the TUC] reported that the draft had been accepted without amendment .... There was a changed atmosphere and I stressed again that there must be an all-out effort, by close relations between the Government and both sides of industry, to ensure that the full force deriving from the agreement was directed to dealing with the strike problem ....

Barbara Castle and I then went to report to the Cabinet ... I read out the text of the TUC undertaking. There was great excitement, even cheers, as I went on reading and at the end an ovation unparalleled at Cabinet meetings so far as my experience goes."

F3 Richard Crossman was a Cabinet Minister at this time. The extract is taken from his diary for June 1969.

F3

"Bob [Mellish, the Chief Whip] had been telling me how violent Harold had been that afternoon and how he was refusing to climb down but there was one very big difference. Last night he had been talking about resigning but he had obviously reflected during the night that this was not sound policy. Harold had said to Bob. 'I'm not going to resign. They won't chase me out'. The moment I heard this I knew that he was going to settle .... *He had to leave Barbara in the lurch to save his own muttons and his own Prime Ministership*. I have no doubt that this was the motive which drove him and of course there is nothing like the prospect of certain death to concentrate energy."

F4 The verdict of two historians. A. Sked and C. Cook, in Post-War Britain *published in 1979.*

F4

"Wilson and Castle had no option but to capitulate [give way completely]. On 18 June a face-saving formula was announced in which the TUC General Council gave a 'solemn and binding undertaking' that member unions would observe the TUC's own guidelines on regulating unofficial strikes. Since the General Council had no powers to compel anyone, the undertaking, though no doubt solemn, could hardly be described as binding. Labour's attempts to reform the unions had failed but the government survived intact."

1 *What changes did Wilson and Castle want to make in the 'In Place of Strife' proposals? How important did Wilson (source F1) consider them to be?*

2 *Who opposed the proposals? Why?*

3 *What eventually did Wilson and Castle agree with the TUC leaders? How does Wilson describe their agreement in his Personal Record (source F2)?*

4 *How does Richard Crossman describe the agreement (source F3)? What does he mean by the sentence in italic?*

5 *Whose version do Sked and Cook indicate is closer to the truth? Explain your answer.*

***The 1973
energy crisis***

Worse followed in 1973. The Arab-Israeli War caused first serious oil shortages, then a fourfold increase in the price of oil. Britain was then dependent on foreign oil for 50 per cent of her energy needs. The government was more than ever determined to keep control of inflation by limiting rises of prices and incomes. It fixed 7 per cent as the limit for pay increases and refused a miners' pay claim above that figure (see source G). The National Union of Mineworkers first banned overtime in November 1973 and then, in February 1974, struck in support of their claim. Heath believed their action to be a threat not just to his government but to the authority of a democratically elected Parliament. He announced emergency measures in January 1974 which included industry going on to a three-day week since the miners' overtime ban, supported by other groups of workers, was affecting power supplies. Then in February 1974 he called a general election, asking the country to support his policies of wage and price controls and of resisting unreasonable union demands. The country could not give a clear answer. The result was as follows: Labour 301, 37.1 per cent, Conservative 297, 37.9 per cent, Liberals 14, 19.3 per cent, Scottish and Welsh Nationalists 9, 2.6 per cent. The Conservatives lost more than a million votes and 36 seats; Labour lost 500,000 votes but gained some seats from the Conservatives. The main gains went to the Nationalists and to the Liberals but the latter were unable to turn their great increase in votes into a proportionate increase in MPs. Talks about a Conservative-Liberal coalition failed. Heath resigned and Wilson became Prime Minister of a minority Labour government. He called another election in October 1974 in the hope of winning a workable majority. The result was again very close but there was a small shift to Labour (Labour 319, 39 per cent, Conservative 277, 36 per cent, Liberals 13, 18 per cent, Nationalists 14, 3.5 per cent). This second defeat was the end of the road for Heath. In the election for the Conservative Party leadership in 1975 he lost to Margaret Thatcher. If Heath's four years as Prime Minister ended in dramatic failure, he did achieve one of his main aims, Britain's entry to the Common Market (see page 259). This was a matter of justifiable personal pride to him, since he was one of the most convinced and energetic campaigners for entry since he had led Britain's negotiating team during the first application of 1961–3.

***The three-day
week***

***February 1974
general election***

***October 1974
general election***

***Thatcher
replaces Heath
as Conservative
leader***

Northern Ireland (Ulster)

***Protestants
versus Catholics***

One problem which every British government would have happily done without was the state of near civil war which existed in Northern Ireland from 1968. Unlike the rest of Ireland, which was mainly Catholic, Ulster, the most northerly province, had had a large Scottish settlement in the seventeenth century and the majority of its population was Protestant. Six counties of the historic Ulster province had stayed part of the UK when the rest of Ireland had broken away in 1921. It sent seventeen MPs to Westminster and had its own assembly at Stormont Castle. While most Catholics believed that before long the whole of Ireland should be united in a single republic, the Northern Irish Protestants (Loyalists) fiercely opposed the idea of being ruled from Dublin in a Catholic-dominated state. They saw the substantial Catholic minority with Northern Ireland as part of the enemy. The Ulster police force (the Royal Ulster Constabulary) was Protestant, and Catholics got the worst jobs and the worst housing.

Riots

In 1968 serious rioting occurred when Northern Irish Catholics demonstrated against the misuse of power by the Loyalists. The Irish

Source G: Industrial and political crisis 1973–4

G Daily Mail *11 January 1974.*

1 *What were the miners doing in January 1974? Why does the* Daily Mail *talk of a great industrial and economic crisis?*

2 *What was Heath's policy on prices and incomes? Why did he think that it was necessary?*

3 *When did Heath hold a general election? How did its results compare with those predicted by the* Daily Mail *National Opinion Poll?*

4 *Can you see any bias in the* Daily Mail *reporting? Where do you think its political sympathies lay? Explain your answer.*

The British Army sent to the province

Republican Army (IRA), a small guerrilla group dedicated to uniting Ireland by force, made the Royal Ulster Constabulary its main target. In 1969 the British Army was sent in to restore order. Its arrival provoked the IRA and other guerrilla groups to greater efforts (the Provisional IRA which had split away from the IRA, was one of the most active.) The first British soldier was killed in 1971. During that year 175 people died, victims for the most part of bombings and shootings. The next year was worse. In Londonderry, on what became known as Bloody Sunday, British troops opened fire on a banned demonstration, killing thirteen marchers and wounding many more. A Labour government had sent the first troops, a Conservative one increased their number to 20,000. Violence continued, suspects were interned without trial. The assembly at Stormont was suspended and the province ruled directly from London. The IRA exploded bombs in England.

*The
Sunningdale
Agreement,
1973*

In 1973 a valiant attempt was made by Heath's government, in discussions at Sunningdale with representatives of the Irish Republic, to find a settlement acceptable to both Protestants and Catholics. There was to be a new assembly in Northern Ireland in which Catholics would have a stronger voice through proportional representation. In addition a Council of Ireland was proposed which would include representatives from the Republic and from Northern Ireland. The Loyalists would have nothing to do with this agreement and ended the new assembly by a general strike.

Its failure

More violence

*Terrorism in
Northern
Ireland and
the mainland*

Violence continued (see sources H1–2). In 1979 Neave, who was to have been the minister responsible for Northern Ireland in Thatcher's 1979 government, was killed by a car bomb in the House of Commons car park. In 1981 ten IRA prisoners, led by Bobby Sands, starved themselves to death in protest against their conditions inside the Maze prison, Belfast (see source H3). Sympathisers, mainly in the USA, provided the IRA with money and arms while within Northern Ireland the extreme republican party, Sinn Fein, gained in popularity and in 1983 won five seats in the election to a new provincial assembly. Once elected they and other Catholic representatives refused to attend the assembly. There was no let-up in the killings and woundings. In 1984 an IRA bomb exploded in the Grand Hotel in Brighton during the Conservative Party Conference. Four people were killed, many more injured and the Prime Minister only narrowly escaped. In Northern Ireland itself murders continued week by week. The endless violence silenced moderate opinion and strengthened the extremists on both sides.

Race relations

*Effects of
immigration*

Another difficult issue in British politics was immigration and its social effects. For many years all Commonwealth citizens had been allowed free entry into Britain and during the 1950s many West Indians, Indians and Pakistanis arrived both to work and settle. Between 1959 and 1961 the arrivals increased considerably, from 20,000 to 115,000 a year. Though they were valuable workers in a period of high employment, they tended to concentrate in a few major cities and sometimes put the health, education and social services under strain. Racial rioting took place in Notting Hill, London, and elsewhere in 1958. The reaction of Macmillan's Conservative government to these developments was the Race Relations Act of 1952 which placed strict controls on immigration.

*The Kenyan
Asians, 1968*

While in opposition, Labour strongly criticised the Act but did not repeal it when it came to power two years later. Labour was in power when there was the likelihood of the arrival of thousands of Kenyan Asians. An Act was quickly passed which limited the numbers to 1,500 per year (see source I1). However, Labour worked at the same time to improve the position of black and Asian people already in Britain. The Race Relations Act of 1968 made discrimination more difficult in housing and employment. Race Relations Boards and Immigration Tribunals were set up. None the less there were many Britons who were unready to accept that their country was multiracial. Powell, a former Conservative minister who warned of a future of racial strife and bloodshed, became their spokesman. He opposed any further immigration and hoped that many recent immigrants could be 'repatriated' to their former homes.

During the 1970s immigration controls were tightened further, though 28,000 refugees from persecution in Uganda were allowed to enter in 1973. The Conservatives added further restrictions by the British Nationality

Source H: Violence in Northern Ireland, 1978–85

H1 *A secret British Army Intelligence document about the Provisional IRA leaked to the press in 1978, included as an appendix to S. Cronin's* Irish Nationalism, *1982.*

H1

"The Provisional Movement is committed to the traditional aim of Irish nationalism, that is the removal of British presence in Ireland. The PIRA leadership is dedicated to the belief that this can only be achieved through violence. *Leadership:* PIRA is essentially a working-class organisation based in the ghetto areas of the cities and the poorer rural areas .... *Technical Expertise:* PIRA has an adequate supply of members who are skilled in the production of explosive devices .... *Rank and File Terrorists:* Our evidence ... does not support the view that they were merely mindless hooligans drawn from the ranks of the unemployed and unemployable ... the mature terrorists are usually sufficiently cunning to avoid arrest. *Popular Support:* Republican terrorists can no longer bring out crowds of active sympathisers on the streets at will as a screen for gunmen. Indeed there is seldom much support even for traditional protest marches ... but the hardening segregation of the communities also operates to the terrorists' advantage .... There are still areas of the Province where terrorists can base themselves with little or no fear of betrayal and can count on active support in an emergency. The fear of a possible return to Protestant repression will underpin this kind of support for many years to come."

H2 (**Below**) *A youth stands ready to throw a petrol bomb at an armoured vehicle outside the RUC police station on the Barnsley Estate in Belfast. The date is 5 June 1981, only a few hours after the announcement of the death of Maze Prison hunger striker Bobby Sands.*

1 *How reliable would you expect source H1 to be?*

2 a) *What were the Provisional IRA trying to do?*
   b) *Where did their members come from?*
   c) *How capable were they on the whole?*

3 a) *Had popular support for the Provisional IRA increased or lessened?*
   b) *In 1978 what kind of support could they count on?*
   c) *Was such support likely to prove lasting?*

4 *If you had been the British Army Chief in Ireland who had received that report in 1978, what steps would you have recommended that the British Government should take a) militarily, b) politically, to end the Provisional IRA threat?*

5 *In source H2, who was Bobby Sands? To which religious group would the youth with the petrol bomb be likely to belong? What was the RUC? Why should it be a target for these rioters in 1981?*

The 1981 riots

Act of 1981. They presented themselves as the party of strict immigration controls, while Labour and the Liberals gave priority to improving race relations (see source I2). During the summer of 1981 widespread rioting by young people in Britain's inner cities had racial aspects. The Scarman inquiry, which looked particularly at the riots of Brixton in South London, discovered that racial discrimination had been a major cause of unrest there. Not surprisingly most of the two million black and Asian voters tended to vote Labour rather than Conservative.

The Labour government, 1974–9

Inflation

Inflation was the major problem which Wilson's government faced. At 9.2 per cent in 1972–3, it rose to 24 per cent in 1974–5. Labour was supposed to have a 'social contract' with the unions whereby the government would not need a prices and incomes policy, since the unions would voluntarily restrain their wage demands. The unions could not deliver. Some wage rises were about 30 per cent. The government had to introduce a tough budget and wage controls. Unemployment rose while the value of sterling fell.

The Common Market referendum, 1975

In 1975 the first referendum in British history took place about Britain's membership of the Common Market. Since there was a strong opposition to the Common Market within the Labour Party, the idea of a referendum had been included in its 1974 election manifesto. While Wilson himself favoured staying in, he allowed his party a completely free vote. The result was a two to one majority for staying in.

Wilson resigns, 1976

An assessment

To everyone's surprise Wilson resigned in 1976. He had been at or near the top of British politics for thirty years which in his view was long enough for anyone. His career was a controversial one. He was without doubt very clever and strong on political tactics. He won four elections by skilful timing and the persuasive presentation of Labour's case and of himself as a leader. At a time of serious and growing divisions within the Labour Party he prevented it from an open split. However his critics said that he had no realistic strategy for Britain between 1964 and 1976, that his economic policies were, if anything, less successful than those of the Conservatives which he himself so brilliantly attacked, and that the 'white-hot technological revolution', to which he was going to give so much well-informed support, simply did not happen. By placing too much importance on keeping Labour united he failed to give determined leadership when it was most needed, for instance over trade union reform.

Callaghan Prime Minister

His successor Callaghan had three exceptionally difficult years as Prime Minister. Unemployment rose fast (to 1,420,000 in 1977) and inflation stayed uncomfortably high. Another serious financial crisis in 1976 made necessary another IMF loan, a condition of which was higher taxes and cuts in public spending. During 1977 and 1978 the economic situation improved. North Sea oil was extracted in greater volume and brought about an improvement in the balance of payments. The pound strengthened against the dollar and inflation fell back at last to single figures. Had Callaghan called a general election in 1978 Labour might have won again. He waited, however, until 1979. During the winter of 1978–9, the country was swept by a wave of strikes – of lorry drivers, water workers, ambulance drivers, sewerage staff and dustmen. Violent picketing accompanied the strikes, which not only destroyed the government's pay policy but caused much public anxiety and anger. In March 1979 Labour lost a vote of confidence in the Commons and had to call

The winter of discontent, 1978–9

Source I: The Labour Government and the Kenyan Asians

I1

I1 The limit of 1,500 entering the country each year had just been fixed. Richard Crossman, who was then a Cabinet Minister, went to a dinner party on 4 March 1968. The guests were what he called 'the intelligentsia' readers of The Times *and the* Guardian, *journalists, bishops and the like. They attacked him strongly for the Government's illiberal and racist immigration policy. This is what Crossman noted in his diary.*

"I was on the top of my form arguing an unpopular case and showing that our whole immigration policy ever since 1964 had been right. It had been bitterly attacked, but it had worked – it had taken the poison out of politics so that in the 1966 election immigration was no longer a political issue – we were getting the social problems in the Midlands under control by severely limiting the incoming stream of immigrants and taking trouble in schools. The intake was now at about maximum. We could digest 50,000 at the very most. If that were doubled, the whole of the good work which we'd done in the last three years would break down and Powellism would become the philosophy of the Birmingham area."

I2 'At school we dance, tomorrow we . . .' Immigrant children at school in Haringey, London, May 1968 (Illustrated London News).

1 What was Labour's policy towards the Kenyan Asians in 1968? Why did many people think that it was 'racist' and 'illiberal'?

2 What reasons did Crossman give (source I1) to support Labour's policy?

3 What did he mean by Powellism?

4 Crossman talks about 'taking trouble in schools'. Would he have approved of the photograph (source I2)? Explain the caption.

5 How do you think race relations today compare with those in 1968? How can one measure the extent of racial prejudice and discrimination a) in the present, b) in the past?

The 1979 general election

The popular mood

a general election. The Conservatives won a comfortable victory: Conservative 339, 44 per cent, Labour 268, 37 per cent, Liberals 11, 4 per cent, Nationalists 4, 2 per cent).

The Callaghan years were gloomy. More and more of the British electorate came to believe that the country could not go on as it was. Within the Labour movement the influential left wing argued that the best way forward lay in more nationalisation and government spending, coming out of the Common Market, supporting unilateral nuclear disarmament and making radical reforms. The Conservatives were also keen to make a clear break from the immediate past. They would end inflation by 'monetarist' policies. Public spending would be cut right back and private enterprise encouraged wherever possible. With it would flourish individual freedom and responsibility. Trade unions would be brought under control. As the election result showed, the country preferred the Conservative alternative.

Conservatives in power, 1979

Conservative plans

Thatcher, the new Prime Minister well supported by Howe, her Chancellor of the Exchequer, showed her monetarist colours straightaway. For a time inflation rose but fell back again to single figures in 1982. In contrast unemployment rose and went on rising, from 1,253,000 in 1979 to 3,021,000 in 1983. Businessmen taking firm measures to restore ailing industries to genuine profitability, like Edwardes at British Leyland and MacGregor at British Steel, were solidly supported. Plans were made to denationalise (privatise) those industries which might be attractive to private industry (e.g. British Telecom). Local government spending was placed under tight control. Acts to reduce the power of trade unions were passed in 1980 and 1982. Secondary strikes (for example railwaymen in support of miners) were made illegal and unions taking part in illegal disputes were made liable for damages. There were many fewer strikes in the early 1980s than in the 1970s. While the government claimed that this was the result of their policies, their opponents argued that it was due to high unemployment. Council houses were put on sale to their tenants and more than 500,000 were sold between 1979 and 1983.

The Falklands War, 1982

Active though the government was, it was not at all popular between 1979 and 1981. With inflation still out of control, unemployment rising and manufacturing industry in obvious decline, Mrs Thatcher was in 1981 the most unpopular Prime Minister since opinion polls began. Then, in April 1982, Argentinian troops invaded the Falkland Islands. When they refused to withdraw the British government sent a task force which in a brilliant and risky campaign won the islands back. Thatcher proved an effective war leader and her no-nonsense patriotism won a warm response across the country. Victory in the Falklands conflict transformed her standing and that of her party. She also took an uncompromising line with the Russians over disarmament and with the Common Market over Britain's financial contribution.

Divisions within the Labour Party

The formation of the SDP

The 1983 general election

The political opposition was weak and grew weaker as time passed. When Callaghan resigned as Labour leader in 1980, Michael Foot was elected in his place. Foot's victory was the last straw for a number of Labour moderates. The move to the left had gone so far that they could no longer remain party members. In 1981 four – Rodgers, Jenkins, Owen and Williams – resigned and formed the Social Democratic Party (SDP). From the first it co-operated with the Liberal Party with the intention of capturing the moderate centre of British public opinion. In one sense the SDP was very successful, since it immediately became a force to be reckoned with in both local and national elections. At the same time, however, it made it easy for Thatcher to win the 1983 election. Though the Conservatives polled nearly 700,000 fewer votes than in 1979, they won a huge majority since the SDP/Liberal Alliance took many votes from Labour, without being able to turn votes in to MPs: Conservatives 397, 42 per cent, Labour 209, 28 per cent, SDP/Liberals 23, 26 per cent, Nationalists 4, 1.5 per cent. While 33,000 votes were needed to elect a Conservative MP, 338,000 were required for an SDP/Liberal one, since their support was spread very evenly across the country. Not surprisingly the Alliance cried foul play and demanded a voting system based on proportional representation. Neither the Conservatives nor Labour showed any readiness to consider such a change.

Index